WALES AS IS

DAVID HURN

Essay by RICHARD KING

Seren is the book imprint of
Poetry Wales Press Ltd
Derwen Road, Bridend, Wales

www.serenbooks.com
Find us on social media @SerenBooks

Image captions by Ceri Jackson

Book design by Brian Carroll

ISBN 978-1-78172-753-9

A CIP record for this title is available from the British Library

The publisher works with the financial assistance
of the Books Council of Wales.

EU GPSR Authorised Representative
Logos Europe, 9 rue Nicolas Poussin, 17000,
La Rochelle, France
E-mail: Contact@logoseurope.eu

WALES AS IS

DAVID HURN

Essay by **RICHARD KING**

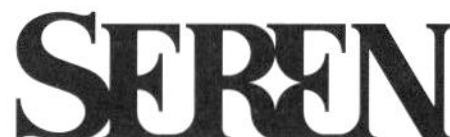

With thanks to:

Eva, Rob, Brian, Gareth, Emyr, Glenn, Ceri, Bella, John and Rudi.
Each in their own way held my hand and helped me over hurdles.

cover image: **TŶ NEWYDD, ANGLESEY** *(page 37)*

Contents

INTRODUCTION

David Hurn

In 1970, after a successful time working as a photographer in London,
I returned to Wales to try to discover what I understood about the word 'culture'.
I spoke with the renowned cultural theorist Raymond Williams who suggested
that an important part of culture was landscape.

I had never really tackled landscape photography before so had no idea what I
actually wanted to do. However, I knew what I didn't want to do. I had no desire
to ape Ansel Adams: he had done what he did so very well. Neither did I want to
do the equivalent of sentimental or picturesque postcards. Again, others do it so
much better. And I certainly didn't wish to go on long trips shooting pictures out
of the window every quarter of a mile and then write about why 'this and that'
was particularly significant. Frankly, I don't think it ever is.

What I did know was that my idea of landscape involved people.

It was while in a café/second-hand bookshop in Talgarth, as I browsed an early
geological book of Wales, I was struck by the accuracy of the text written by
trained scientists alongside woodcut illustrations. I thought to myself, 'Well I can
do that but in photography'.

Ostensibly this meant letting various experts suggest what I should photograph
when it came to exploring the human effect on the landscape. Once I had
reached the various recommended locations, I could then photograph them
however I liked.

I could document 'Wales As Is'.

A BENCH IN WALES

Richard King

The picture is of a roadside scene on the B4574 in the hamlet of Cwmystwyth, in which the principal image is of a bench. It is located in the familiar Welsh countryside of a hillside in varying shades of green. The sky is an even grey hue; the half-beam headlights of an oncoming car indicate it may be producing a haze of light drizzle.

In the middle distance, past the bench, is a tree on its way to being in full leaf. This suggests the month might be April, though the random fluctuations in conditions precipitated by the climate crisis make such signifiers of the time of year less reliable. Alongside the bench is a well-maintained encased notice board, at the foot of which are two flower baskets. In the adjacent field is another object, a flag, Y Ddraig Goch (the Red Dragon) caught lightly in the breeze, flying non-committedly at roughly half its extent.

A spotlessly clean and well-maintained bench and a notice board accompanied by a modest flower display. The hallmarks of municipality and community, of local order and social energy are amplified by the patriotism implicit in the flag, which has been placed here as this location is understood to be the central point of Wales.

The photograph demonstrates that this mid-point is also an epicentre of a particular type of topography, of pitching fields and hillsides, of broad skies occupied by small communities. Its territory is the centre of the smallest country in Great Britain and the poorest country in the United Kingdom, where debates centred around nationhood, identity and place draw their energy from the landscape and language of Wales and are as overfamiliar and wearing as driving through the lambent grey drizzle.

To the north and south of Cwmystwyth lies high open moorland; to the east and west is the sheltered floor of the Ystwyth Valley, where another characteristic of this panorama is revealed. The area is often included in what visiting travel and nature writers since the nineteenth century have called the Desert of Wales, or by the Cymraeg place name Elenydd,

the largely unoccupied interior of heather moorland, expansive fields of purple moor grass, squares and rectangles of conifers grown spindly in the Welsh rain, hills and very little else. But the valley of the Ystwyth is historically a place of industry. Its U-shaped aspect is dramatically steep. Its rugged slopes littered with scree are considered by archaeologists to be the product not of glacial erosion but of mining. There are historical artefacts of the industry on the valley floor and on its hills, including the extensive ruins of Cwmystwyth lead mine that cover Copa Hill on the valley's steep northern gradients. A picture of one such spoil is contained within these pages.

On its opposite side, smaller remains of minor workings are visible: a dressing mill, a mining office and smithy. The presence of these disused industrial buildings gives the hillsides an absorbing atmosphere as they alert the visitor to the lead veins beneath their feet. However seductive the alchemical properties of Wales' open spaces may be in the collective or folkloric memory, it is the historic excavations of the raw mineral substrata that provide the scenery of the Cwmystwyth with its authority. The surviving ruins are robust, if dangerous. The brickwork of the Copa Hill mine endures beside a side wall whose door frame has long collapsed, as have the nearby remnants of a mine shaft.

The abandonment of these buildings to the raw weather of these hills suggests the wind that tears through the valley carries with it the weight of good or bad fortune that shone on the generations of prospectors as they set about their tasks in this remote working environment.

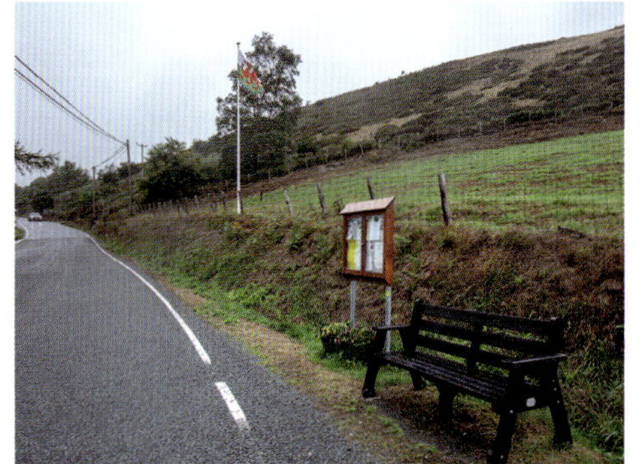

Cwmystwyth, Ceredigion – page 198

If the driver of the car, headlights on, continued their journey on the B road past the bench in Cwmystwyth heading east they would, in roughly twenty miles reach the A470, a main road that similarly reveals the past excavations of the Welsh landscape and, like the ruins in the Ystwyth Valley, allows the driver to experience, or at the very least imagine, a similar sense of deep time.

This feeling of engaging with the infinite while travelling through the slow miles of undeveloped surroundings may not always be fanciful. The A470 is the sole transport route that directly links Wales' North to its South, or if one were to change direction, the country's capital Cardiff to the coast at Llandudno. Despite its regular and irregular accentuated bends, anomalous turnings, long approaches and the occasional feeling of having entered differing altitudes, the road more or less manages to convince the driver they are travelling in a straight line along a vertical meridian.

The southernmost end of the 186-mile-long road starts in Cardiff and makes its way northwards, climbing through the reclaimed slopes of the post-industrial South Wales Valleys, where the densely built terraces of former mining communities, which followed the coal seam, are clearly visible. There is an image in this book of Ferndale, where in 1857 the first coal mine shaft was sunk, thereby creating the first industrial community of the Rhondda Valley.

The image includes a quotation from Gwyn Thomas, the novelist, dramatist and broadcaster, born in the Rhondda and brought up by his sister in poverty. Thomas evokes the back-to-back housing of the industrial Valleys:

> Scattered here and there are tiny communities dropped as casually as
> a curse on some old mining project… The streets buck like broncos.
> The housing pattern is so fantastically complicated even pigeons
> returning from races have been seen poised in a long hover.

The 'long hover' aptly describes the sensation of driving near and above these 'tiny communities'. It also captures the enduring lack of conviction with which successive governments and agencies have attempted to address the role of the Valleys in a deindustrialised society. These settlements include Aberfan, the site of one of the country's greatest tragedies. David Hurn was among the first photographers present on the scene. The images he took of the enfolding tragedy were subsequently syndicated around the world and used as evidence in parliamentary debate.

Within twenty miles the road opens up into the contrasting expanse of the mountains of Bannau Brycheiniog National Park. For a major arterial highway, the A470 is slow going, especially when the driver is sharing the road with the inevitable haulage and agricultural vehicles going about their business.

Further north, after the road passes through the small market town of Rhayader in the Elan Valley, where the driver from Cwmystwyth would join the road, the pace of travel begins to be dictated by yet steeper climbs that require the occupants of the vehicle to accept that time is no longer of the essence but has turned fundamental. In due course the driver experiences views of another mountain range, now contained within the Eryri National Park. These are juxtaposed with the decommissioned nuclear reactor at Trawsfynydd – an impressive, and for Wales rare, piece of Brutalist architecture that looms on the horizon. Its muted grey dignity enhances the strange charge provided by the feeling of travelling through the Welsh version of canyons. The feeling might be described as a comforting eeriness, an inarguable sense of connection with place and past that defines a national character. And it is a feeling on which Wales has grown somewhat over-reliant in terms of understanding itself.

Further along the A470 passes through the singular, vivid shards and hard edges of the slate mines of Blaenau Ffestiniog. And the sense of the journey having fragmented, from the outside world, into the dark-hued inner escarpment of Welsh identity, is complete. Some thirty miles later, the road ends at the sea front of Llandudno.

On 16 October 2002, during an archaeological excavation of a Roman and early Medieval lead bole (or lead smelting hearth) at Banc Tynddol in the upland of Cwmystwyth, not far from the roadside bench, a metal object was discovered. The small (39 mm diameter) disc was made of gold foil and unearthed a mere 15cm below the surface remains of a medieval hearth. Further examination revealed the significance of the find. Archaeologists established the object was likely to be an Early Bronze Age sun disc dated to around 2000 BC. The disc exhibited no visible signs of wear implying it may have been utilised, or even created, as a funerary ornament – an object to be interred in a grave alongside its occupant. Another theory posited that the disc may have been used as a button and the item of clothing to which it belonged had been included in a burial. In either case, there was no certainty as to whether the disc had been deposited intentionally, nor were any further archaeological artefacts identified. Rather than having been placed deliberately, the disc may have been dropped there while being worn or carried from a different location.

As a result of the initial discovery, a further excavation was commissioned, for which work began in March 2003. The investigation did in fact reveal an oval-shaped 1.75m-long grave cut enclosing the initial find-spot, lending weight to, if not quite confirming, the theory that the sun disc had been deliberately placed in the grave fill as part of a burial rite. The area around the grave had been heavily disturbed, both by burrowing animals and the activities of the Roman or its early Medieval operators of the smelting hearth, by the heat and debris of which ensured any remains of a skeleton or any further grave goods or artefacts were essentially lost, leaving only a scant trace of degraded bone film.

The find-spot of the sun disc was located above the position where the upper torso of a corpse would lie in its grave, with its head looking south-west directly down the V contour of the Ystwyth Valley and out to the horizon beyond.

The excavation was highly notable, providing as it did the discovery of the first sun disc in Wales. The thin foil disc was decorated on one side with a modest set of points and concentric rings, created using the repoussé technique – a gentle hammering of the object from its reverse side to craft a design in low relief. Repoussé gold work is typical of the Copper Age / Early Bronze Age Beaker period, which is attributed in Britian to c. 2450 BC until as late as 1700 BC. People living in this period often practised single burial rites. Examples of similar artefacts have been unearthed in Ireland, where more than twenty have been found, as well as in Scotland (six) and England (five). The Banc Tynddol sun-disc is a rare artefact and the oldest gold object to be found in Wales.

Some 200 metres north of Banc Tynddol lies the site of the Early Bronze Age copper mine on Copa Hill, which since 1986 has been investigated by the Early Mines Research Group. Their work has established that prospecting works took place at the site from 2100 BC or earlier, which raised the possibility that the sun disc was associated with an individual or community connected to this industry. As a report by the Early Mines Research Group stated, the disc 'provides a possible link with Beaker prospectors, and perhaps even the very start of mining at the end of the 3rd millennium BC.'

Here in the centre of the country, in the middle of Mid Wales, within sight of where Y Ddraig Goch is now flown, was possibly the earliest example of the metallurgical extraction with which the Welsh landscape has become synonymous. Alongside those who visited the major Neolithic axe quarries of Wales, the Beaker people and the Romans that followed them participated in the process of unearthing Wales that would continue for millennia.

During the Middle Ages the Ystwyth Valley fell under the jurisdiction of the Cistercian Strata Florida Abbey, now another ruin some fourteen miles further west into Ceredigion and once considered to be among the most significant abbeys in Wales. The estate included approximately two hundred and fifty square miles of land and a charter to excavate that land's 'possessions.'

The Abbey's rights endured until the dissolution of the monasteries. For the next hundred and fifty years, during the Elizabethan Age, the title fell under the ownership of the Society of Mines Royal.

During the eighteenth century the technique of 'hushing' – prospecting for lodes by scouring the surface of the ground by flushing through a sudden rush of water – was practised. Channels and reservoirs associated with this process are still visible, as are many other relics of mining practices such as tips, shafts, tramways, inclines, open-casts, crusher houses and the remnants of more buildings, including workers' cottages.

By the middle of the eighteenth century, private leaseholders, some of whom, records suggest, came from the Peak District, were successfully mining Cwmystwyth. Once the price of lead crashed in the 1830s, its then owners were forced into declaring bankruptcy. This precedent, of riches followed by insolvency, was set for the next century with a small succession of owners whose fortunes tracked the market fluctuations in minerals, before mining was abandoned entirely in 1921.

A quotation from a letter entitled 'A derelict village – plea for Cwmystwyth unemployed' appears later in this book. It was originally published in the *Welsh Gazette* in January 1934 during the Great Depression and attributed to M.R:

> No lead mines in Wales were better known or more profitable at one time than the Kingside Mines, Cwmystwyth. They stand today derelict, forsaken and forgotten like dark sentinels overlooking the River Ystwyth, ever reminding passers-by that here, once upon a time, prosperity and fame went in hand with happiness. For what village lad was not happy who had the good fortune to be a miner in his own native place?

That Wales was for centuries excavated for its natural mineral resources is inarguable and David Hurn has photographed the places of origin of each industry that exploited the seams and veins of its landform: stone, gold, copper, iron, lead, steel, slate and coal. The sense of extraction, of providing both the domestic labour and fuel for the industrial revolution while receiving only a negligible return, has frequently engendered a sense of grievance and of exploitation within Wales, a sentiment that has been known to provide an inverted form of solace. Or in the phraseology of Raymond Williams, a Welsh author whose relationship to the hillsides near his native Pandy and its surrounding area may have been overdetermined, a 'structure of feeling' – in this instance, a feeling that the terrain has been ransacked and that Wales struggled to share in its rewards.

This ransacking has continued and has by now taken myriad forms. The extractive nature of agriculture is permanently contested. The lack of biodiversity in the landscape, particularly for visitors to the Desert of Wales, is a regular source of commentary as is the health of Wales' rivers. An inevitable consequence of tourism, which has been of greater value to the Welsh economy since the end of the last century and heavily promoted by the Senedd, is an interest in the country's coastline and its rural hinterland. As properties in these locations were and remain relatively inexpensive compared to the national United Kingdom average, the housing market worked in favour of those in a

position to increase their market share. In response, the Senedd introduced legislation accompanied by questionnaires from local authorities that conflated the ability to speak Cymraeg with Wales' housing stock. This has the effect of placing geography, language and culture in an unsteady and uneven dialogue with each another. The Welsh prospect of the twenty-first century has many contemporary examples of economic extraction to complement the Bronze Age and Roman smelting site at Banc Tynddol in Cwmystwyth.

There is as well another method of extraction, that which the driver lapses into when journeying through the plains and vistas of the A470: the extraction of identity and sense of belonging. It is a recognition, perhaps even an indulgence, of the sentiments evoked by that most overused of Cymraeg words, hiraeth – customarily defined as a singularly Welsh form of grief, nostalgia, homesickness or wistfulness, a habitual gaze at the landscape to seek confirmation of who we think we are; it was an activity I enjoyed while writing this essay.

To excavate the fields and hillsides in search of the spoils of our identity is to participate in the same activity practised by the mine owners, the steel masters, the farmers and the second homeowners in whom we have grown accustomed to locating our grievances. Instead, we might consider only the surface of our land, a decision that would allow us to look outwards, at ourselves and at Wales, as is. We could then commence the difficult process of asking how we go about plausibly constructing our future rather than continually disturbing the subsoil, prospecting for our past.

Wales's oldest identified rocks, part of the Stanner-Hanter Intrusive Complex found in the Old Radnor district. One of three hills formed along major fault zones 700 million years ago when the land lay deep in the Southern Hemisphere and part of a continent named Avalonia.

The UK's oldest rocks are 3,300 million years old and found in the Isle of Lewis, relative newcomers compared to the oldest in the world found in Acasta, north west Canada, dated 3,962 million years.

"The stones are its soul"

— **Ruskin**

GEOLOGY

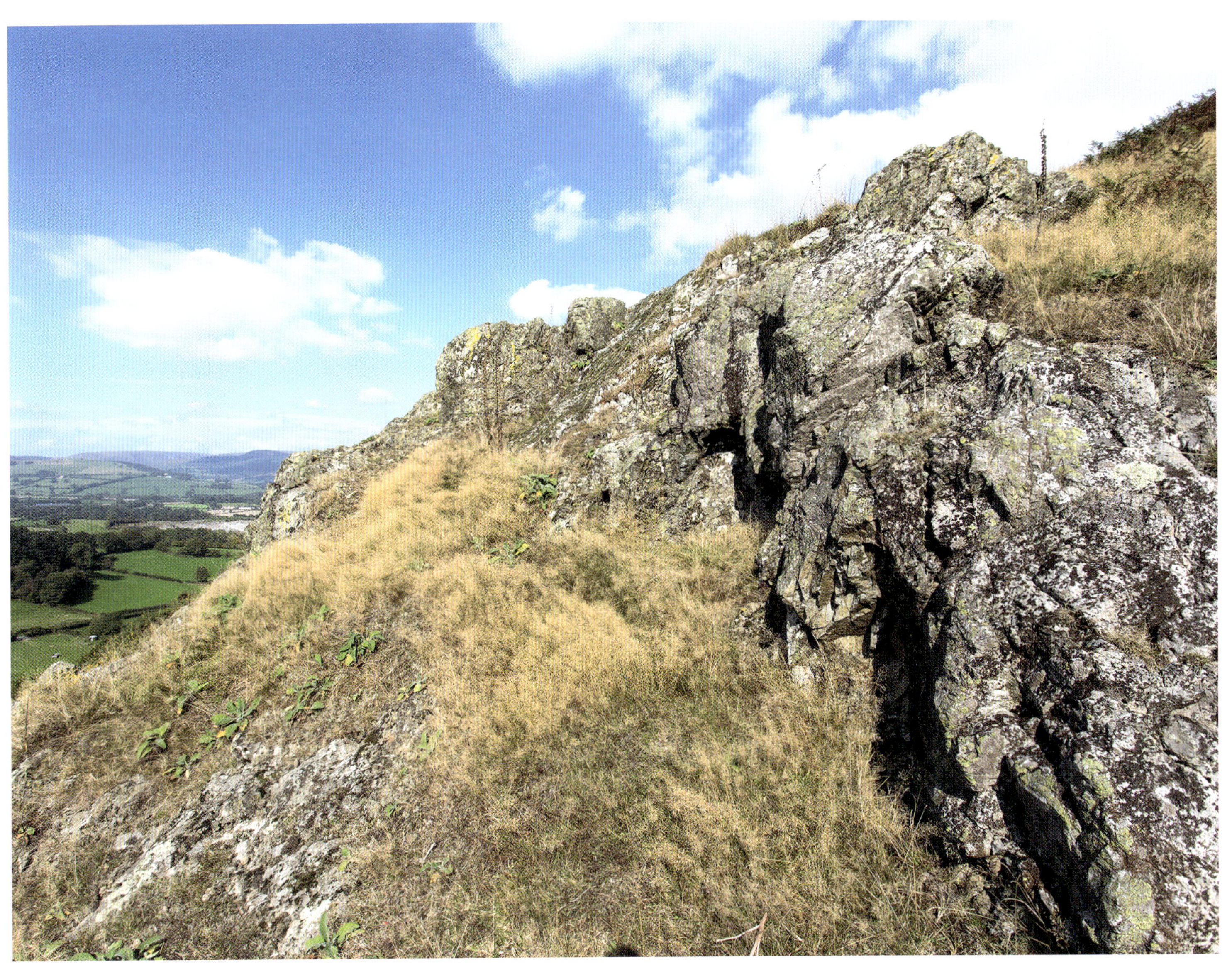

SN 58574 84188

HANTER HILL, POWYS

2014

A wider perspective. In 2024 Keep Wales Tidy urged action to protect the environment against a "litter crisis worsening at an alarming rate".

On average, each person in the UK throws away their own body weight in rubbish every seven weeks.

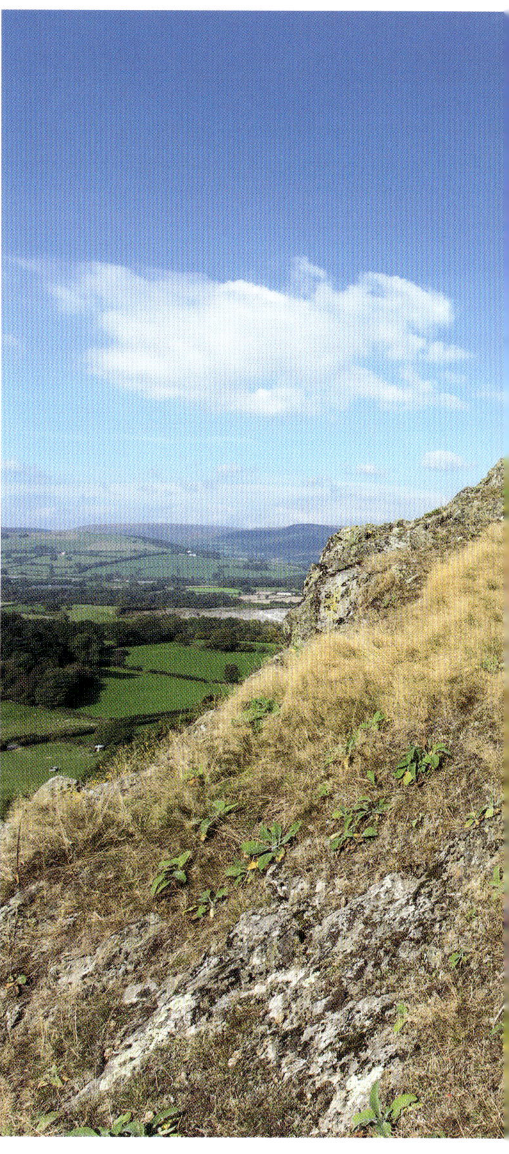

SN 58574 84188

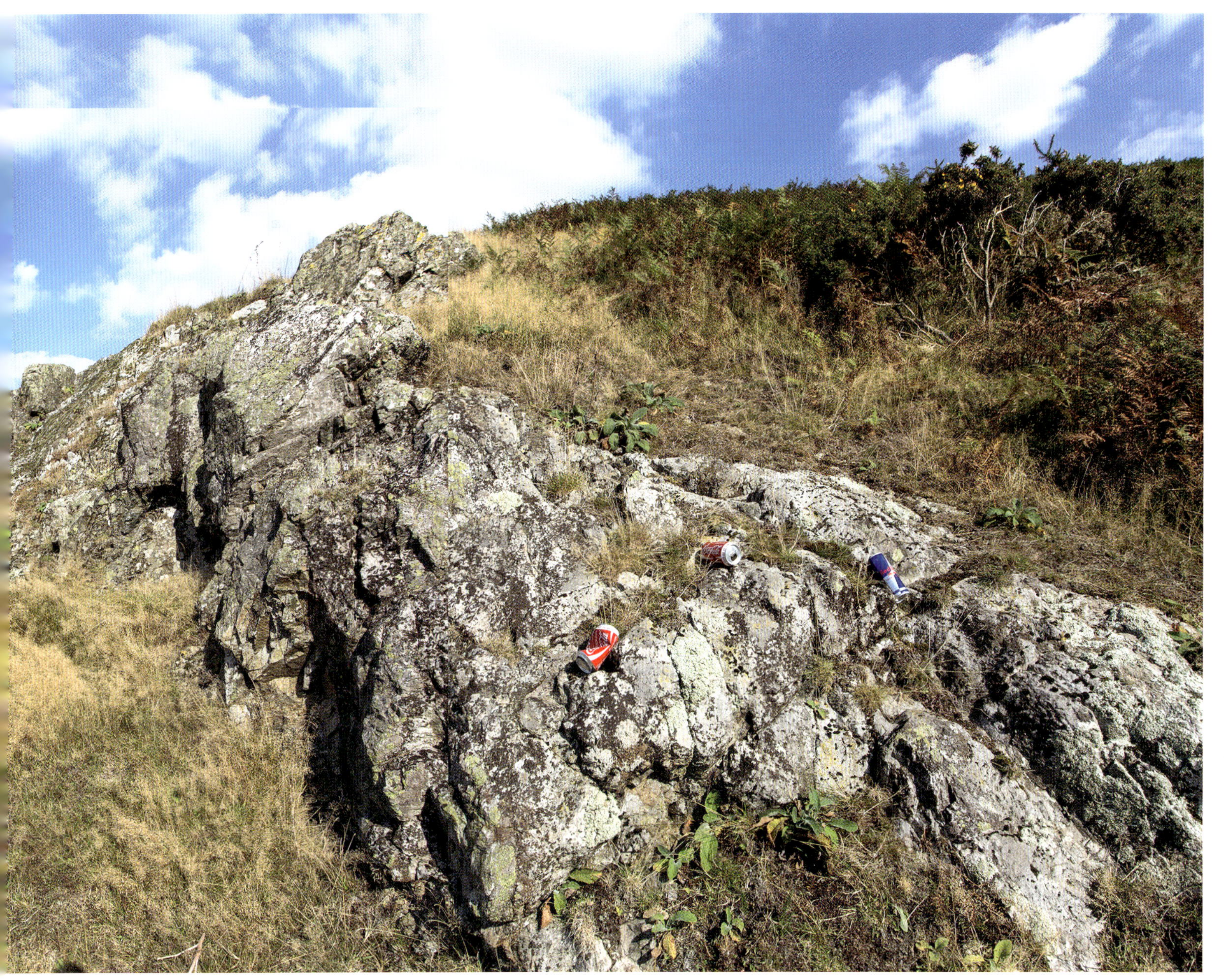

CWM SODEN, CEREDIGION

2011

A striking example of folds of sedimentary rock buckled and twisted during collisions within the earth's crust.

These examples occurred 440 million years ago during the Silurian period, named after the Silures, a Welsh Iron Age people which occupied the area where rocks of this age were first studied. During this geological epoch the earth underwent significant changes including the evolution of fish and the earliest clear evidence of terrestrial life.

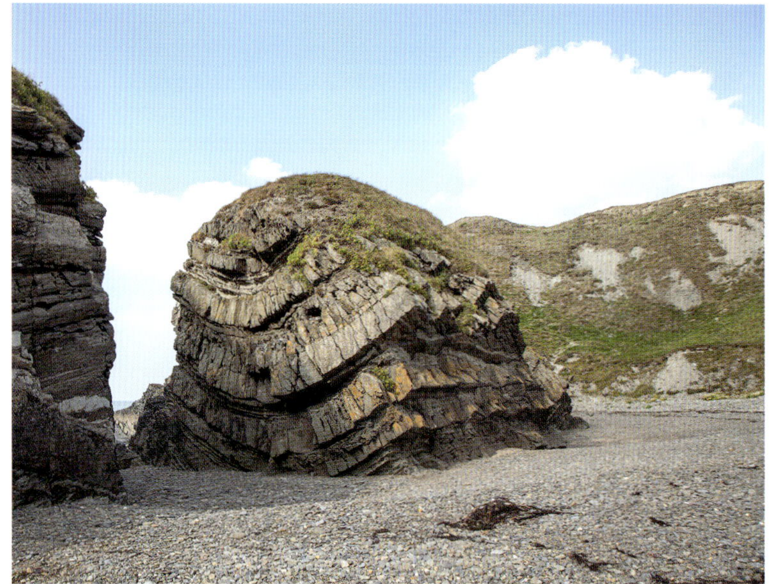

SN 35959 57987

COBBLER'S HOLE, PEMBROKESHIRE

2007

The folding and faulting of the sheer Old Red Sandstone cliffs at St Ann's Head, the near vertical 110ft walls drop from a flat plateau, the result of wave-cut erosion some 400 million years ago when sea levels were 200 feet higher.

The peninsula is also the sunniest place in Wales, recording some of the lowest rainfalls.

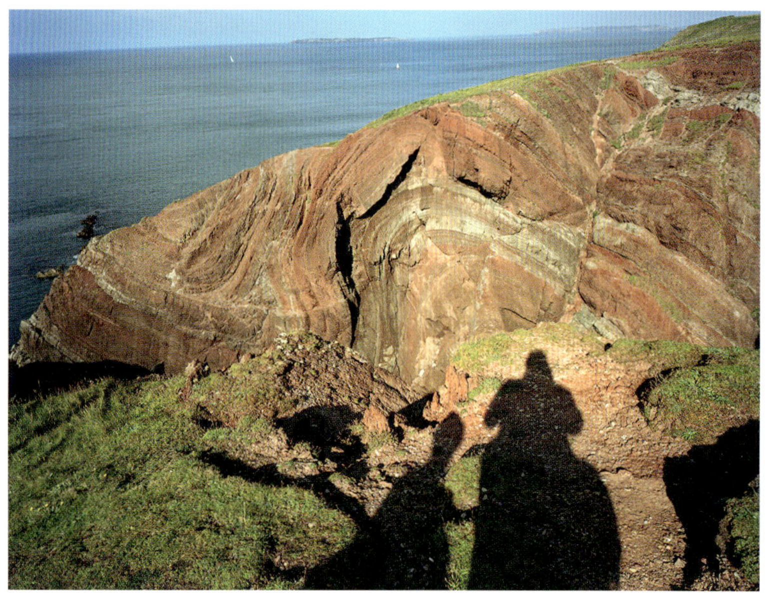

SM 80528 03162

SOUTHERNDOWN, VALE OF GLAMORGAN

An example of an ancient rocky shoreline, a 300-million-year-old mosaic pavement spreads in waves of deeply-fissured Carboniferous Limestone beneath the Jurassic Blue Lais cliffs of the Glamorgan Heritage Coast.

The fossil-encrusted beds are the remains of cliffs eroded, tilted and claimed by the relentless ebb and flow of the tide.

The area, designated a Site of Special Scientific Interest for its geological and botanical value, is also rich in history, once notorious for wreckers who lured ships onto rocks.

Today, it might be more recognisable from the scenes of many TV programmes and films shot there.

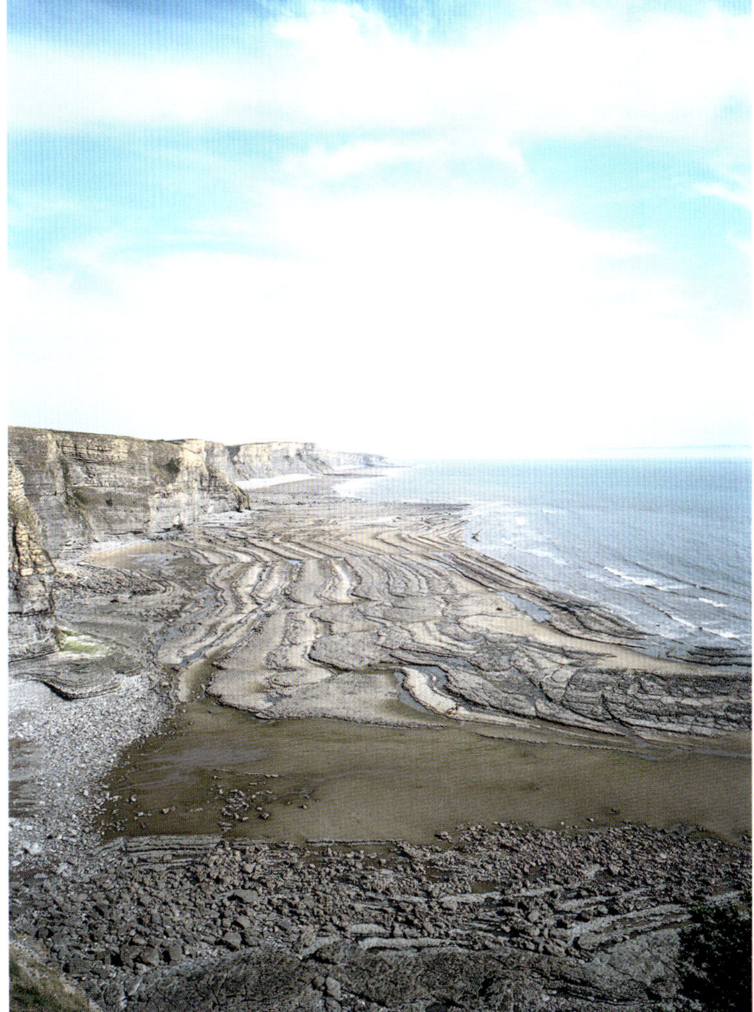

SS 88946 72707

LLANBERIS PASS, GWYNEDD

2013

Carved by ice into a narrow, steep valley at the foot of Yr Wyddfa (Mt Snowdon), the pass was one of the first in Britain to be investigated as the Glacial Theory was developed in the 1840s. The Cromlech boulders, distinctive rhyolite outcrops of volcanic rock, cling ominously to the side of the road.

In 1973 a local council plan to blow them up in order to widen the road was met with outcry prompting a six-year, ultimately successful, campaign.

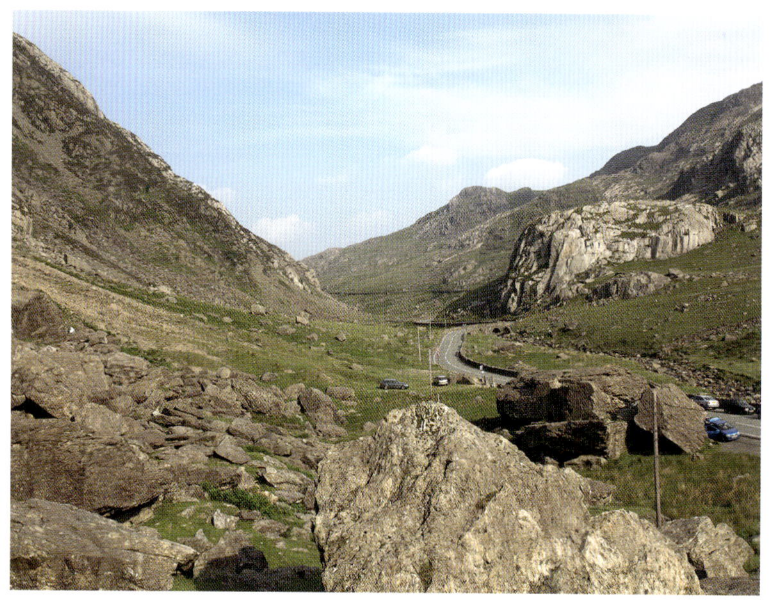

SH 62797 56764

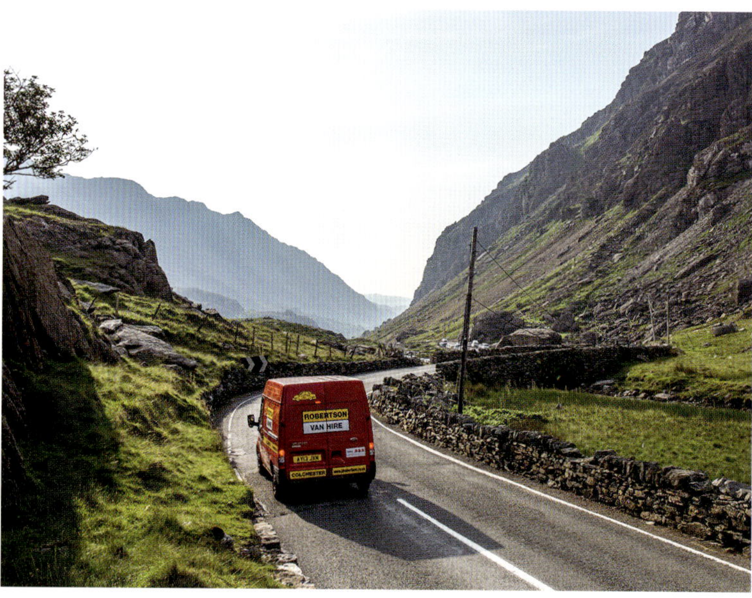

SH 63035 56521

The Cromlech boulders photographed by celebrated landscape photographer Francis Bedford circa 1875.

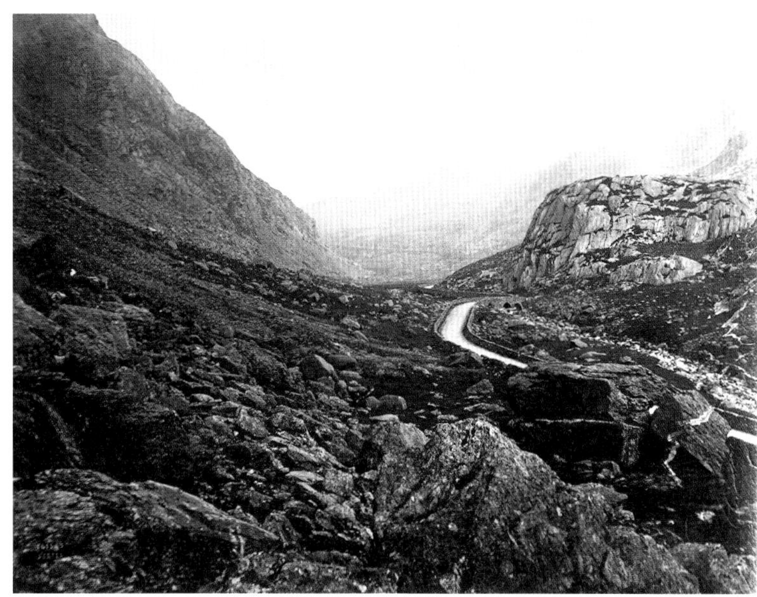

Francis Bedford, circa 1875

A shot of the nearby bridge by early commercial photographer Francis Frith during a visit circa 1890.

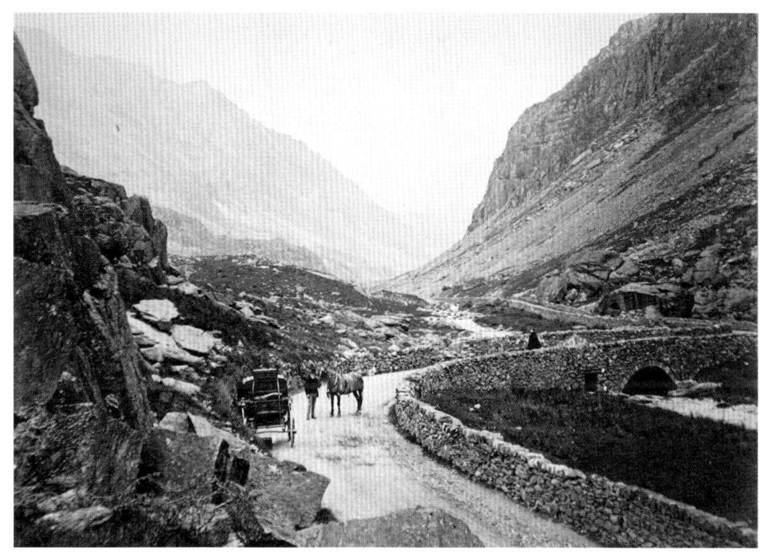

Francis Frith, circa 1890

PRESELI HILLS, PEMBROKESHIRE

2007

Two viewpoints:

An advert for 'Healing crystals'

Preseli Bluestone is the same stone that the ancient monoliths at Stonehenge are made from. These crystals are strong aids to enhance your spirituality, as they connect you to the mystical energy of Merlin and his magic. Their vibration resonates strongly with the solar plexus chakra, to stimulate your willpower and inspire courage… a primordial vibration with an ancient energy. They may assist in the development of psychic gifts.

National Monuments Record of Wales

A series of natural outcrops of spotted dolerite which naturally fragments into pillars, blocks and screes. Noted as a geological source of the Stonehenge bluestones but debate is still active as to whether the stones reached Salisbury Plain in Wiltshire through glacial or human agency. There is however evidence for quarrying on this outcrop.

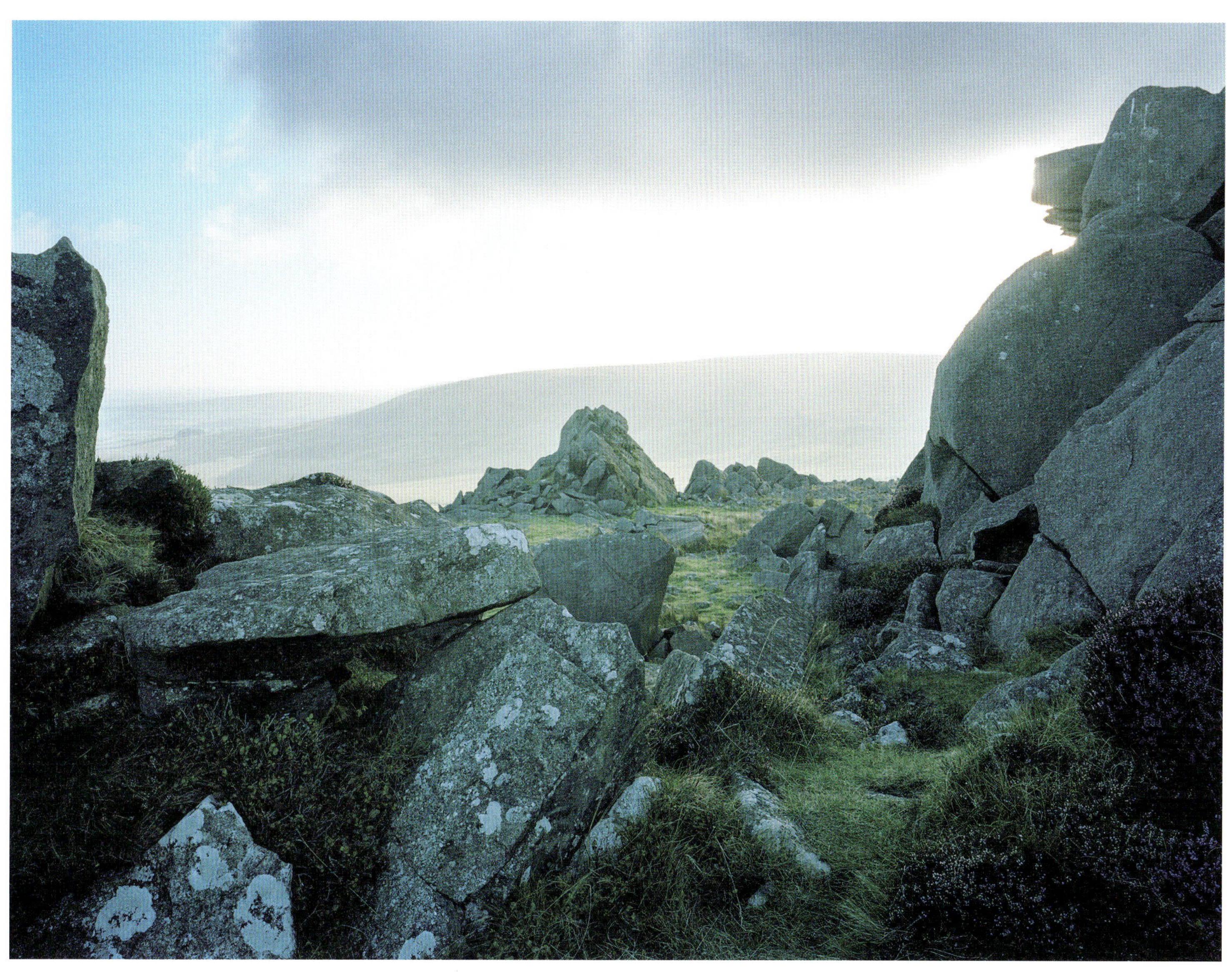

SN 14512 32521

A thick sequence of Cambrian metasediments folded into quartz-veined anticline in a geological area known as the Precambrian of Anglesey or the Mona Complex. It boasts a greater variety of rocks than anywhere in the UK, a spectacular geology spanning twelve periods over 1,800 million years.

It has been referred to as 'the mother of Wales', separated from the mainland by the Menai Strait.

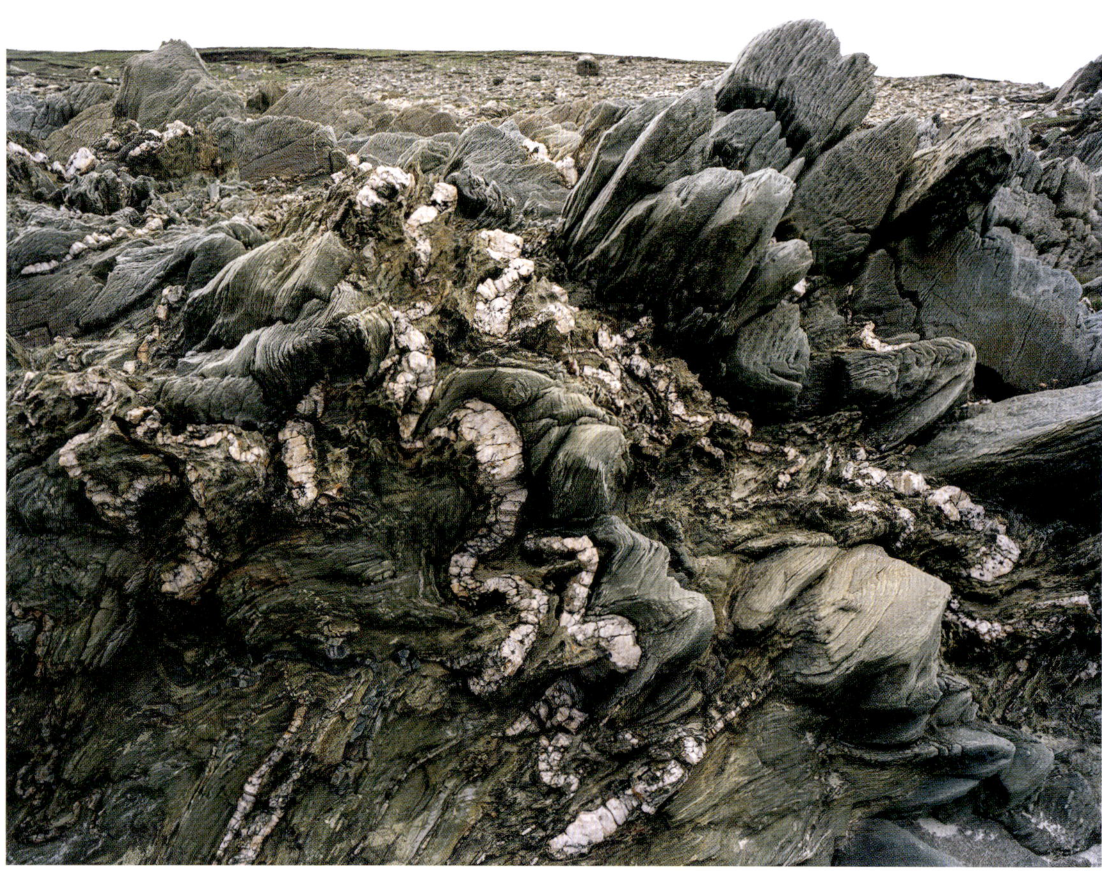

SH 26466 79439

PILLOW LAVAS, ANGLESEY

2007

The ancient pillow lavas on Ynys Llanddwyn off the west coast
of Anglesey, are regarded as some of the best preserved and
most accessible in the world. They were formed by
underwater eruptions of molten rock from a volcanic vent
during the Precambrian age around 580 million years ago.
As the magma surfaced, it cooled and set into lobes, patterned
with a mix of sea water minerals including red jasper grey
quartz, green epidote and creamy calcite.

It was largely down to these rocks that the island was
afforded its status of Geological Sites of Special Scientific
Interest in 2010.

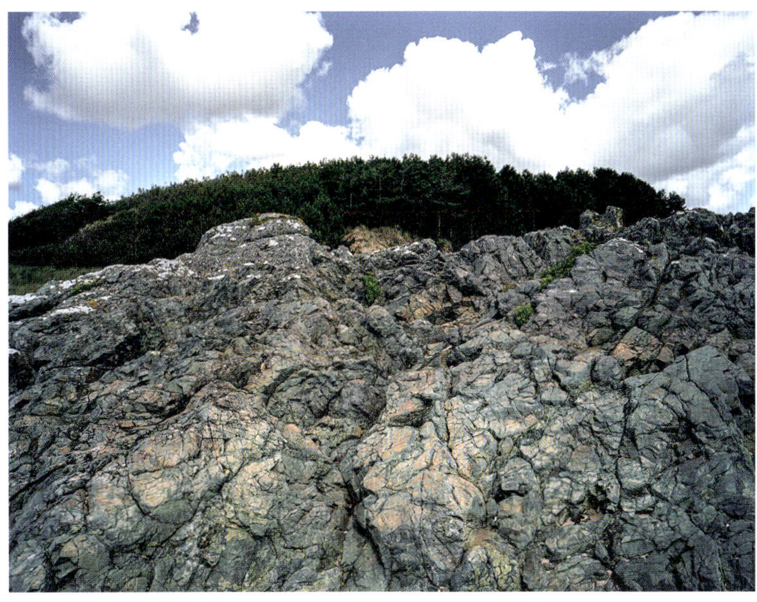

SH 39198 63479

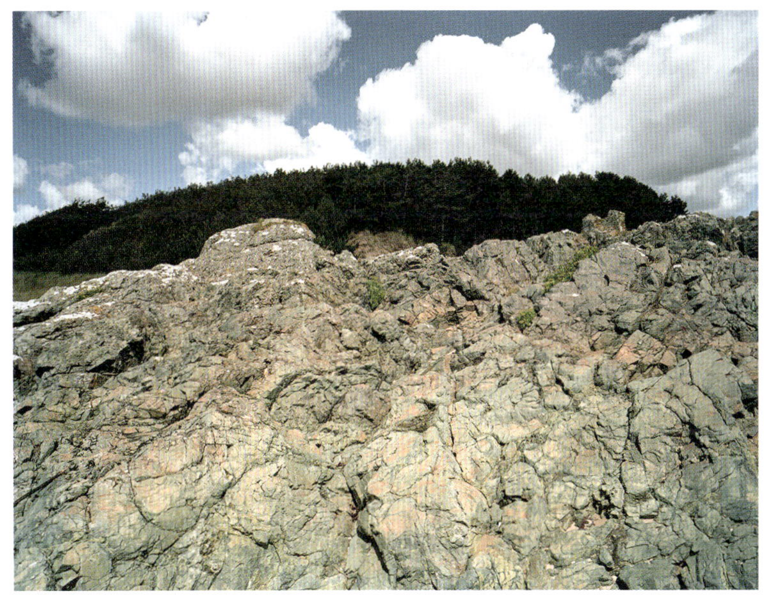

SH 39198 63479

CLARACH BAY, CEREDIGION

2013

The dramatic rock formations on a popular holiday beach
– once pliable mudstones, grit and sandstones on the ocean
floor, moulded and shaped by the sea over 400 million years –
was deemed the perfect environment to replicate the surface
of Mars.

In July 2010, scientists from Aberystwyth University involved
in research to find life on Mars, put its state-of-the-art robot
named Bridget through its paces around the bay's rock pools
and cliff faces.

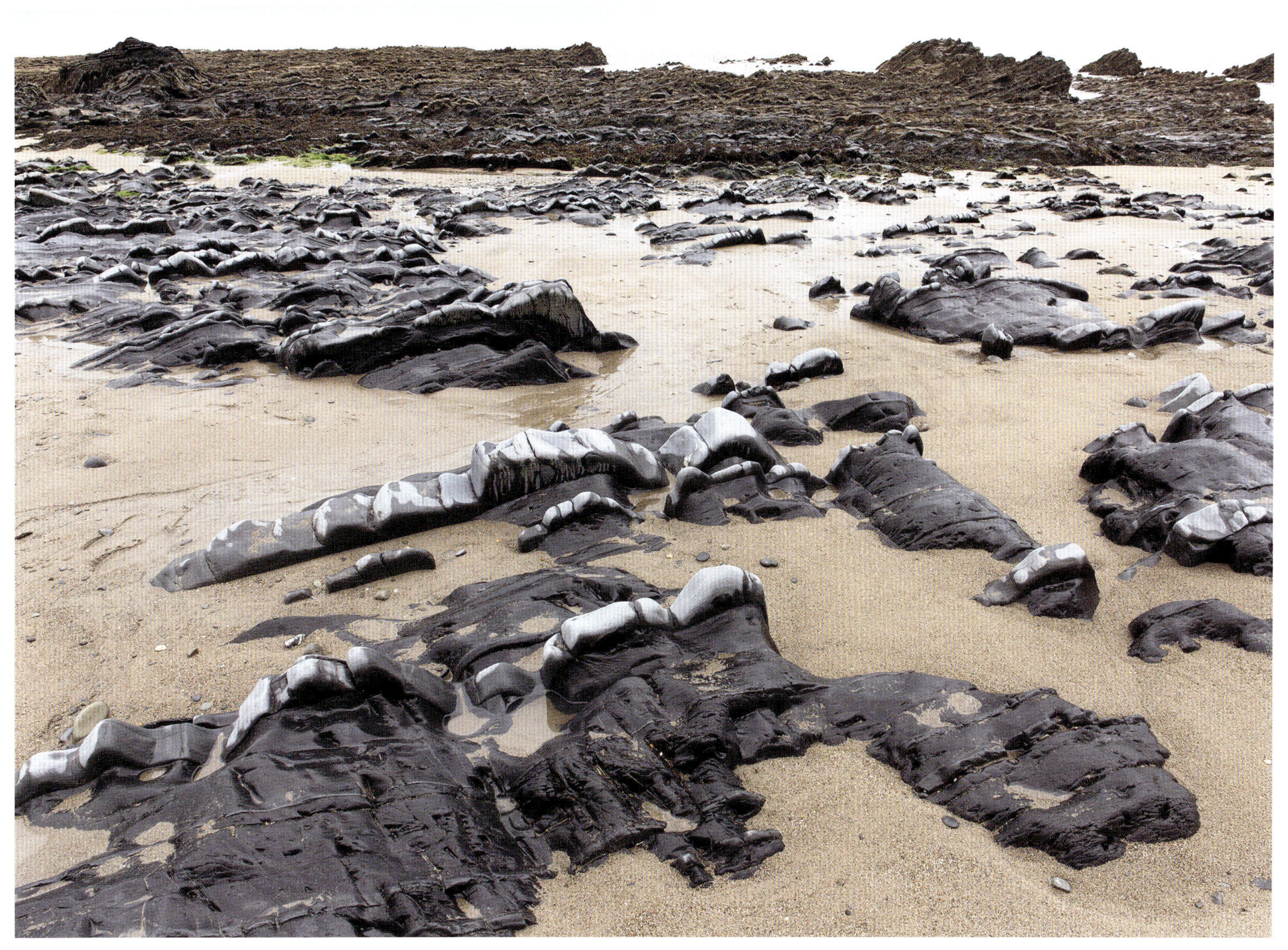

SN 58574 84188

A mile-or-so north of Borth, the remains of an ancient submerged forest revealed at low tide. Embedded Bronze Age stumps of oak, pine, birch, willow and hazel, which radiocarbon dating suggests died around 1500 BC, are evidence of rising sea levels and a receding coastline.

Many associate it with the legend of Cantre'r Gwaelod, a low-lying mythical city surrounded by a sea wall. One-night Seithennyn, the man responsible for closing the gates, got drunk and fell asleep allowing spring tides to breach, forcing its people to run for the hills.

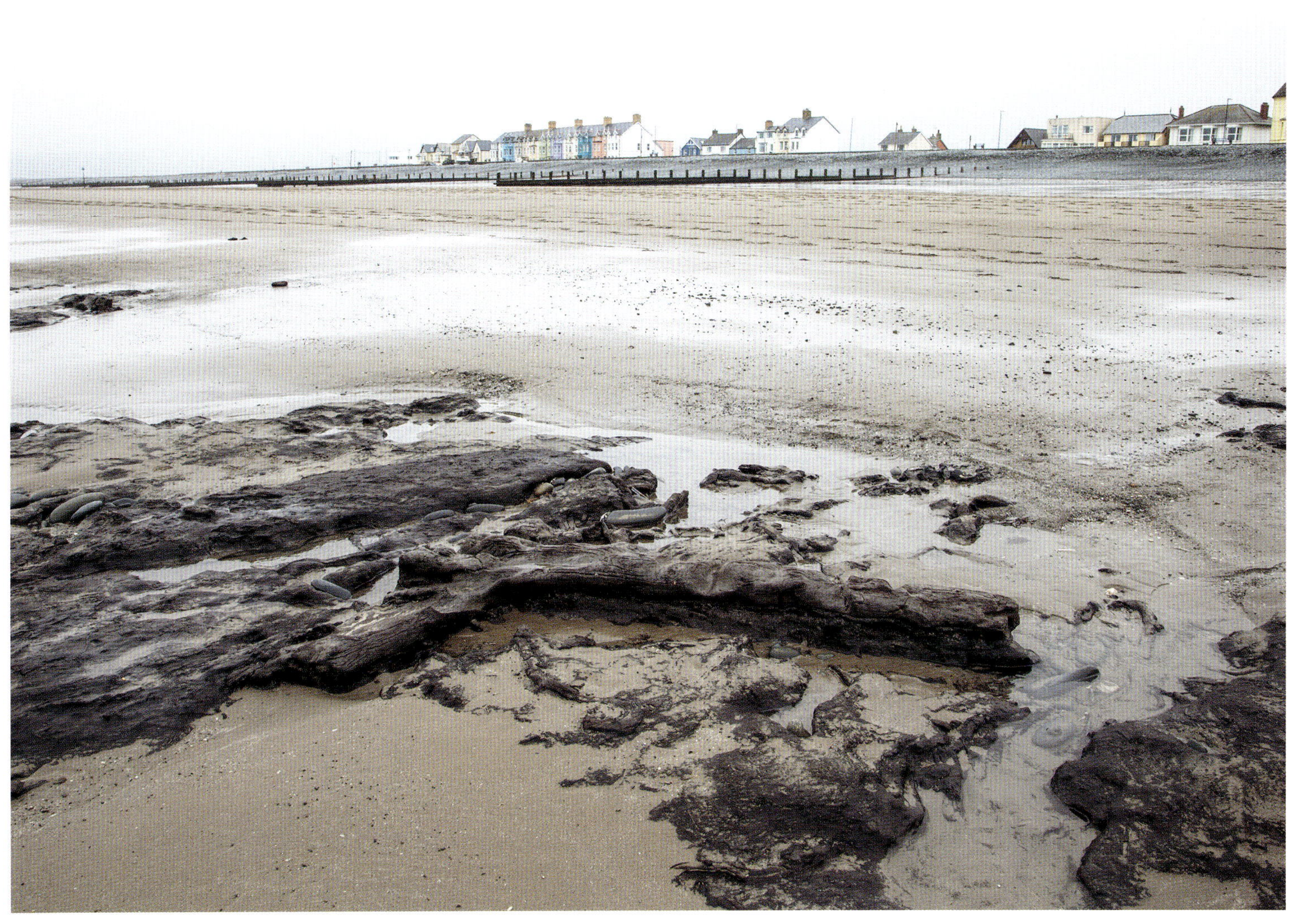

SN 60612 90506

The Palaeolithic site within the Elwy Valley is the only location in the UK to produce fossils of a classic Neanderthal, a branch of the human family tree that became extinct. Excavations by the University of Wales began in 1978 and unearthed nineteen teeth from at least five individuals. Among them was a jawbone of a child containing a heavily worn milk tooth and newly-erupted permanent molar dated as 230,000 years old.

One of the most important archaeological sites in the UK, the cave, on a privately-owned estate, is bricked up with three doors barring access.

ANTHROPOLOGY

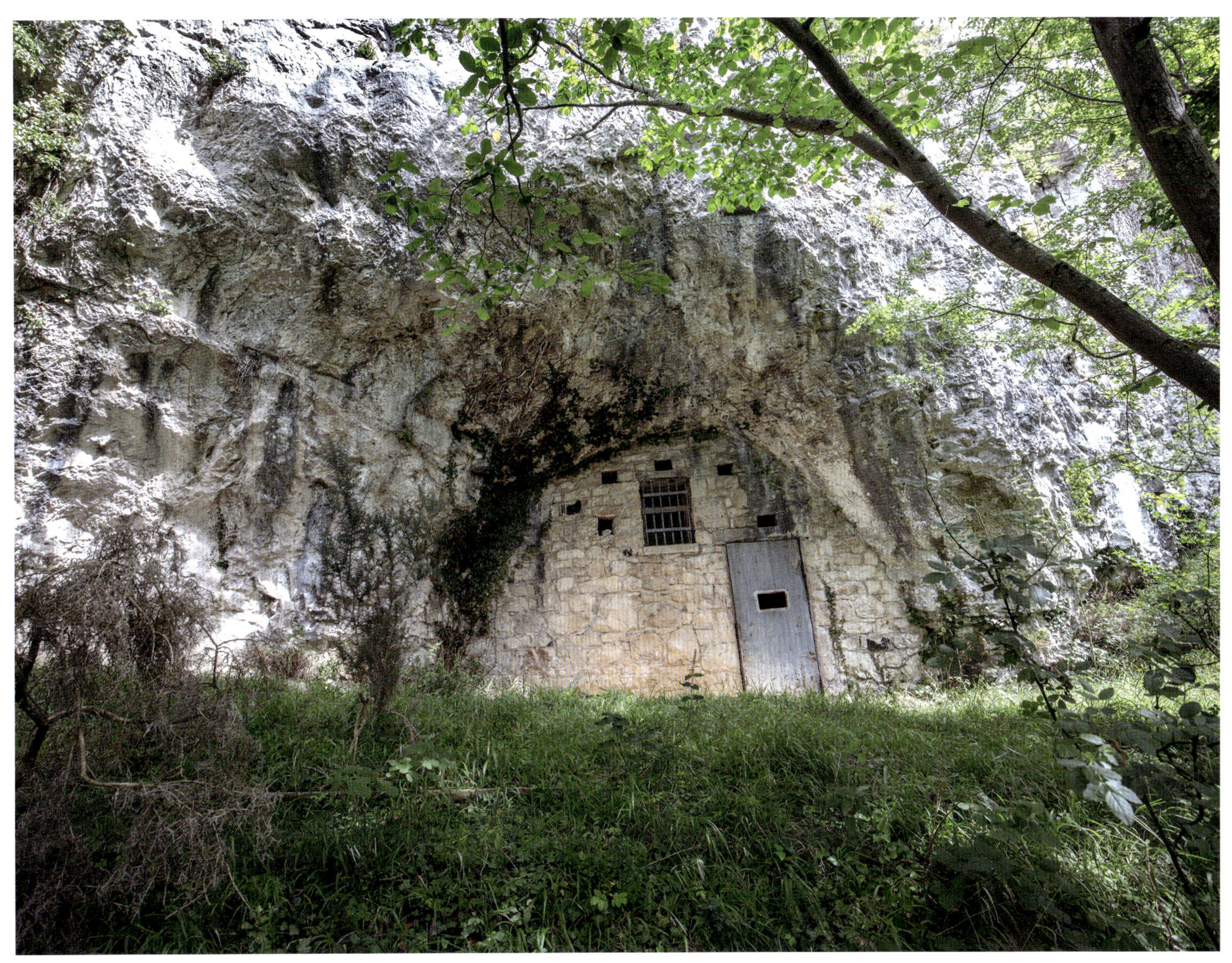

SJ 01526 71040

DYFFRYN ARDUDWY, GWYNEDD

2015

A pair of Neolithic tombs on a hillside overlooking Cardigan Bay. Built around 4000 BC, the chambers are described by heritage body Cadw as the finest surviving examples of a portal dolmen, where two upright stones support a large, flat capstone.

As with similar structures, the openings are to the east to face the rising sun.

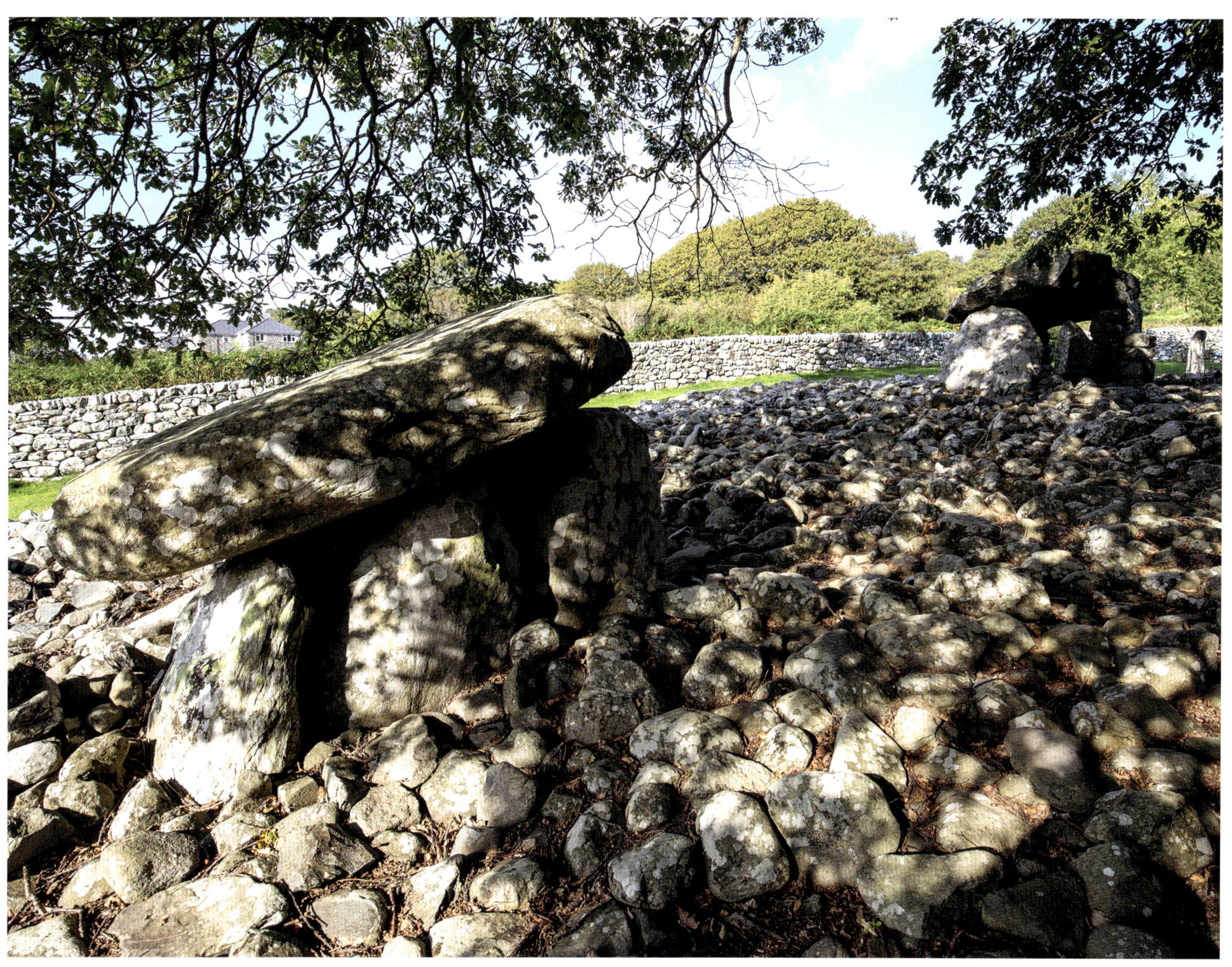

SH 58862 22841

TINKINSWOOD, VALE OF GLAMORGAN

2014

One of the UK's best-preserved Neolithic chambered cairns
built 1,500 years before Stonehenge's famous trilithons. Its
capstone is one of the largest recorded, weighing in at 40
tonnes. Placing it would have been the equivalent of lifting an
articulated lorry. The remains of up to 50 people were found
during an excavation in 1914.

Folklore has it that anyone who spends the night there on the
eve of May Day, Midsummer or Midwinter Day, either goes
mad or becomes a poet.

HAROLD'S STONES, MONMOUTHSHIRE

2014

No-one knows for certain why three Late Neolithic or Early
Bronze Age stones stand in a farmer's field in Trellech, near
Chepstow. Theories range from ritual, astronomical, part of
a larger stone circle and commemoration of three chieftains
who fell in battle, to the remnants of a throwing competition
between a giant and the devil.

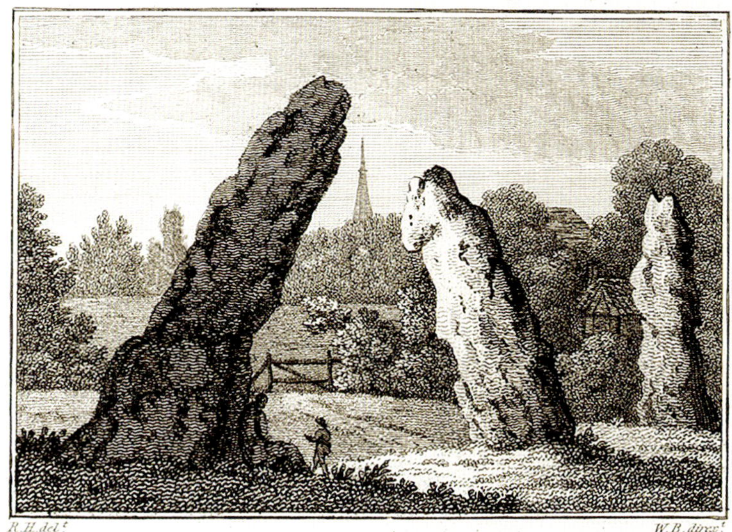

Sir Richard Colt Hoare, 1793

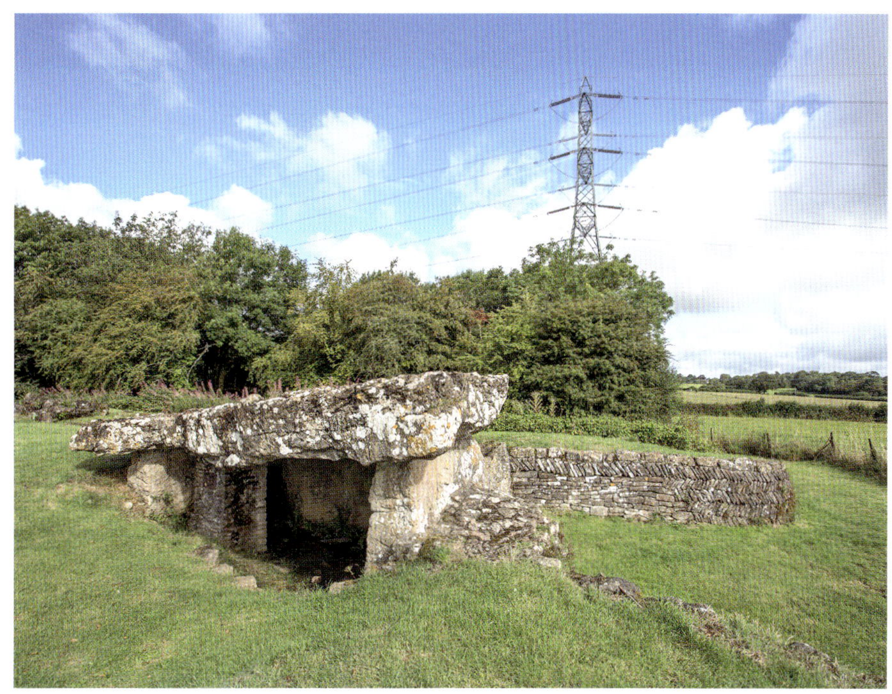

ST 09237 73296

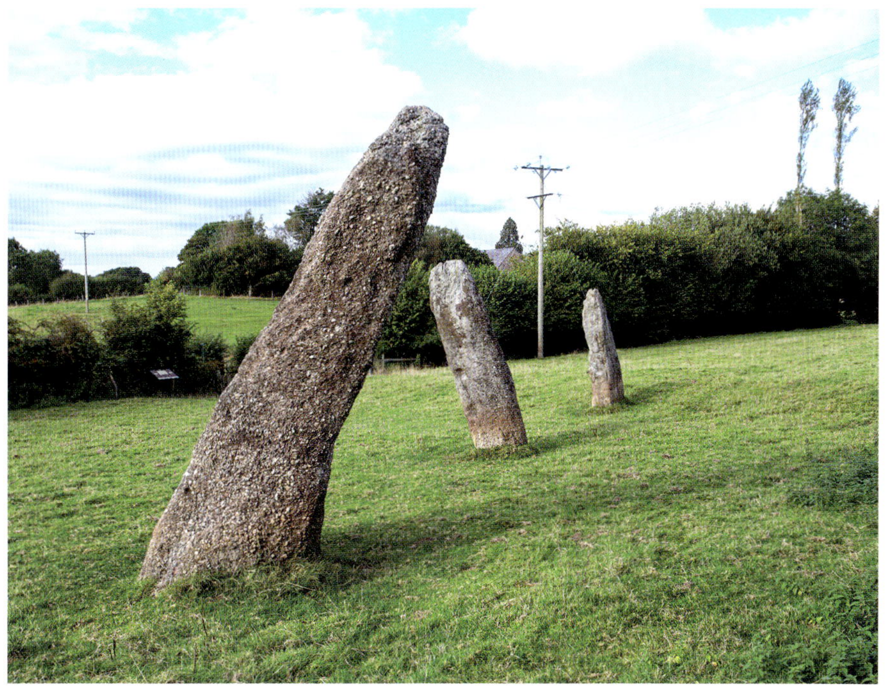

SO 49926 05136

THE TRETOWER STONE, POWYS

2014

Also known as the Cwmdu Stone, the two-meter-high
prehistoric relic can be found inside a hawthorn hedge dividing
fields near Brecon. Close by are the ruins of a medieval castle
with an impressive circular tower after which the area gets its
name 'settlement of the tower'.

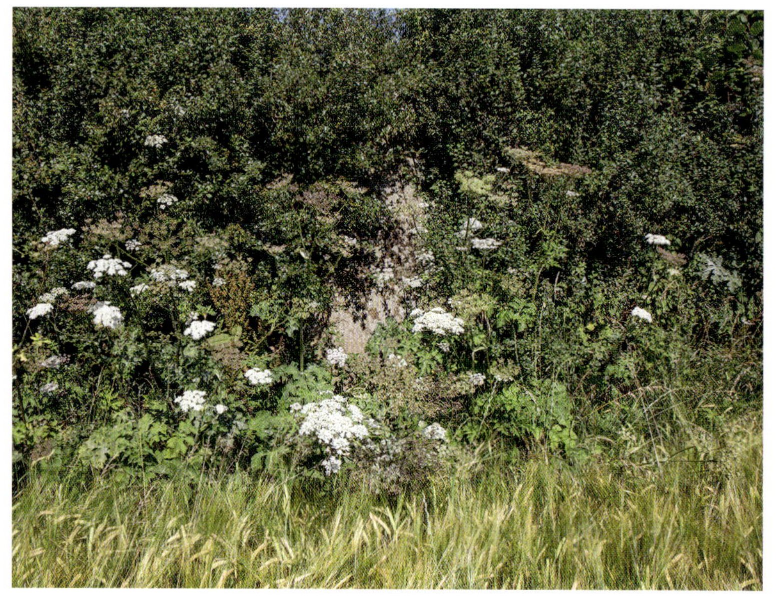

SO 18045 21920

THE TRETOWER STONE, POWYS

2015

The stone is best viewed in winter.

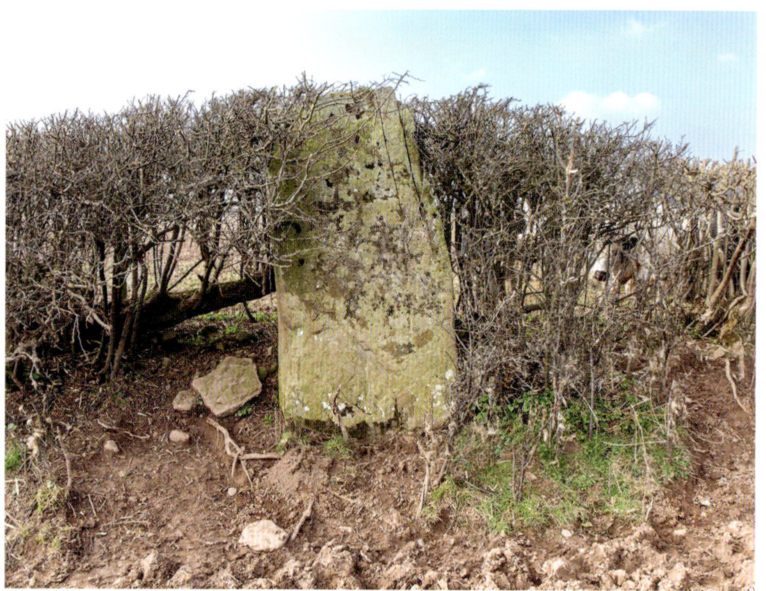

SO 18045 21920

PENTRE IFAN, PEMBROKESHIRE

2014

The bare bones of the dolmen or burial chamber, Pentre Ifan, or Ifan's village in English, is missing its original Neolithic covering of a curved earthen and stone mound. The scheduled monument, one of three in Wales to receive legal protection under the Ancient Monuments Protection Act 1882, was studied by early antiquarians and became famous as an image of ancient Cymru.

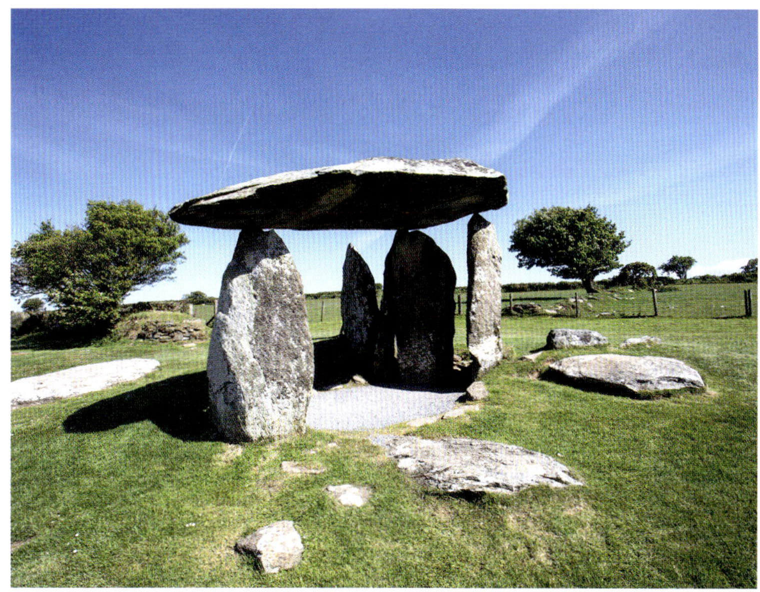

SN 09940 37025

MAEN LLIA, POWYS

2018

A towering, four-metre-high, diamond-shaped Bronze Age Old Red Sandstone monolith stands alone in an isolated moorland in the heart of the Brecon Beacons National Park. At an altitude of 573m, it is said to be the highest standing stone in South Wales. Its visibility for some distance suggests it could have marked an ancient trackway. In 2013, it was graffitied with a white painted smiley face.

Local legend tells that on Midsummer Eve, the stone moves to the edge of the nearby Afon Llia to drink. It is at this time that its shadow stretches down towards the river bank.

The charming manifestation of someone's originality and imagination in the foreground where, in place of the usual tourist information board, is an inscribed, small-scale replica of the scheduled ancient monument.

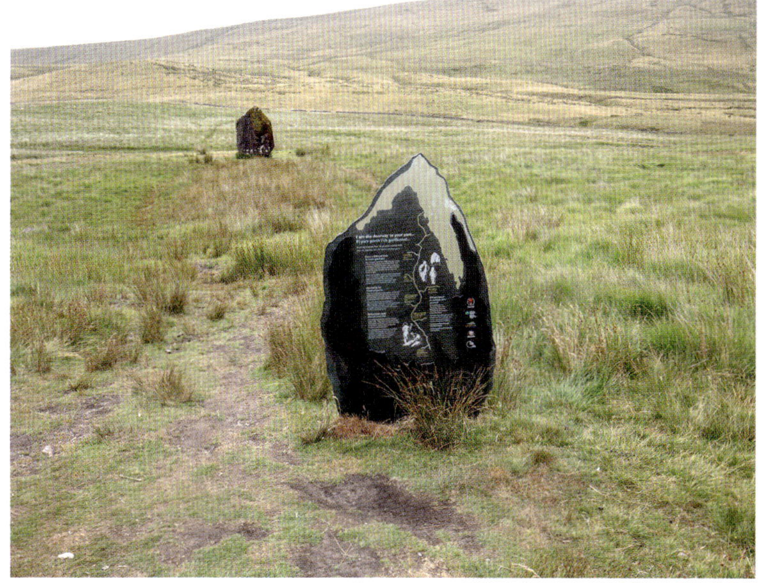

SN 92373 19179

TŶ NEWYDD, ANGLESEY

2007

The old and the new… likely to have been the cheapest and easiest material to hand, brick pillars now partially support the Neolithic capstone of the burial chamber found within the boundaries of a farm by the same name near the village of Llanfaelog. Pottery and arrow heads were found in 1935 by Charles William Phillips, who went on to lead the excavation of Sutton Hoo.

In more recent years, prehistoric 'cup marks' (which might be artwork) have been detected on the capstone.

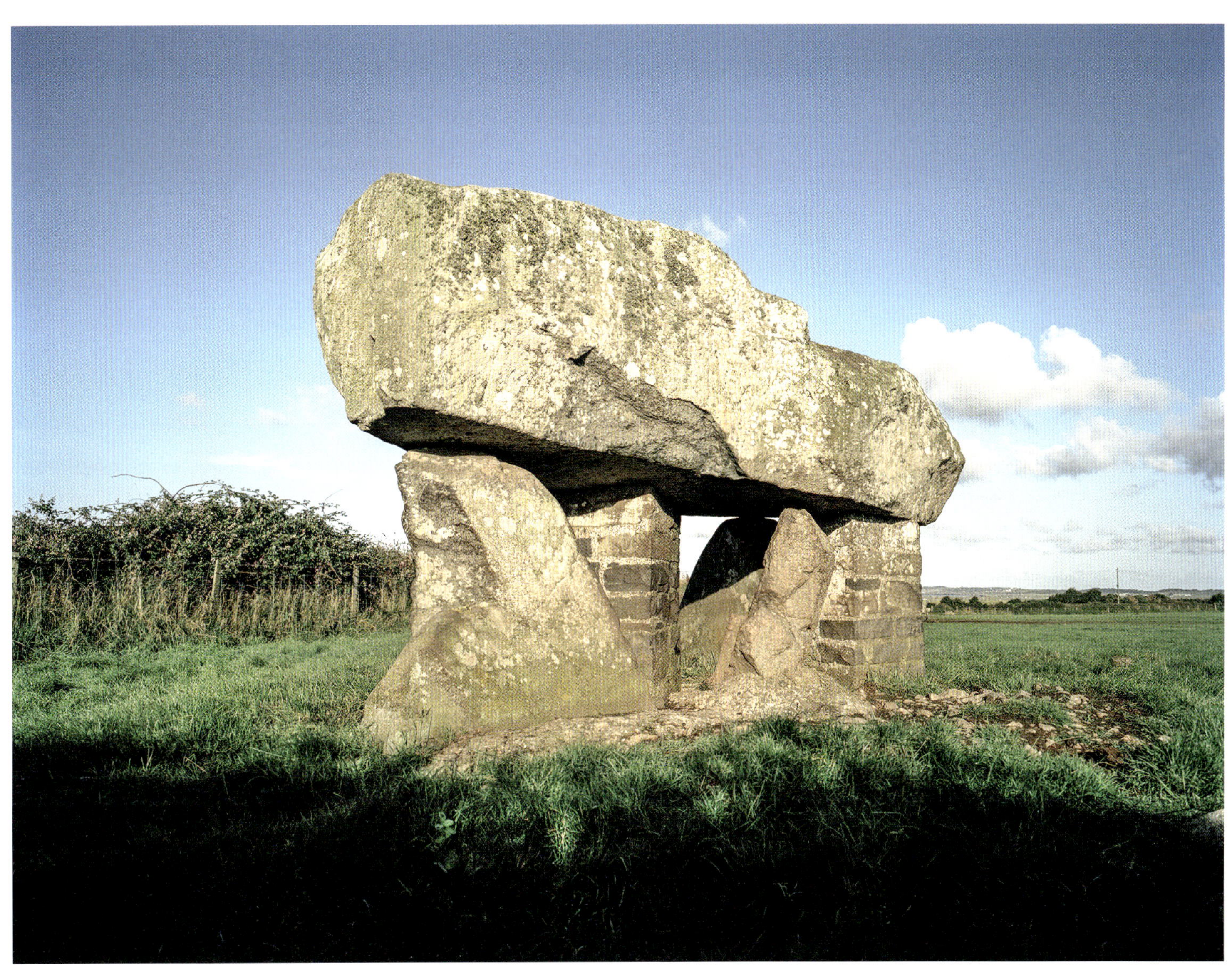

SH 34421 73861

THE ROCKING STONE, RHONDDA CYNON TAF

2024

A central rock carried down the valley during the last Ice Age lies at the heart of the Garreg Siglo Bardic Complex, a scheduled ancient monument of national importance as the focus of Wales' eighteenth century cultural renaissance.

The first of two stone circles was erected to mark the 1795 inaugural meeting of the Gorsedd y Beirdd – a collective of writers, artists and poets supposedly based on the ancient Celtic Druidry – established by antiquarian and scholar Edward Williams, who went by the bardic name of Iolo Morganwg. A man fixated with the revival and, in some instances, reinvention of Wales' medieval past, Morganwg's legacy is described by the University of Wales Centre for Advanced Welsh and Celtic Studies as 'an inspiring, if frustrating, mesh of fact and fiction.'

The gorsedd, which literally means 'throne' in Welsh, was later co-opted into the nineteenth century eisteddfod revival. Today, its members conduct ceremonies at the annual Eisteddfod Genedlaethol dressed in coloured robes.

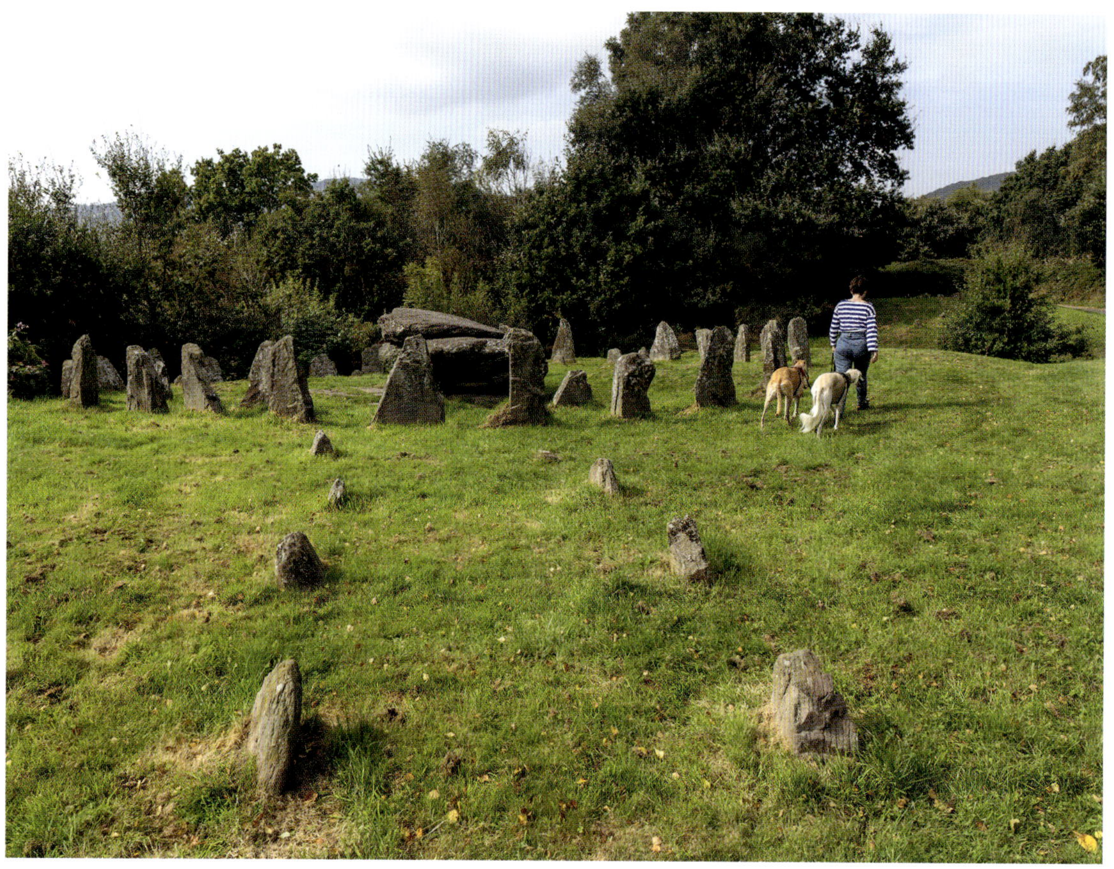

ST 08126 90116

Looking for all the world like a Bronze Age relic, the circle of unhewn stones is in fact only 120 years old, erected in 1904 for the Eisteddfod Genedlaethol the following year.

Cardiff Times, **July 1904:**
"The site in the centre of a handsome grove of oak trees is admirable. It stands on the centre of a natural amphitheatre, which lends itself to the ceremony, as it will be visible from either side."

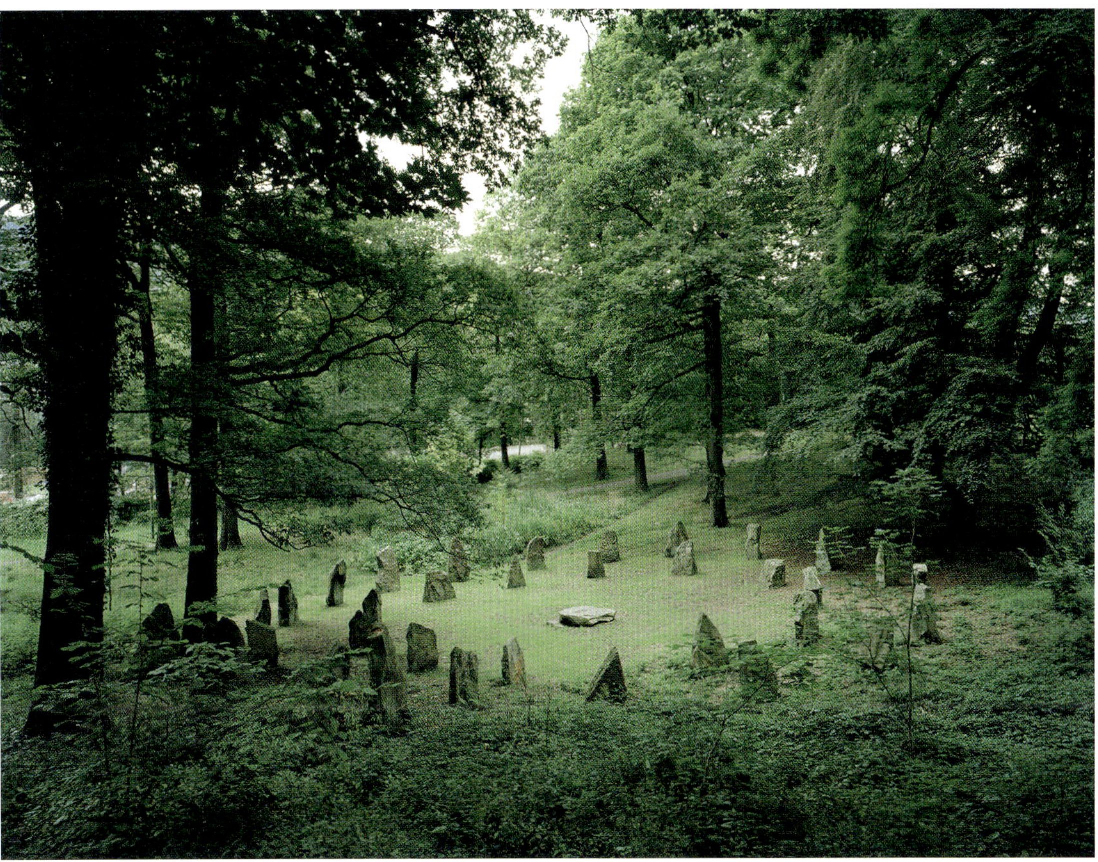

ST 04421 99801

MY TELEVISION SCREEN, MONMOUTHSHIRE

2019

North Wales Live, February 2004:
"Fake rocks are likely to be used for next year's Gorsedd ceremony in North Wales.

"The traditional Gorsedd circle, made of huge granite stones, will in future be replaced with plastic or fibreglass ones.
The main stone structures are arranged in a circle, usually consisting of twelve stone pillars.

"The board recommended the switch to stop bards being bussed to standing stones, often miles away.
Consultants have told the Eisteddfod it needs a complete facelift if it is to survive by attracting more people."

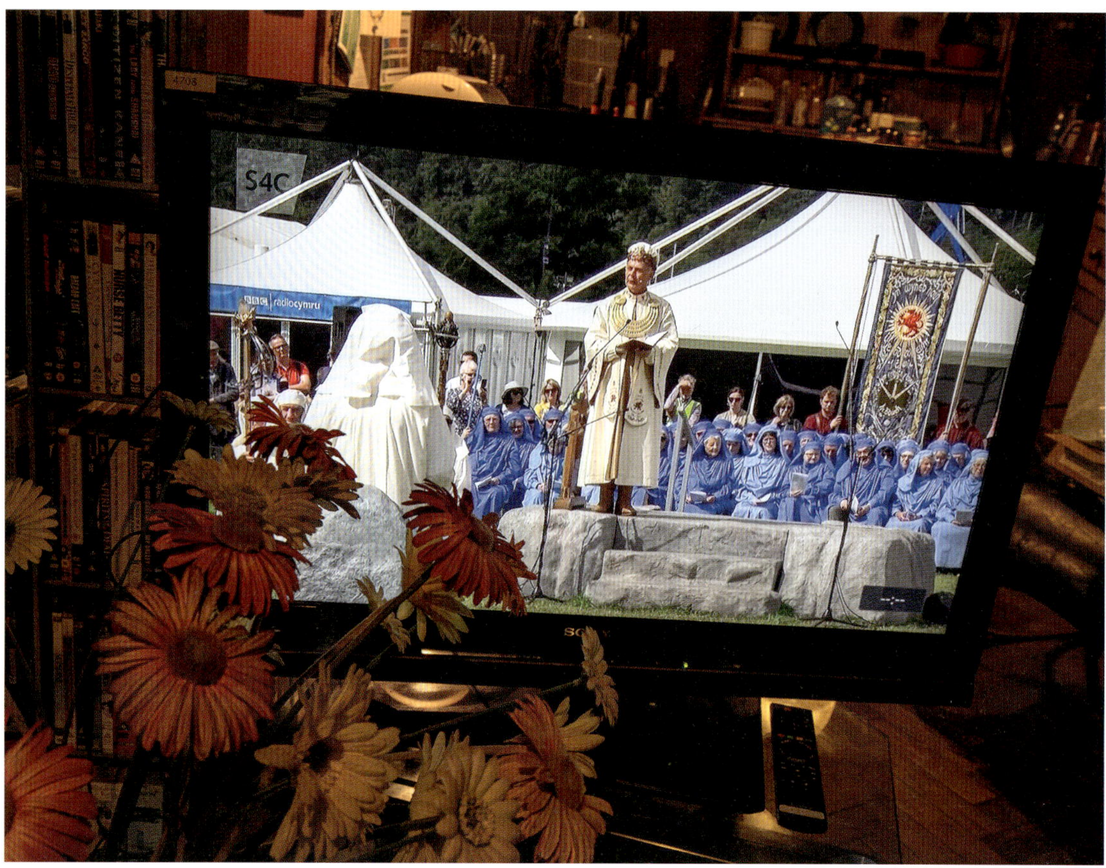

SO 52890 00759

STEPPING STONES, ST BRIDE'S MAJOR,
VALE OF GLAMORGAN

2015

St Teilo's steps or Stepsau Teilo, offer a path across a ford of the
Ewenny river. One story holds they were built to enable two young
lovers to meet unimpeded by tides and floods. The couple, both
from Norman noble families, were Hawise de Londres, resident in
the nearby (now ruinous) Ogmore Castle, and Walter de Braose, and
were later married.

BRIDGES

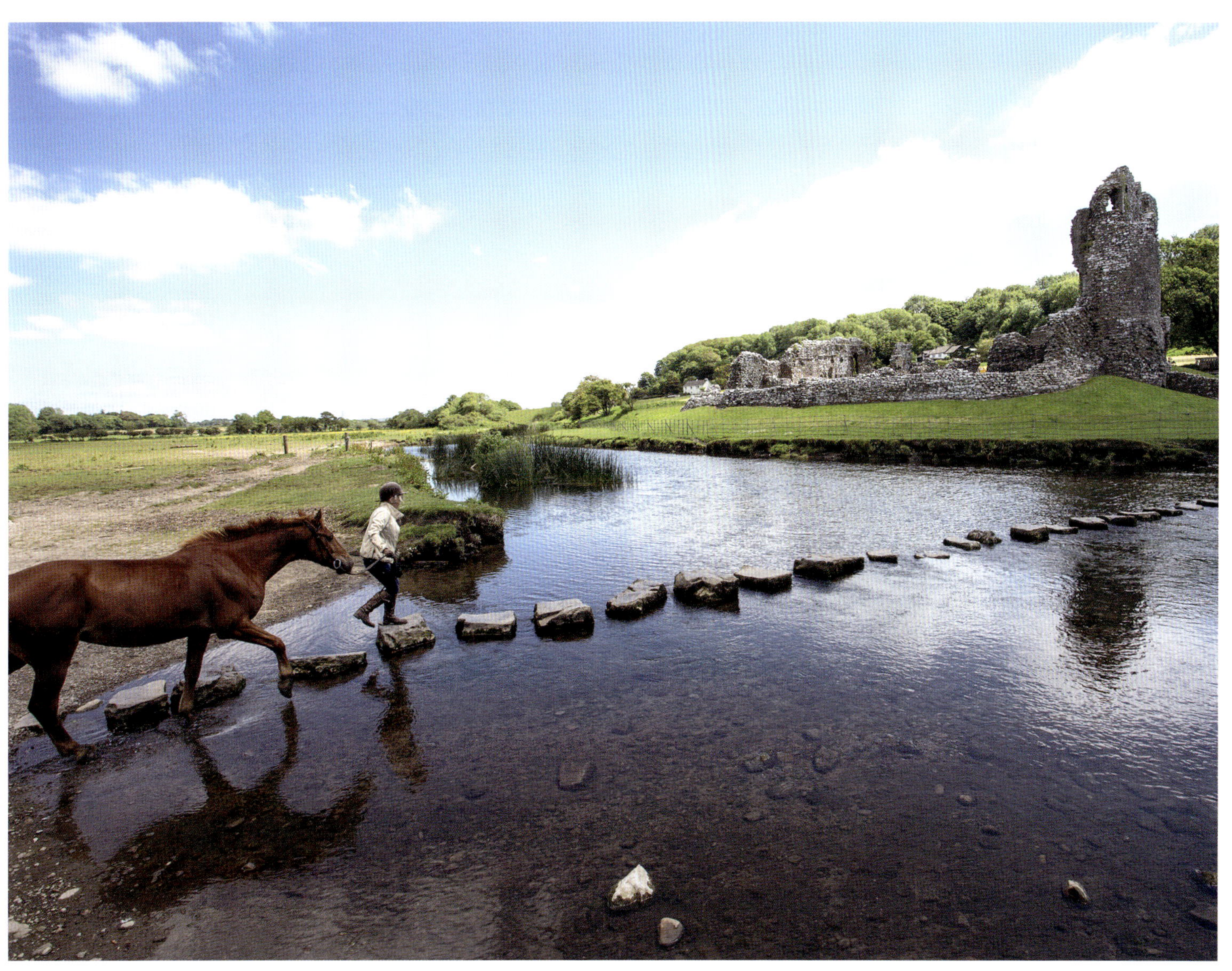

SS 88131 77014

The heavily-worn path of sixteen 'stepsau duon' or black steps, were laid as far back as the tenth century near a ford of the Afon Alun, a tributary of the Ewenny.

The site is a scheduled monument deemed of national importance for its potential to enhance our knowledge of early transport networks.

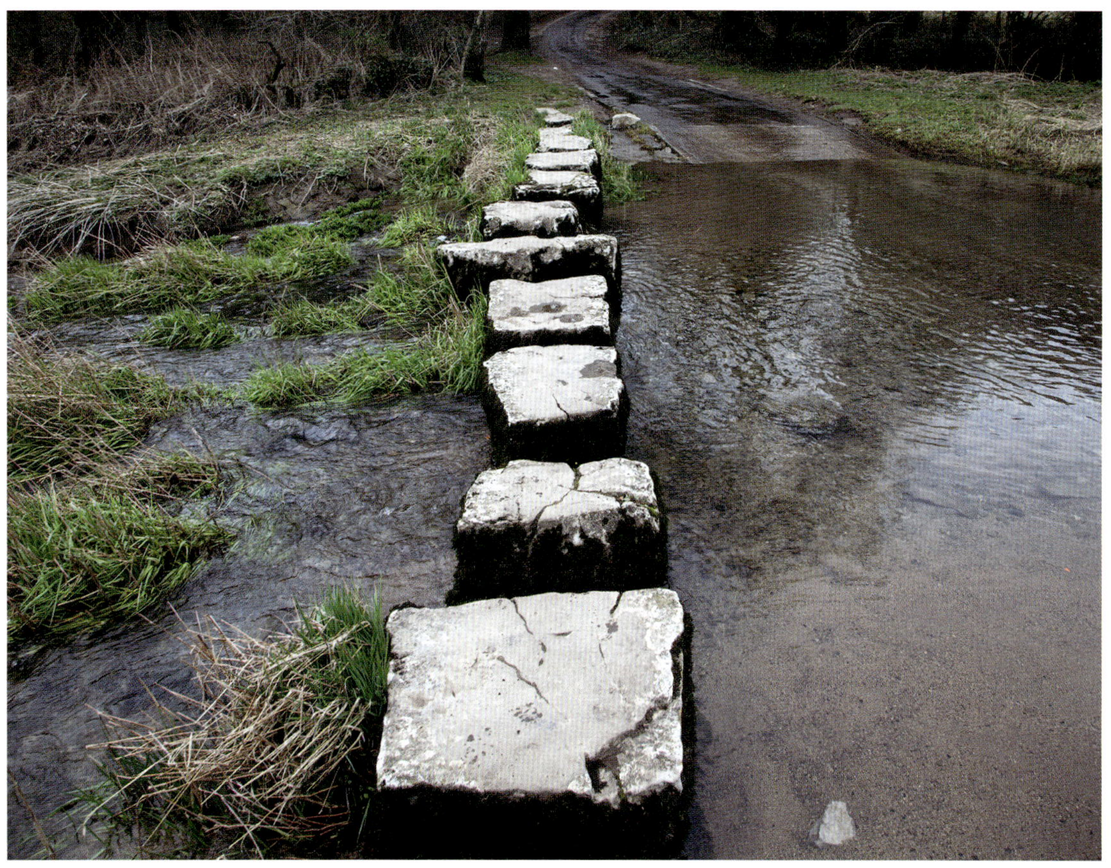

SS 90906 75673

CWM CADNANT, ANGLESEY

2016

An ancient clapper bridge over the Afon Cadnant downstream from a nearby mill. There are two theories of the origin of 'clapper'.
One holds it derives from the Anglo-Saxon word cleaca meaning bridging the stepping stones. The Oxford English Dictionary cites the medieval Latin word clapus, a pile of stones.

An unsightly modern handrail fitted by the local council has since been removed.

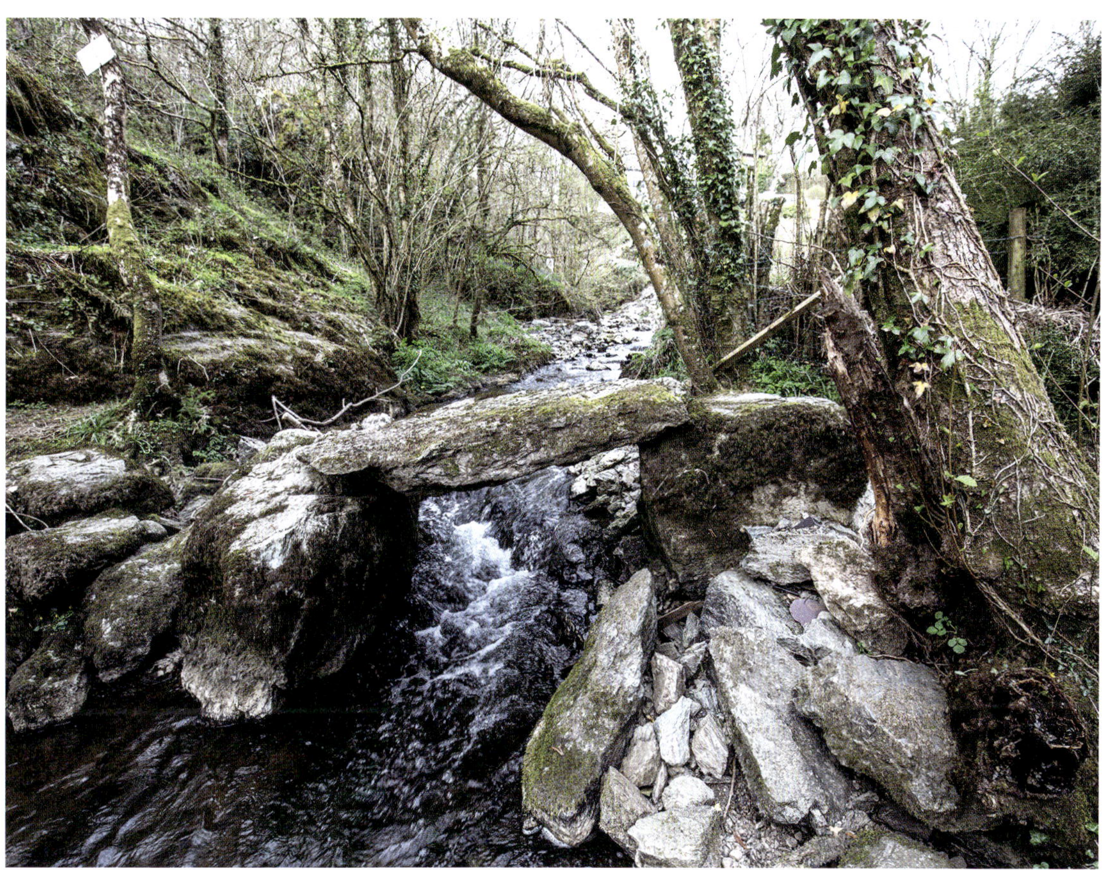

SH 55940 74033

A little-known, well-preserved example of an eighteenth century clapper bridge using an ancient construction of large limestone slabs laid across the natural bedrock, spanning 35 yards under which the River Alun, more of a steam, freely runs.

In his book *The Bridges of Wales*, Gwyndaf Breese notes that some of the openings are original whereas others have been crudely rebuilt, one 'badly repaired in concrete, over an earlier effort of stone blocks supported on a rusting iron bar'.

Considered an historical monument, the bridge is in a hamlet near the village of St Bride's Major, dating back to the medieval period where it is thought a pre-Norman castle once stood.

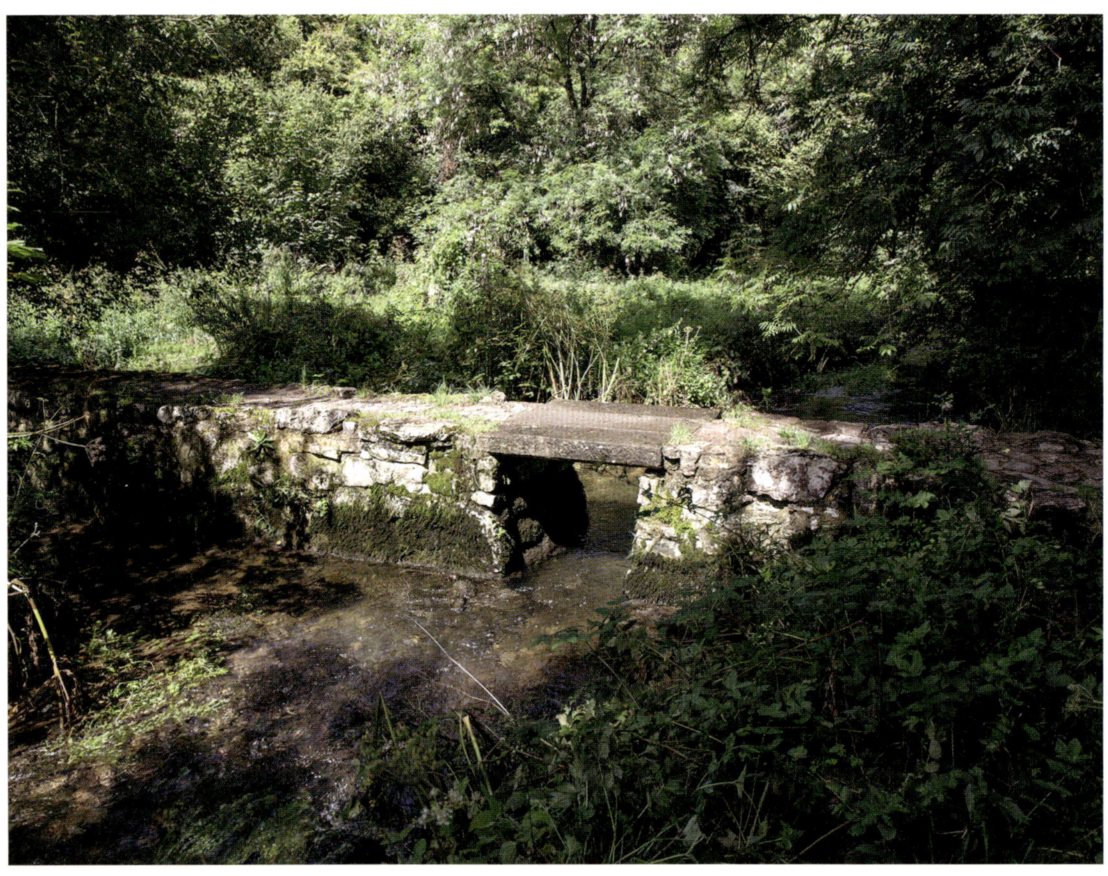

SS 90995 75088

Packhorse routes were the medieval arteries across Britain with narrow bridges built to provide transport over rivers. Low parapets accommodated mules loaded with heavy panniers.

A lack of records makes it difficult to put an age on the bridge which still links the villages of Caergwrle and Hope. In his book *Hidden Highways of North Wales*, R.J.A. Dutton writes: 'It is probably one of the oldest bridges over the river Alyn and is the best example of this type of bridge in North Wales. It is assumed to be of the late seventeenth century and is a picturesque and historical survivor of an age gone by.'

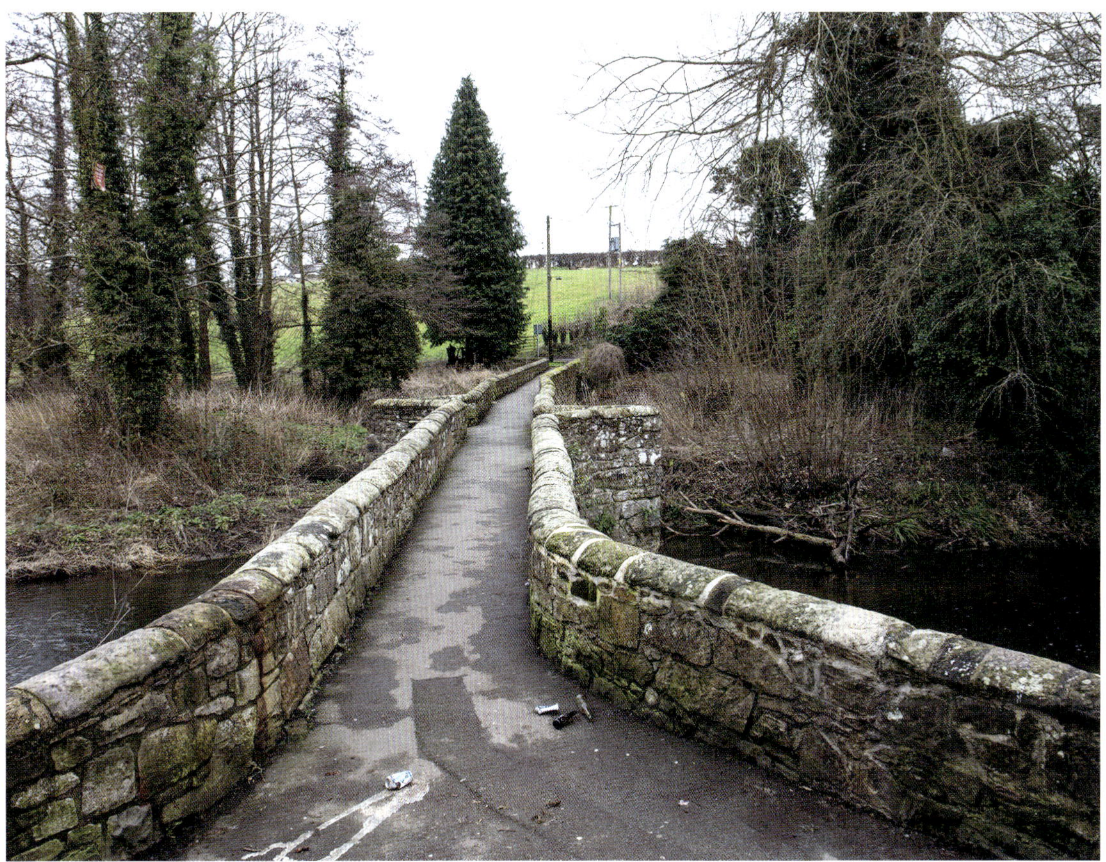

SJ 30605 57610

DIPPING BRIDGE, BRIDGEND

2015

The holes in the parapets of the four-arched fifteenth century bridge at the entrance to the village of Merthyr Mawr were once used to dispatch sheep for their annual dip.

A feature on the landmark in the *Western Mail* published in June 1951 drew an angry response in the letter section:

"Sir," AA Williams of Llanstephan wrote, "With a drop of more than 15ft, please grant me space to strongly protest against such methods which must cause shock and injury to helpless creatures."

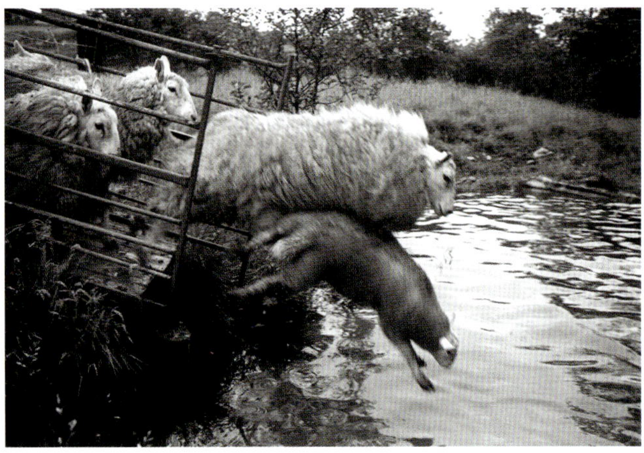

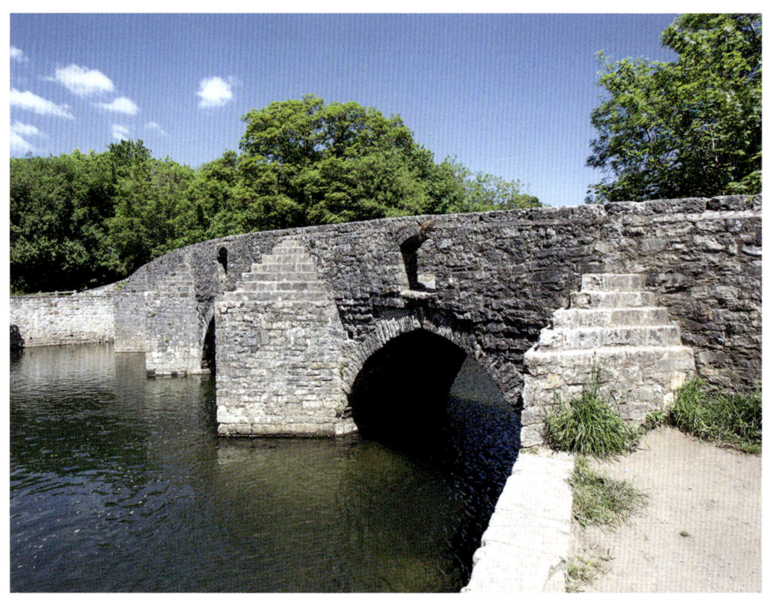

Upper Chapel 1973

SS 89089 78406

PONT-Y-CAFNAU, MERTHYR TYDFIL

2014

Acknowledged as the world's oldest surviving example of its kind, the cast iron railway bridge built in 1793 at the confluence of the River Taff, is double-decked; the upper for rail, the lower an aqueduct.

An important early prototype, its construction influenced Thomas Telford's feats of engineering.

It is now a footbridge.

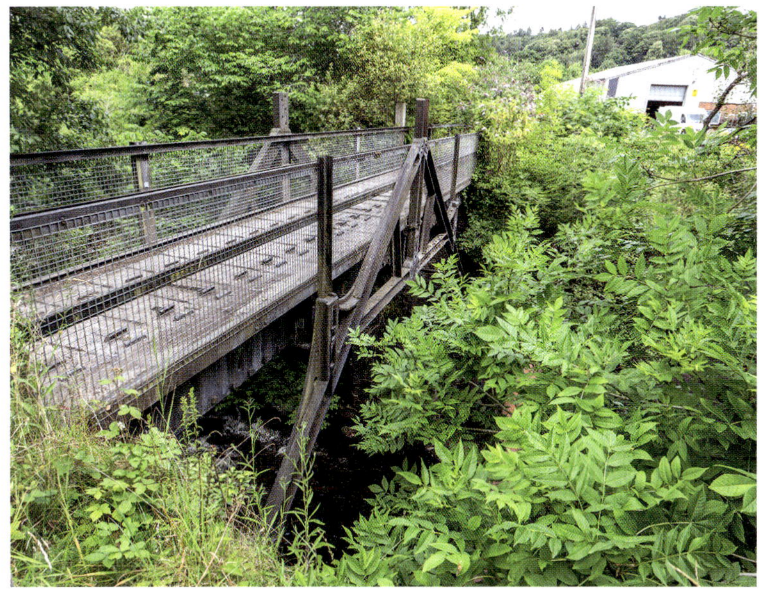

SO 03764 07130

OLD BRIDGE, RHONDDA CYNON TAF

2016

One of Pontypridd's most distinctive landmarks was constructed in the middle of the eighteenth century – the fourth attempt by self-taught William Edwards to build a single-span crossing over the River Taff. Stretching 140ft, at one time it held the record as the longest of a masonry bridge in Europe, exceeding the Rialto Bridge in Venice by 40ft.

Its cylindrical holes were made to lighten the otherwise heavy construction.

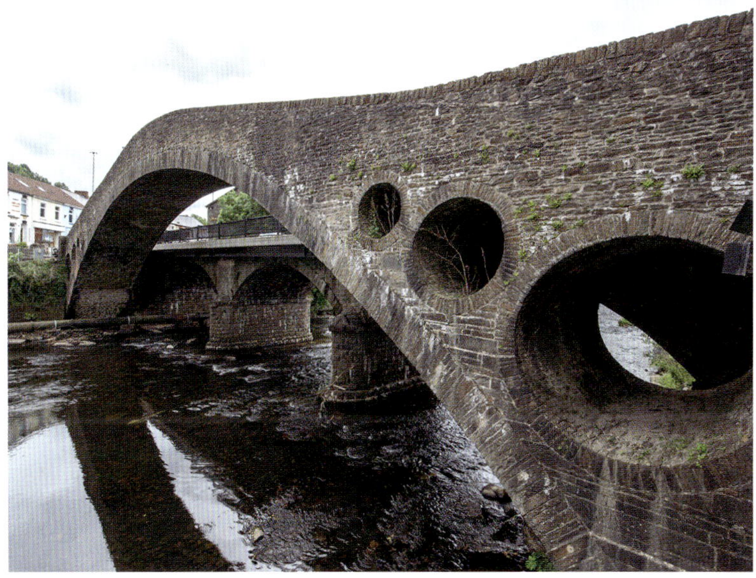

ST 07403 90442

MONMOUTH BRIDGE, MONMOUTHSHIRE

2014

The only remaining medieval fortified bridge in the UK,
its construction began in 1272 and replaced a Norman timber
bridge. Its primary function was defence and was last used
as such in 1839 when an attack by the Chartists in Newport
was feared.

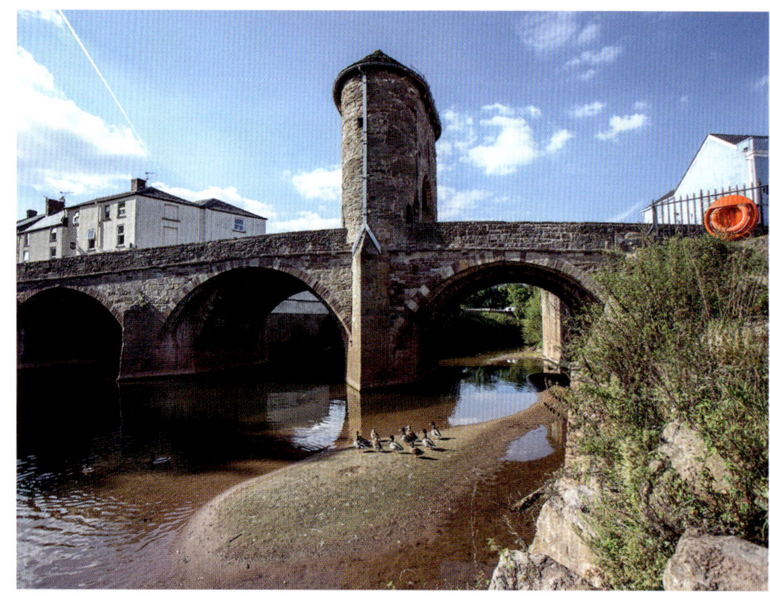

SO 50483 12501

SECOND SEVERN CROSSING, MONMOUTHSHIRE

2024

Britian's longest river bridge opened in 1996 uniquely built
over the 110-year-old South Wales to London railway tunnel.

Soon after its completion, the *South Wales Echo* invited
readers to suggest a name. Suggestions included:
Celtic Crossing, the Gateway Bridge, Atlantic Gate,
Severn Western, Bassey Bridge, Merlin's Bridge,
St David's Crossing, Millennium Bridge, Dick Turpin (on
account of the 'highway robbery' tolls).

It remained officially unnamed until shortly before the tolls
were abolished in 2018, when it was confirmed as the
Prince of Wales Bridge.

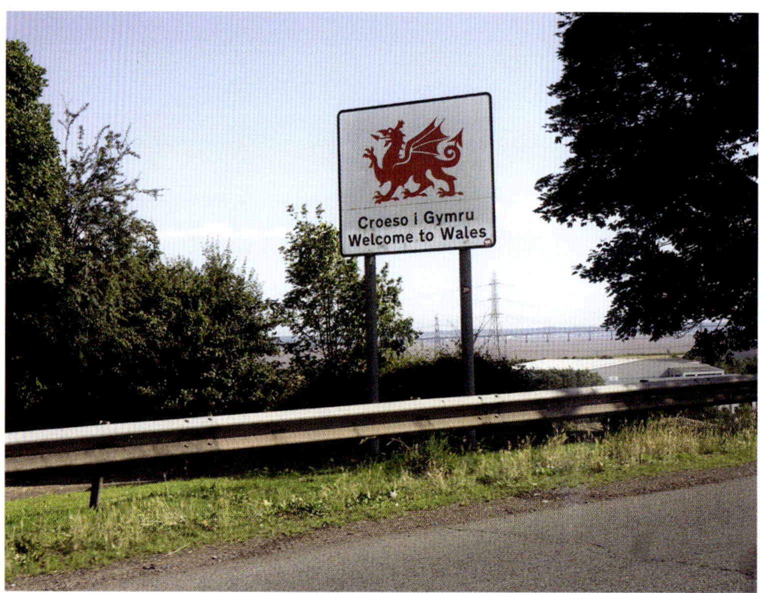

ST 53556 91487

2018

"The stream in the sky," noted Sir Walter Scott,
"The most impressive piece of art I have ever seen… where fish
swim above birds in flight."

Holding aloft the canal 120ft over the river Dee, the 18-arch
aqueduct completed in 1805 is the longest in the UK and one
of the highest canals in the world. One of Thomas Telford's first
engineering feats, it has both Grade One listing and is part of
the Llangollen Canal UNESCO World Heritage Site status.

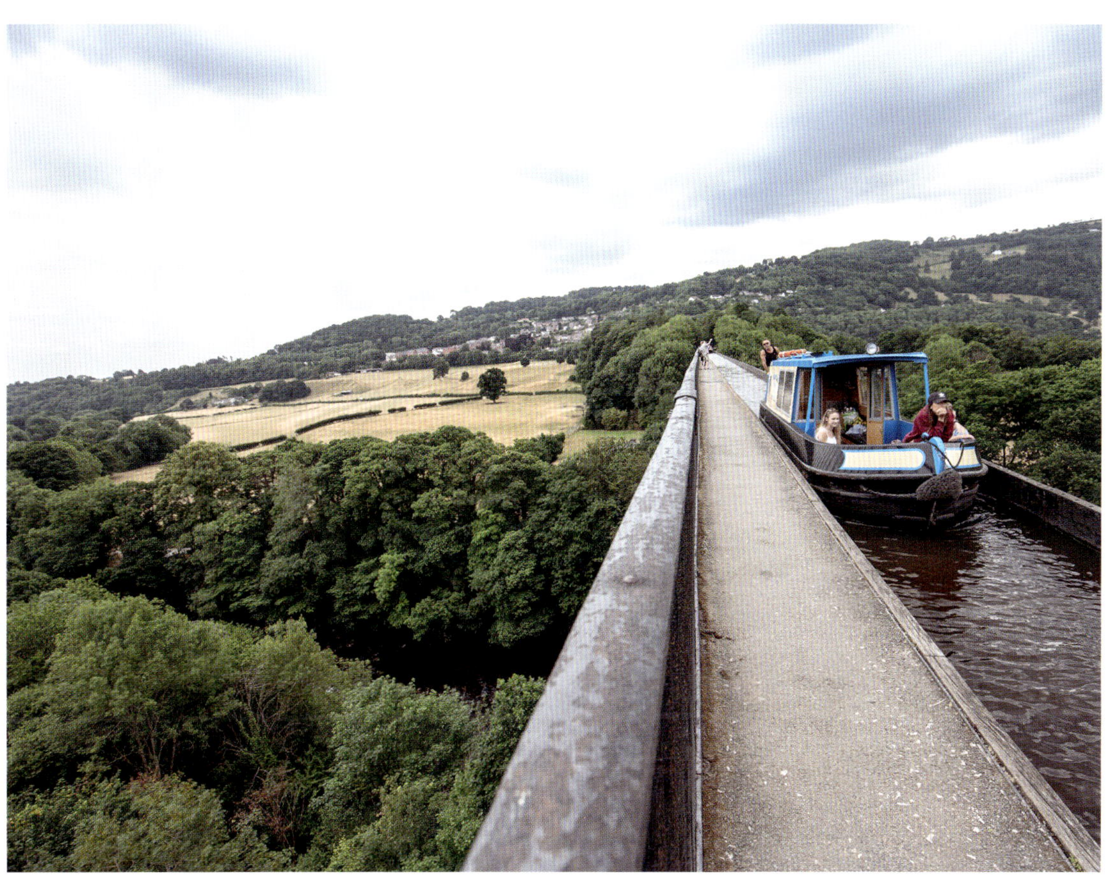

SJ 27072 42083

Stretching across the Church Village by-pass, wire solid mesh tubes suspended between trees provide safe passage for dormice to meet European Union rules. In 2010, the Countryside Council for Wales criticised 'negative reporting' over the £190,000 construction costs.

Surely more noteworthy was the revelation that dormice live in trees. Who knew?

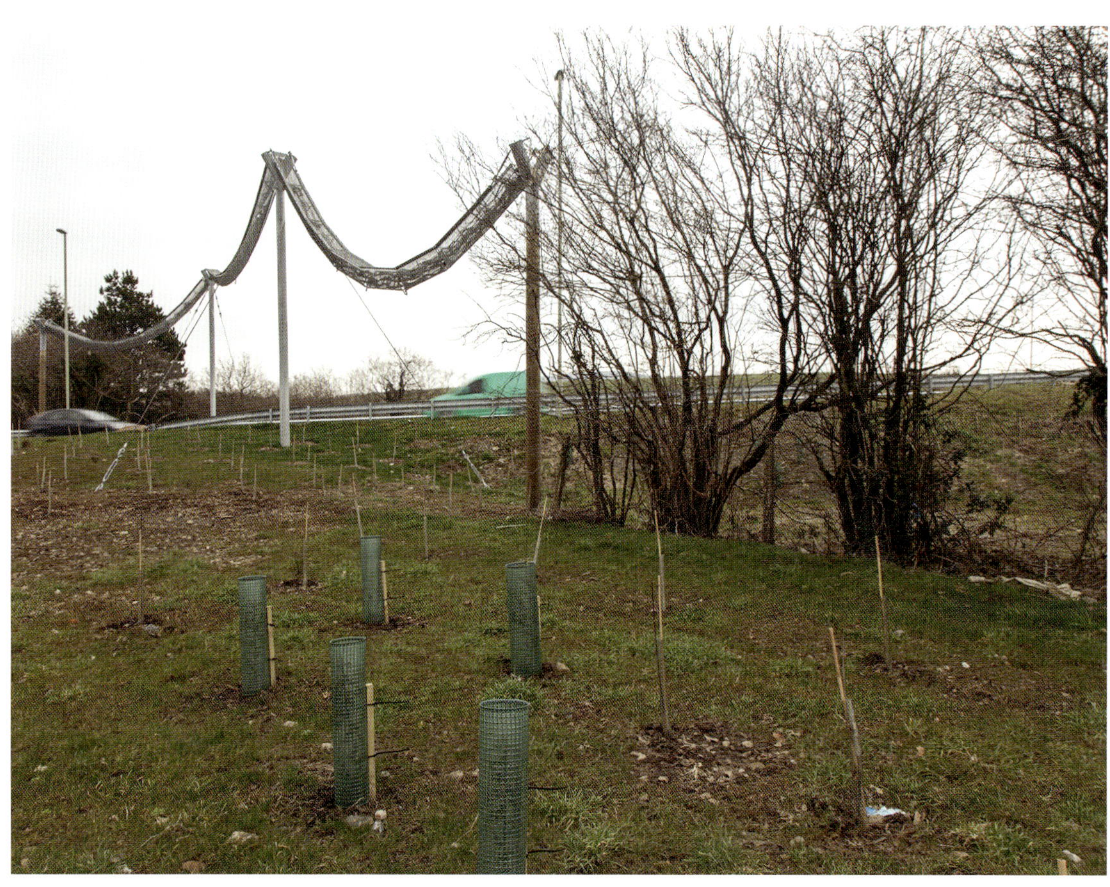

SS 06491 83914

DOLWYDDELAN, CONWY

2016

The oak, poetry-inscribed replacement of a rickety and dangerous
crossing over the River Lledr in Roman Bridge, Dolwyddelan.
Completed in 2010, the project was funded by Bob Borzello,
a retired businessman and former Chicago newspaper editor who
has a home in the area.

The Borzello Trust, formerly known as the Camden Trust, supports
Welsh poetry and the words of poets Menna Elfyn and Paul Henry
are inscribed in slate steps either side of the bridge.

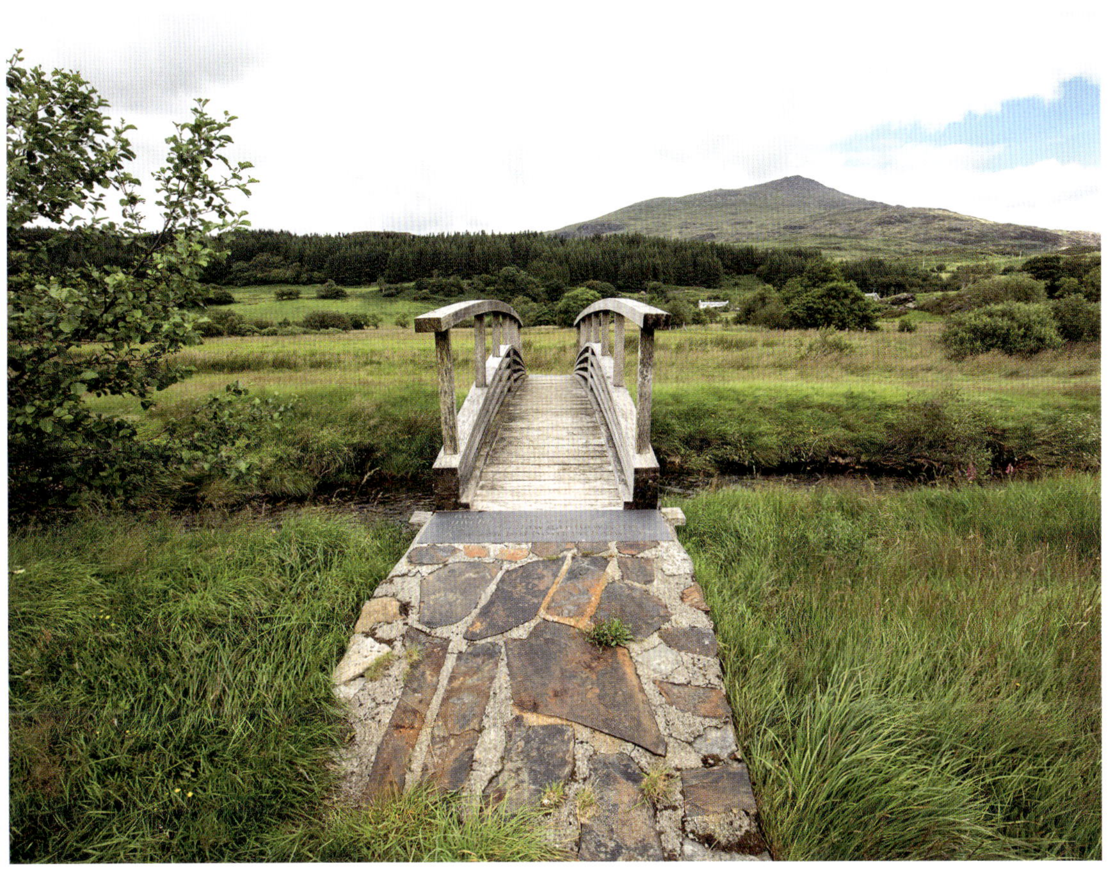

The well-preserved stone-built Romano-British settlement known as the Din Lligwy Hut Group is now shrouded by woodland but its original dwellers, local Britons who adapted their lifestyles to the invading Romans, enjoyed wide views over Lligwy Bay.

"The astonishing things about this place," a journalist wrote in the *Liverpool Daily Post* (Welsh edition) in October 1964, "is that there is a feeling that the people who once lived, ate, slept, loved, laughed and cried, are not far away.

"Yet Din Lligwy has lain asleep under soil and green grass until 1905 when it was discovered and excavated back into time."

Amid the ruins of roundhouses, rectangular barns and metal workshops, archaeologists recovered Roman coins of the third and fourth centuries AD, glass, pottery and a silver ingot.

HOUSING

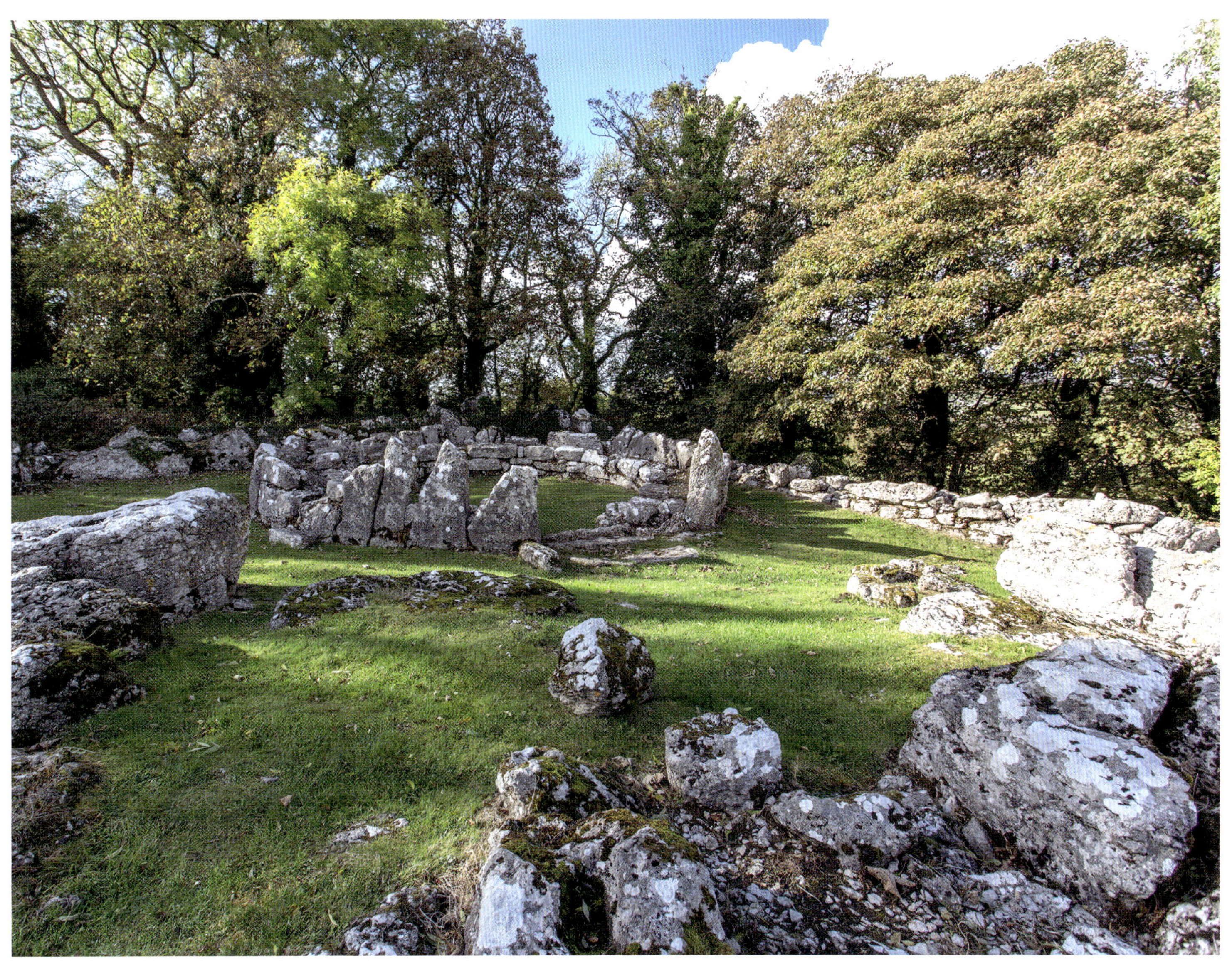

SH 49686 86144

Cytiau'r Gwyddelod or the Irishmen's Huts near Trearddur on Holy Island. Originally thought to date from the Roman occupation in Wales, the huts in fact originated in prehistoric times. Around 20 of the original 50 circular foundations remain and would have been topped with conical thatched roofs.

Our ancestors were inspired by nature when it came to building homes, by the curves of stones, tree trunks, nests and dens. Circular structures were also more energy efficient, and are perhaps more pleasing to the eye than modern homes.

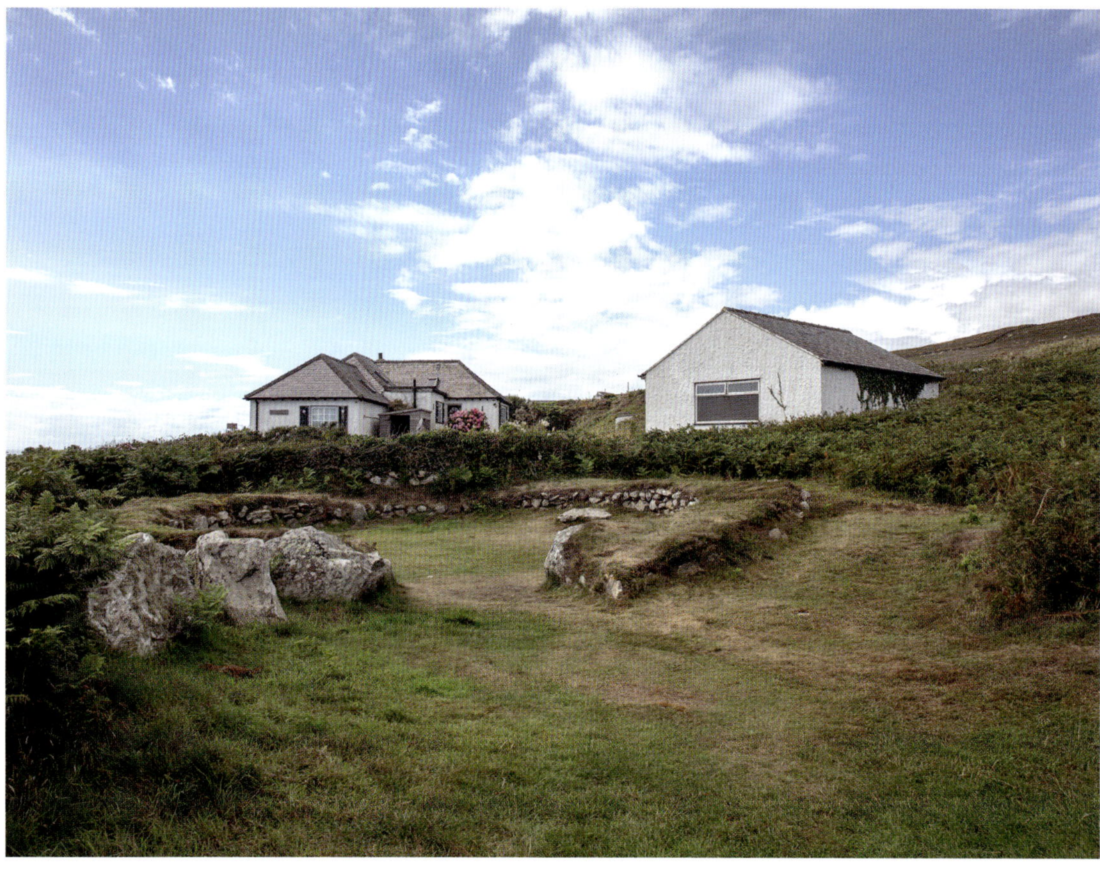

SH 21107 81920

The National Showcaves Centre for Wales leaflet explains:
"Our reconstruction of an Iron Age village has been made using similar raw material to those used in 700 BC, including tree trunks, straw for roofing, bracken and turf."

(Video installation and plastic livestock from more modern period.)

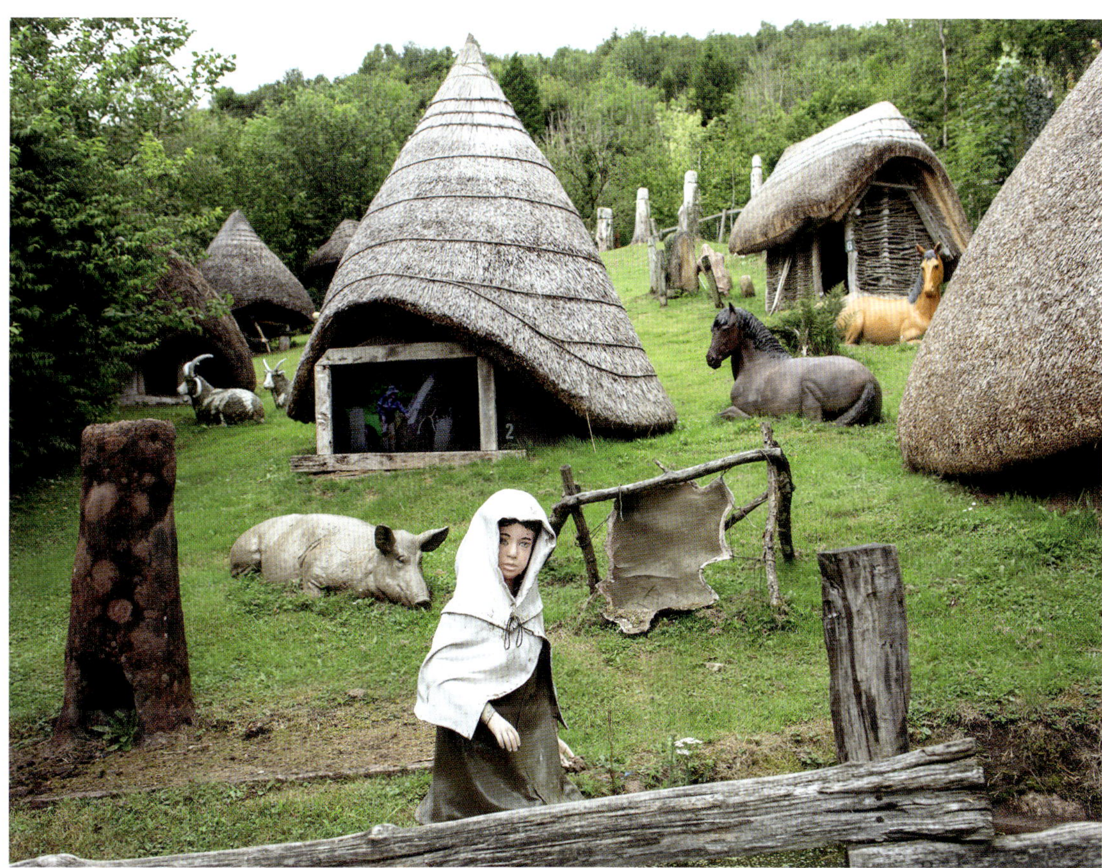

LLANGORSE LAKE, POWYS

2011

The only example in Wales of a crannog; an ancient, man-made island dwelling. Set in the middle of the largest natural lake in the southern half of Wales, it was ignored until its oak planks were exposed in the exceptionally dry summer of 1868.

More recent surveys determined it was built out of the water as a defensive homestead in 916 AD.

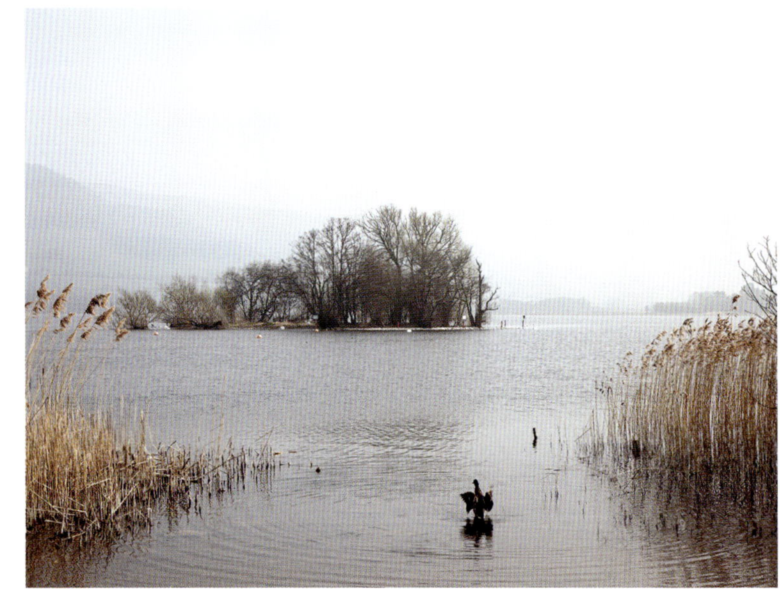

SO 12737 27012

WISTON CASTLE, PEMBROKESHIRE

2019

Said to have been built by an early Flemish settler with the questionable name of Wizo, the castle first appears in documents from 1147 and is described by the historic monuments body Cadw as one of Wales' best-preserved motte-and-bailey castles.

The castle survived numerous attacks until 1220 AD when it was destroyed by Prince of Gwynedd, Llywelyn ab Iorwerth also known as Llywelyn the Great.

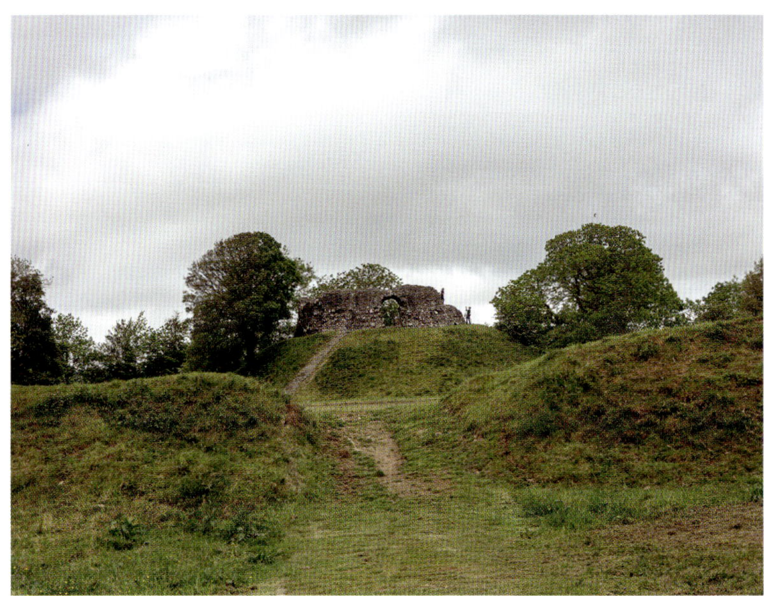

SN 02260 18102

LLANGELYNNIN, GWYNEDD

2016

High above the Conwy Valley in the foothills of Eryri's Carneddau mountains, is one of the remotest and oldest places of worship in Wales, its rubble construction dating back to the twelfth century.

The National Churches Trust:
"In the corner of the walled churchyard is a well associated with sixth century Saint Celynnin, after whom this church is named. Its waters were reputed to have the power to heal children. Today it shelters a colony of newts."

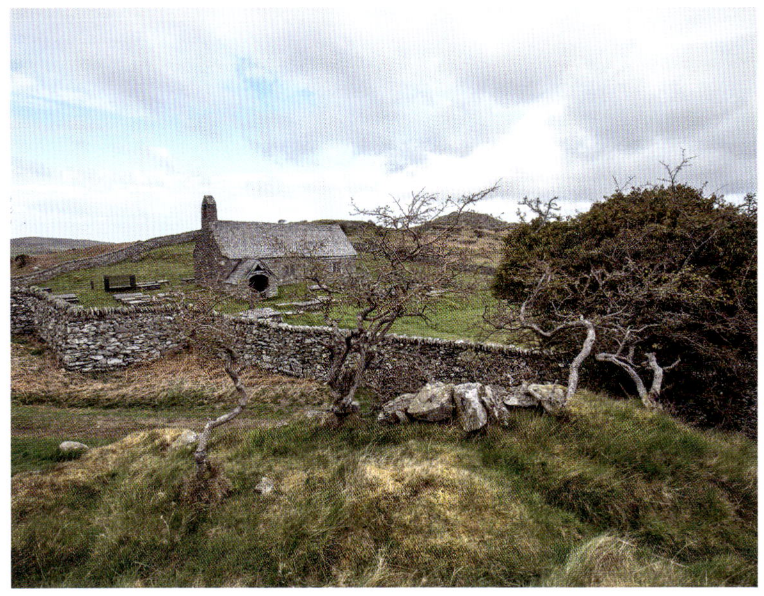

SH 75108 73692

LLANRHYCHWYN, CONWY

2006

Staking its claim as the oldest site of Christian worship in Wales, the slated church might have been used for worship as far back as the sixth century.

The oldest part of the existing building dates from the eleventh century.

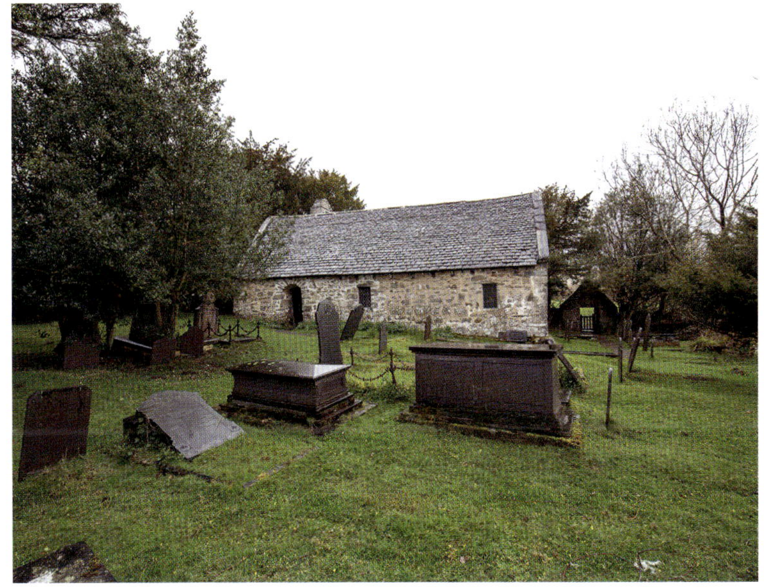

SH 77531 61621

TINTERN ABBEY, MONMOUTHSHIRE

2010

Founded in 1131 by Cistercian monks headed by Abbot Henry, a reformed robber, the abbey started life as a simple timber building.
In 1269, renovations began to create what is often described as one of the masterpieces of British Gothic architecture.

After surrendering to the sixteenth century's dissolution of the monasteries, its haunting remains set on the Welsh side of the winding Wye Valley, attracted poets and painters of the Romantic period such Williams Wordsworth, Thomas Gainsborough and J.M.W. Turner.

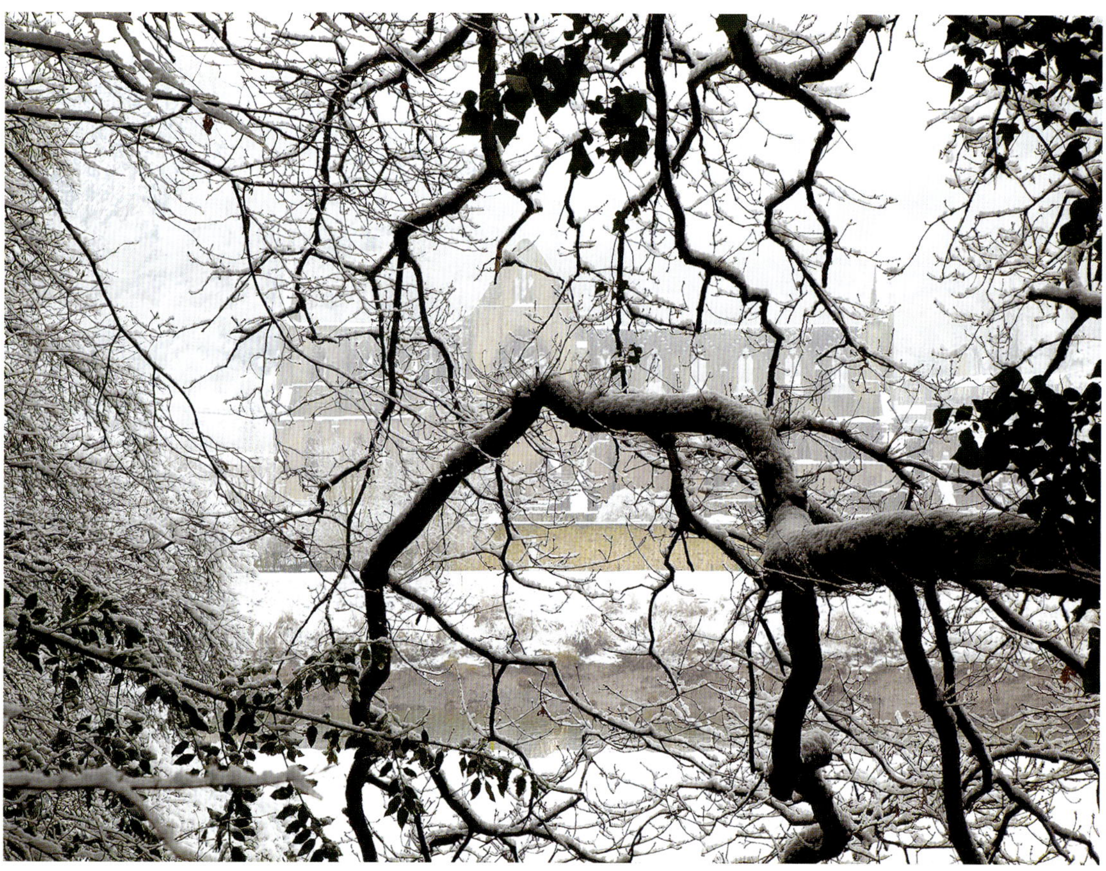

SO 53380 00281

2024

In 2024 the first of five phases of conservation works began to address extensive erosion and decay of soft sandstone masonry which was not designed to survive without a roof.

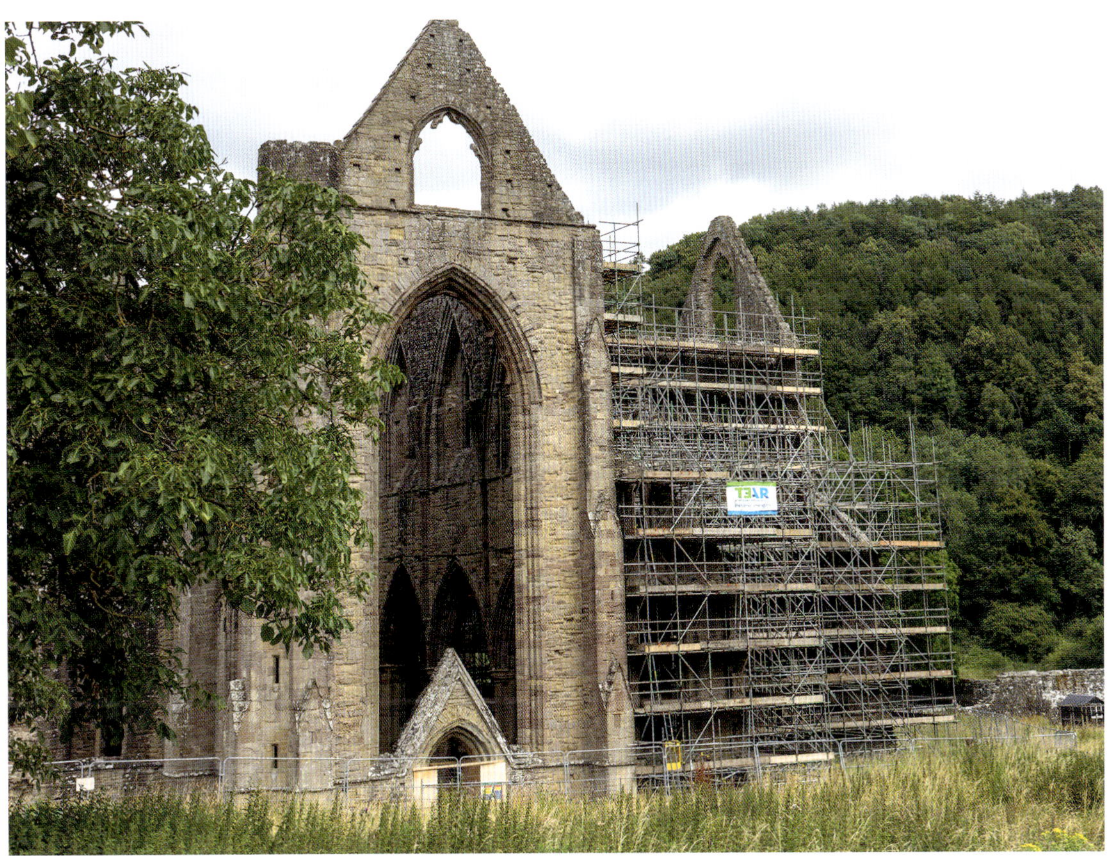

ST 53260 99939

2024

Tŷ Hyll is a dwelling so steeped in the Welsh tradition of myths and legends, it is difficult to discern any verifiable facts about its history. One theory holds it is a fifteenth century tŷ unnos (one night house), when a home built on common land between sunset and sunrise which could be claimed by its builders. Other stories tell of it being a robbers' hideout. The Snowdonia Society, which acquired the building in 1988, notes that it was unmentioned by travel writers until 1853, giving rise to speculation it might be a folly for a rise in tourists at the time.

Comprising a single living room with the large fireplace and a ladder up to a sleeping loft, the house was occupied until 1961 and is now a tearoom.

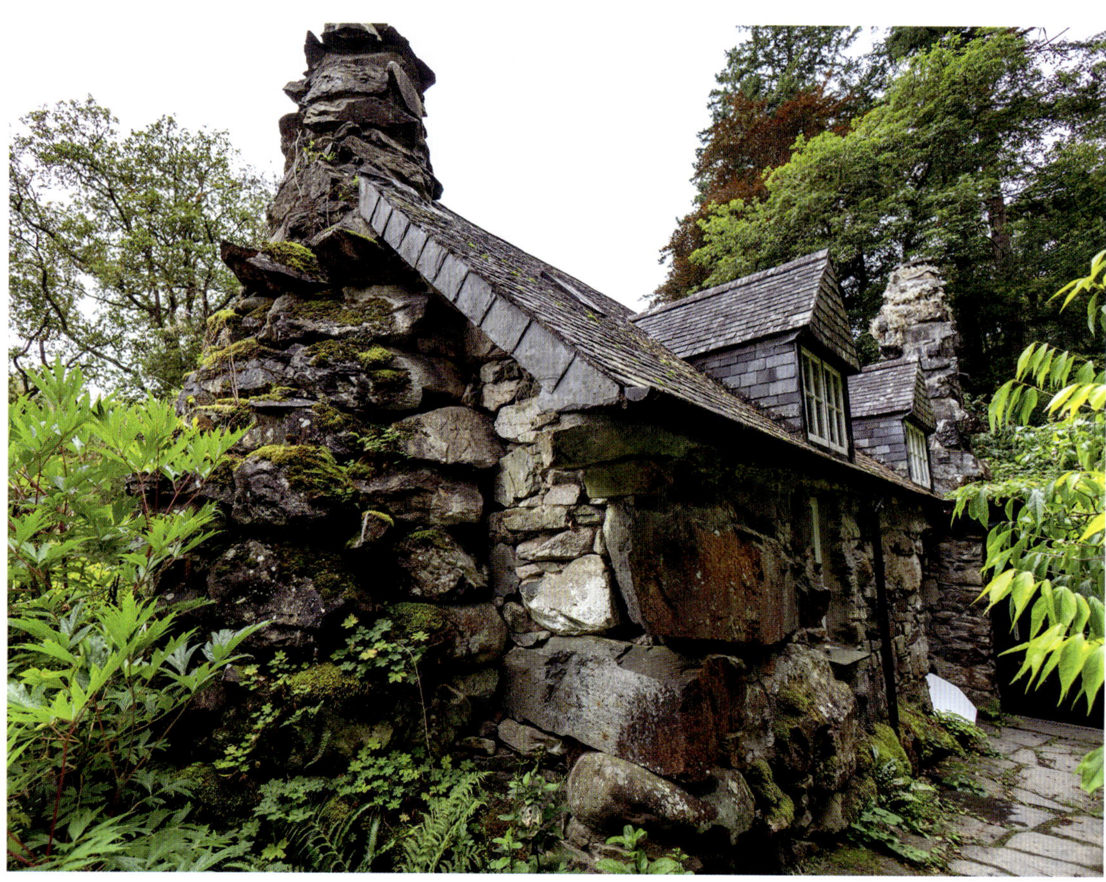

SH 76493 57728

2016

Birthplace of William Morgan, the son of tenant farmers of
Penmachno, near Betws-y-Coed, who translated the Bible from
Hebrew and Greek into Welsh in 1558. Taking ten years to complete,
his work proved to be a seminal moment in the history and status
of Welsh as a language of worship and learning.

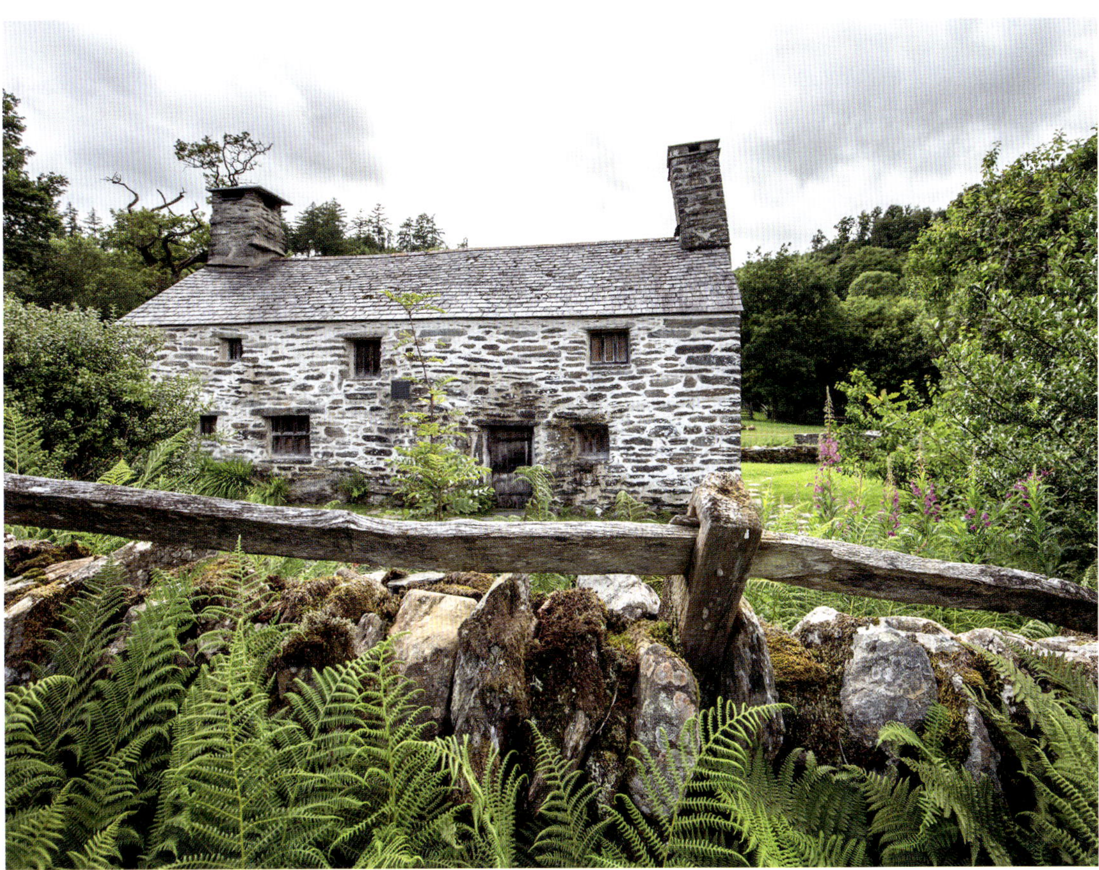

SH 77020 52412

Plas Mawr, or Great Hall, deemed to be Britain's finest surviving house of the golden Elizabethan age, is both Grade One listed and a scheduled monument. The sixteenth century townhouse was built by Robert Wynn, the son of a local landowner, who served in the Tudor court of Henry VIII.

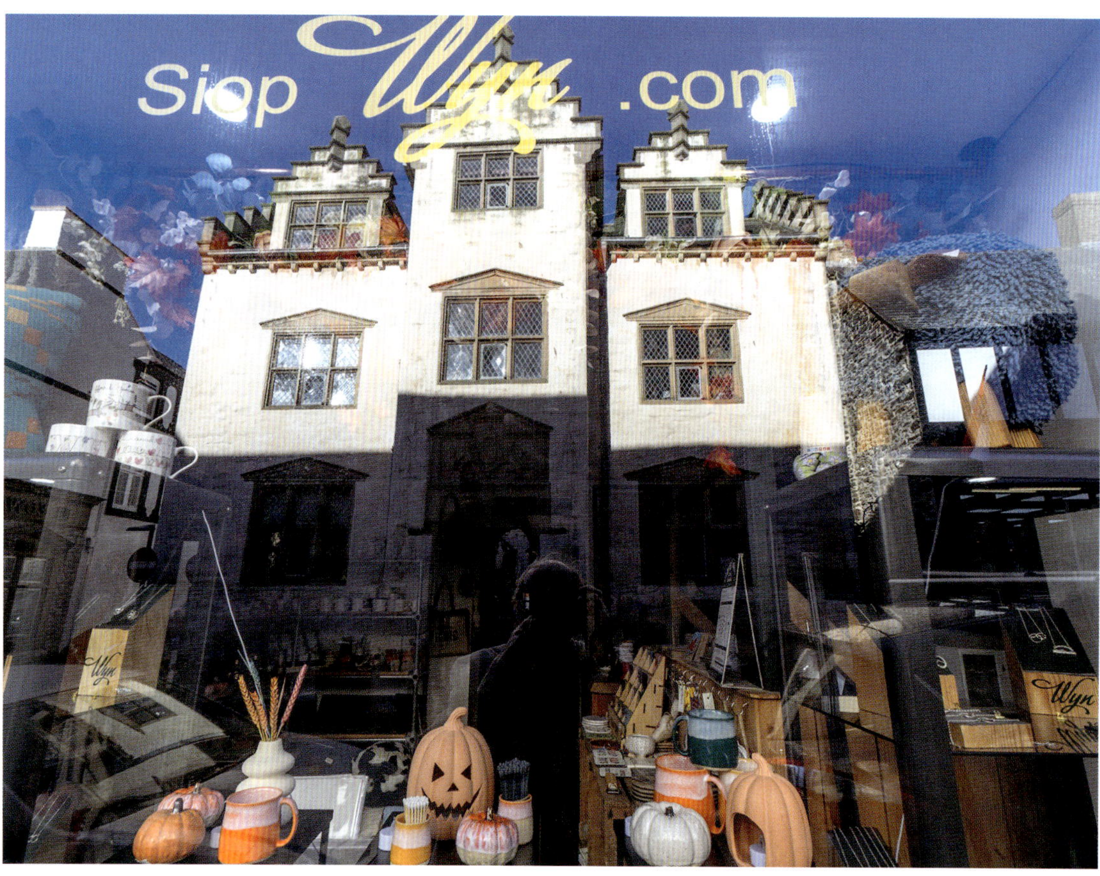

SH 78114 77572

QUAY HOUSE, CONWY

2024

Standing 122 inches high and 72 inches wide, Britain's smallest house as confirmed by the *Guinness Book of Records*.

Built in the sixteenth century, the home remained occupied until 1900. Its final tenant, Robert Jones, a local fisherman, was 6ft 3ins tall, and unable to fully stand up inside.

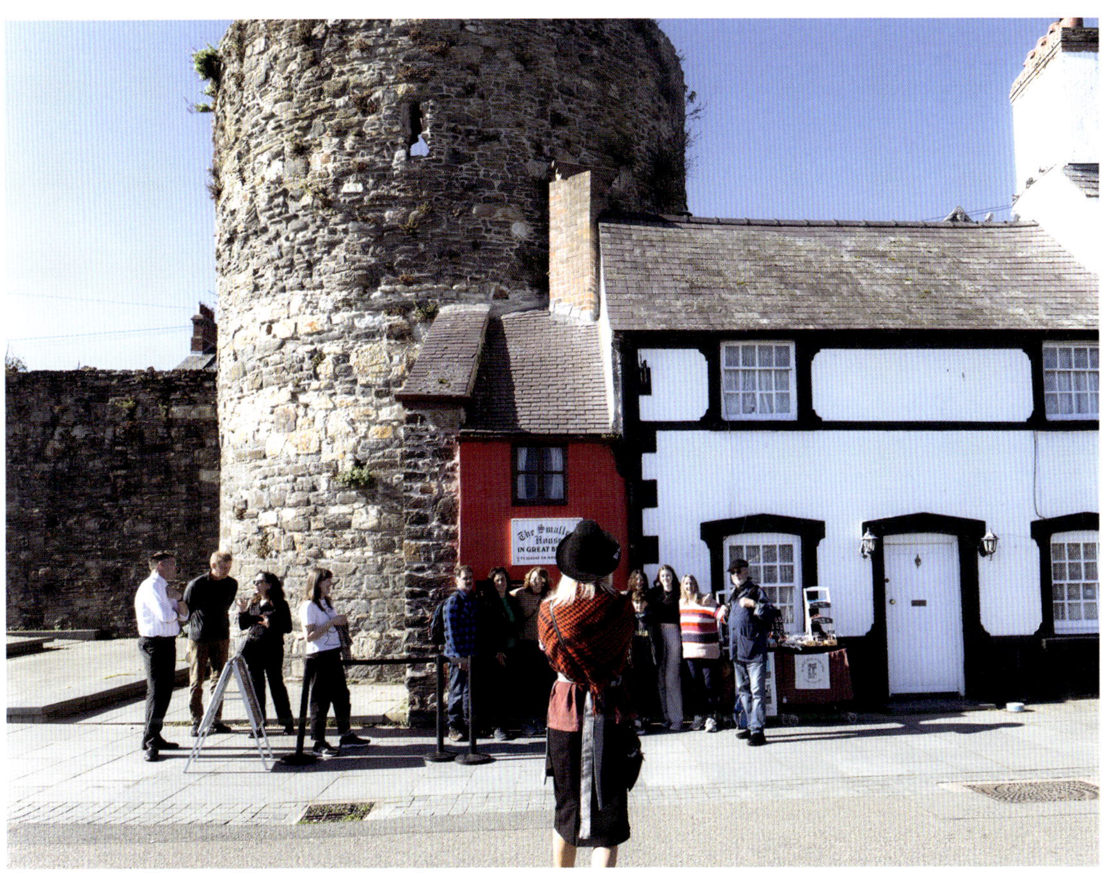

SH 78195 777225

2018

London's *Daily Herald*, May 27, 1931:
*In search of Wales – The Fair Vale of Llangollen… and the ladies who
held court there.*

"There is one thing in Llangollen which everyone goes to see, a queer
black and white house called 'New Place'. Here 150 years ago lived those
two strange women 'the most celebrated virgins in Europe', as they were
called. Lady Eleanor Butler and Miss Sarah Ponsonby – the 'Ladies of
Llangollen'…

"At first sight this house, standing back against smooth lawns and
gardens, looks like a very impressive half-timber Tudor mansion, but
when you come near to it you discover that a very ordinary square
Georgian house has been literally plastered, inside and out, with old oak
carvings.

"What a query story it is. In the year 1776, two Irish women arrived
suddenly in the Vale. They had run away from Ireland, mutually pledged
to resist matrimony and to devote their lives to friendship, celibacy and
the knitting of blue stockings."

The architectural wonder drew fashionable guests including –
the Duke of Wellington, Wordsworth, Sir Walter Scott and Charles
Mathews, a celebrated comic actor.

"Oh, such curiosities," Mathews later wrote of the women. "I was nearly
convulsed… As they are seated there is not one point to distinguish them
from men… It is difficult to understand why these two improbable people
achieved immortality. I suppose they were one of life's side-shows."

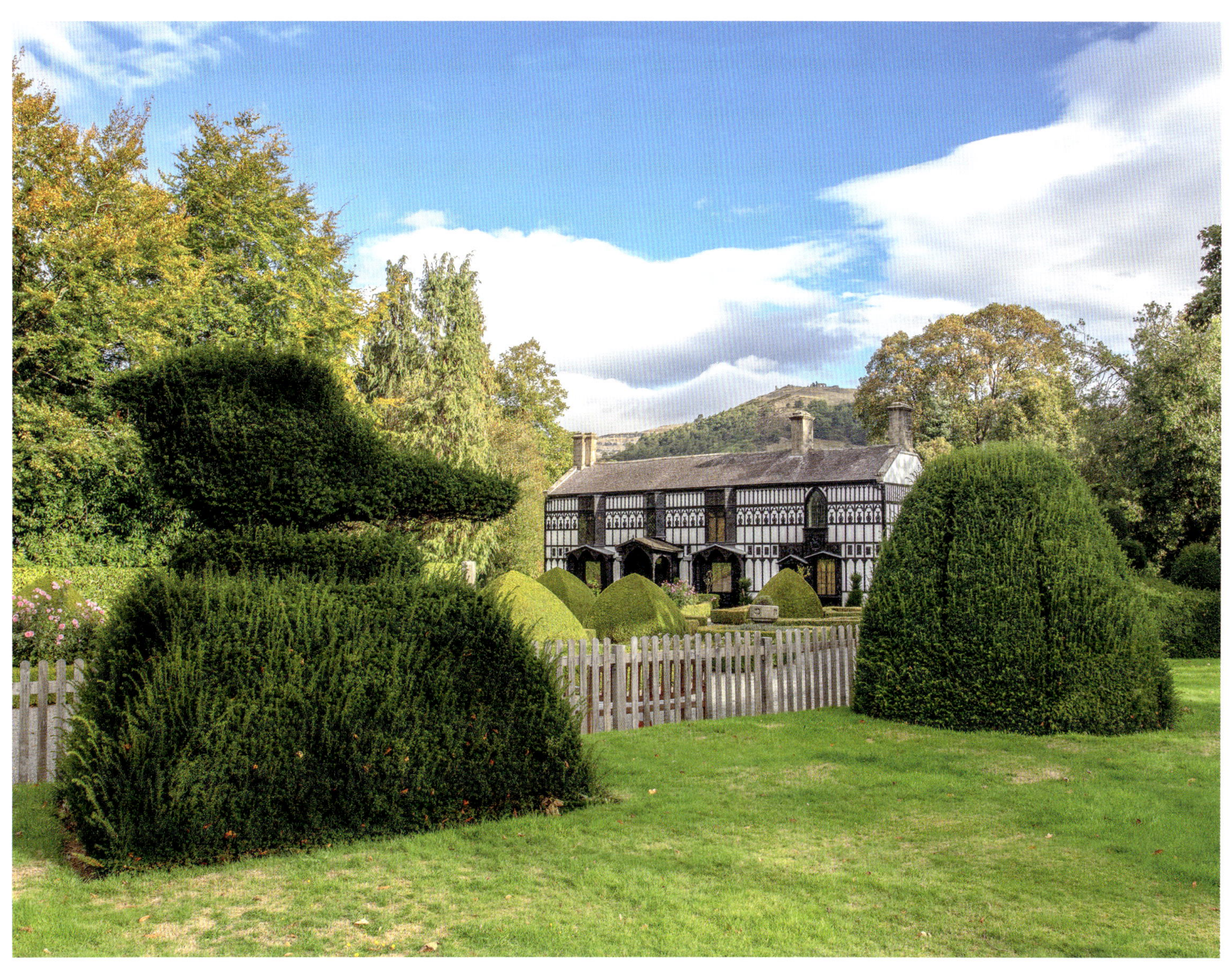

SJ 21810 41674

FERNDALE, RHONDDA CYNON TAF

2011

The first community in the Rhondda Valley to be industrialised when the first coal mine shaft sunk in 1857, set above its rugby field presenting a quintessential view of the south Wales valleys, rows of uniform terraces densely packed on the side of steep hillsides.

"Scattered here and there are tiny communities dropped as casually as a curse on some old mining project…" wrote the late Rhondda-born Gwyn Thomas, heralded as the true voice of the English-speaking Valleys.

"The streets buck like bronchos. The housing pattern is so fantastically complicated even pigeons returning from races have been seen poised in a long hover."

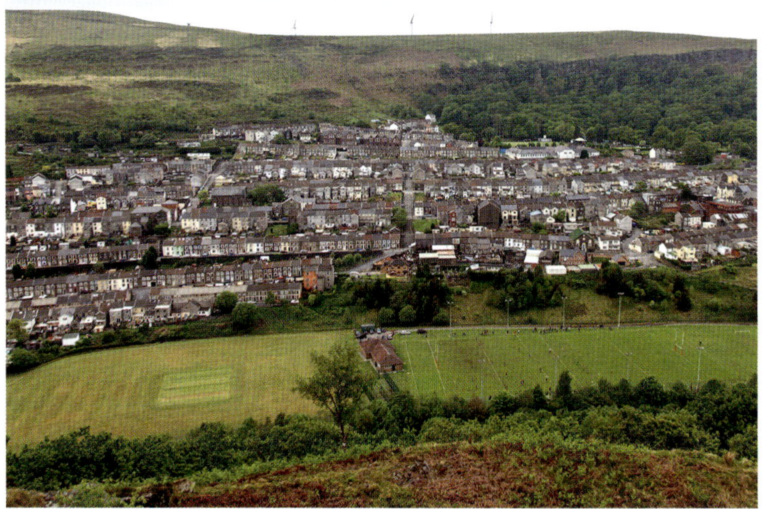

SO 17173 08815

BANGOR, GWYNEDD

2024

Some of Wales' earliest council houses on the Maesgeirchen estate, built as part of Prime Minister David Lloyd George's 'home for heroes' programme. It aimed to clear slums and reward returning World War I soldiers.

The estate – a satellite township within reach of Bangor yet separate to it with homes 'suitable and convenient for the ordinary man, his wife and children' – was completed in 1937 with the building of 534 dwellings for 1,871 people.

Maesgeirchen was the shape of things to come. Between 1945 and 1959, 120,000 council houses were built in Wales.

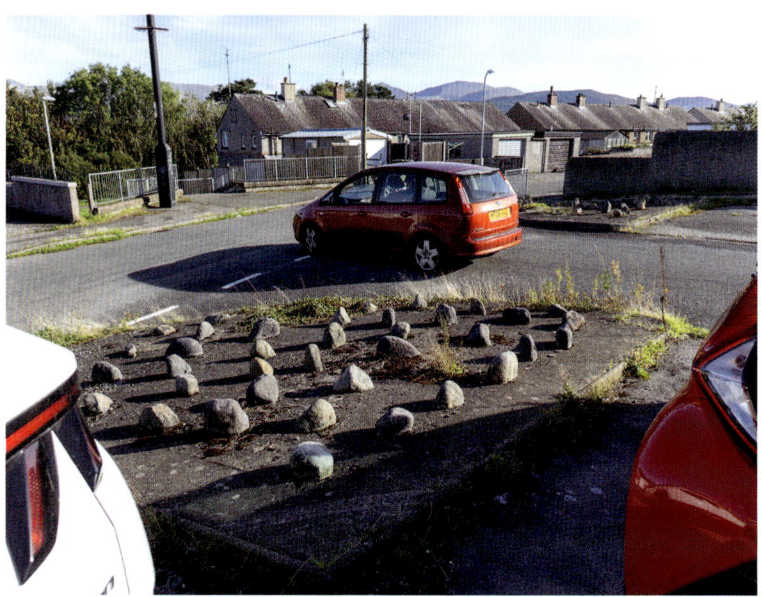

SH 58940 71016

NEW TREDEGAR, CAERPHILLY

1972

The back-to-back terraces of South Wales. It must have been a
Monday, the traditional washing day.

Tuesday was reserved for ironing.

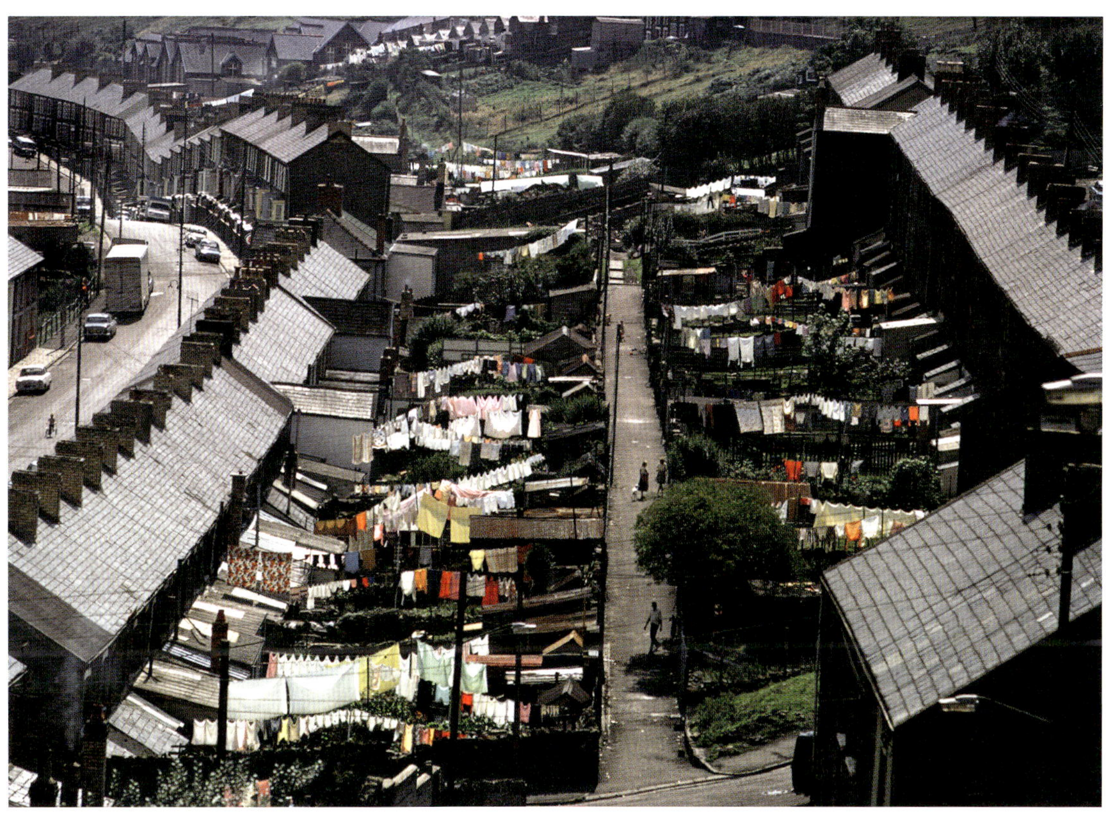

PREFAB, CARDIFF

The last remaining B2-type prefabricated bungalow in Wales.

A once common feature across the UK amid the post-war housing initiative, this aluminium bungalow was one of 40 in Llandinam Crescent in Gabalfa, Cardiff, for half a century before it was dismantled and its four sections reassembled four miles away at St Fagans National Museum of History.

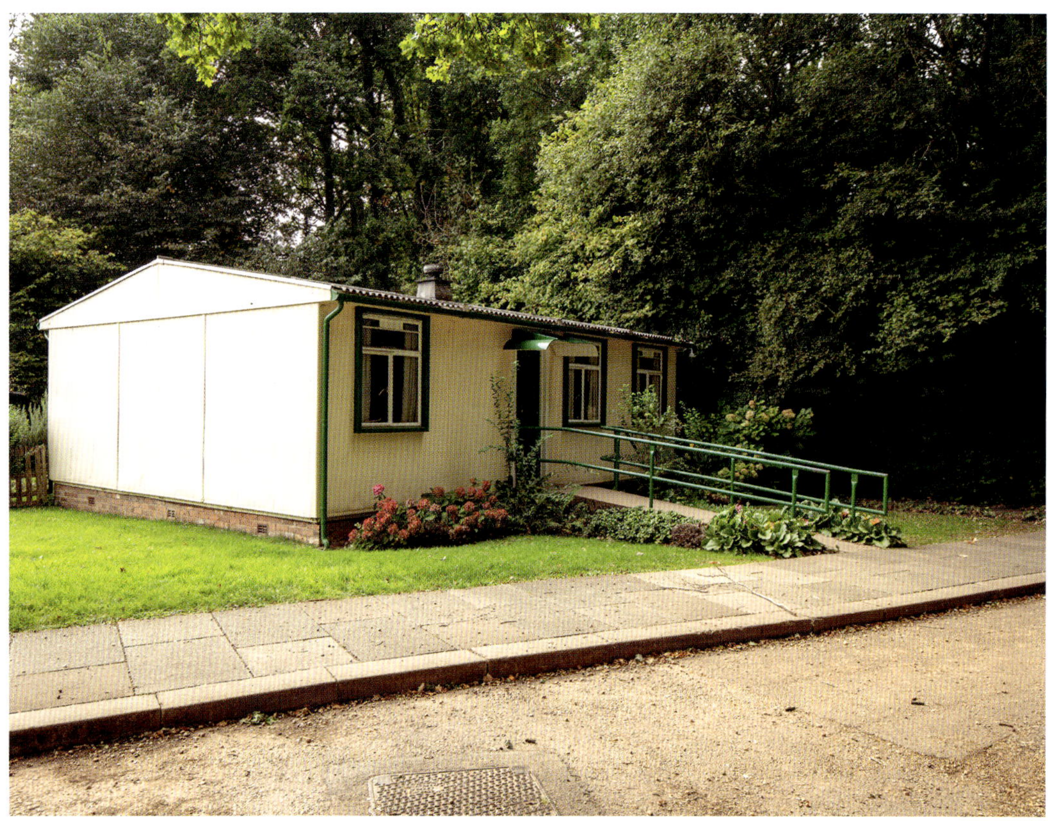

ST 11388 77402

PORTMEIRION, GWYNEDD

2024

The hanging ram on the toll house entry to the village of Portmeirion, a baroque, vibrantly-coloured childhood fantasy realised by architect Sir Clough Williams-Ellis between 1925 and 1975. The ornate Italianate folly was, held Sir Clough (an ardent campaigner against the destruction of the visual beauty of UK towns and countryside), proof it was possible to 'develop even a beautiful site without defiling it, and given sufficient loving care to improve on what God had provided'.

A master of illusion, his use of tapering walls, small windows, twisting, sloping walkways and a lack of cars create the impression everything is bigger than it actually is. It was heralded by some as the future of urban design.

Containing many listed buildings and gardens, Portmeirion is a noted source of inspiration for musicians and artists, perhaps best known as 'The Village' in the surreal sixties spy TV series The Prisoner.

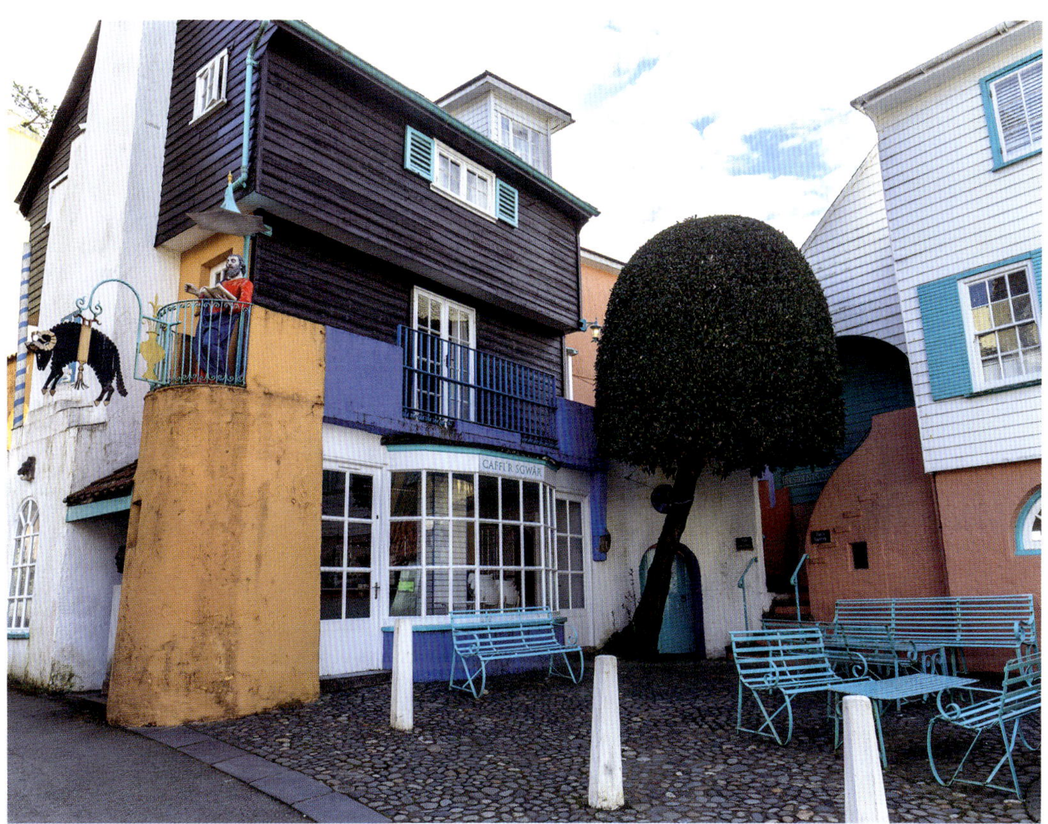

SAS KILL HOUSE, POWYS

2010

In 1939, the 'Epynt clearance' evicted 400 people and seized 54 farms across 30,000 acres of land for one of the UK's largest military training grounds at Sennybridge, north of the Bannau Brycheiniog or Brecon Beacon's National Park.

The area became a traditional practice range for the Special Air Service Regiment.

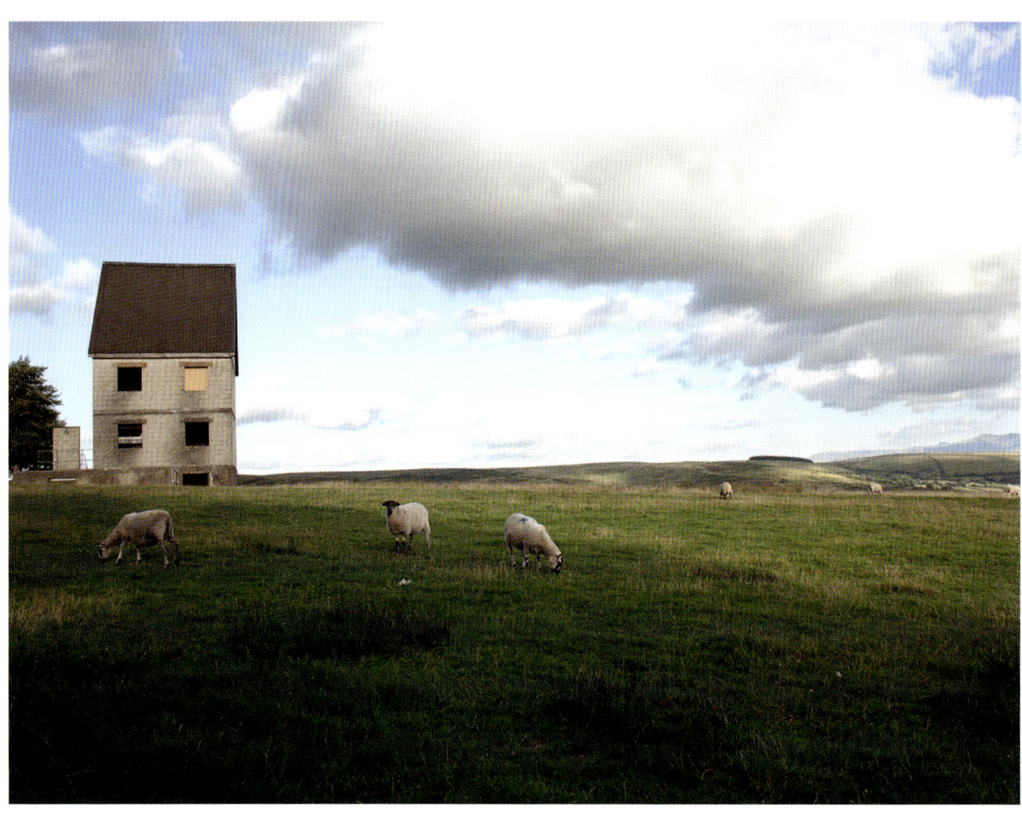

SN 90000 39233

2013

Eco village modelled on King Charles' new town of Poundbury in Dorset.

Country Life, July 2006:
"Detailed plans for the first phase of a proposed new Coed Darcy Urban Village to be built on the 1,000-acre site previously occupied by Britain's first crude oil refinery at Llandarcy, have been submitted to Neath Port Talbot Council by a consortium of public and private sector partners. The houses and apartments designed by the classical architect Robert Adam, are based on a mixture of traditional local architectural styles."

Daily Mail, November 2023:
"The long-suffering residents of a 'new' Welsh village that is supposed to have schools, parks and shops say they are still waiting for them to be built 10 years later. Coed Darcy, a village being developed near to Llandarcy in Neath Port Talbot, Wales, was sold to homeowners as the perfect place to start a family. But locals say they've lived there for 10 years now and they're still waiting for schools and shops to be built."

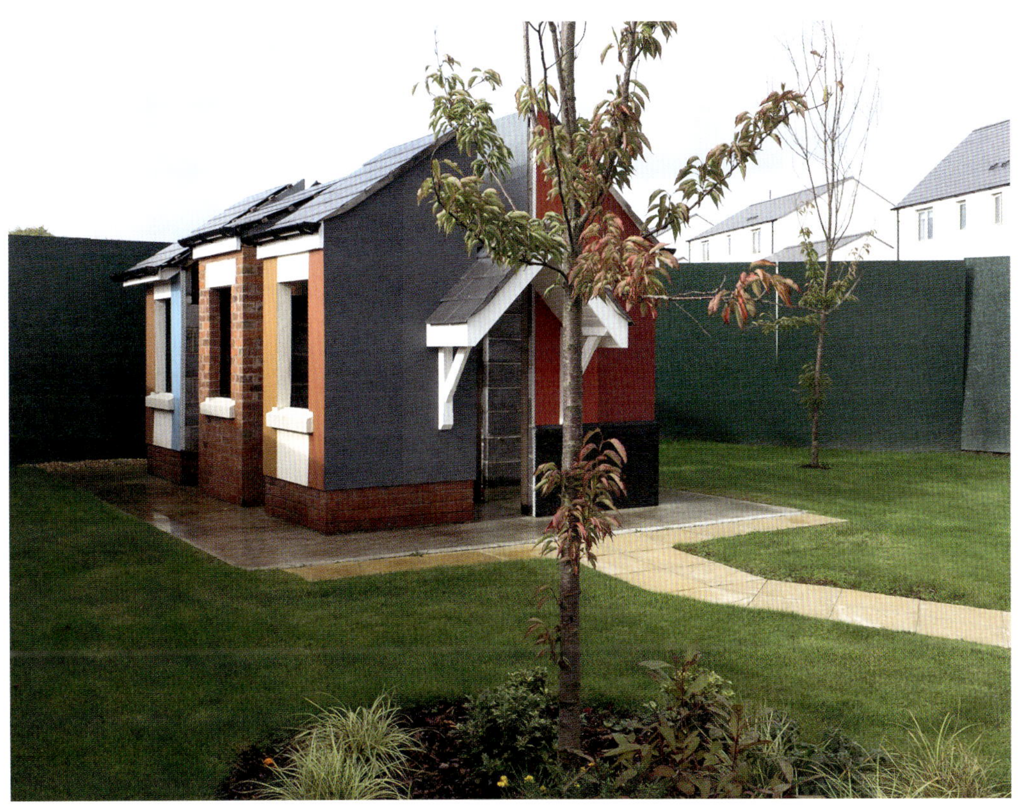

SS 71750 95674

A cluster of eight space age creative arts business studios nestled in the woodland setting of Aberystwyth University's arts centre.

The unique 'dimpled', ultra-thin stainless-steel foil clad over a basic timber frame was fabricated on site using a contraption similar to a Victorian mangle. The award-winning design by Heatherwick Studios was completed in 2009 and is designed to reflect its surroundings like 'broken mirror', firmly embedding the cabins into the environment.

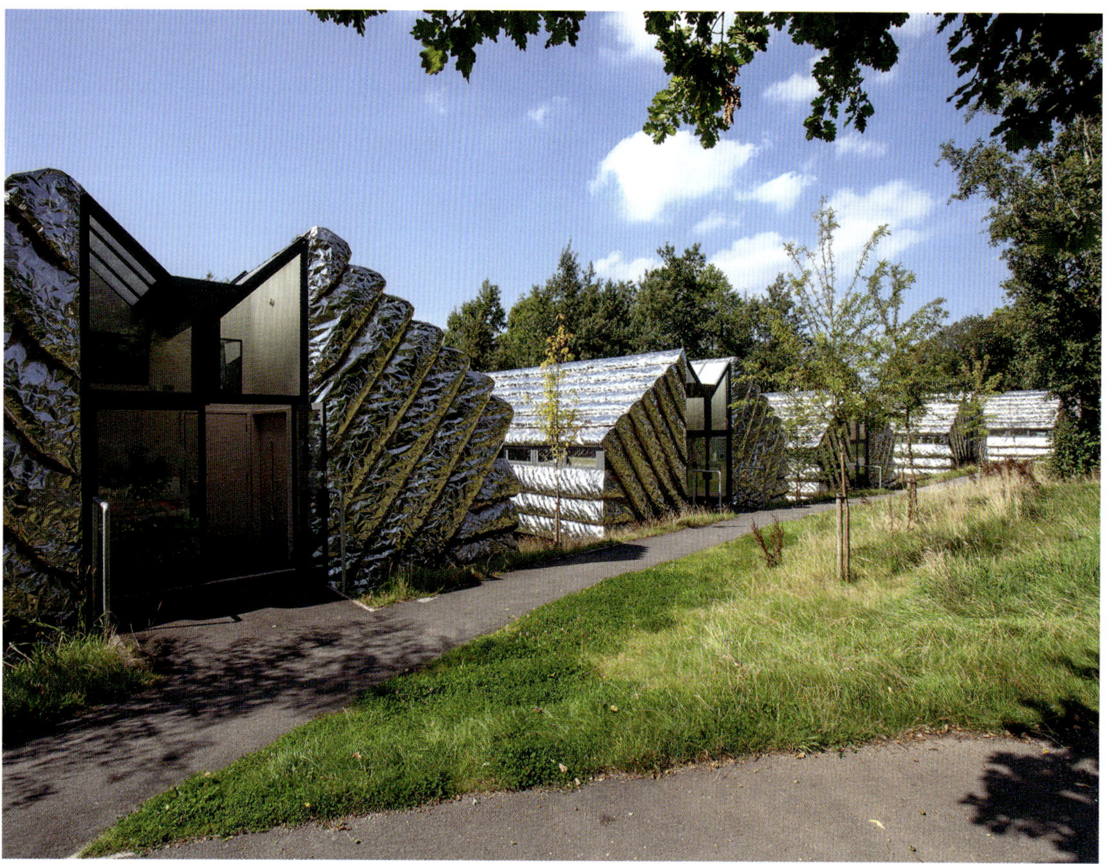

SN 59896 81766

Caravans. Since the rise in ownership of the both static and mobile varieties in the 1950s, rural and coastal Wales has become studded with around 580 caravan parks.

Spectacular countryside, sandy beaches and theme parks continue to offer a retreat from densely-packed cities ever since, albeit weather permitting!

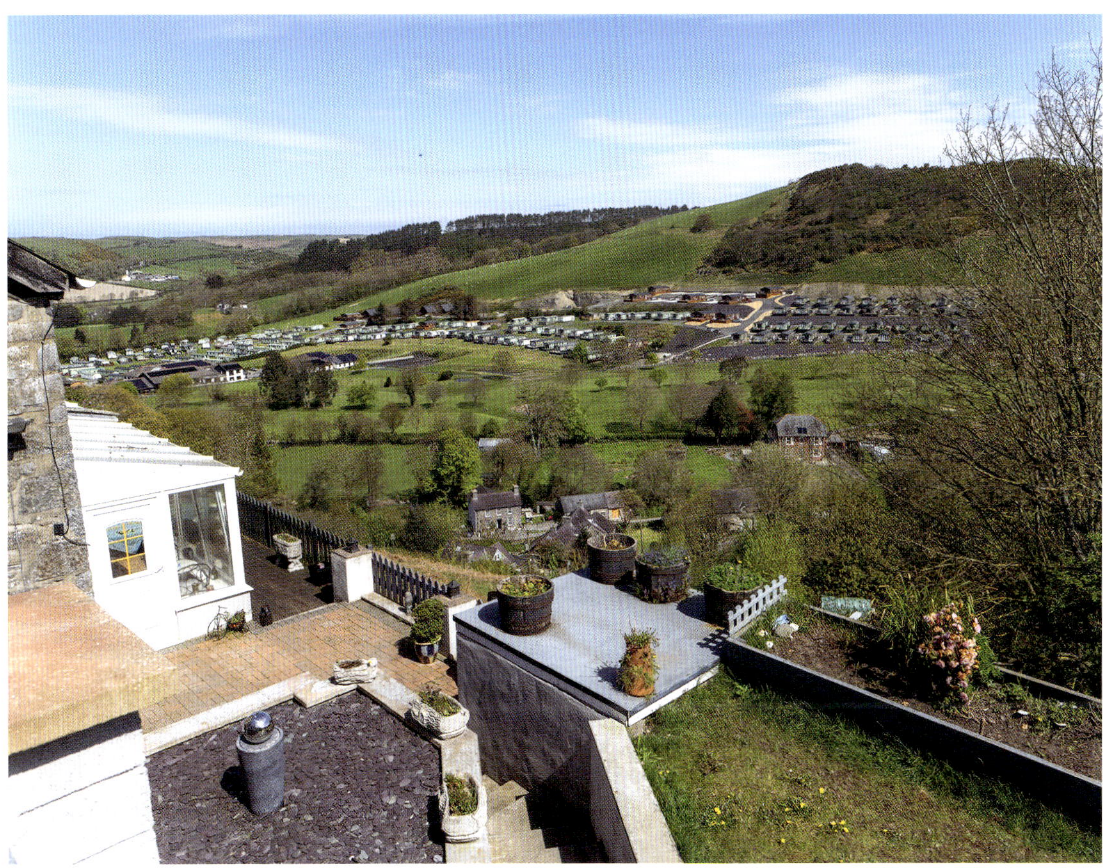

SN 54718 69109

BBC News website March 2019:
"A distinctive 1930s ice cream kiosk which was painstakingly repaired after a car crashed into it 10 years ago has been granted listed building status.

"The Big Apple at Mumbles has been one of Swansea's most recognisable landmarks for generations… The granting of listed status follows a campaign by local supporters.

"Cadw said the elliptical concrete building had 'special architectural interest' and was an 'iconic' feature from the heyday of seaside entertainment.

"The kiosk was built in the early 1930s to promote a cider brand called Cidertone. Others materialised in coastal towns in the UK, including Porthcawl, but Mumbles historian John Powell said the kiosk in Bracelet Bay was the last one standing."

LISTED

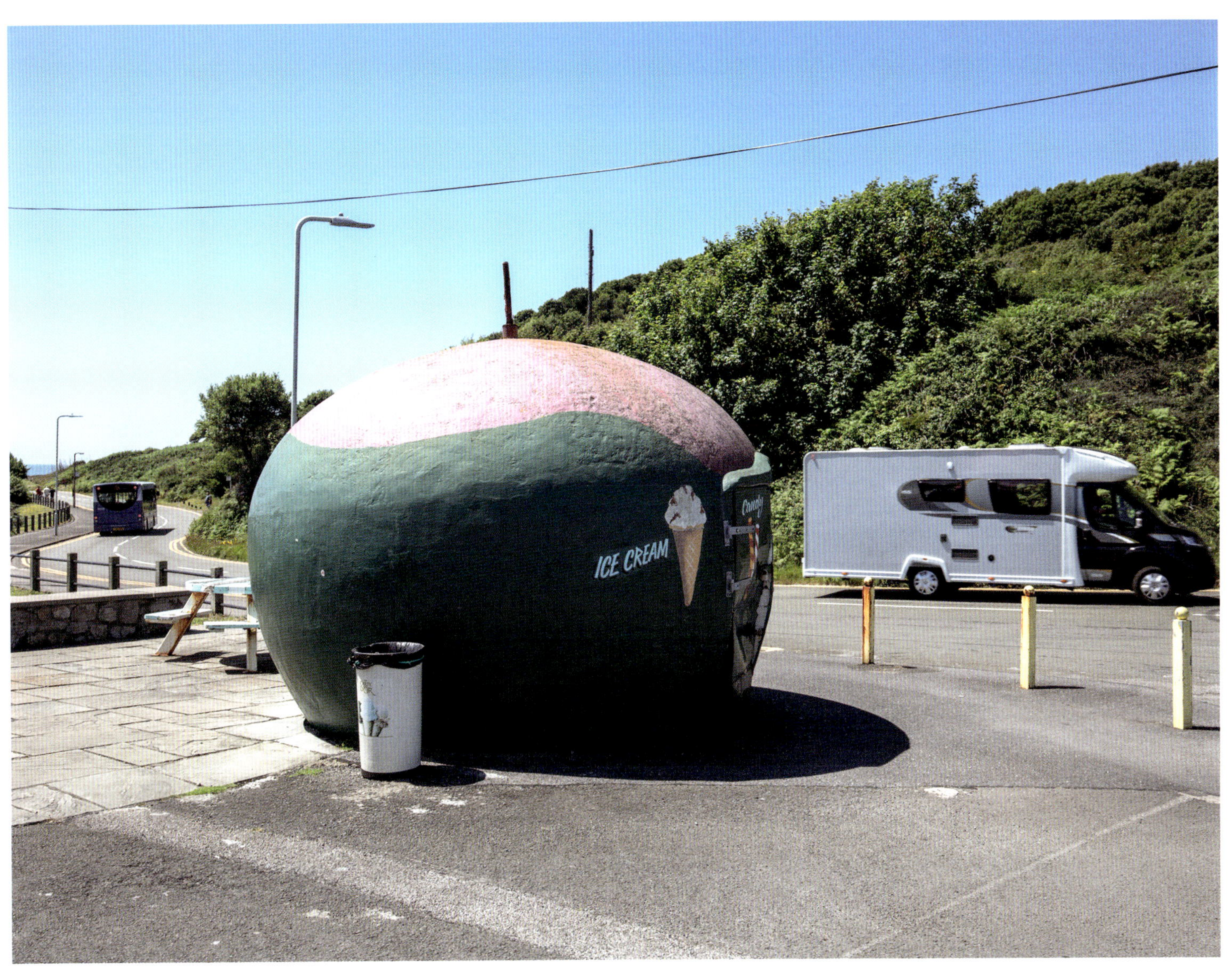
ICE CREAM
Candy

Man verses nature. Nature wins.

As Cardiff's suburbs expanded around the turn of the twentieth century, a London plane sapling, one of a line along Ninian Road, was planted alongside a post box.

The engulfed pillar box has now been decommissioned but it meant enough to someone for them to recommend it for listed building status.

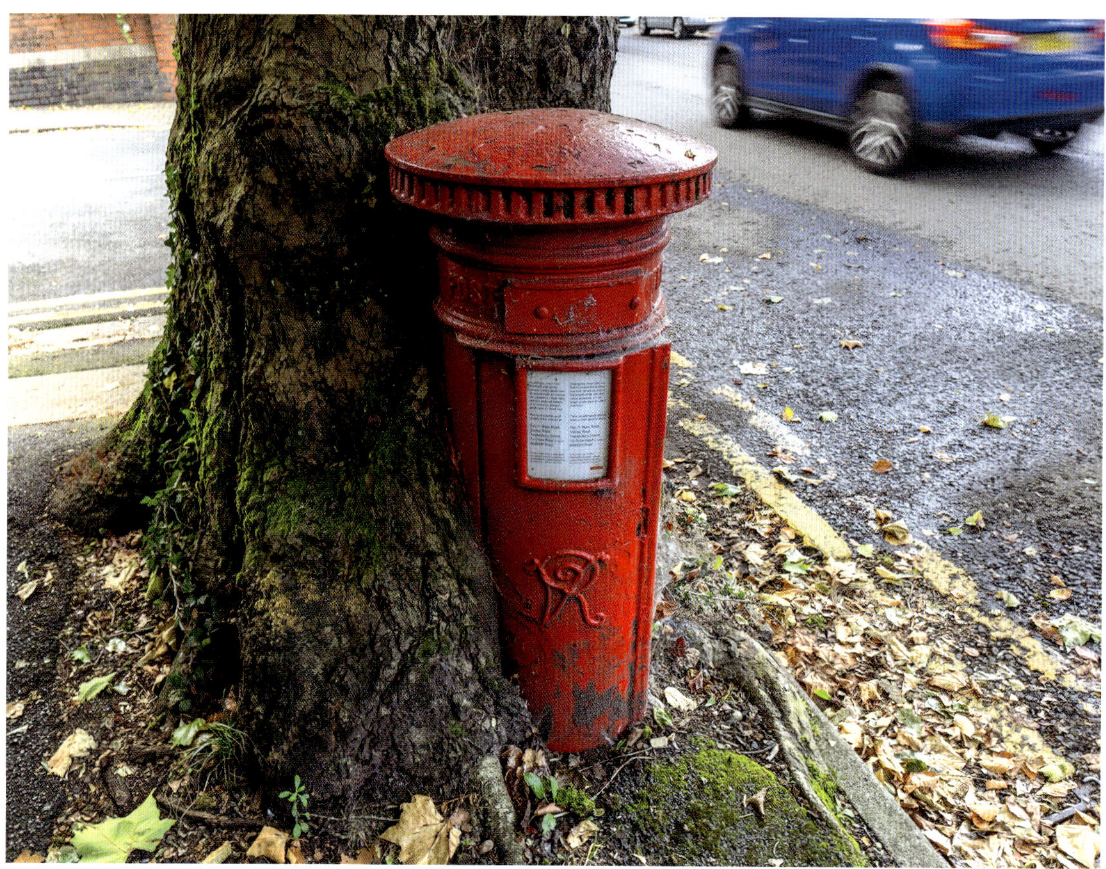

ST 18687 78558

Still operational in the remote community until the early nineties, this Grade Two listed fuel tank was operated by hand and run by the Happy Union Inn, the village pub which would add the bill to a drinker's tab.

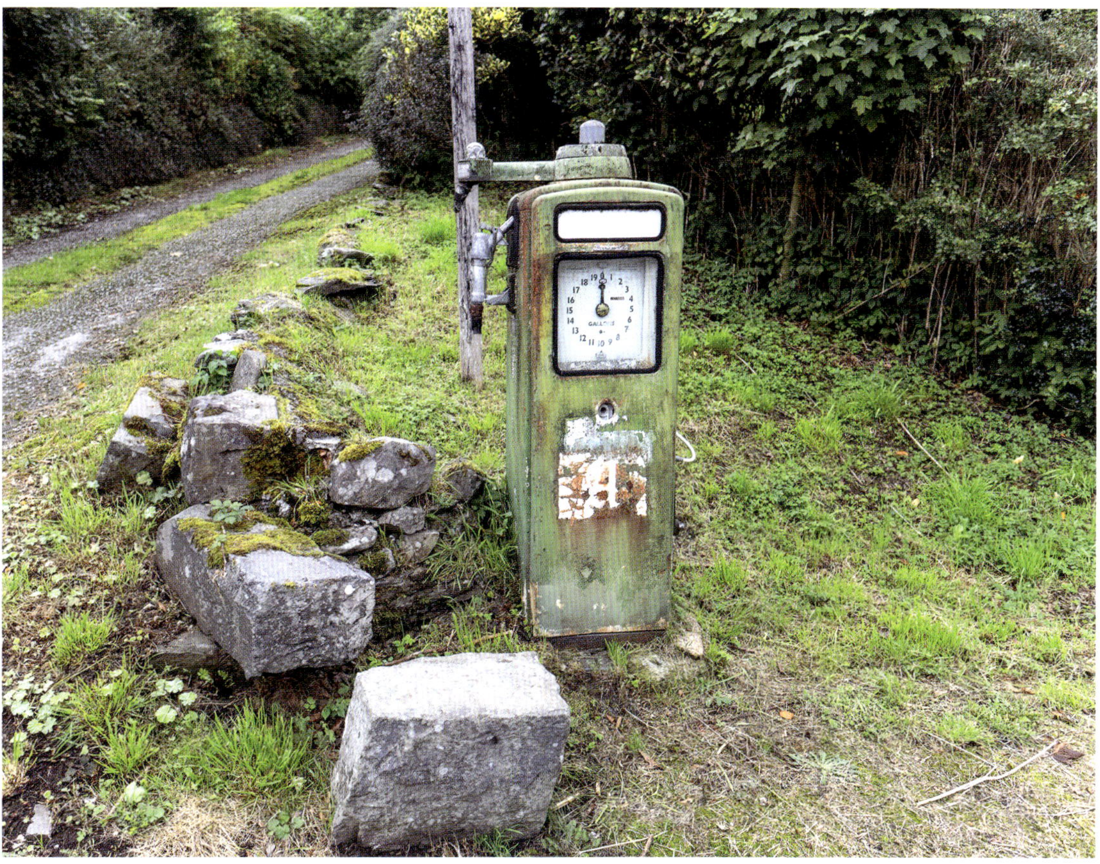

SO 05397 71254

THE HAYES, CARDIFF

As well-known as any other landmark to Cardiffians, the capital's first public toilets opened to great fanfare in August 1898 as the city's coffers swelled thanks to its teeming coal port.

The once opulent Grade Two listed subterranean building was shut by the council in 2013 not long after a £148,000 refurbishment.

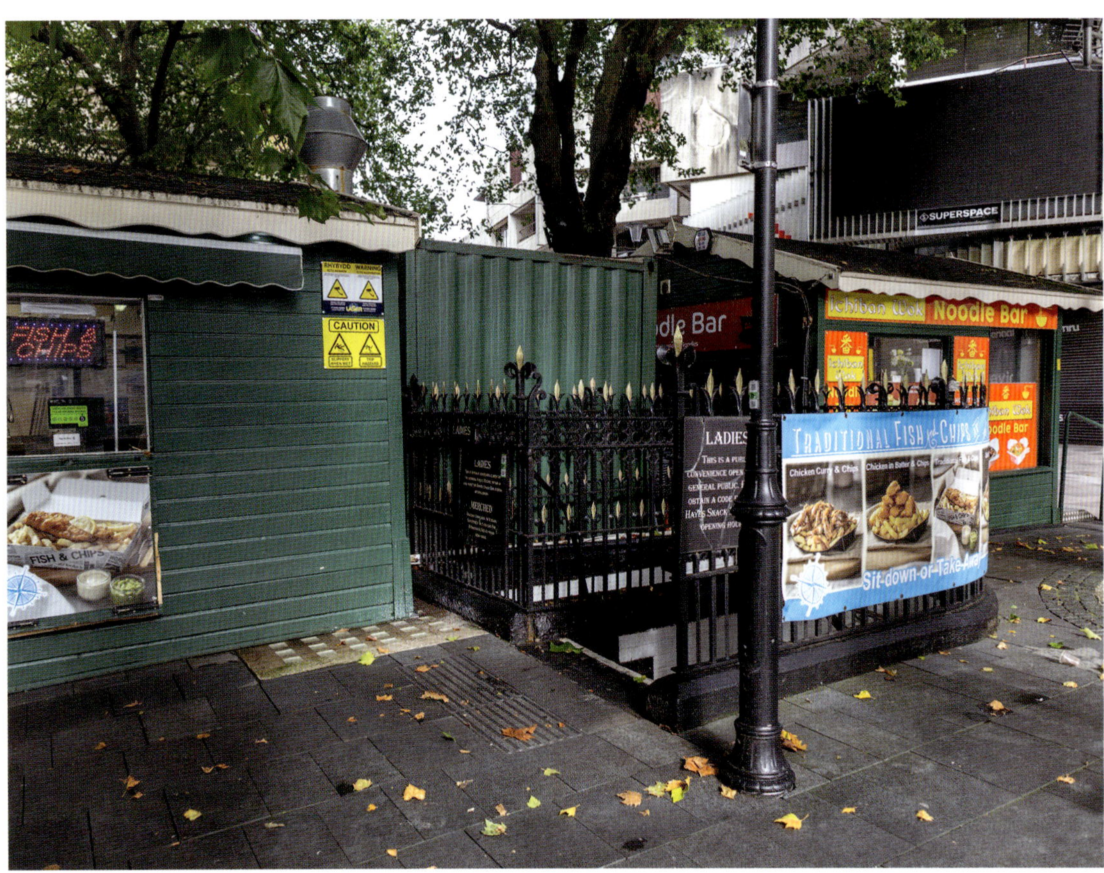

ST 18349 76321

Wales' only major new town was built following the New Towns Act of 1946 was regarded as a significant post-war event with new areas of industrial development to provide employment.

Announcing its decision to afford the sign Grade Two listing in 2019, historic monuments body Cadw said:

"A classic example of post-war design, the tall, three-sided painted steel structure perfectly embodies the spirit of the age of Cwmbran's development as a new town".

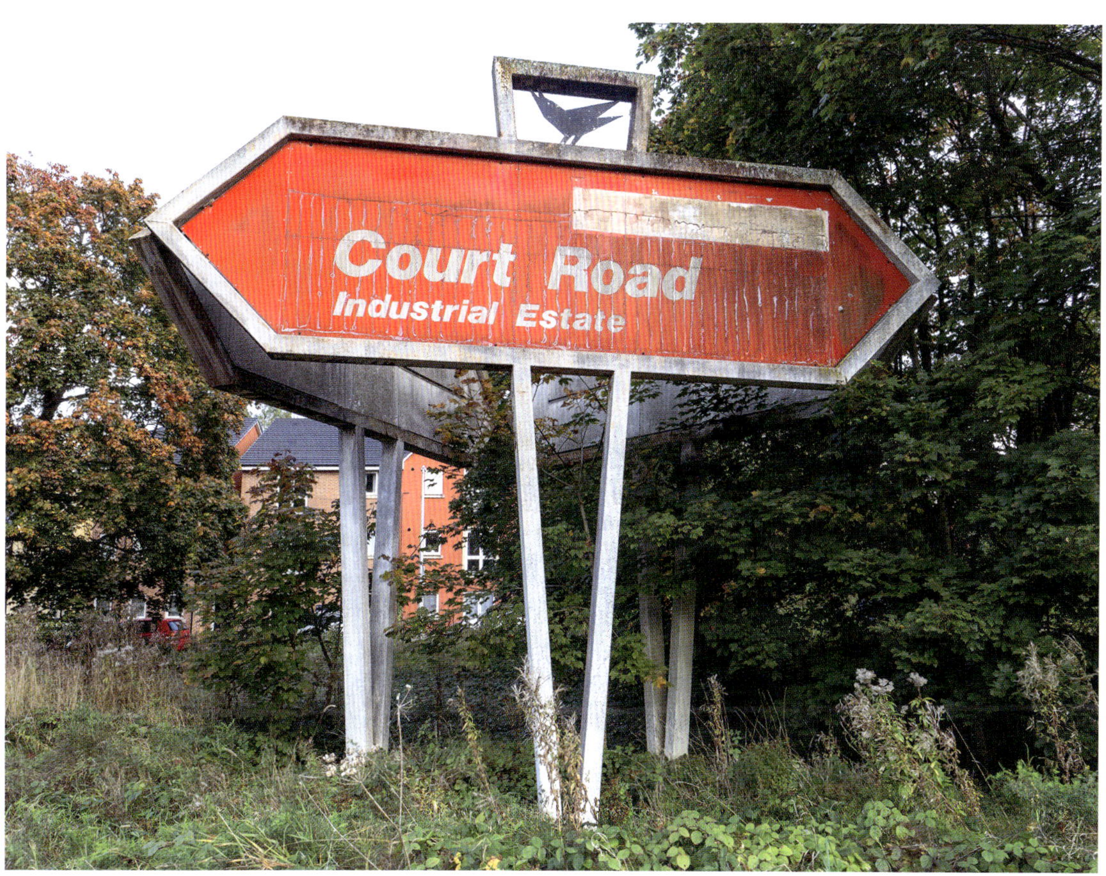

ST 29785 94510

On the gate of St Digain's Church is a certificate signed by celebrated botanist David Bellamy who declared that 'according to all the data we have to hand' the tree was between 4,000-5,000 years old. This pre-dates the Great Pyramids of Giza and if true, it makes the yew one of the oldest non-cloning trees in the world, potentially rivalling the Methuselah in California and even Scotland's Fortingall Yew.

Yew trees are commonly found in church yards. Kew Gardens describes them as a symbolic of everlasting life and rebirth, held sacred by Druids, symbolic of death and resurrection for the ancient Celts. This continued into the Christian era with yew branches carried on Palm Sunday and at funerals for many centuries.

Of vast circumference and gloom profound
This solitary tree! a living thing
Produced too slowly ever to decay;
Of form and aspect too magnificent
To be destroyed.

– **William Wordsworth** on Yew Trees

TREES

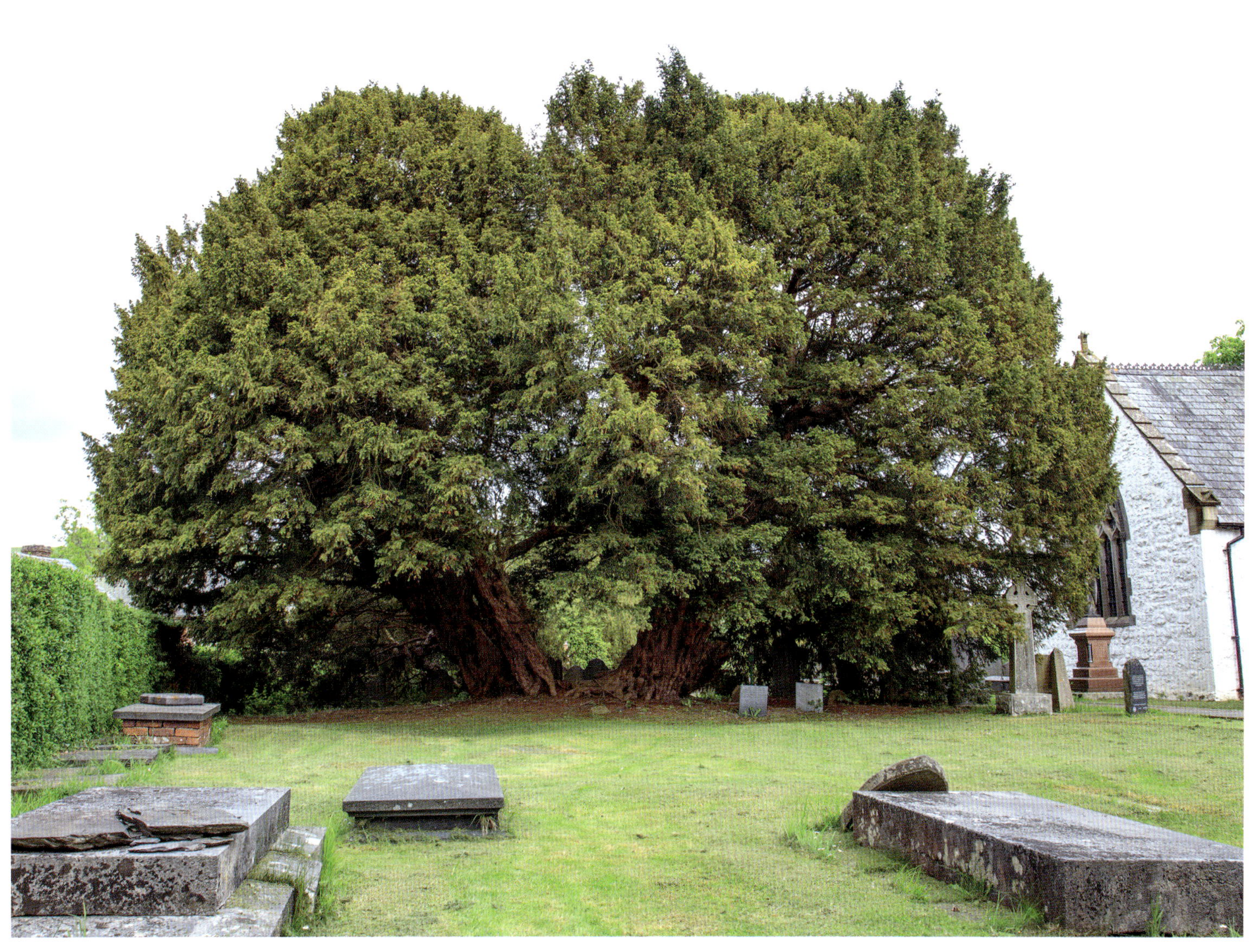

WELSHPOOL, POWYS

2015

The oldest known planting date of any tree in the UK – 893 AD. The yew in All Saints Church yard in the village of Buttington, was planted 1,100 years ago to commemorate victory at the Battle of Buttington when Welsh and English armies defeated invading Vikings.

Known as the Buttington Yew, it has an 8-meter circumference broken by a hollow section allowing access to its interior.

The nearby Buttington Oak, believed to have also commemorated the battle, collapsed in 2018 after being badly damaged by storms the previous year.

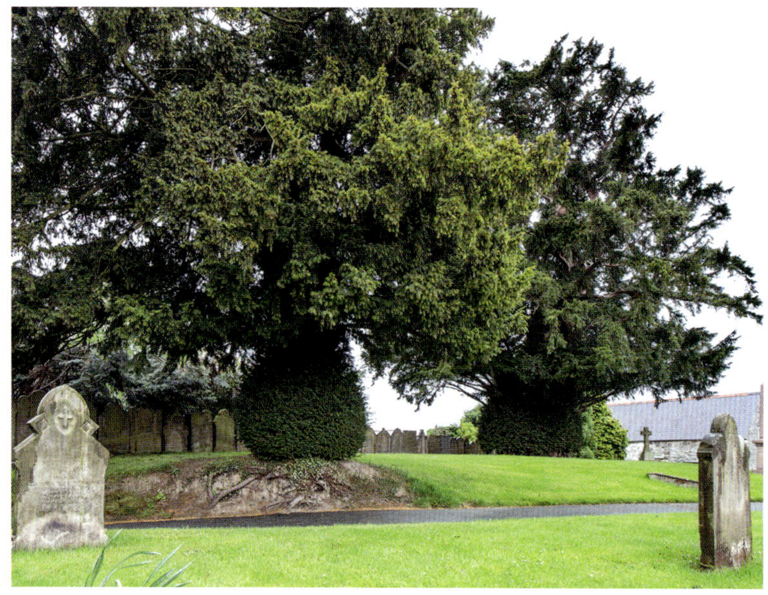

SJ 24911 08971

BANNAU BRYCHEINIOG, RHONDDA CYNON TAF

2014

The rarest tree in Wales. Sorbus Leyana or Ley's 'Whitebeam' is named after the man who discovered it in the late nineteenth century – the Reverend Augustin Ley who rode across Wales on horseback exploring his passion for botany and history.

Only seventeen of the small trees exist in the wild in two reserves within the Bannau Brycheiniog National Park, Penmoelallt and Darren Fach, both protected as Sites of Special Scientific Interest.

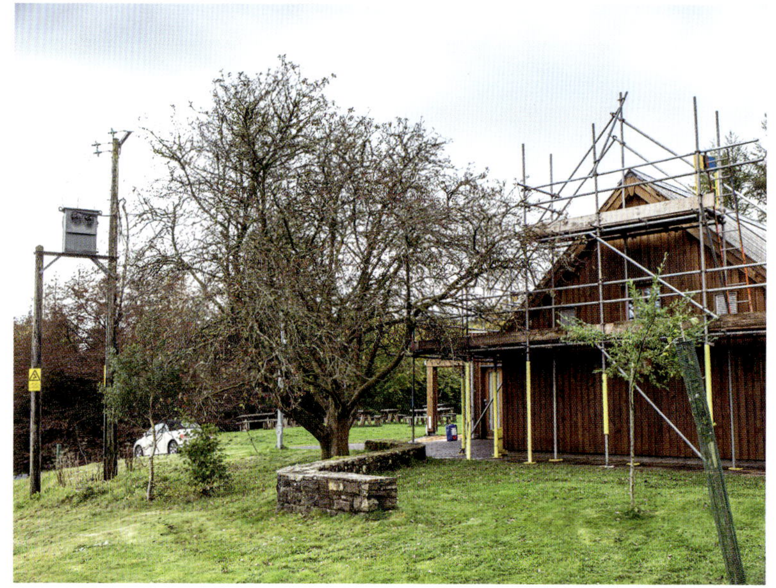

SO 00341 13128

TŶ CANOL WOODS, PEMBROKESHIRE

2007

The stuff of fairy tales.

Close to the village of Felindre Farchog, the ancient wood is home to trees over 800 years old. Its dense carpets of nearly 400 species of lichen, and biofluorescence – glowing and colourful light under certain conditions – have led to the nature reserve being deemed "one of the most magical and special woodlands in the UK".

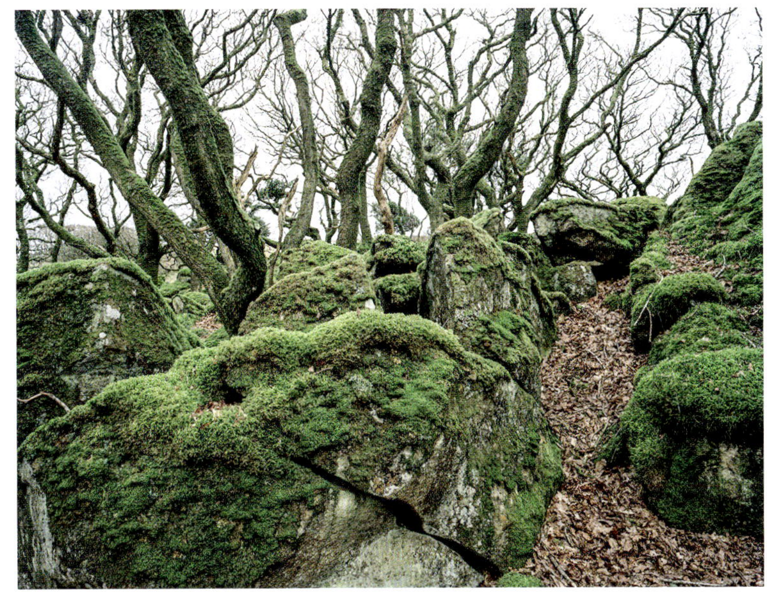

SN 09527 37138

YEW TUNNEL, CARMARTHENSHIRE

2011

One of Aberglasney Gardens biggest tourist attractions began life as a hedge.

Some believe it to be as old as 1,000 years, others say 300. Regardless, the trees have been around long enough to grow so tall they arched over, their branches becoming fused together to form an enchanting walkway.

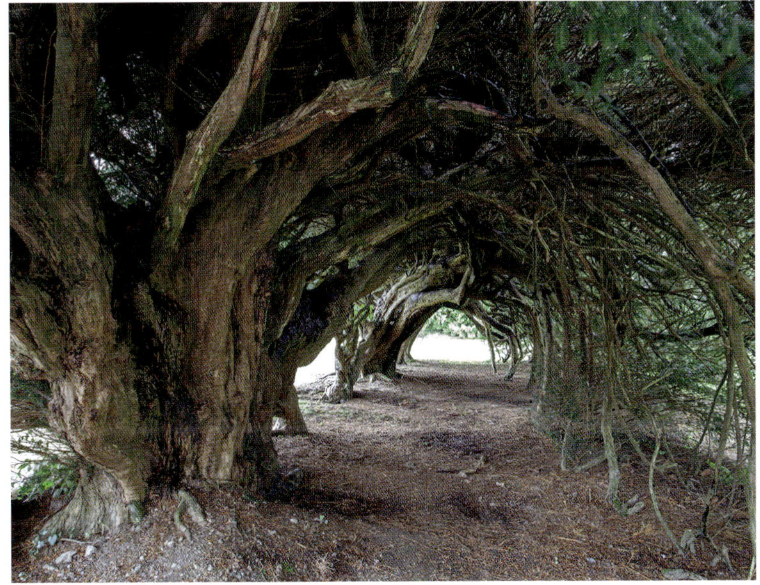

SN 58135 22149

A cedar planted to commemorate the wedding of Charles I in 1625 in the now Grade One listed ten-acre garden, it was inspected by the monarch himself twenty years later when he visited the fourteenth century fortified manor house, close to the market town of Llanrwst.

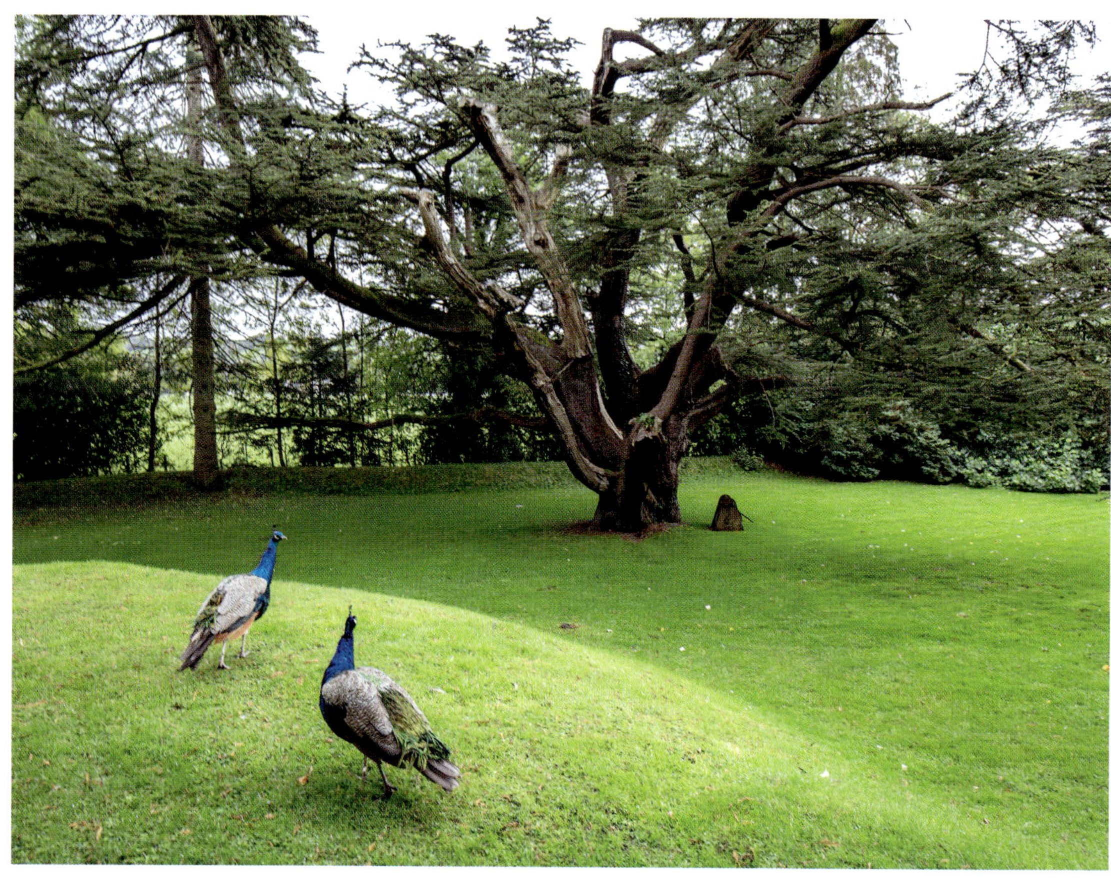

SH 79659 61044

GARWNANT, MERTHYR TYDFIL

2018

The planting of an arboretum to celebrate 100 years of the Forestry Commission in 1919. Since then, the national forestry reserve has grown to an area of 126,000 hectares and supplies half of all timber in Wales.

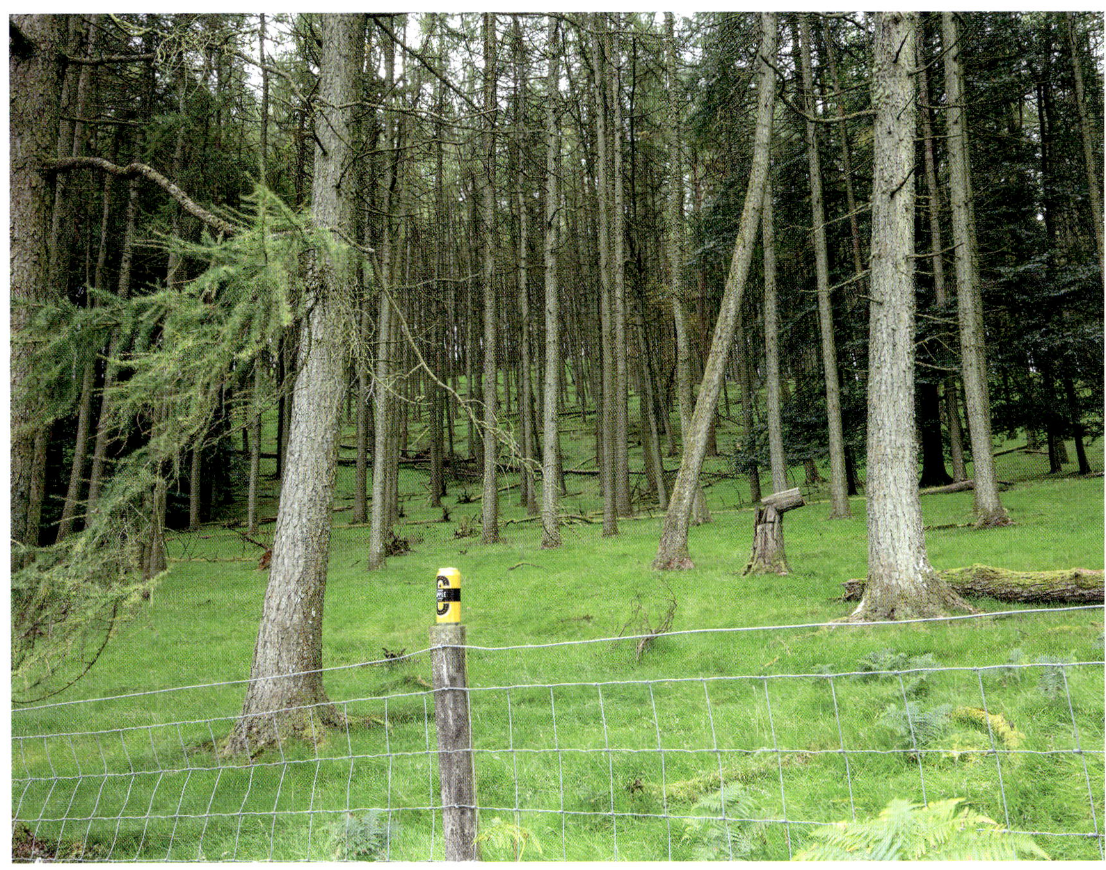

SN 74648 763882

The early stages of a six-year environmental crisis operation at Cwmcarn Forest Drive. The seven-mile area was closed as 160,000 diseased larch trees were felled. The fungus-like virus Phytophthora ramorum, also known as sudden oak death, can spread from tree to tree through air currents, mists, and even raindrops.

A popular visitor attraction off the M4 near Newport, the forest drive was reopened in 2021.

Since 2010 around three million infected larch trees have been felled in Wales.

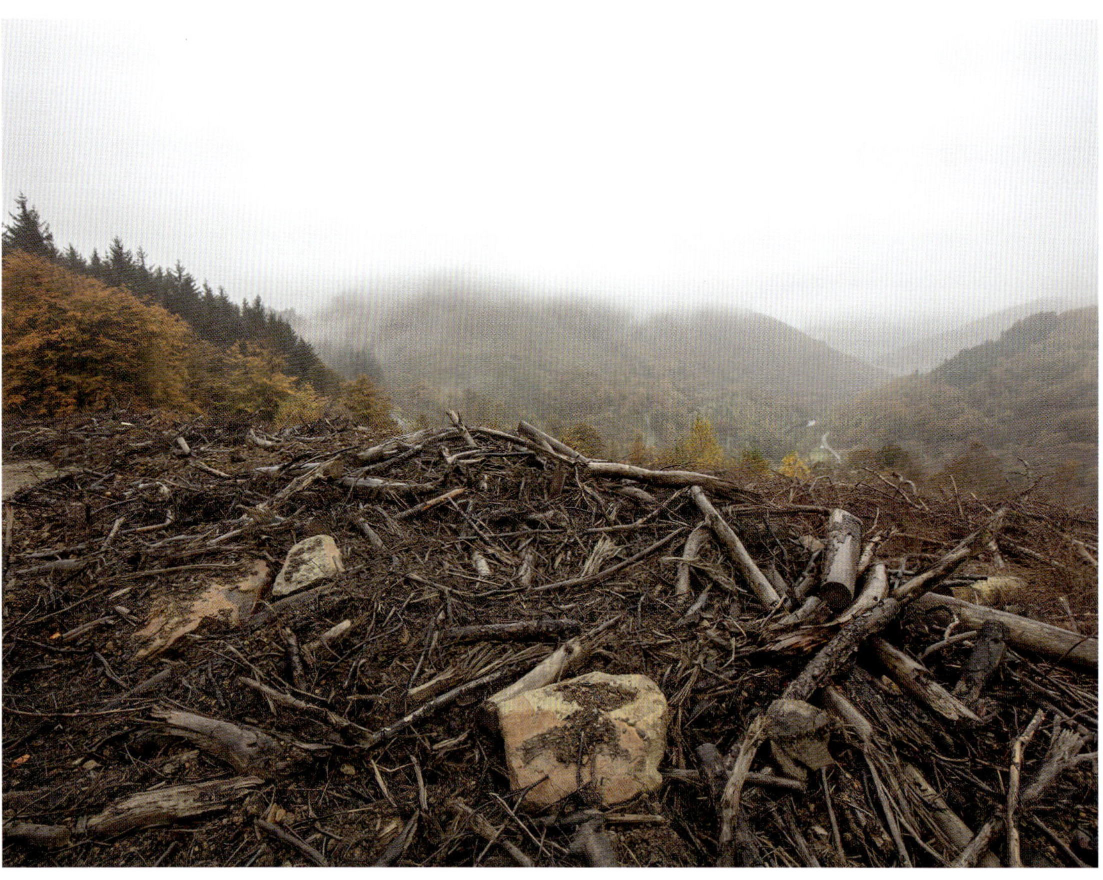

ST 242274 93368

Abandoned to history, the ghostly remains of a once proud avenue of sweet chestnuts guarding the approach to the Tudor mansion of Llanvihangel Court.

Known locally as Armada Avenue, they were possibly planted from nuts carried on board the ships of Armada prisoners who helped build part of the house.

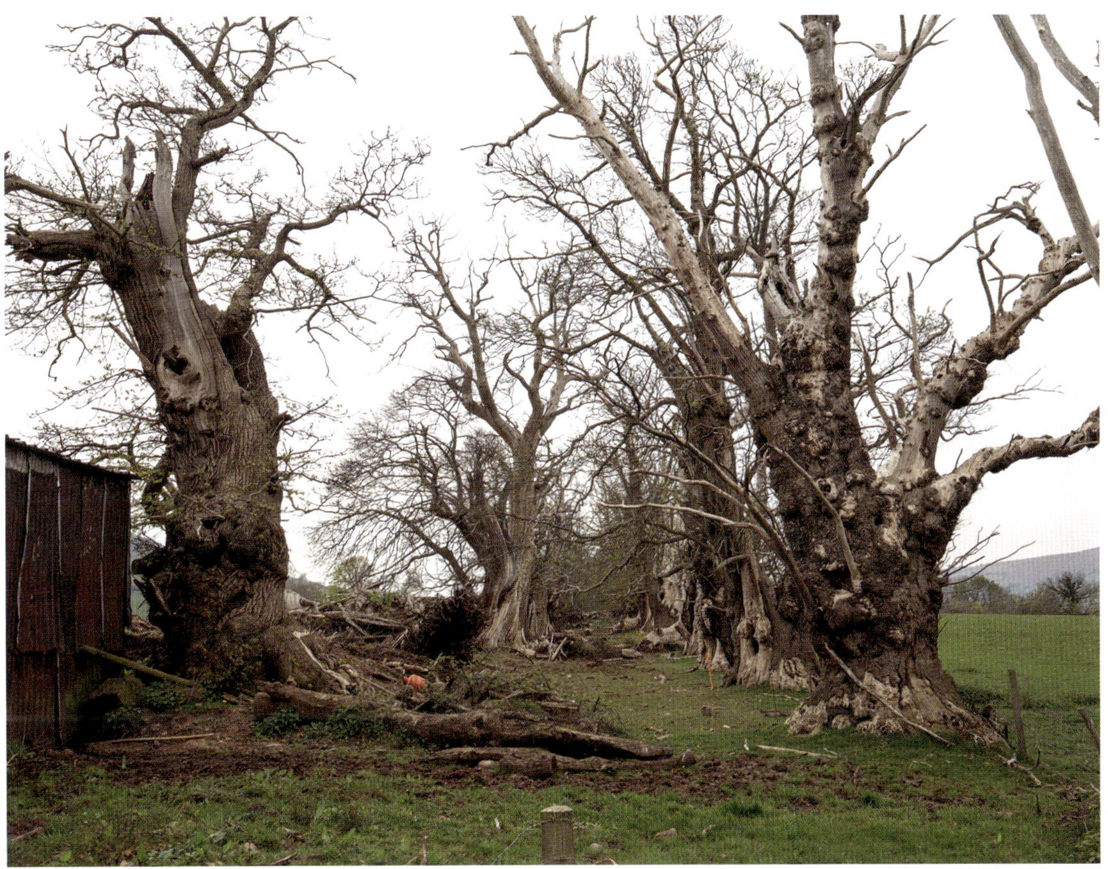

SO 33001 09641

DOLBADARN CASTLE, GWYNEDD

2012

Built in the early 1200s, the fortification served as a symbol of power for Llywelyn the Great, King of Gwynedd, its large stone keep described as 'the finest surviving example of a Welsh round tower'.

Painted by J.M.W. Turner & Richard Wilson.

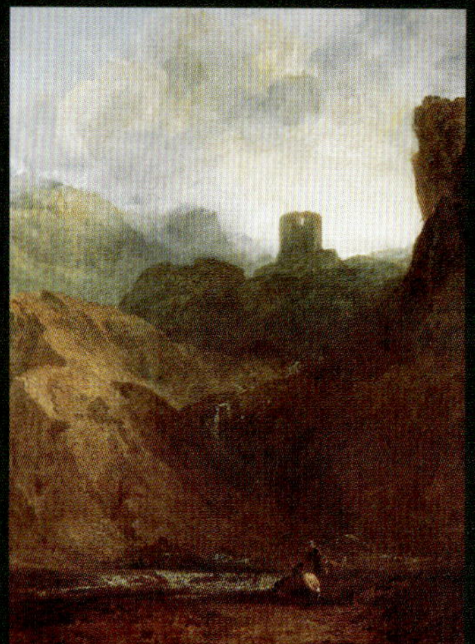

J.M.W. Turner, 1798

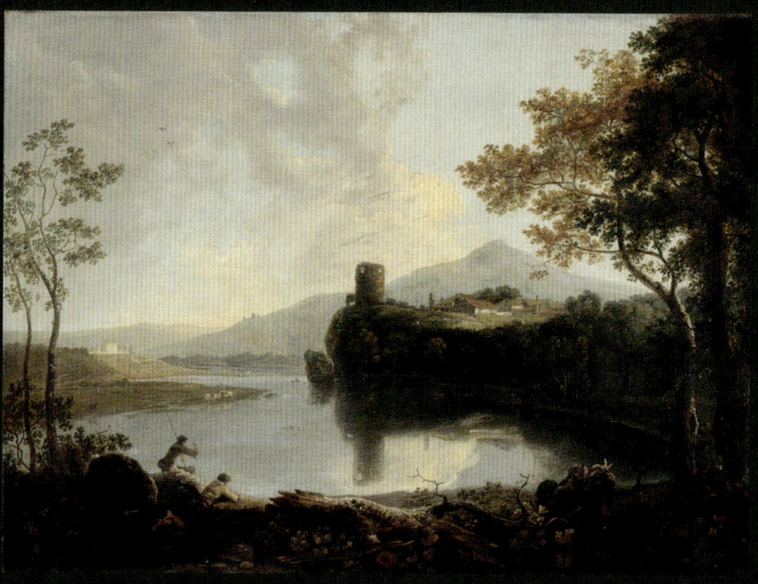

Richard Wilson, circa 1765
Amgueddfa Cymru – National Museum Wales

THEN & NOW

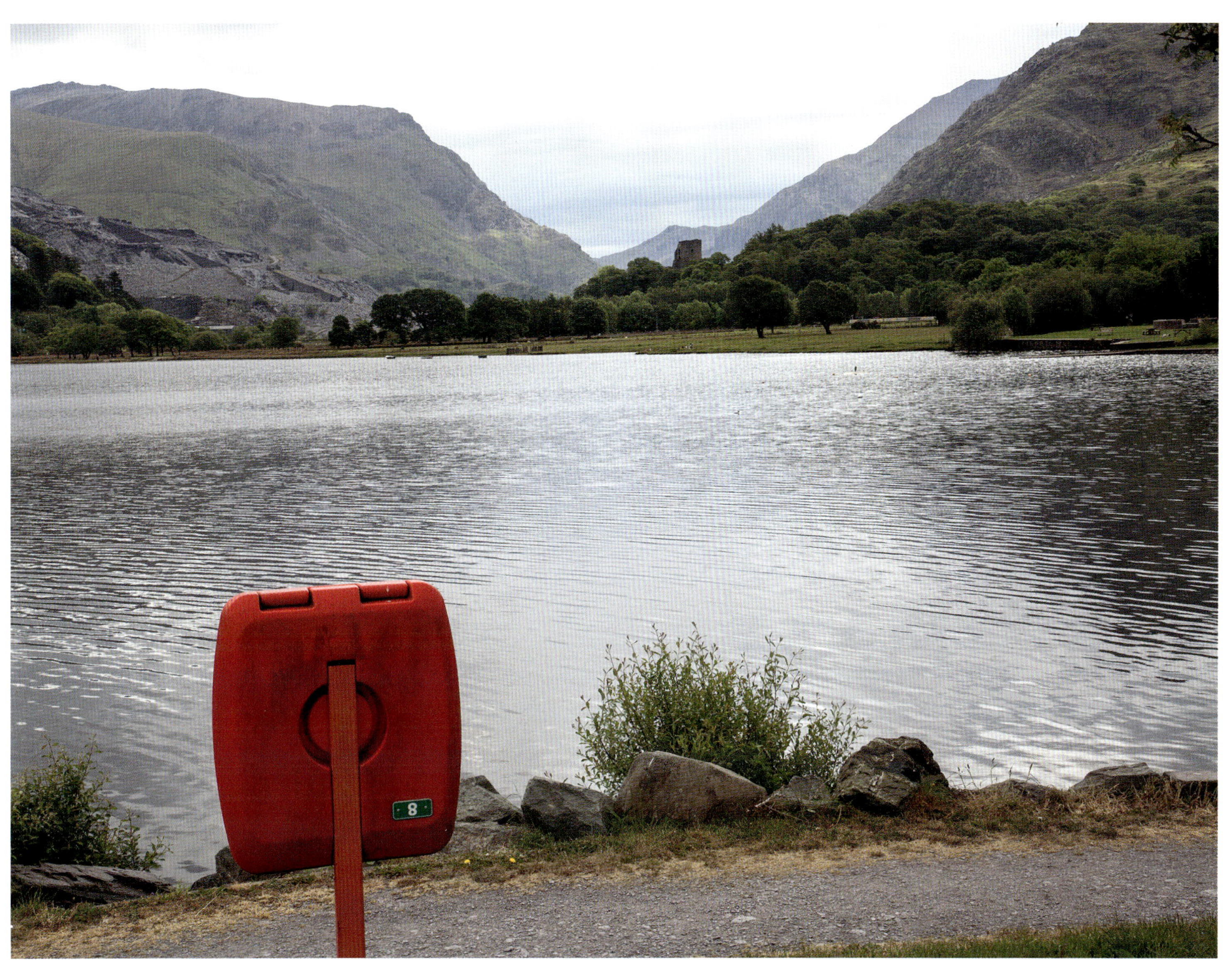

SH 57807 60448

DOLBADARN CASTLE, GWYNEDD

2012

The King's grandson, Prince Llywelyn ap Gruffudd, one of the last
native and independent Princes of Wales, is said to have imprisoned
his brother, Owain, in the castle.

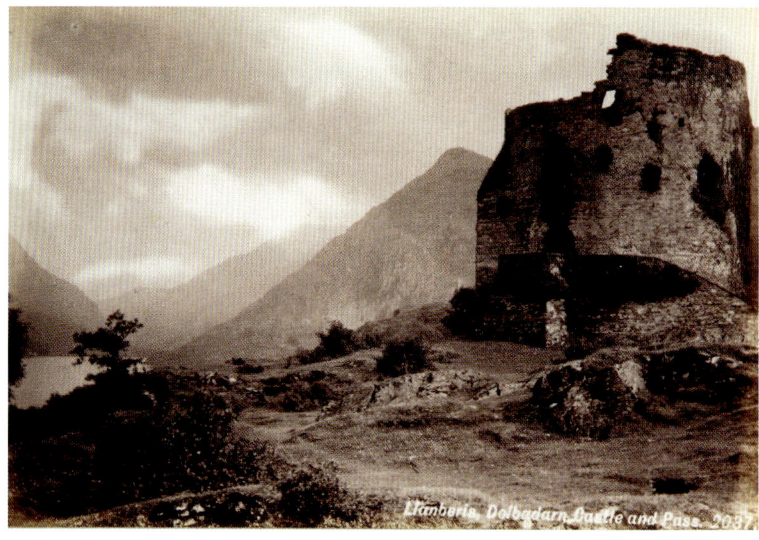

Francis Bedford, prominent English photographer:
View of Dolbadarn Castle and Llanberis Pass, 1859

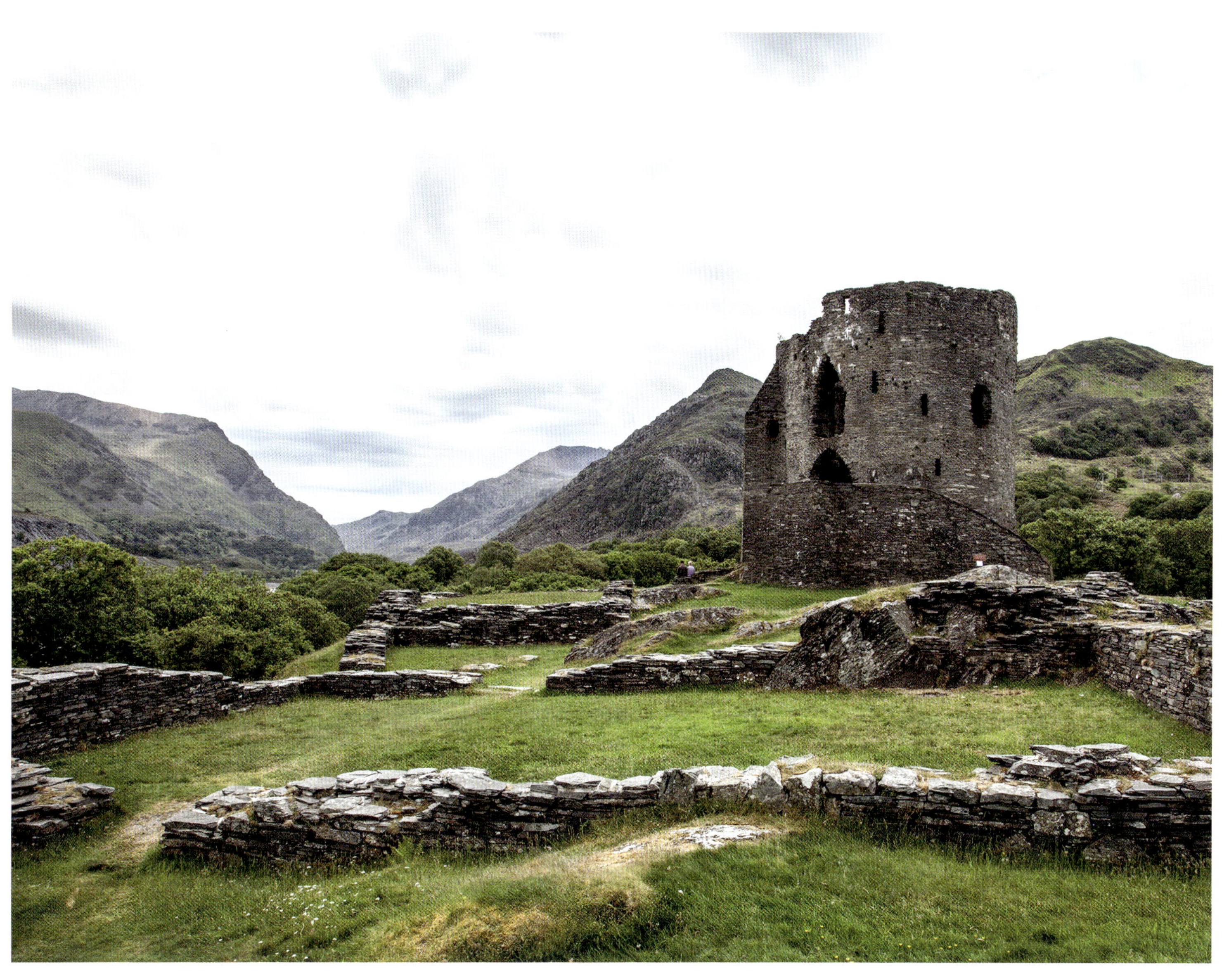

SH 58587 59841

2014

The first photograph taken in Wales in March 1841 by painter and mathematician Calvert Richard Jones, a daguerreotype of the Tudor Gothic-style home of the Mansel Talbot family.

Named after its inventor, Louis Daguerre, the photographic process which used a silver-coated copper plate and fumes to make it light sensitive, was the first publicly available in 1939.

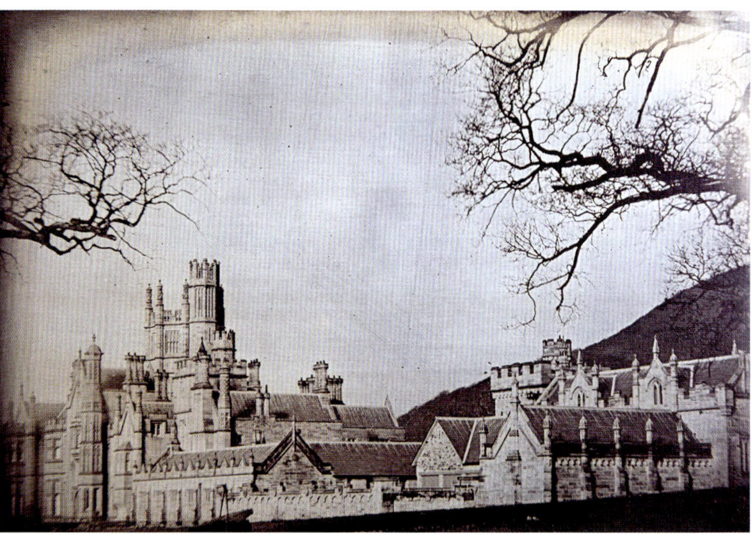

The first photograph taken in Wales:
Margam Castle by Calvert Richard Jones, 1841

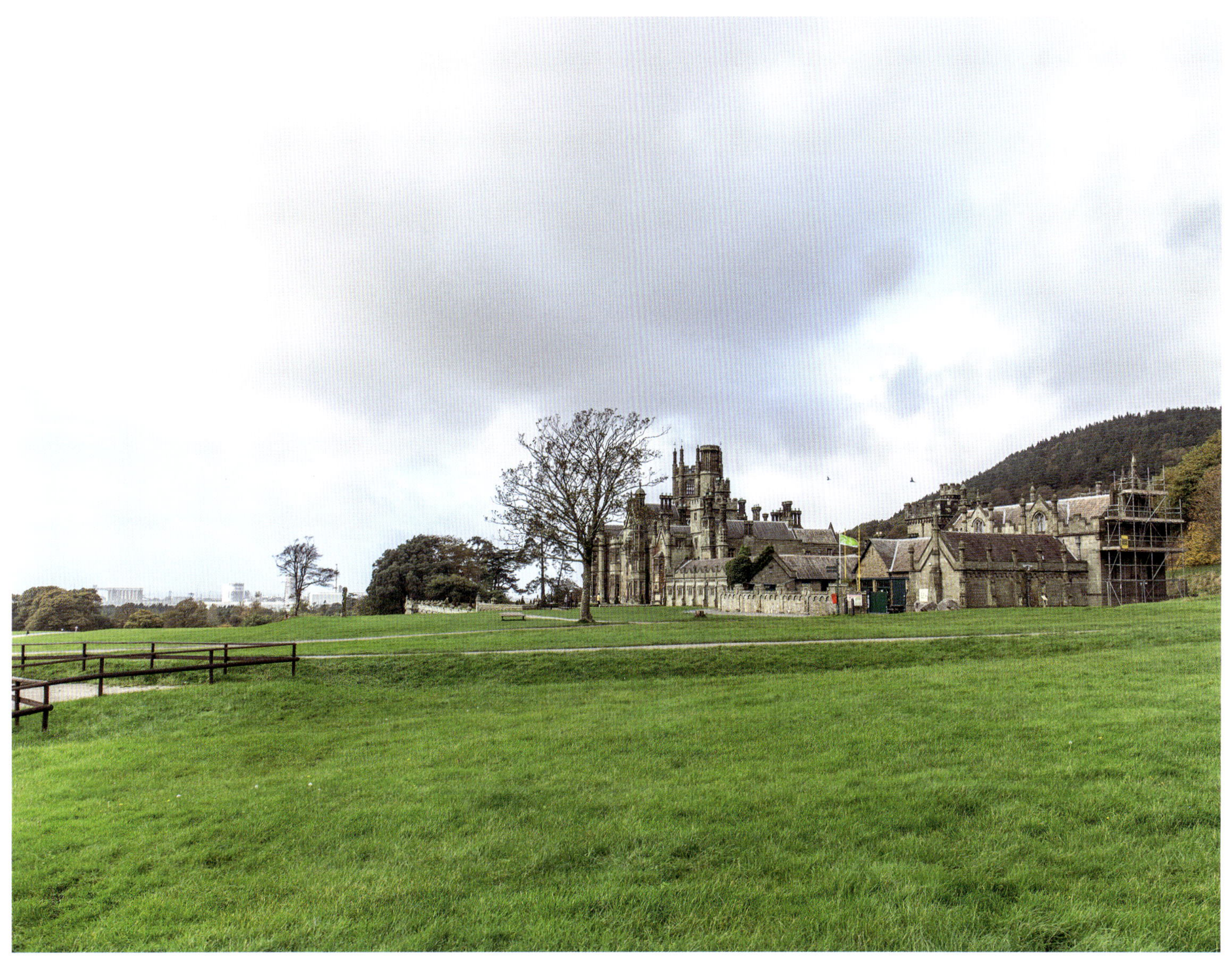

SS 80711 86351

CAERNARFON CASTLE, GWYNEDD

2017

Delving into the history of one of Wales' most magnificent castles, it becomes clear why some in Wales, particularly nationalists, felt aggrieved it was chosen for the investiture of the then Prince Charles as Prince of Wales in 1969.

The remains of the medieval fortress on the banks of the River Seiont, is not Welsh at all but a symbol of English invasion by Edward I in 1282, who conquered the native princes and colonised their land.

Its stone walls – which extend 734 m around the town and include eight towers and two gatehouses – were erected to envelope the original motte-and-bailey castle in a display of wealth and power. Tradition has it that within its bounds, Edward I presented his son to the Welsh as the first English Prince of Wales in 1284, the year Wales was formally incorporated with England by statute.

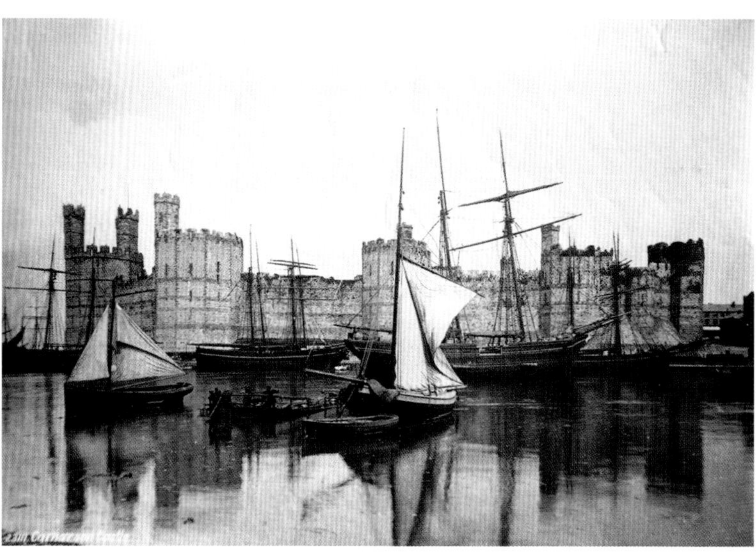

Francis Frith, circa 1890

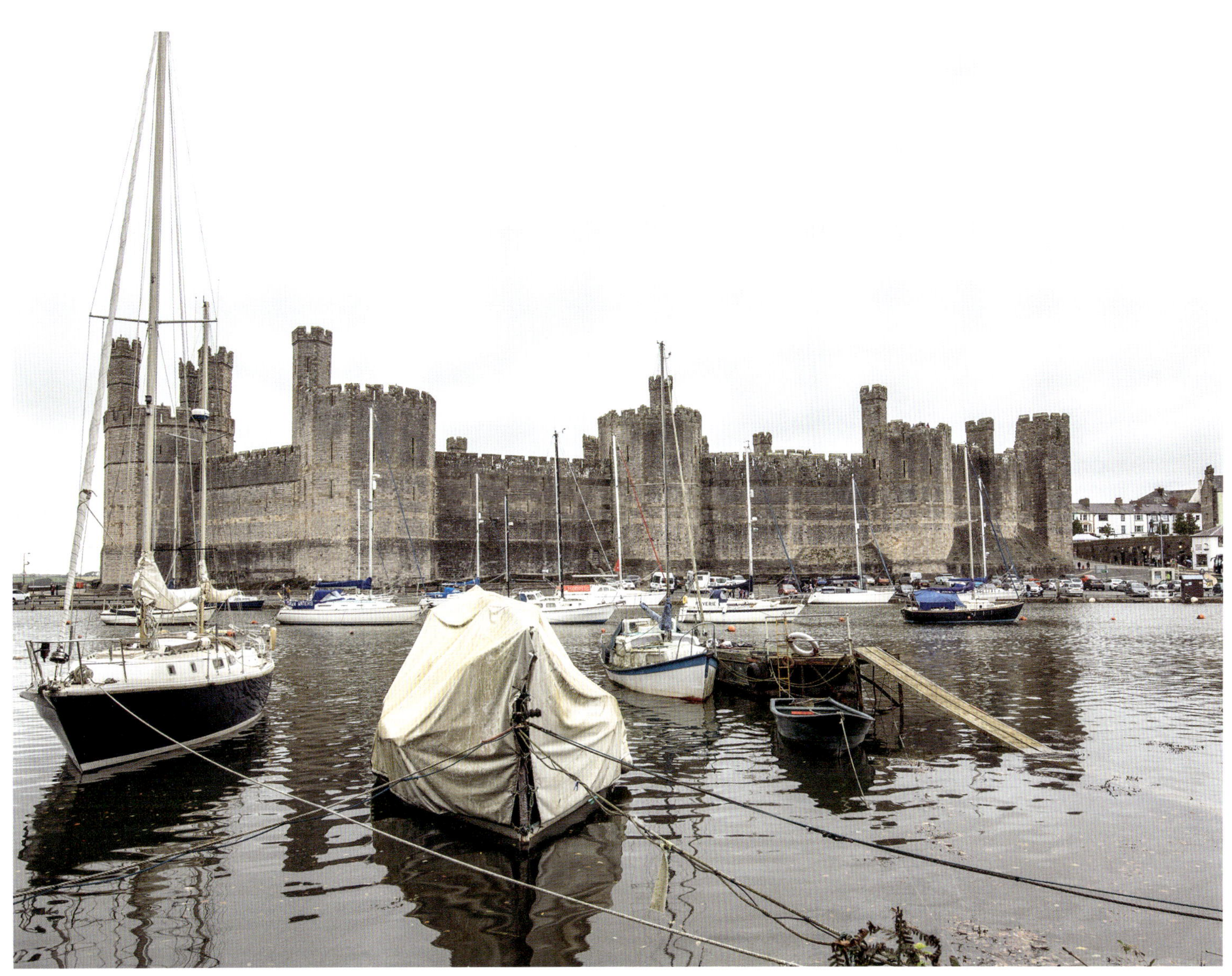

SH 47771 62507

Once the largest copper mines in the world.

Known as 'the great discovery', in 1768 Roland Pugh, a local miner, stumbled across a large deposit of copper ore sparking a copper rush with crowds descending from across the UK seeking their fortune. The minerals processed into sheets helped forge British naval fleets around the time of Nelson.

At the core of the deeply excavated site mined as far back as the Early Bronze Age, is the remains of a volcano.

INDUSTRY

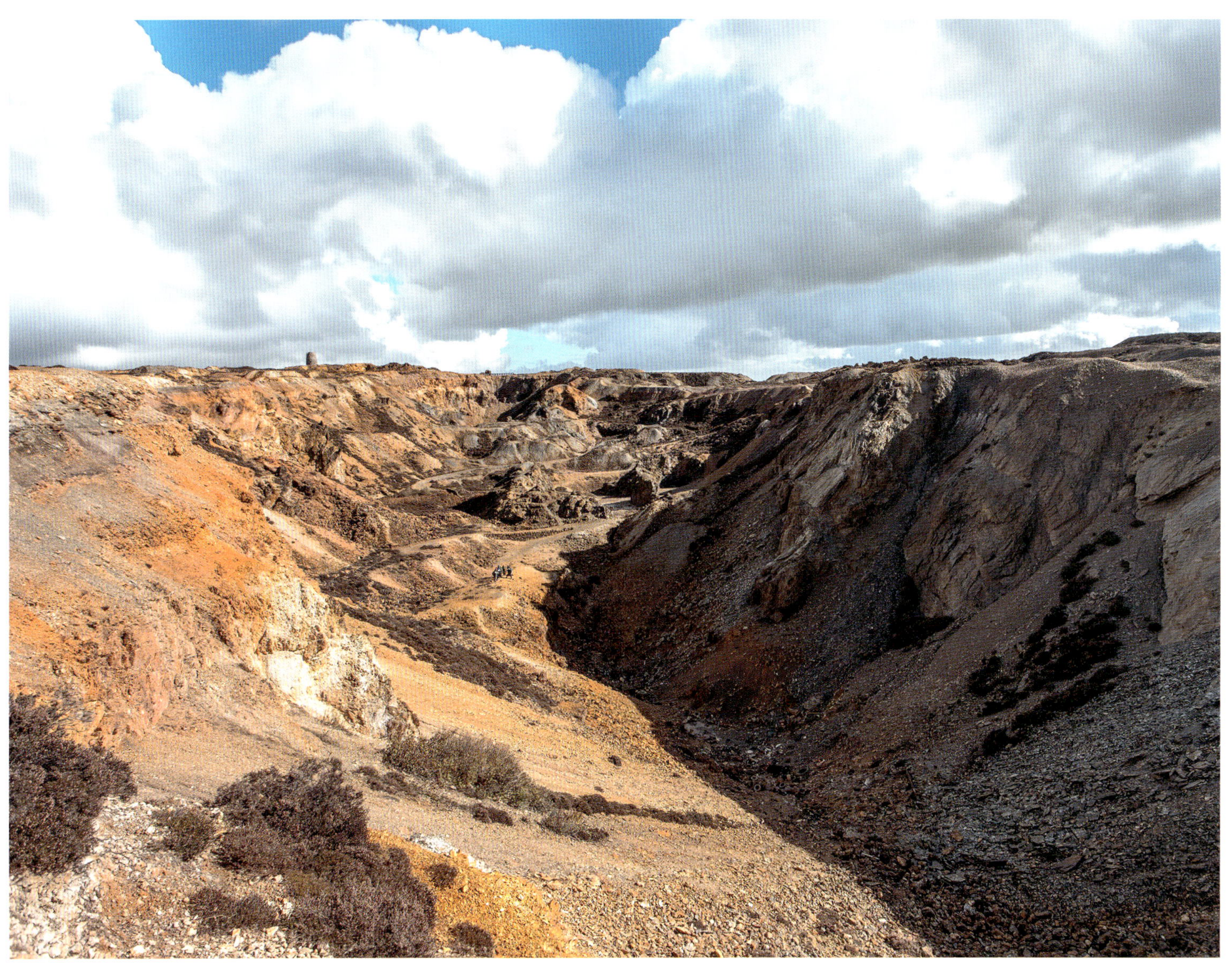

SH 43906 90209

CYFARTHFA IRONWORKS, MERTHYR TYDFIL

2016

On visiting in 1844, the King of Prussia heralded the area as "the fiery city of Pluto". More widely remembered as the 'iron capital of the world' during the industrial revolution, this derelict blast furnace was one of seven at Cyfarthfa. Their remains are the largest and most complete surviving examples of their kind, originally built in 1765 and later developed by ironmaster Richard Crawshay.

At its height in 1803, the works employed 1,500 people including many children. Although closed in 1910, the furnaces were briefly revived during the First World War before being finally dismantled in 1938.

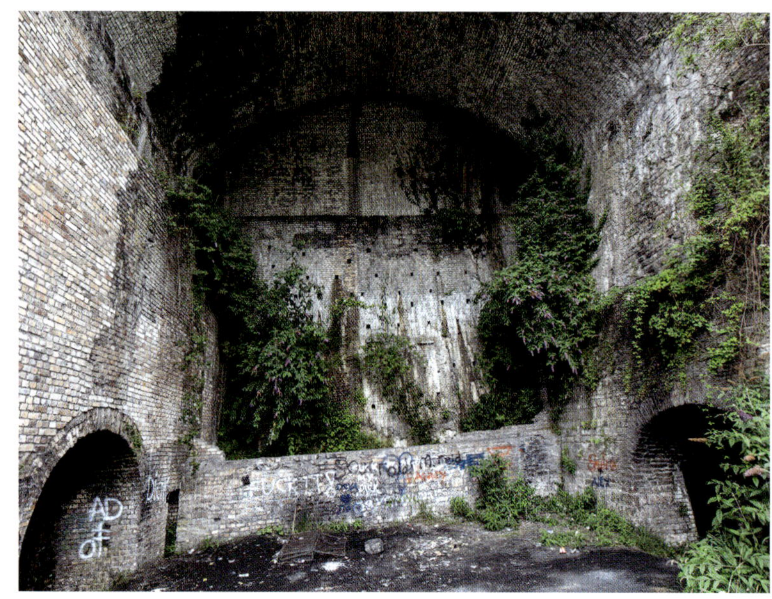

SO 03821 06828

BLAENAVON IRONWORKS, TORFAEN

2016

Historic monuments body Cadw describes the area as one of the finest examples in the world of a landscape created by ironmaking in the late eighteenth and early nineteenth centuries.

Immortalised by Alexander Cordell, the first book in his classic trilogy about a local family, *The Rape of the Fair Country* sold millions and was translated into seventeen languages.

Shortly before his death in 1997, Cordell, petitioning for Blaenavon to be recognised and protected, implored: "All that the people of the past have to commend them for the sacrifices they made, are the dirt monuments they left behind. That is why it is incumbent on people with influence to sacrifice everything to get this done."

In November 2000 it was inscribed as a UNESCO World Heritage Site.

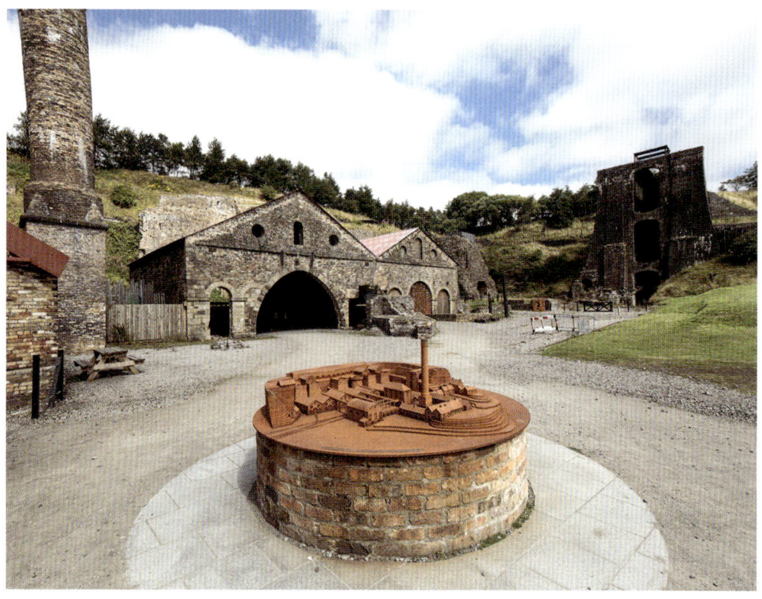

SO 24932 09225

Being reclaimed by nature – one of many monumental spoil heaps across south Wales, testament to the heavy industry of the past. In 2008, the Forgotten Landscapes Project was set up to conserve, restore and open up the landscape beyond the Blaenavon World Heritage Site.

Jointly funded by the Welsh Government and the Lottery Heritage Fund, the project covered 71 square km – home to seventeen scheduled ancient monuments and 109 listed buildings – and ran for six years. Community voluntary action not only worked to promote the area to visitors but also forge understanding and pride in its history.

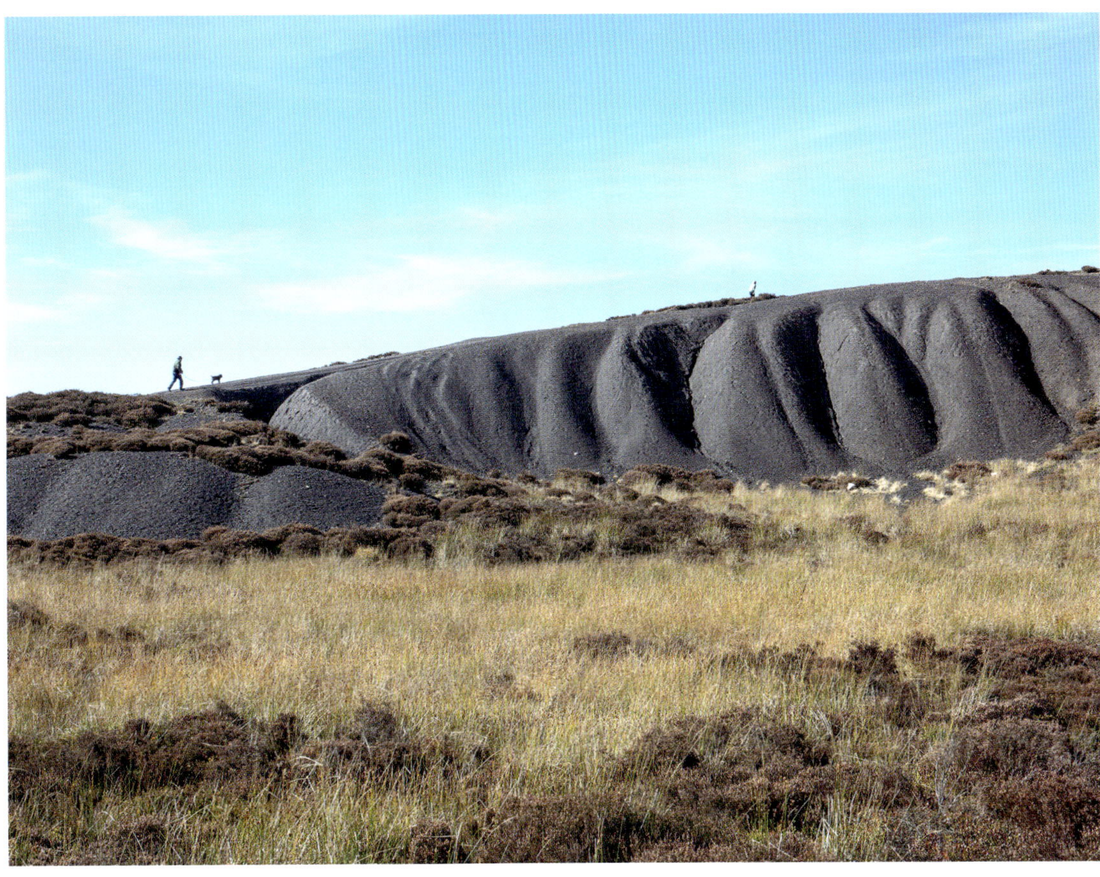

SO 25211 10666

From the Early Bronze Age until 1950, the spoils of opencast mining, which peaked in the eighteenth century, are still evident around the scheduled ancient monument.

Excerpt of a letter entitled 'A derelict village – plea for Cwymystwyth unemployed' signed M.R. and published in *Welsh Gazette*, January 1934:

"No lead mines in Wales were better known or more profitable at one time than the Kingside Mines, Cwmystwyth. They stand today derelict, forsaken and forgotten like dark sentinels overlooking the River Ystwyth, ever reminding passers-by that here, once upon a time, prosperity and fame went hand in hand with happiness. For what village lad was not happy who had the good fortune to be a miner in his own native place".

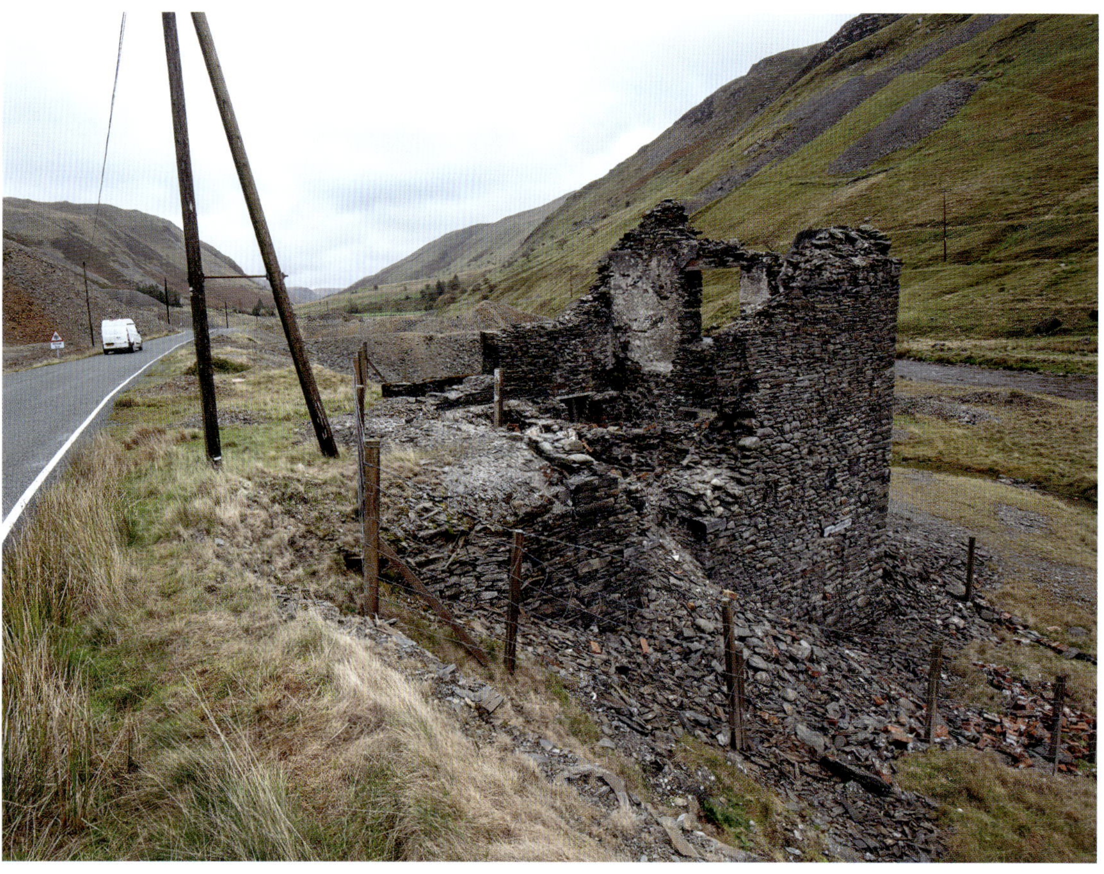

SN 80120 74443

DOLAUCOTHI GOLD MINES, CARMARTHENSHIRE

2019

Abandoned railway track close to the surface and underground workings near Pumsaint.

Last worked in 1938, the mines are the only remaining Roman gold mines in the UK and are run as a visitor centre by the National Trust.

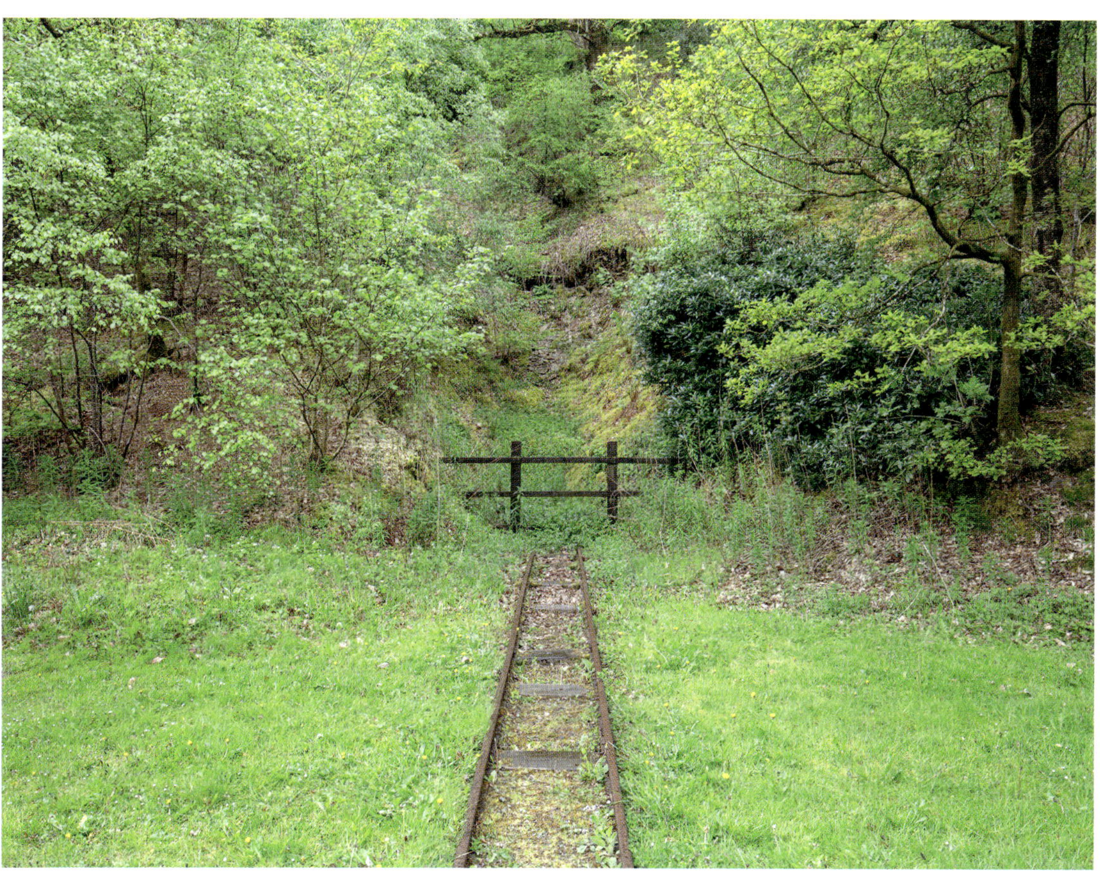

SN 66333 40258

TOTES MEER BY PAUL NASH

1941

The title of the 1941 oil on canvas is German for 'Dead Sea' and depicts a graveyard landscape of wrecked German Luftwaffe aircraft mournfully lit by the moon.

Nash had been asked to work as an artist for the Air Ministry in 1940. Some disliked his surrealist style and his full-time position was terminated before the year was out. The War Artists' Advisory Committee later paid him £150 for the artwork which was presented to the Tate Gallery in 1946, the year Nash died.

DINORWIC SLATE QUARRY, GWYNEDD

2018

The spoils of what was the once second largest slate quarry in the world, the biggest found at neighbouring Penrhyn near Bethesda.

Worked between 1787 and 1969 it covered an expanse of 700 hectares, with two main quarries riven with internal tramways. Today, it is now a museum, filming location and extreme rock-climbing destination.

A glimpse of its landscape while walking through was uncannily reminiscent of an oil painting considered to be one of the most important British paintings of World War II.

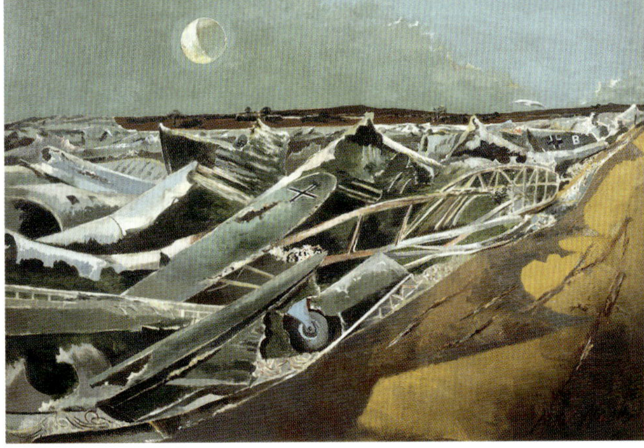

Totes Meer by Paul Nash, 1941
Tate Gallery

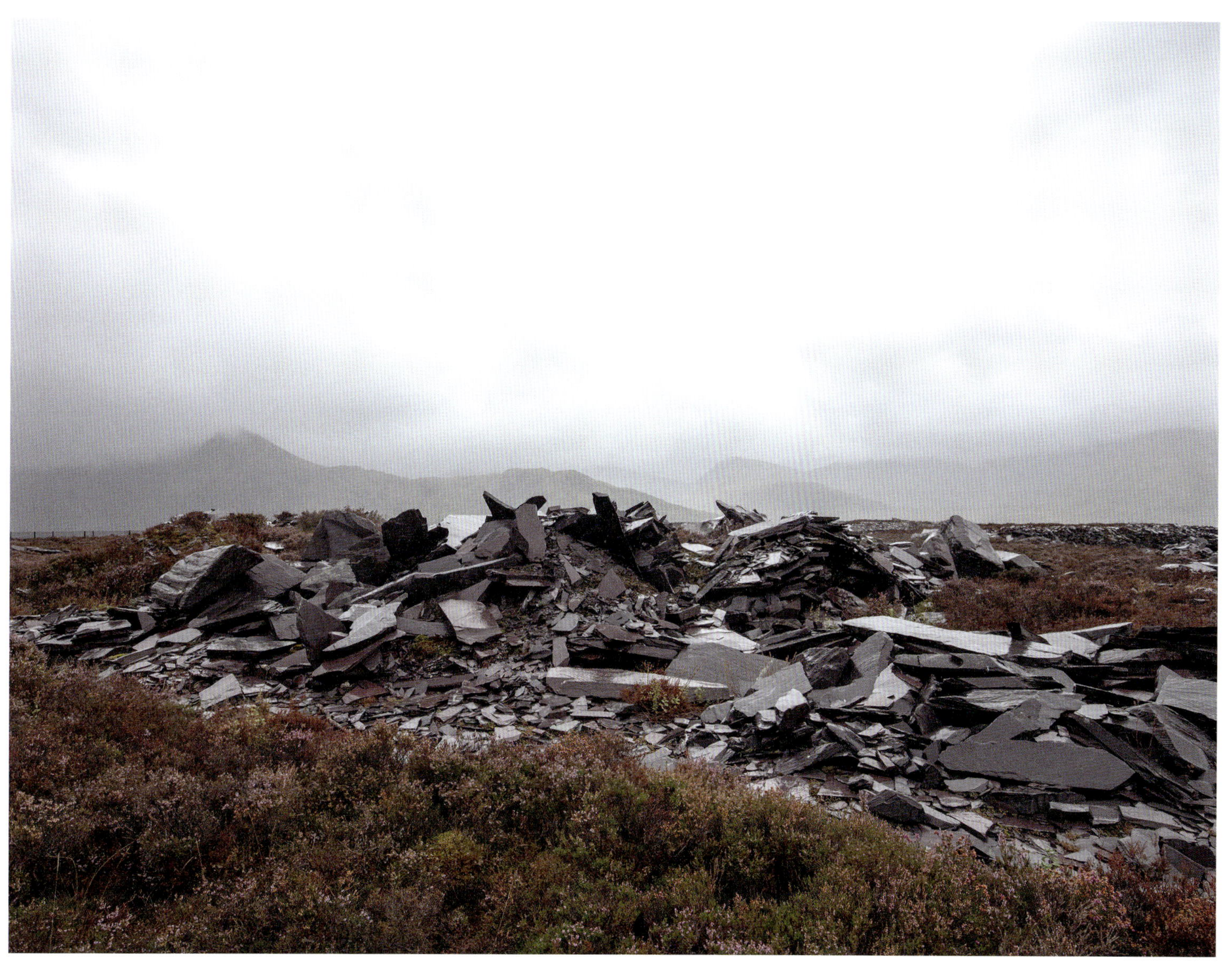

SH 59178 60565

EBBW VALE, BLAENAU GWENT

2015

In the 1930s, the steel works was the largest in Europe exporting
around the world, including to Australia for the building of the
Sydney Harbour Bridge. In the 1960s it employed 14,500 people but
the collapse of the UK's steel industry loomed and by 1981 much
of the site had been demolished, with the remaining tinplate works
closed in 2002.

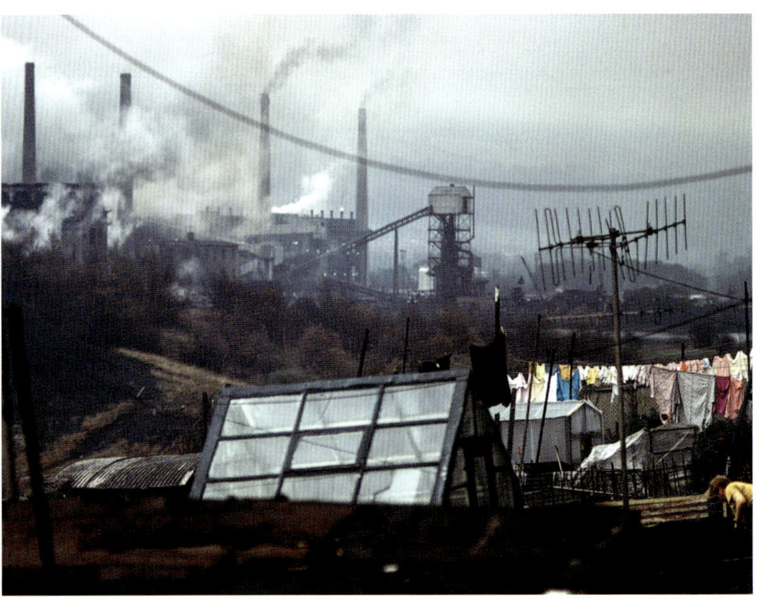

SO 17364 07151

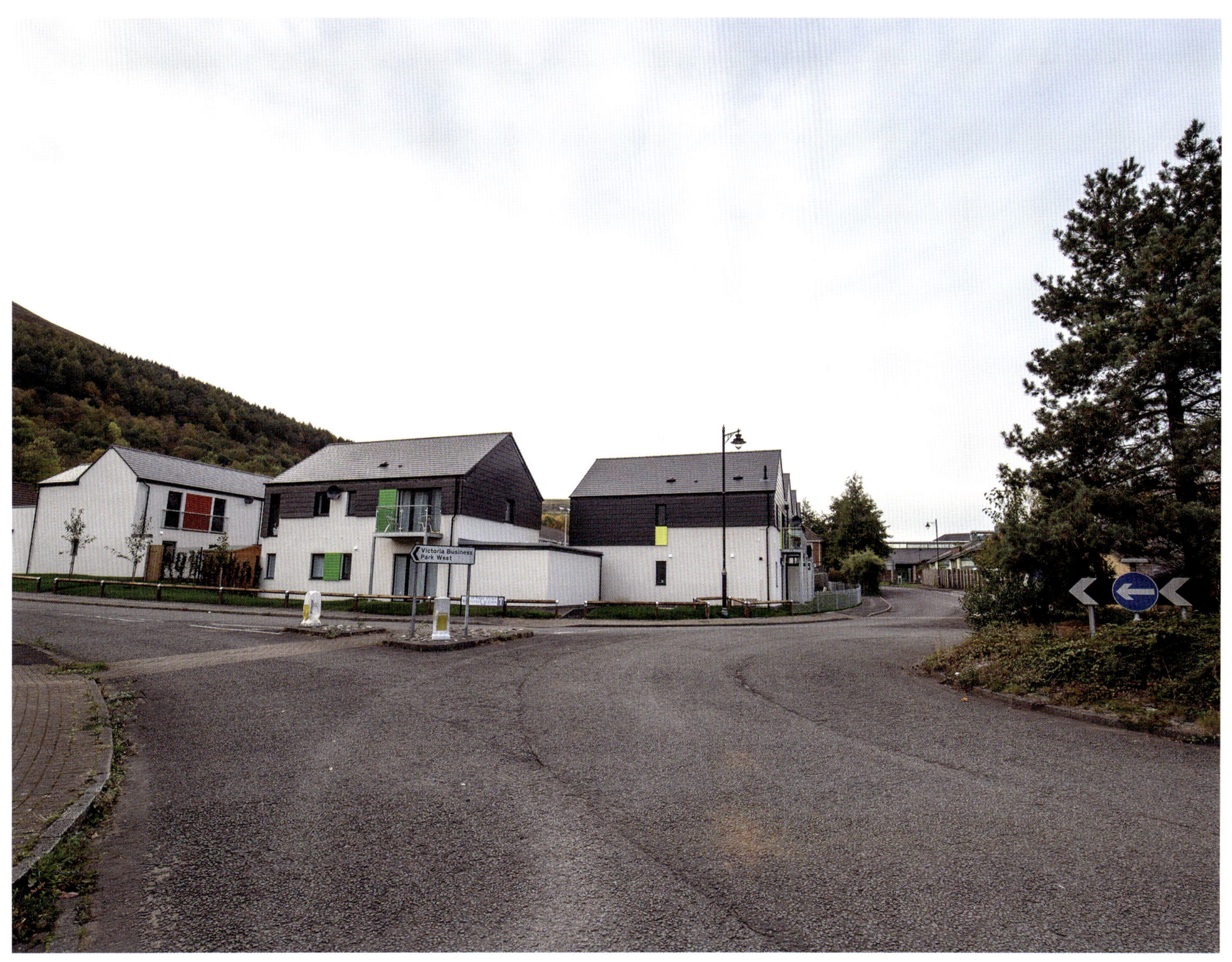

SO 17364 07151

The history of designated playgrounds in the UK is surprisingly short.

It was post-war concern over children playing in the rubble of bombed houses and rising juvenile delinquency that led to them becoming a common landscape feature.

LEISURE

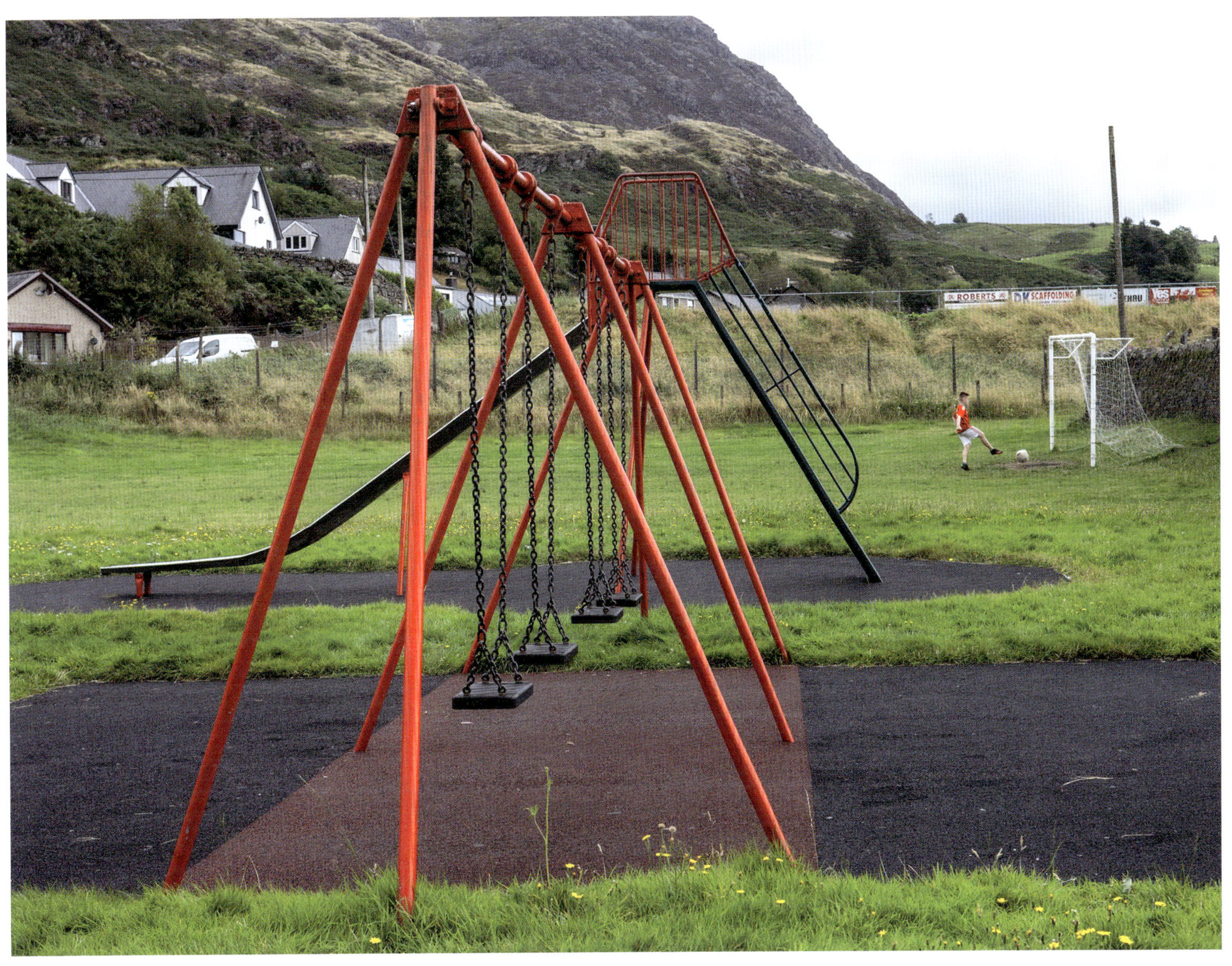

SH 70538 44400

BLAENAU FFESTINIOG, GWYNEDD

2024

The world's first underground trampoline, Bounce Below, part of Zip World Titan, was inspired by an attraction in a French woodland. Founder Sean Taylor – a Royal Marines Commando for 20 years before returning home to North Wales – removed 500 tonnes of rubble from inside the disused Llechwedd Slate Cavern, said to be twice the size of St Paul's Cathedral.

Six trampoline nets are strung on six levels – the highest at 180ft – and are interconnected by a series of chutes.

Of North Wales' global reputation for adrenalised tourism, Taylor says: "I think it's fair to say we are fast becoming the most fun place on earth".

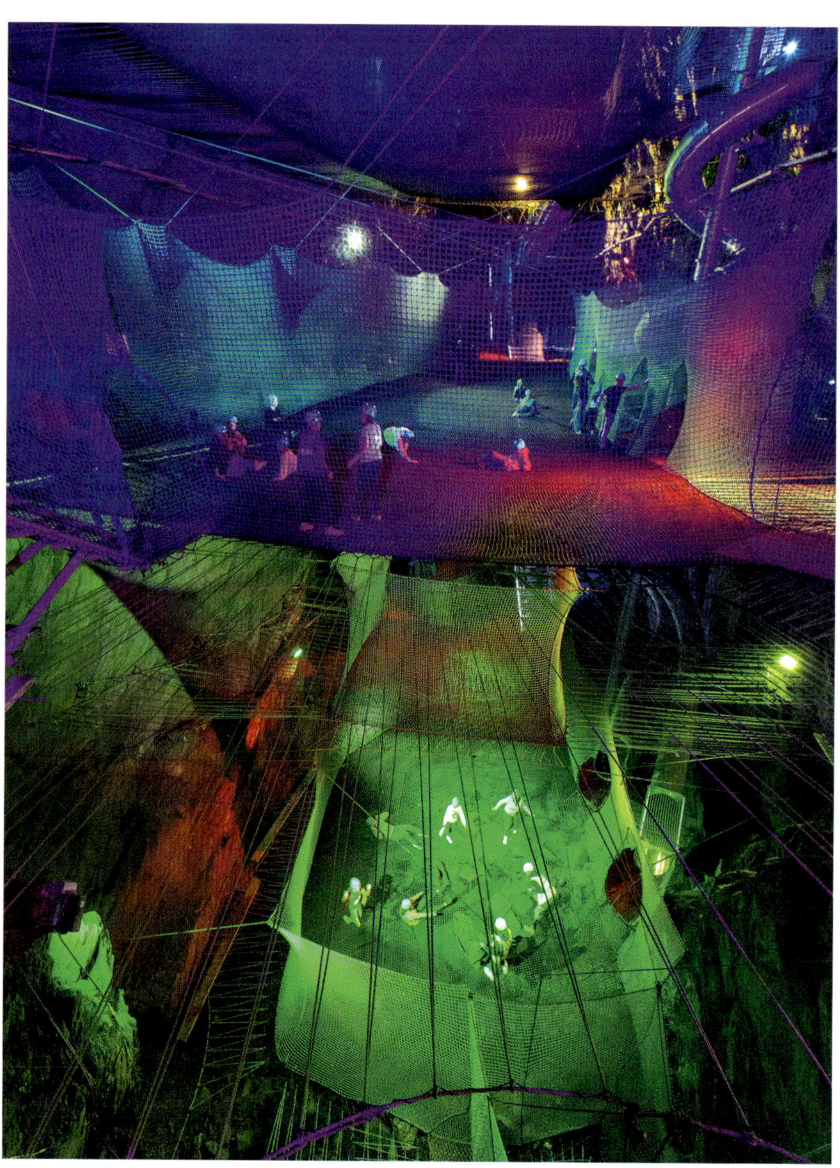

We are not amused! A safety problem closes a newly-opened children's attraction in a sand park along the barrage which crosses the water from Cardiff Bay to Penarth.

The history of play houses stretches as far back as ancient Greece and Rome when small versions of homes were built to educate children as future homemakers. Since then, all cultures have built miniature homes to foster independence and fire the imaginations of their young.

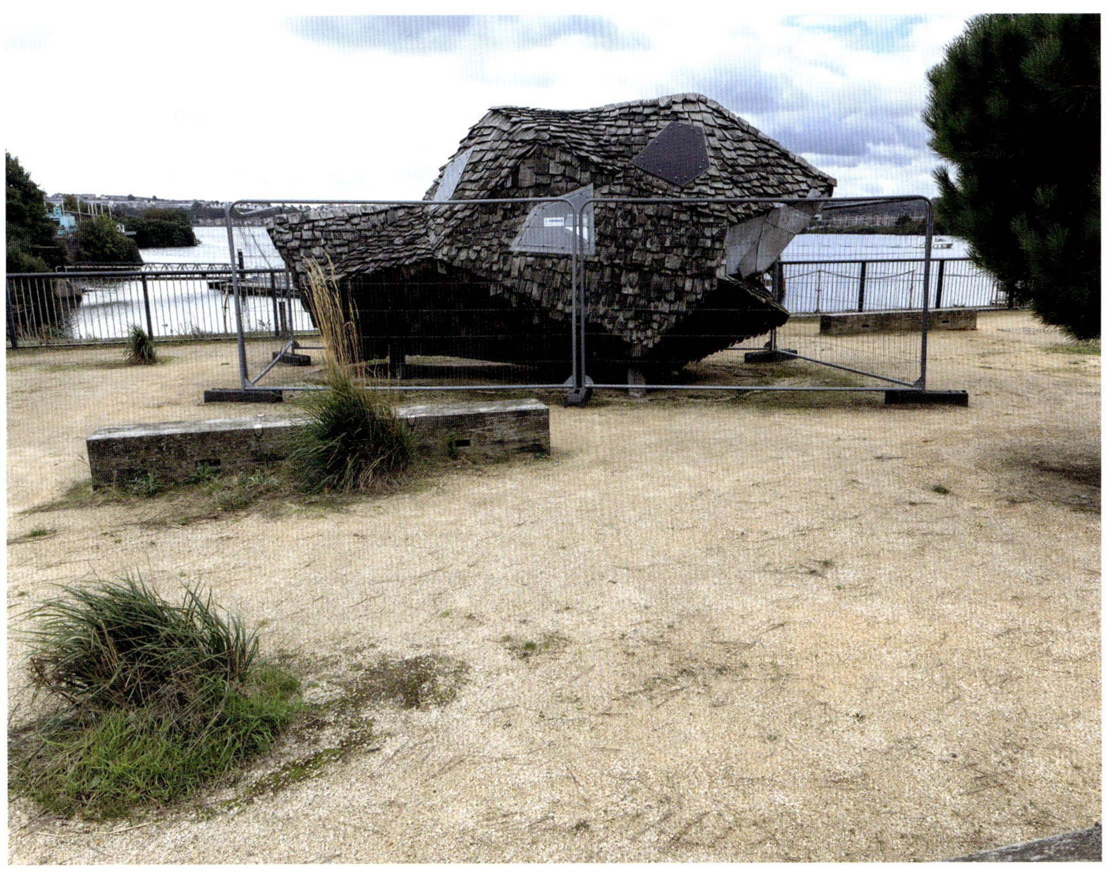

ST 19474 74170

LLYN Y DYWARCHEN, GWYNEDD

2006

Within sight of the Yr Wyddfa (the peak of Eryri), the magical Llyn y Dywarchen 'lake of the turf or clod', is named after a small island that once floated around its shores. In 1188, clergyman and chronicler Giraldus Cambrensis wrote how the island was "driven from one side to the other by the wind, shepherds beholding it with astonishment, their cattle while feeding carried to the distant parts of the lake".

The island is documented again in 1698 and 1798 but has since vanished without trace. He also wrote:
"This is the societies stocked water, providing quality fishing for rainbow trout reared at out own hatchery on the River Seiont at Llanrug. Fish here range from 1.8lbs to 5lbs. Fishing is still by fly only, and boat fishing is a delight".

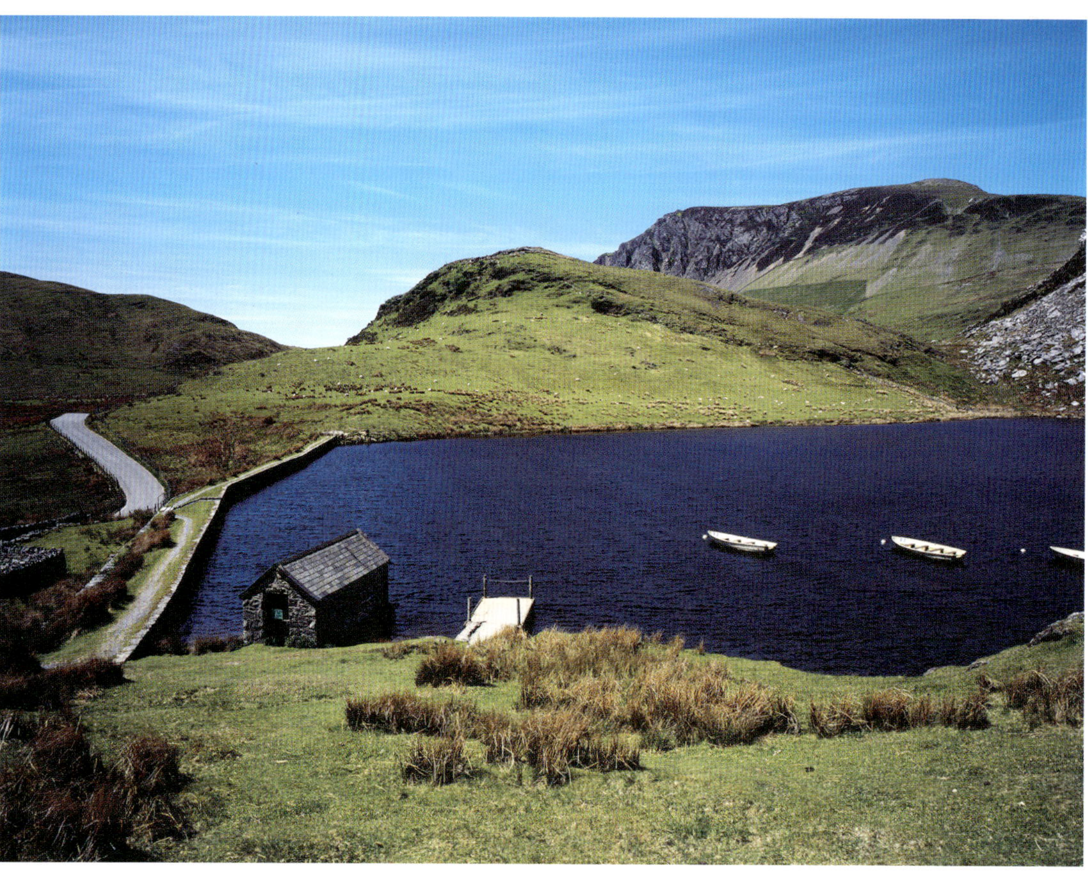

A Manchester United FC flag planted at the top of the mountain by a family in memory of "their darling angel".

Nine-year-old Corey James Watkins, from nearby Blaenrhondda, was killed after colliding with a car while skateboarding in 2007.
The family said at the time, "Everyone loved him. He loved life and was a child any parent would have been proud of. We'll never stop loving him".

A flag still stands in the spot.

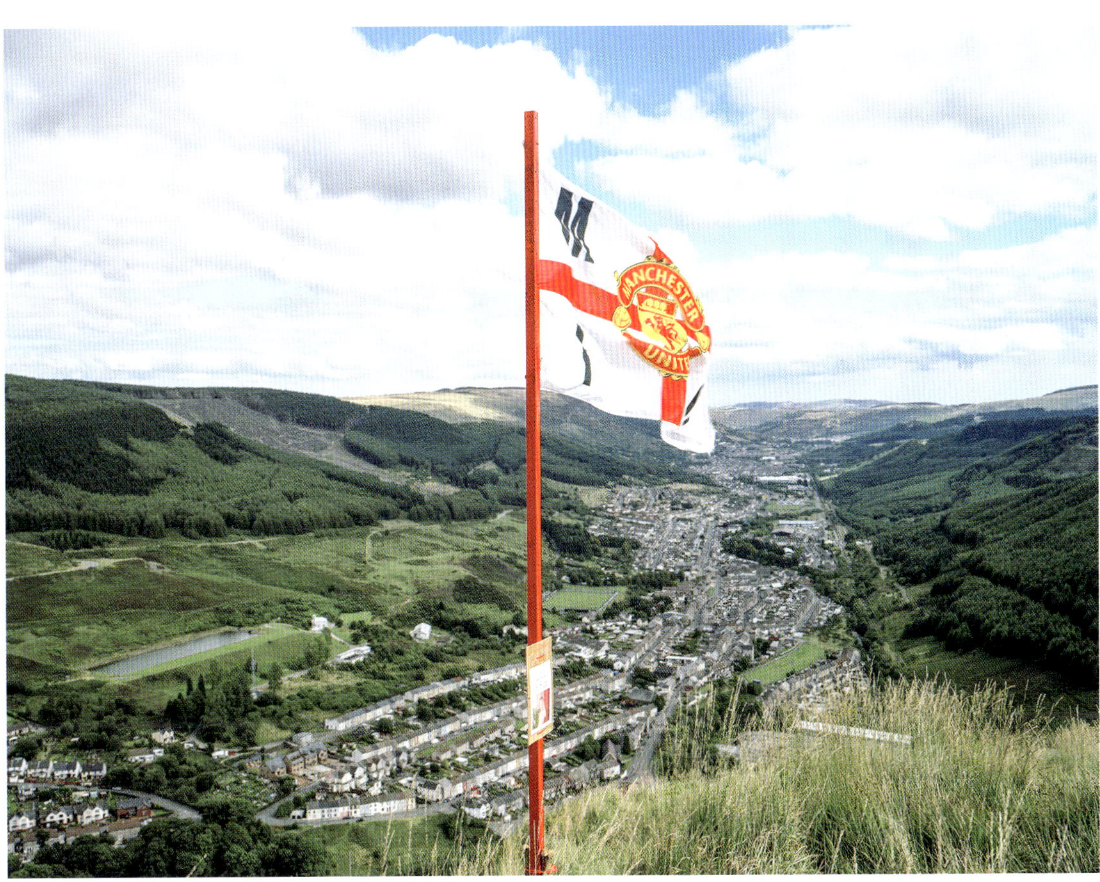

SS 92400 99700

2011

Looking down to the Sirhowy Valley and up to the Bannau Brycheiniog, the highest pitch of the highest rugby football club in the highest village in Wales.

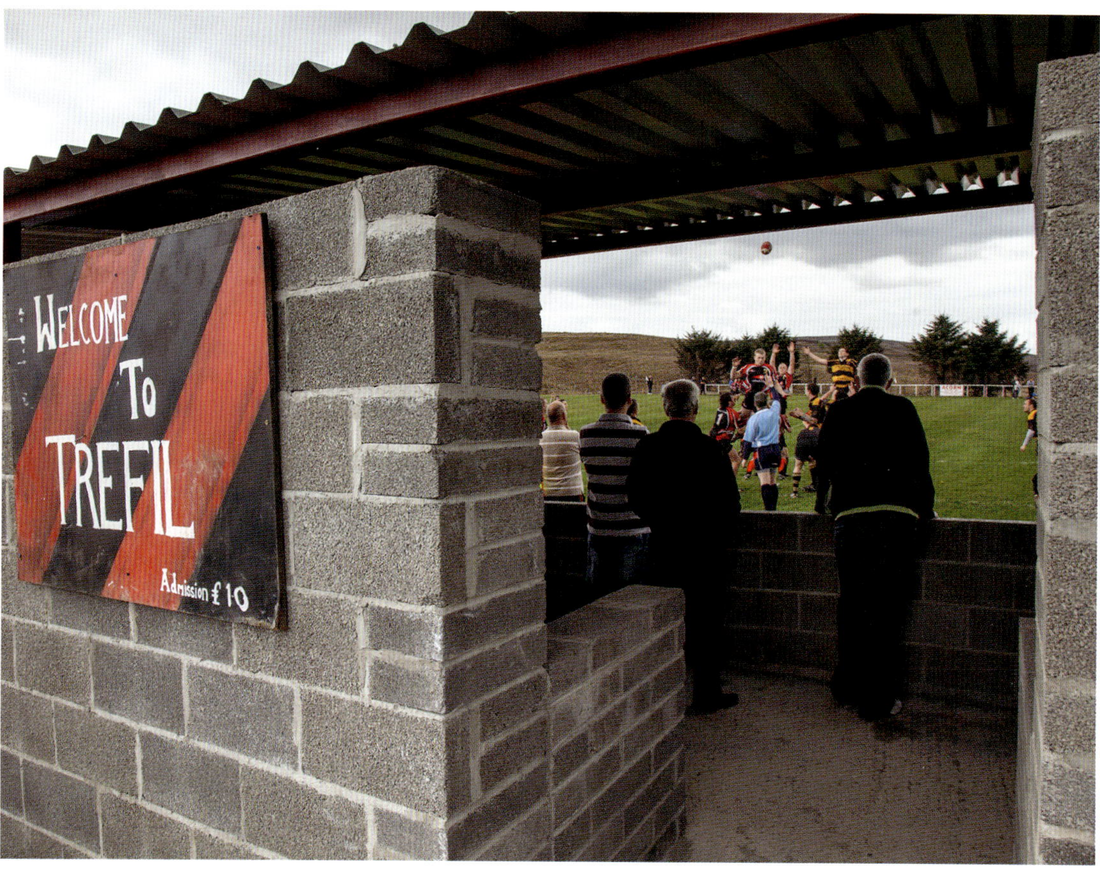

SO 11880 12575

NATIONAL BOTANIC GARDENS OF WALES, CARMARTHENSHIRE

2024

The dish roundabout at the National Botanic Gardens of Wales' children's area.

The amusement, a feature within a large, expertly curated, botanically-themed, safety-first playground, has been designed to be easily accessible for children of all ages and provide good support and security when spinning at high speed. When static, the installation looks for all the world like a fine garden sculpture. Child's play has evolved since the knee-grazing, brutalist concrete and steel of the post-war era.

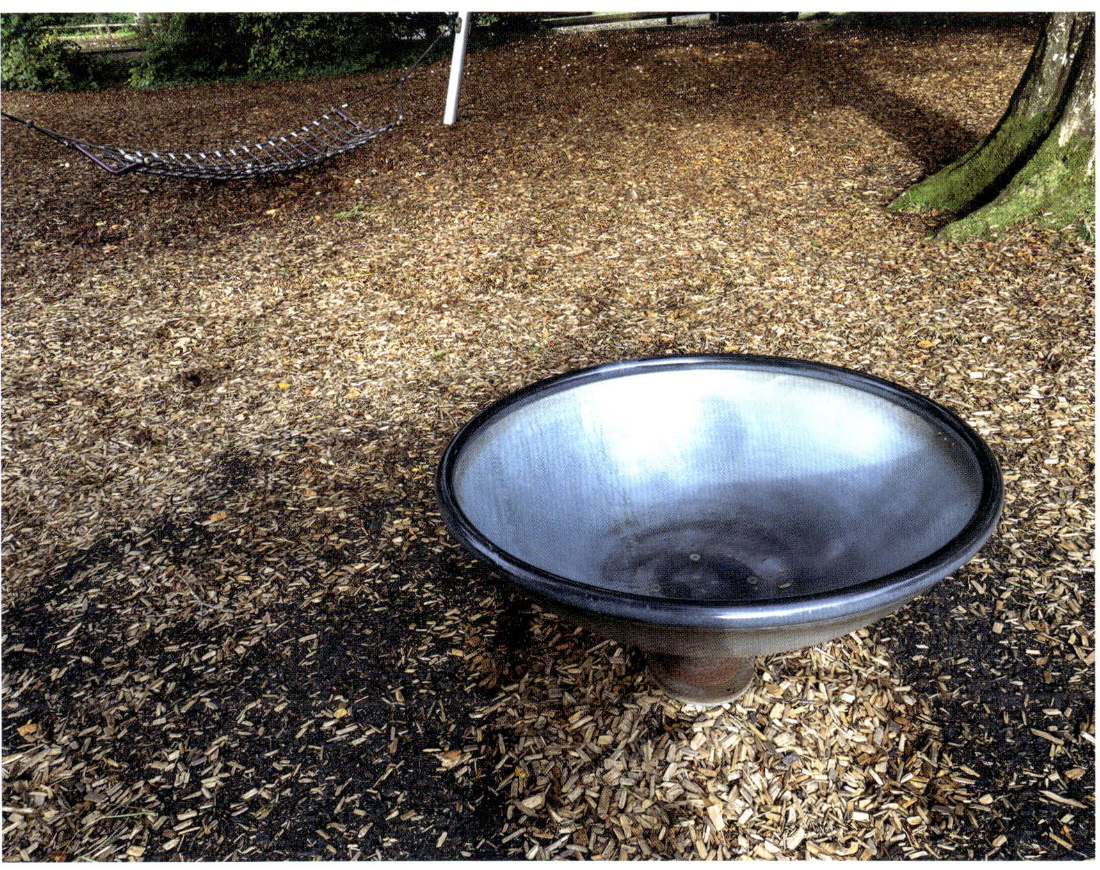

The 10-tonne granite tombstone of one of the last 'iron kings', a man once among the richest in the world, inscribed with the words 'God forgive me'.

"It required thirteen horses, the strongest in the district to bring from Radyr quarry to Vaynor churchyard", newspapers reported at the time, "the massive stone which defies sacrilege to approach the remains of the late Robert Thompson Crawshay, who died on May 10, 1879, age 62 years."

Defies sacrilege? Or defies desecration?

Once a popular man, Crawshay became a tyrant after suffering a stroke. As he lived in luxury, he alienated his downtrodden workers who were thrown further into penury when he closed the Cyfarthfa ironwork four years before his death.

GRAVES

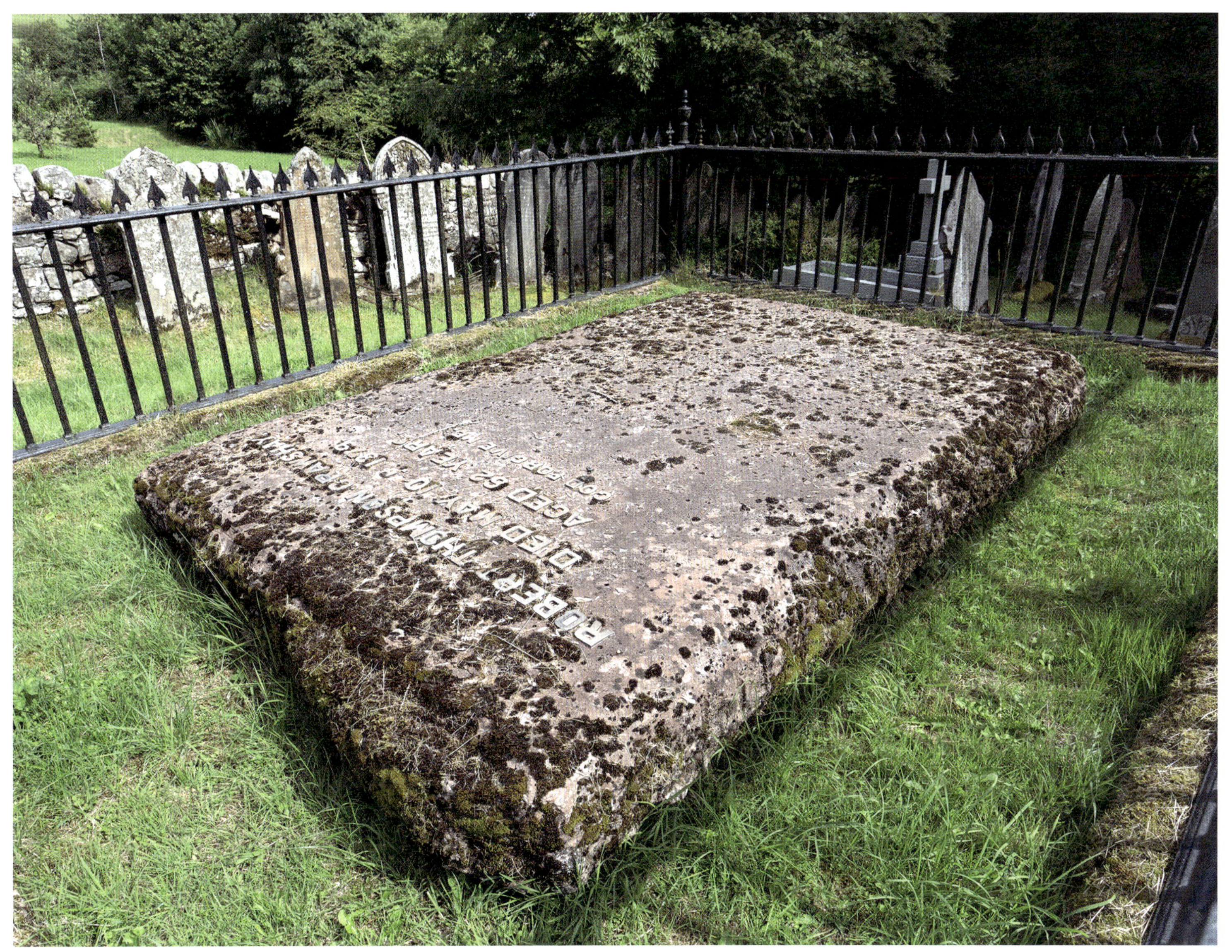

'One night and day I bore great pain,
To try for cure was all in vain,
But God knew what to me was best,
Did ease my pain and give me rest.'

The inscription on the grave of Thomas James, who died 18 August 1849, aged 24 years, sits among many others dated between 1832 and 1855 standing on the windswept site, a scheduled ancient monument. The world-wide epidemic took hold in the area around 1831 and peaked around the time of Thomas' death.

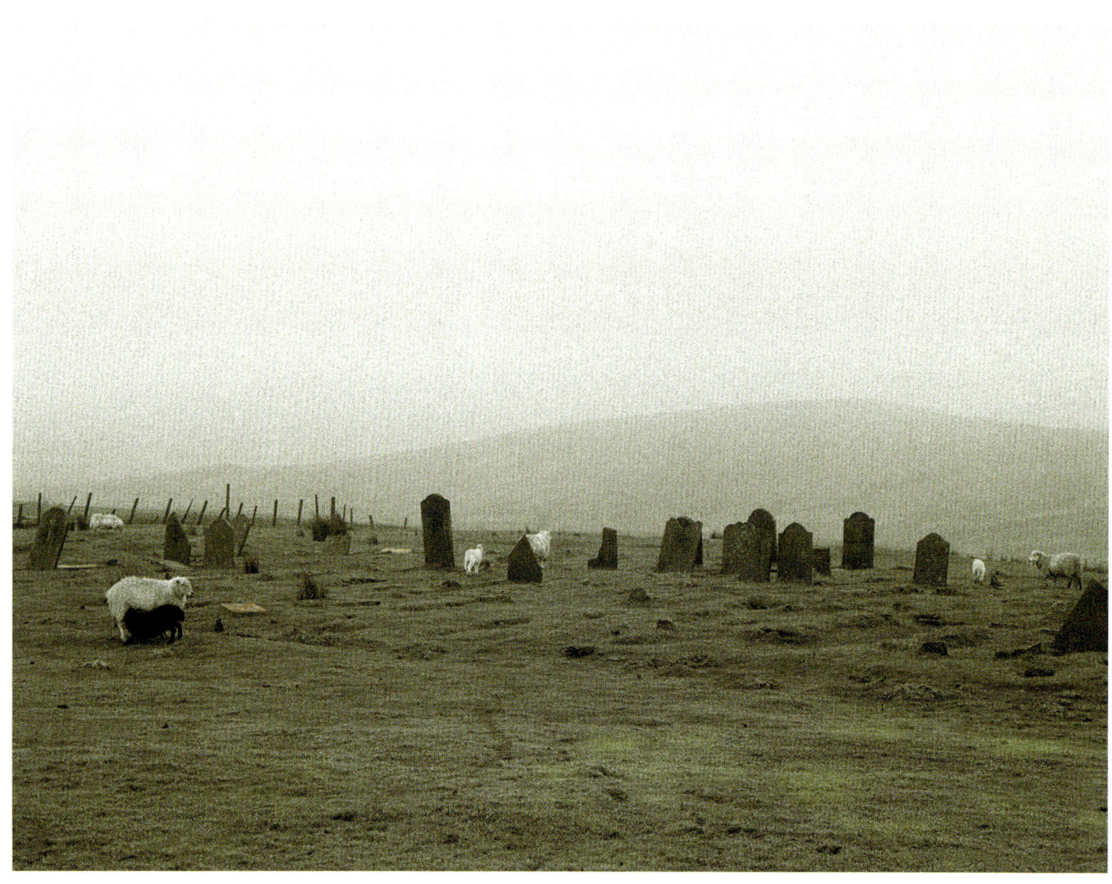

SO 13892 07592

LLANBADRIG CHURCHYARD, ANGLESEY

2014

St Patrick, the story goes, was returning from a mission to Ireland around the year 440 AD when his ship ran aground. In gratitude for finding refuge in a cave, since obscured by rock fall, he founded a church on the headland, said to be one of the oldest in Wales.

Another story tells of a visit by the Dalai Lama who sat on a nearby bench and declared it "the most peaceful spot on earth".

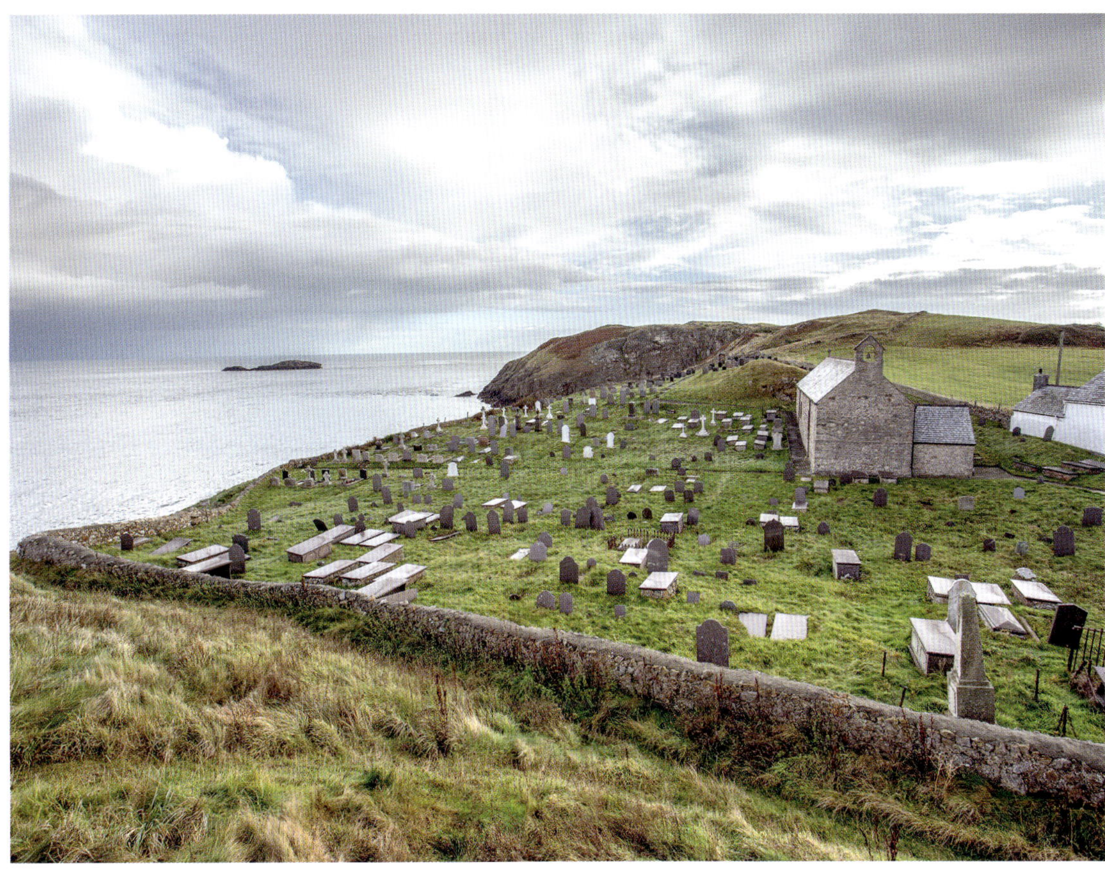

SH 37569 94624

Lest we forget.

The grave of John Collins awarded the Victoria Cross for risking his life to save a number of his men at the 1917 Palestine campaign's Battle of Beersheba. After a fatal fall at his home in 1951, the *Merthyr Express* reported the 70-year-old could not be buried with full honours, as arranged by the local British Legion, because grave-diggers refused to work overtime "to bury anyone".

In 2024 £100,000 government funding was announced to restore the eight graves in Wales of 'the Victoria Cross heroes of the First World War'.

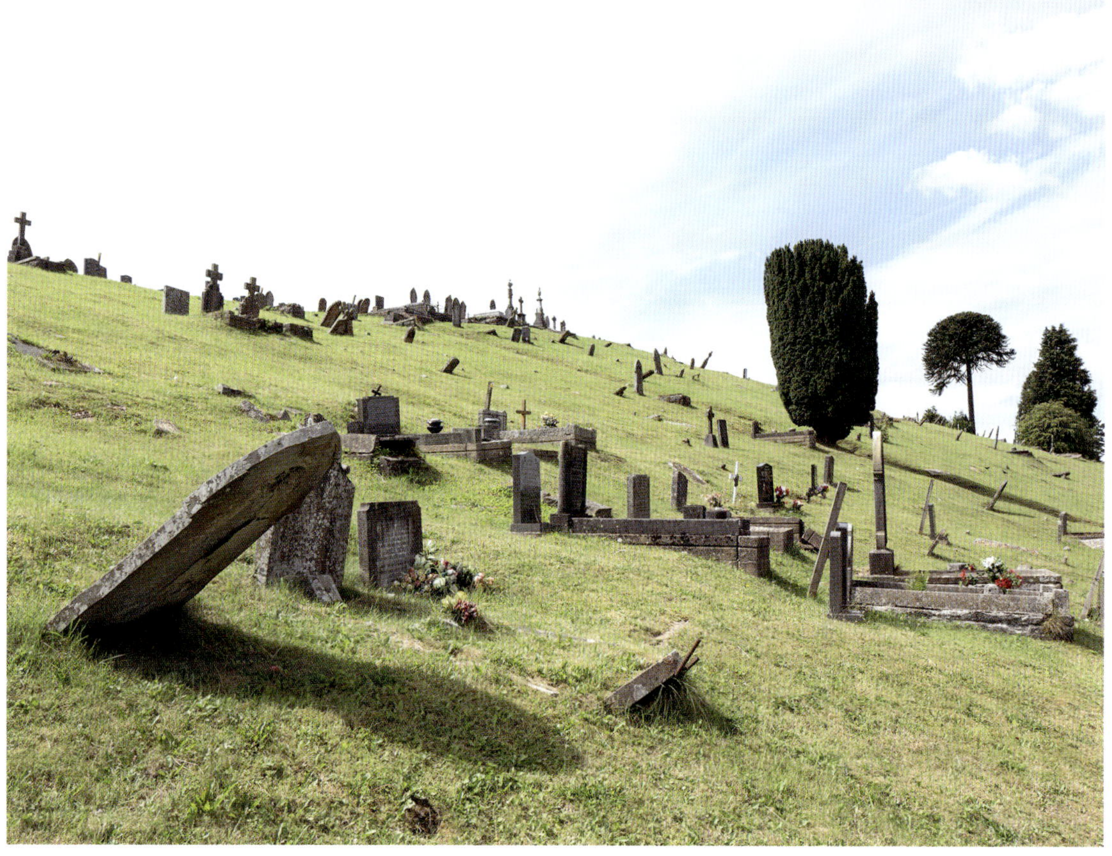

SO 06154 09202

'Deep in our hearts his memory is kept. One we loved and will never forget'

The inscription on the grave of the youngest of 23 servicemen commemorated at the Commonwealth War Graves Commission's cemetery in Aberbeeg.

Brynley Jenkins, aged 18, of the South Wales Borderers, died three weeks after the official end of World War II.

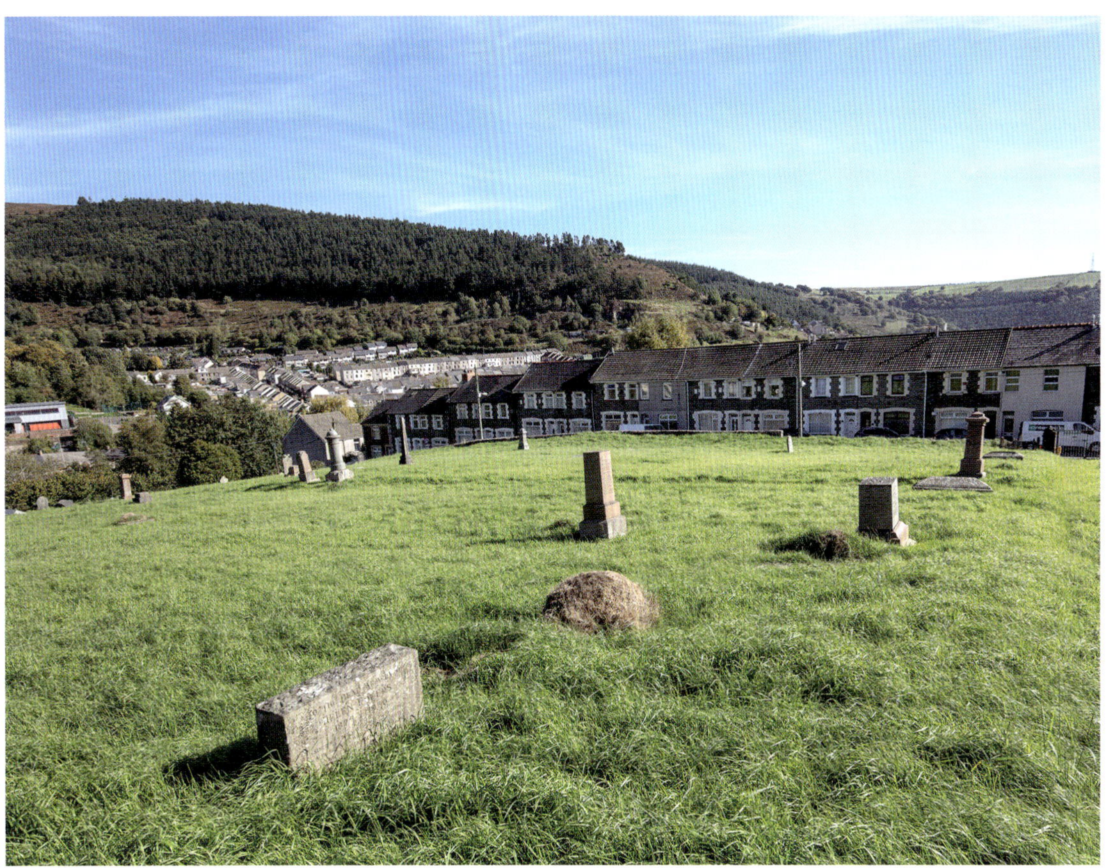

SO 21574 04624

The graves of 35 men of 304 [Polish] Squadron who flew from RAF Dale in 1942 on missions including convoy protection, anti-submarine sweeps and bombing raids on occupied France.

Several of the runway approaches were over cliffs subject to ferocious and, on occasion, fatal crosswinds.

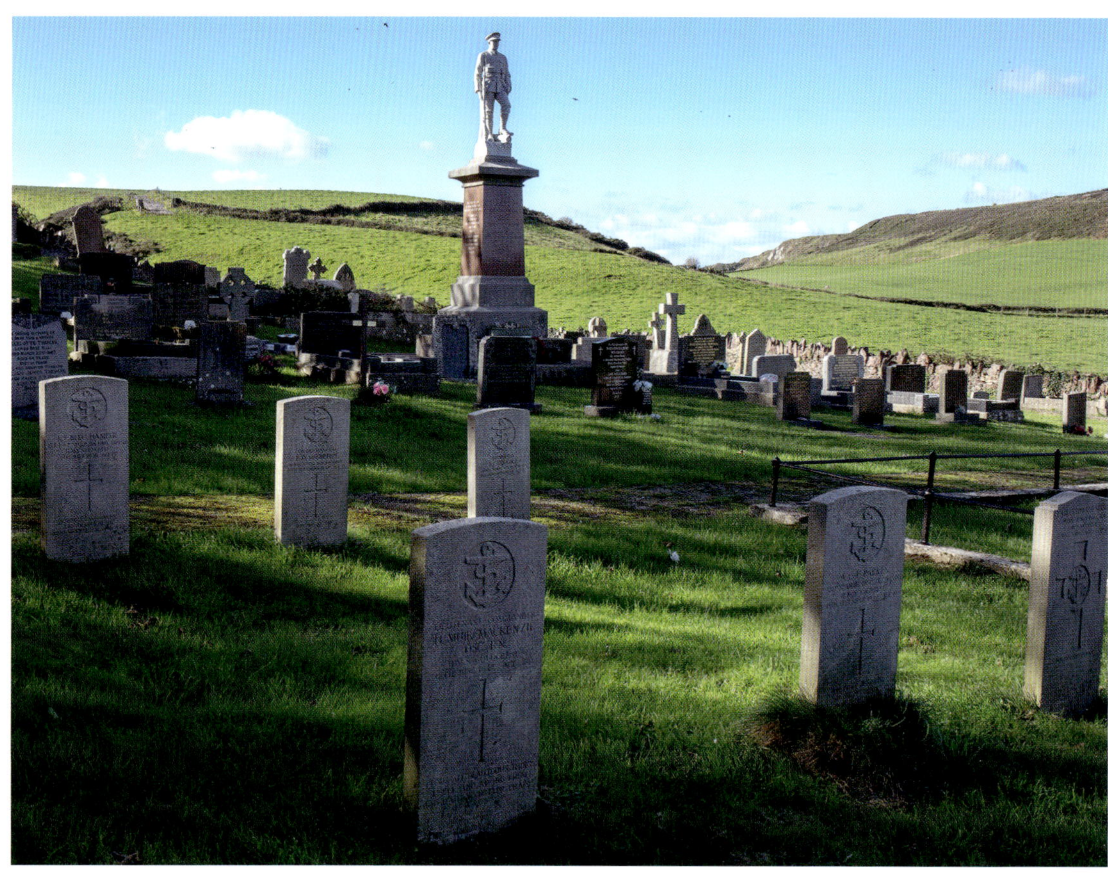

SM 80576 05652

GILESTON, VALE OF GLAMORGAN

2010

A tender mix of real and plastic flowers and a football scarf
commemorate Keith David, 18, who died in 2008 when his off-road
motorbike hit one of a line of concrete boulder on the beach, near St
Athan, known as dragon's teeth, erected during World War I to guard
against tank invasions.

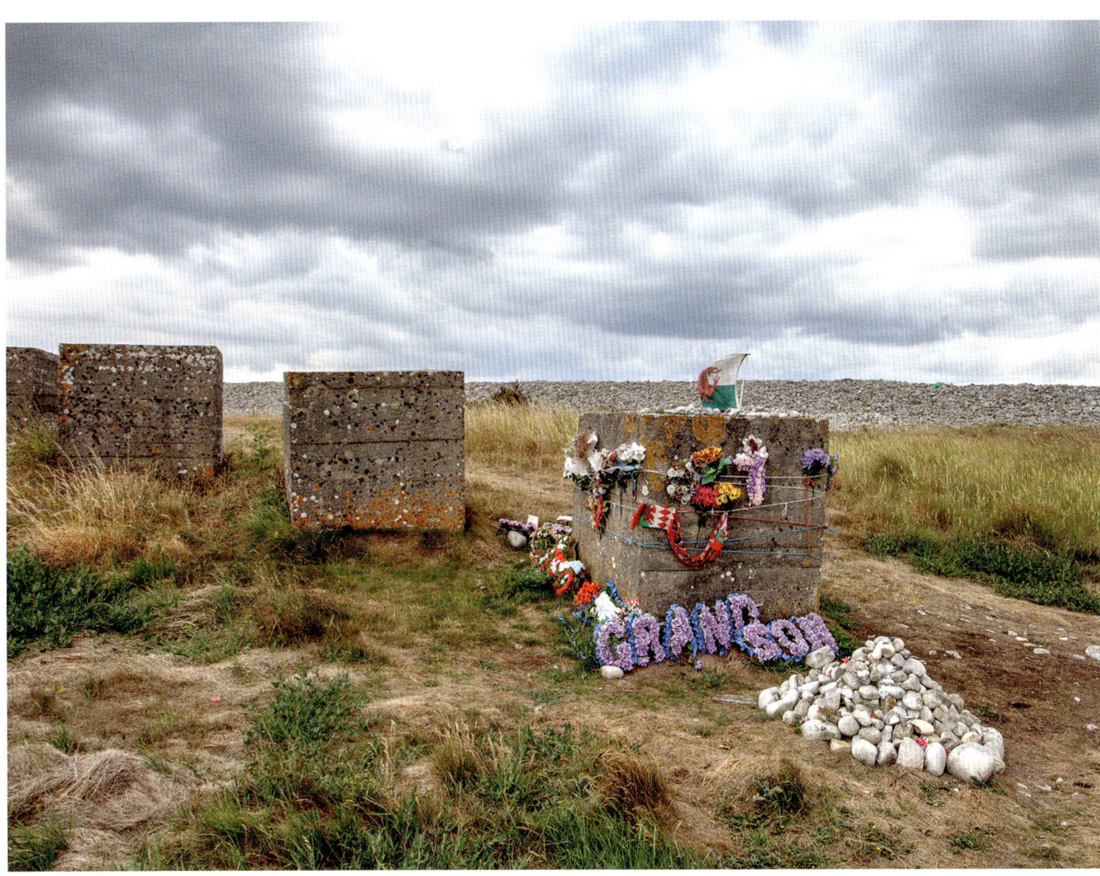

In 1990, a couple facing redundancy ploughed their life savings into a former farm near the village of Brynford and has since helped over 40,000 pet owners.

Graves and memorials are spread over its landscaped gardens, close to a crematorium and chapel of rest in which an animal padre, a retired ordained Anglican cleric, conducts services.

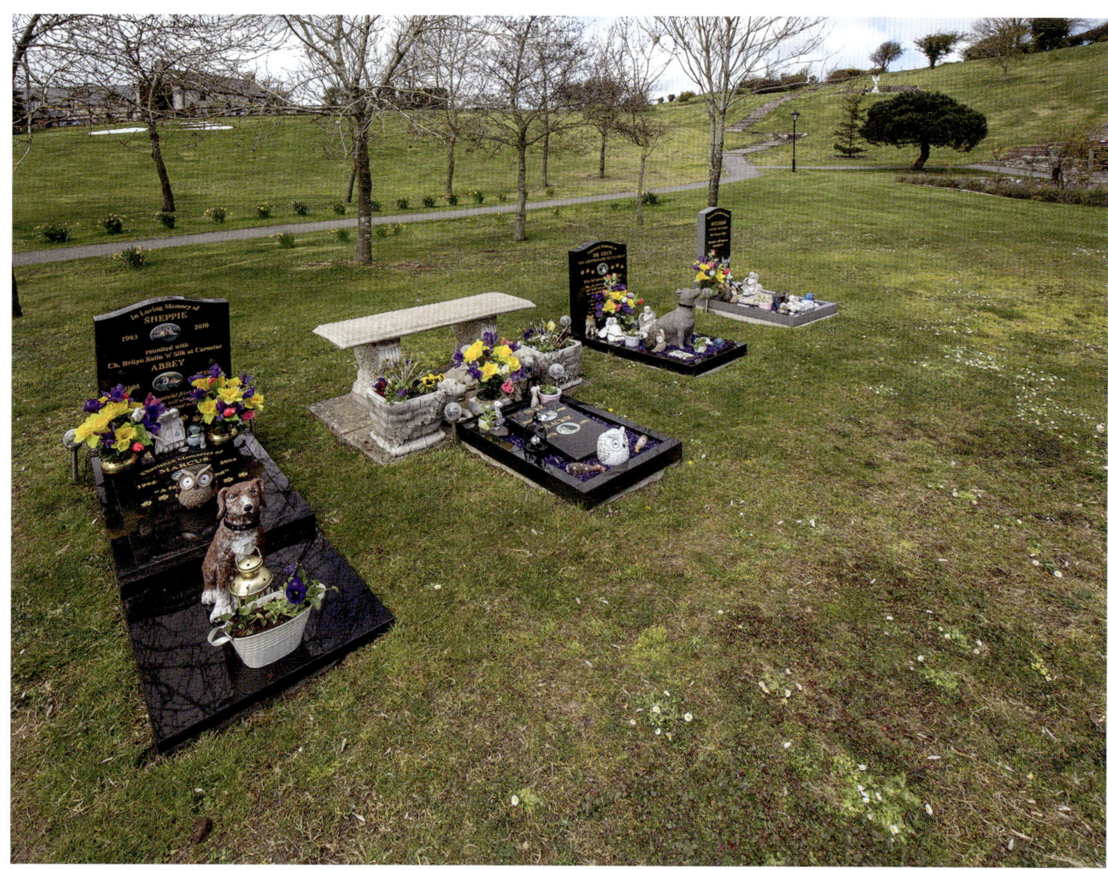

SJ 18262 74994

Self-designated as 'the Energy Island', Anglesey proudly puts itself at the forefront of low carbon research and production.

It is home to three wind farms, two are situated near the north coast while the third is close to Llyn Alaw in the centre of the island.

POWER

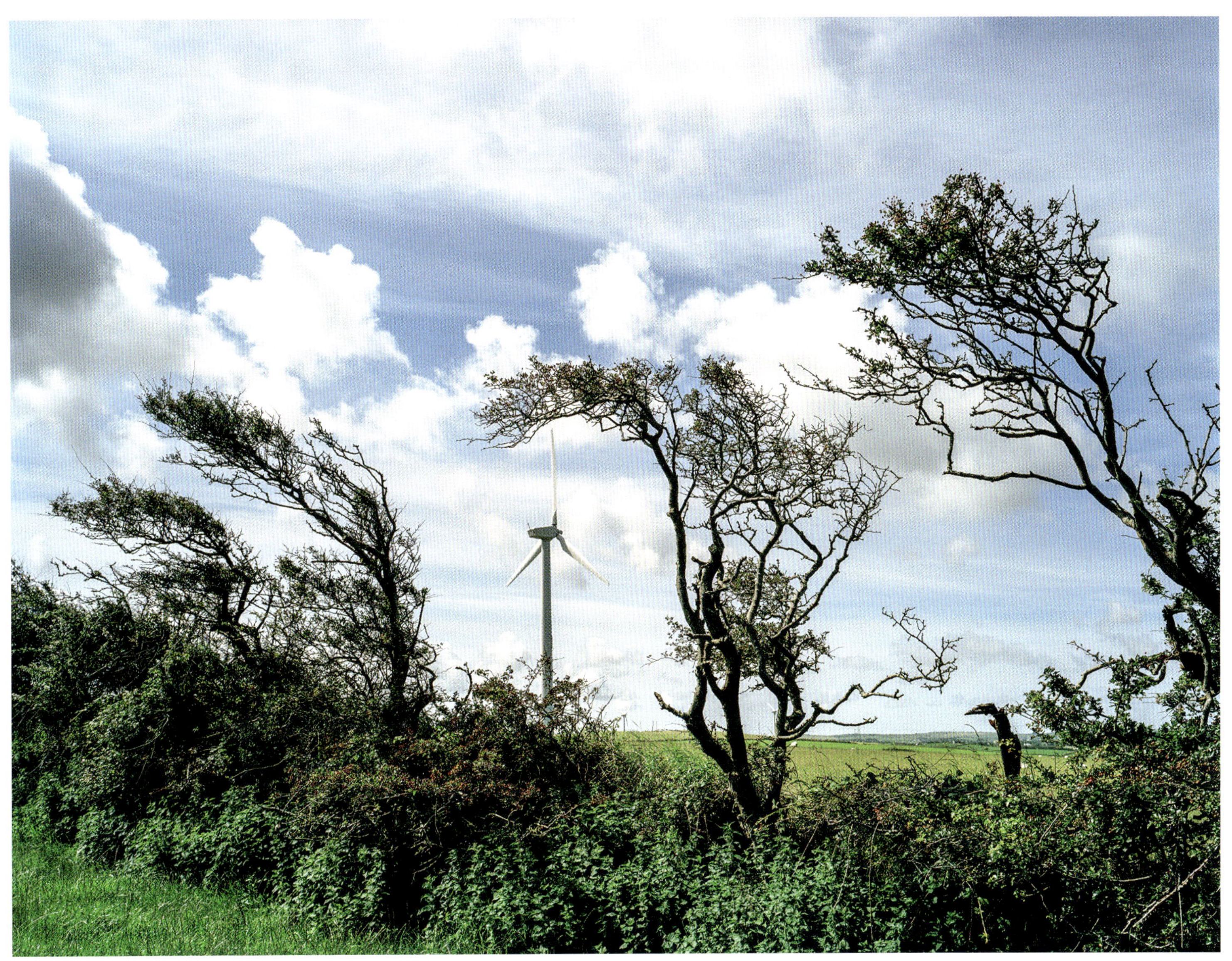

SH 37291 78496

ABERTHAW POWER STATION, VALE OF GLAMORGAN

2024

The site of a former golf course on which two coal-fired and co-fired biomass stations were built, the first officially opening in 1963. The second, Aberthaw B, opened in 1971 and closed in 2020.

It is currently being demolished after decommissioning with plans to redevelop it as a clean energy hub.

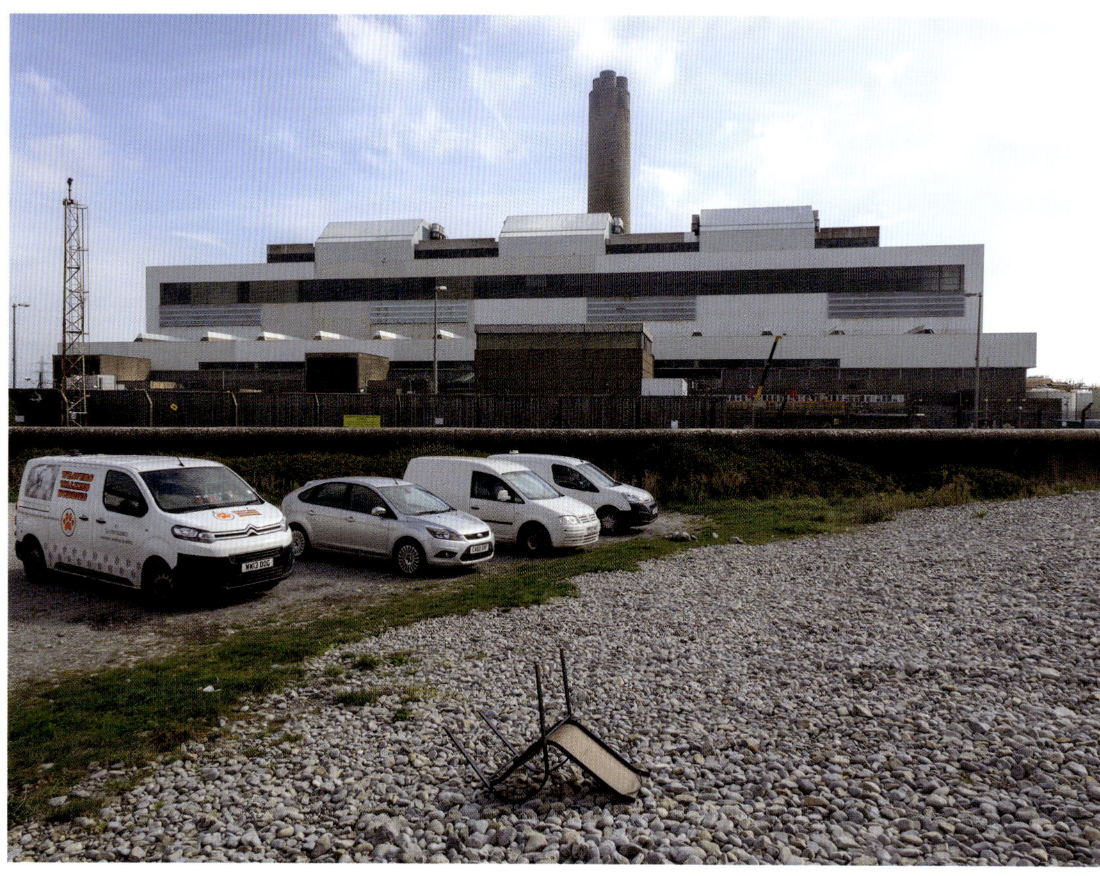

ST 02020 66283

WYLFA POWER STATION, ANGLESEY

2014

After the closure of Trawsfynydd in 1991, this plant became Wales' only nuclear power station until it ceased production in 2015.

It was announced by the then UK Government in 2024 that the site was first choice for a large-scale gigawatt nuclear power plant which would create thousands of jobs.

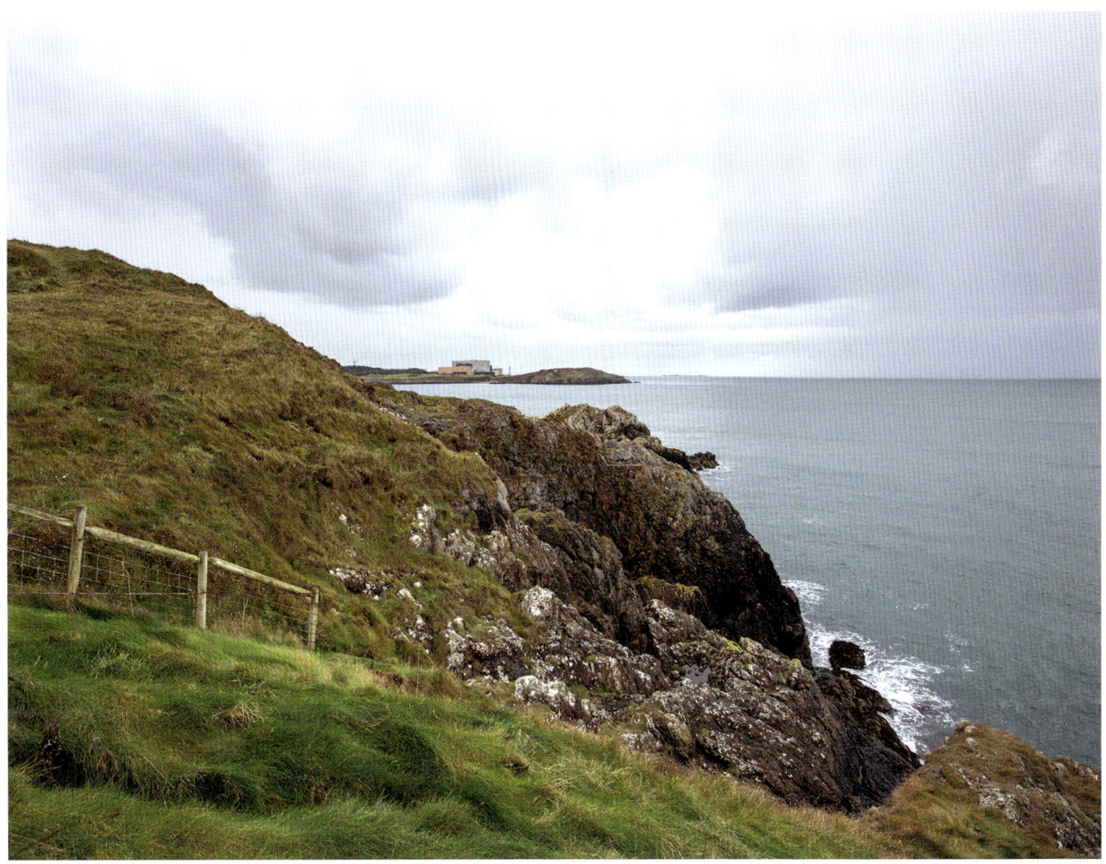

SH 37572 94689

2024

The first inland nuclear power station in the UK, Trawsfynydd Nuclear Power Station started service in 1965, its twin Magnox reactors generating electricity for 26 years until 1991.

In May 2024, the site beside a lake within the Eryri National Park, was ruled out of a plan for new nuclear reactors.

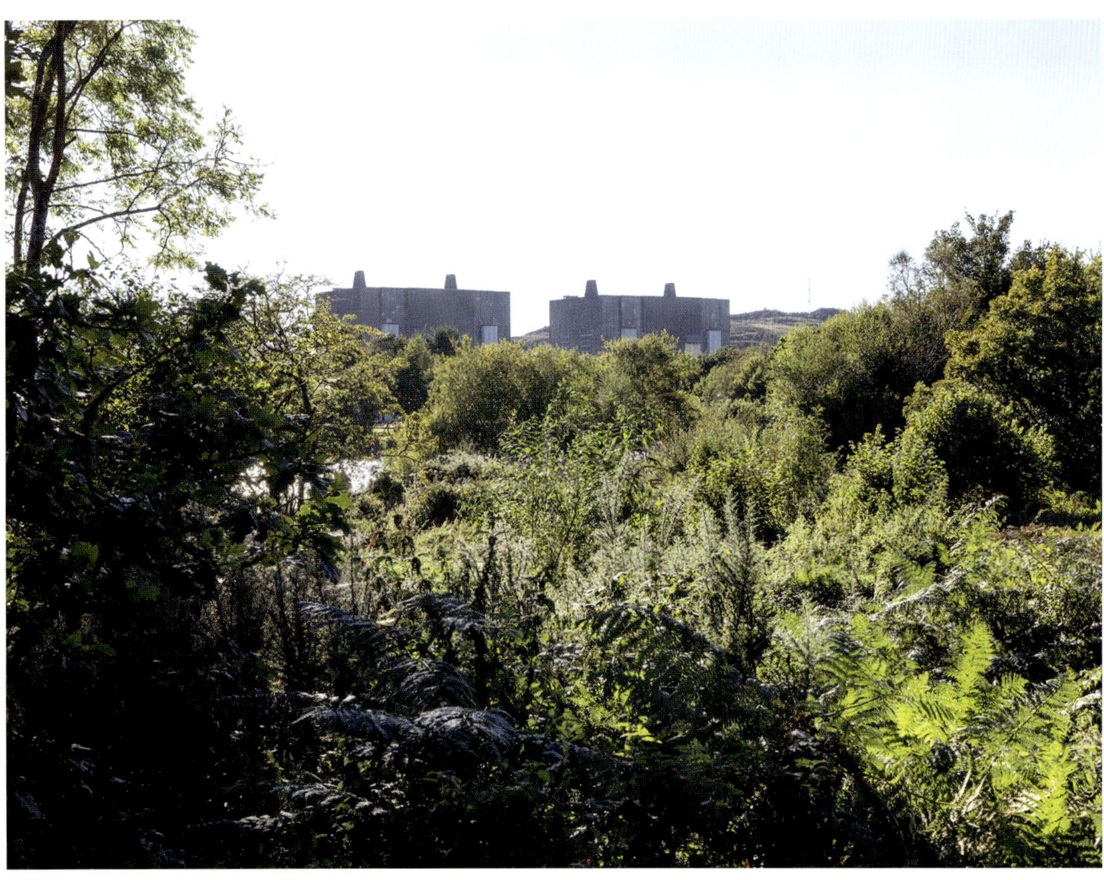

SH 69832 38323

2024

The UK's first purpose-built, affordable solar energy smart house capable of exporting more energy to the national grid than it uses is the result of a joint project between Cardiff and Swansea universities based on the idea of 'buildings as power stations'.

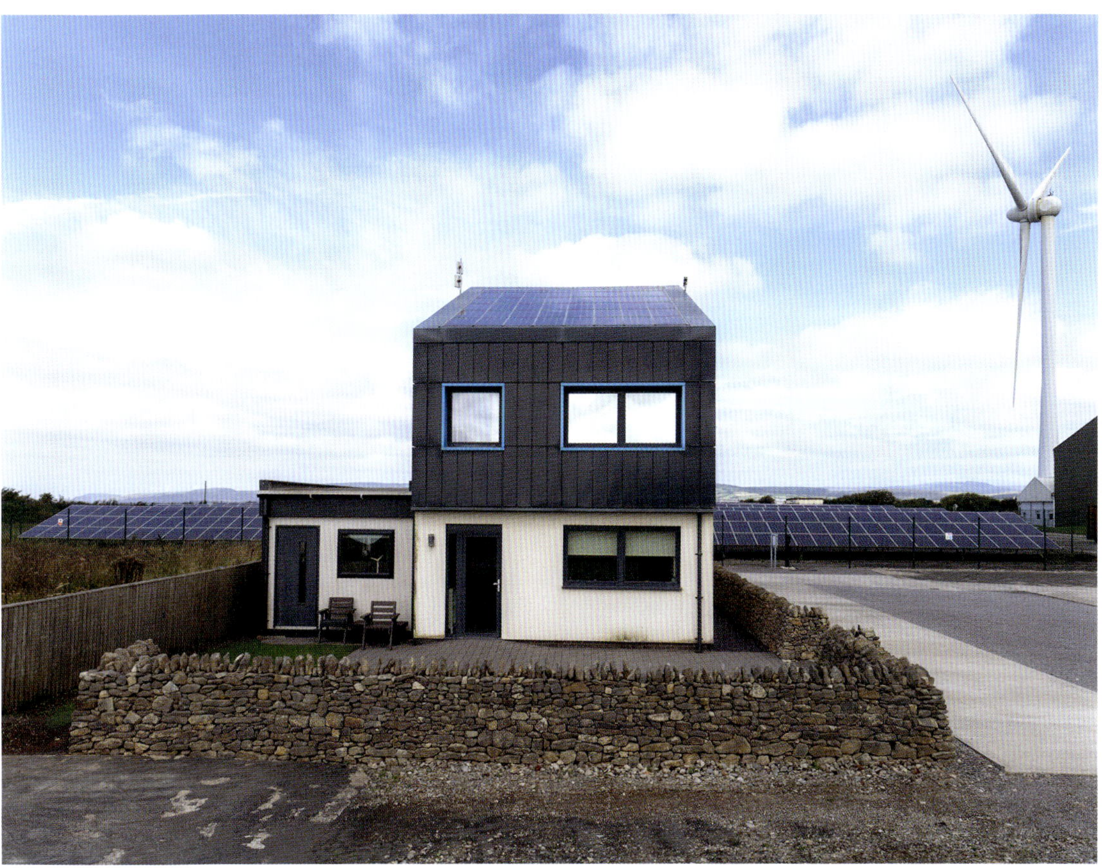

SS 84042 79987

A £7bn tidal lagoon has been proposed on the Denbighshire coast which, it is claimed, would create thousands of jobs and generate enough electricity to power every home in Wales.

The Welsh Government has funded research with ambitions to make Wales a world centre for emerging tidal lagoon technology.

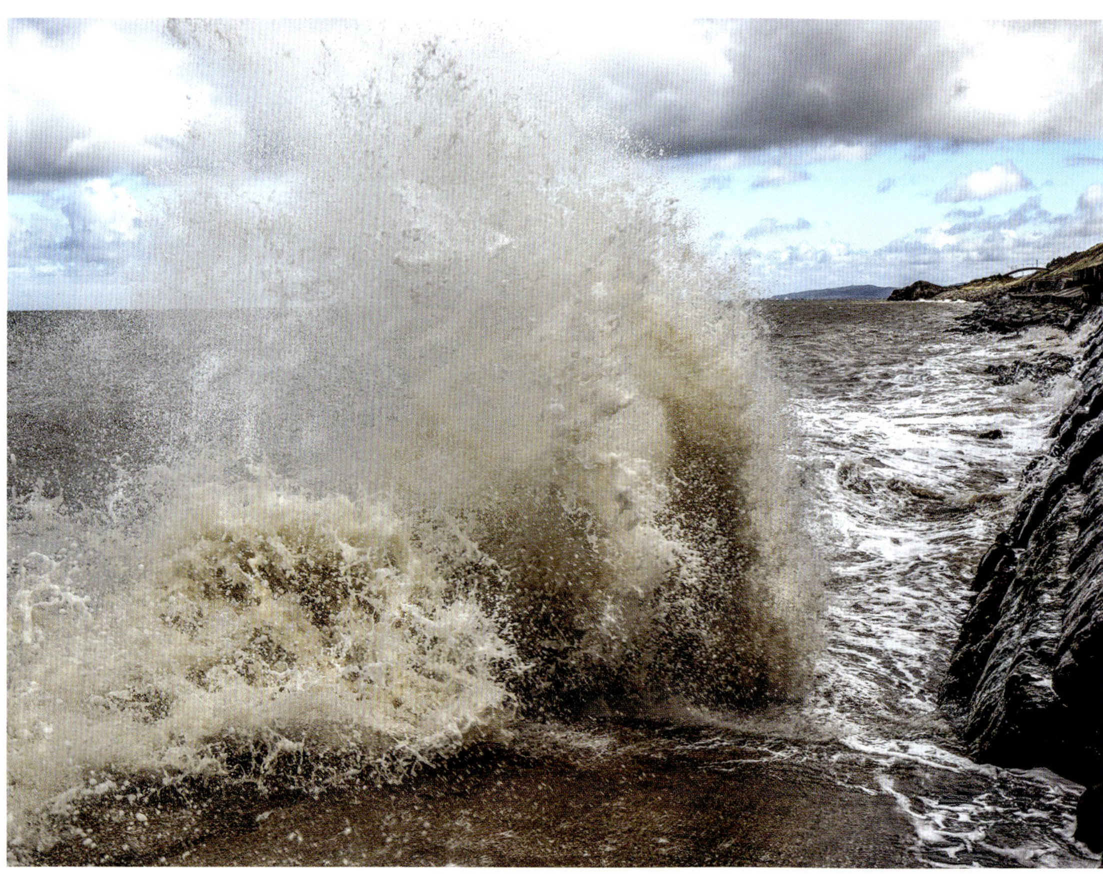

SH 87003 78694

Unveiled in July 1997, a small monument and plaque near the site of
Owain Glyndŵr's victory at Mynydd Hyddgen in 1401 when, hopelessly
outnumbered, he and his men defeated an English army of over 10,000.

The details of Glyndŵr's death and burial remain uncertain. By 1409
his main strongholds had been captured by the enemy and, refusing
two royal pardons, he retreated to continue his fight from the shadows.
He disappeared in 1415, the year Adam of Usk, one of his followers,
recorded his death.

Regarded as a national hero, Owain Glyndŵr Day is on 16 September
and marks the anniversary of his proclamation as Prince of Wales over
600 years ago.

MONUMENTS

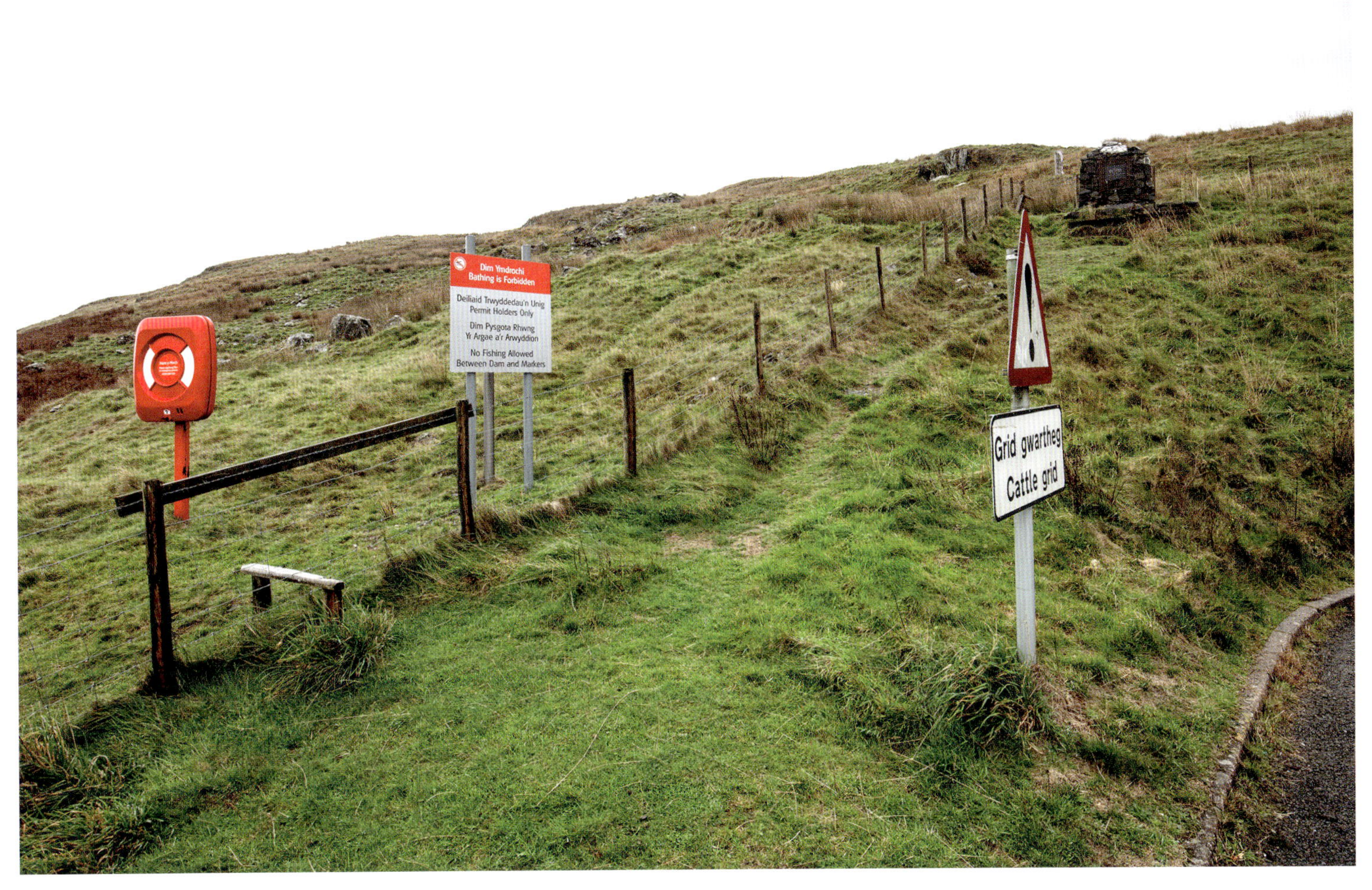

SN 75466 86266

EBBW VALE, BLAENAU GWENT

2006

The Aneurin Bevan Memorial Stones marking the spot where one of the area's most important historical figures
– the architect of the National Health Service and force behind the UK's largest public housing programme – held open air public meetings.

The larger, central limestone symbolised Bevan, the other three the constituency towns of Rhymney, Tredegar and Ebbw Vale which he represented as MP from 1929 to 1960, the year of his death aged 62. The inscription reads:

'IT WAS HERE
ANEURIN BEVAN
SPOKE TO THE PEOPLE
OF HIS CONSTITUENCY AND THE WORLD'

The memorial has been marred over the years by graffiti, broken glass and litter.

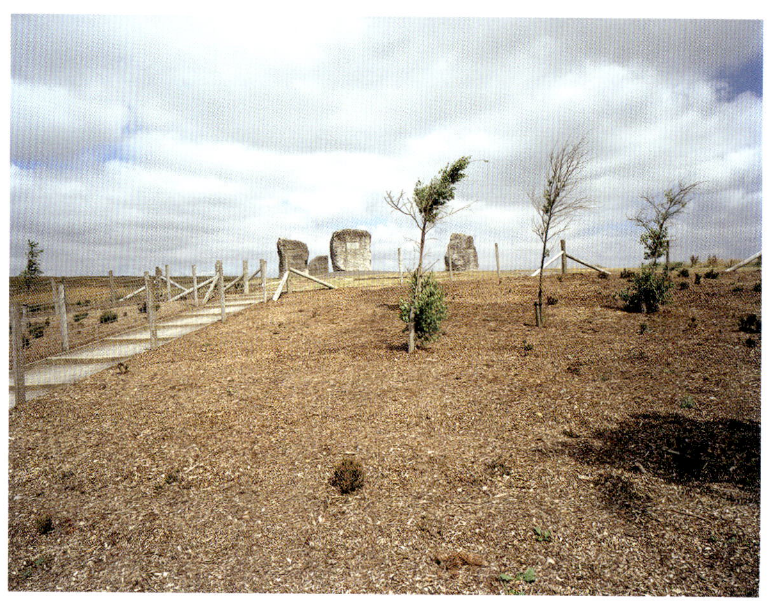

SO 15115 10544

PILLETH, POWYS

2011

A clump of trees marks the site of one of the greatest victories of the Welsh against the English. Led by Owain Glyndŵr in 1402, the Battle of Pilleth, also known as the Battle of Bryn Glas, boosted his rebel army and destabilised English politics.

Over 100 years before, Wales had been conquered by English King Edward I, who killed the native Prince of Wales and bestowed the title on his own son.

Glyndŵr, born into a noble family, had grown up in a time of relative peace. But In 1400, a land dispute on one of his estates ignited a fifteen-year insurgency. Proclaimed as the rightful Prince of Wales, he raised a guerilla army hell-bent on overthrowing the newly-installed King Henry IV, gaining widespread support in Wales and forging alliances with Scotland and France.

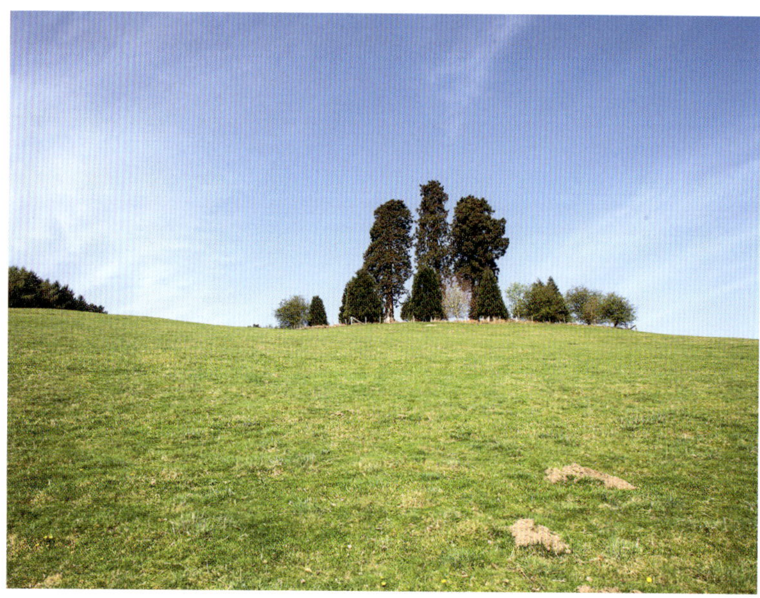

SO 25650 68250

ABBEYCWMHIR, POWYS

2024

Set in the nave of ruins of the abbey in the village near Rhayader,
a stone set in grass marks the burial place of the last Welsh prince of
native descent, Llywelyn ap Gruffydd or Llywelyn the Last, killed
in 1282 by the forces of invading English king Edward I.

It is inscribed with his name followed by 'Tywysog Cymru', meaning
Prince of Wales.

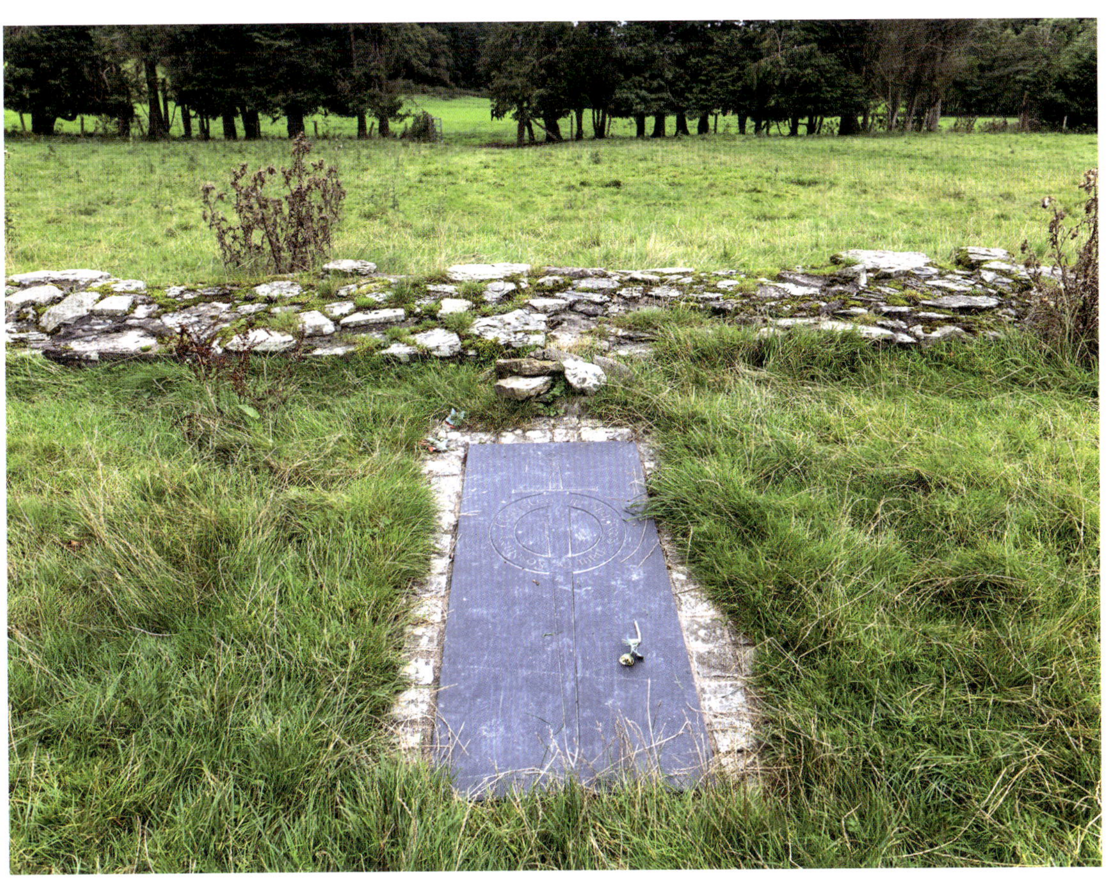

A plaque at the arched stone entrance high on the moors near the summit of Mynydd Llangynidr commemorates the Chartist rebels, a mass workers' movement for political reform.

It is believed the cave was used to stockpile weapons in advance of the Newport Rising in 1839.

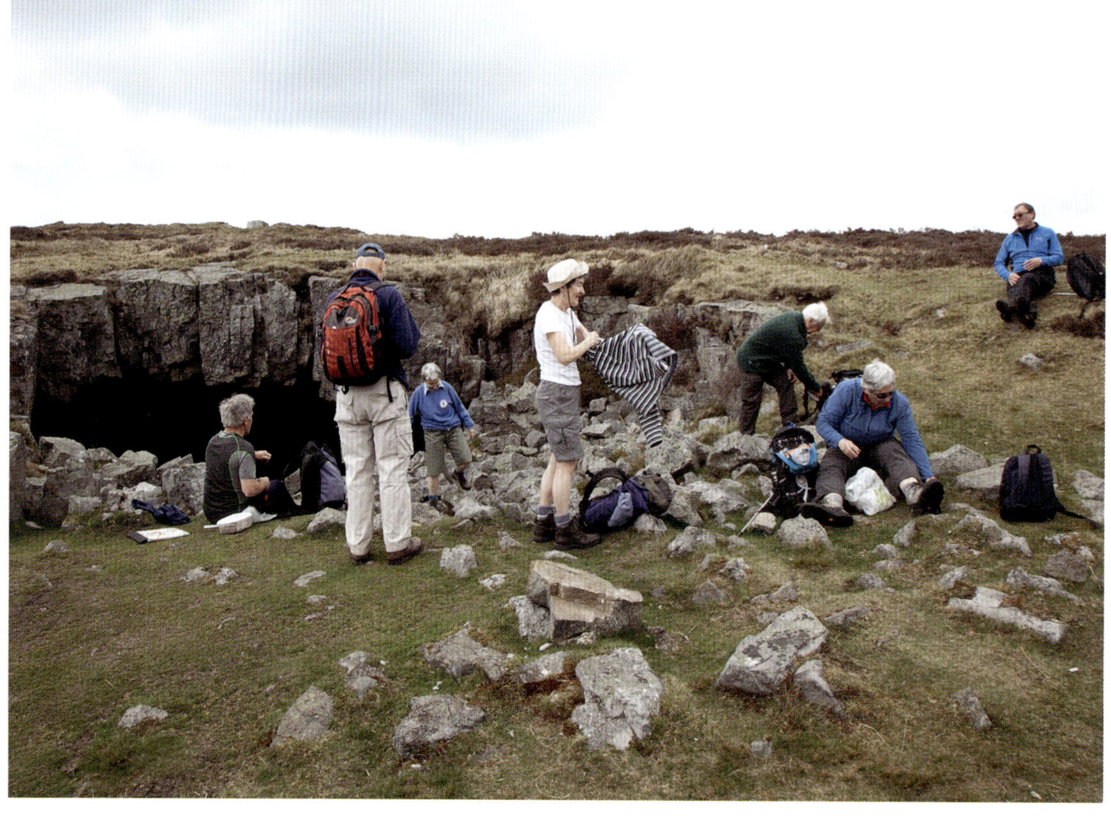

SO 12778 15225

The sight of the 400-year-old former courthouse turned tearooms covered with the red leaves of its Virginia Creeper has become one of the most quintessential autumn views of modern times.

FAVOURITE VIEWS

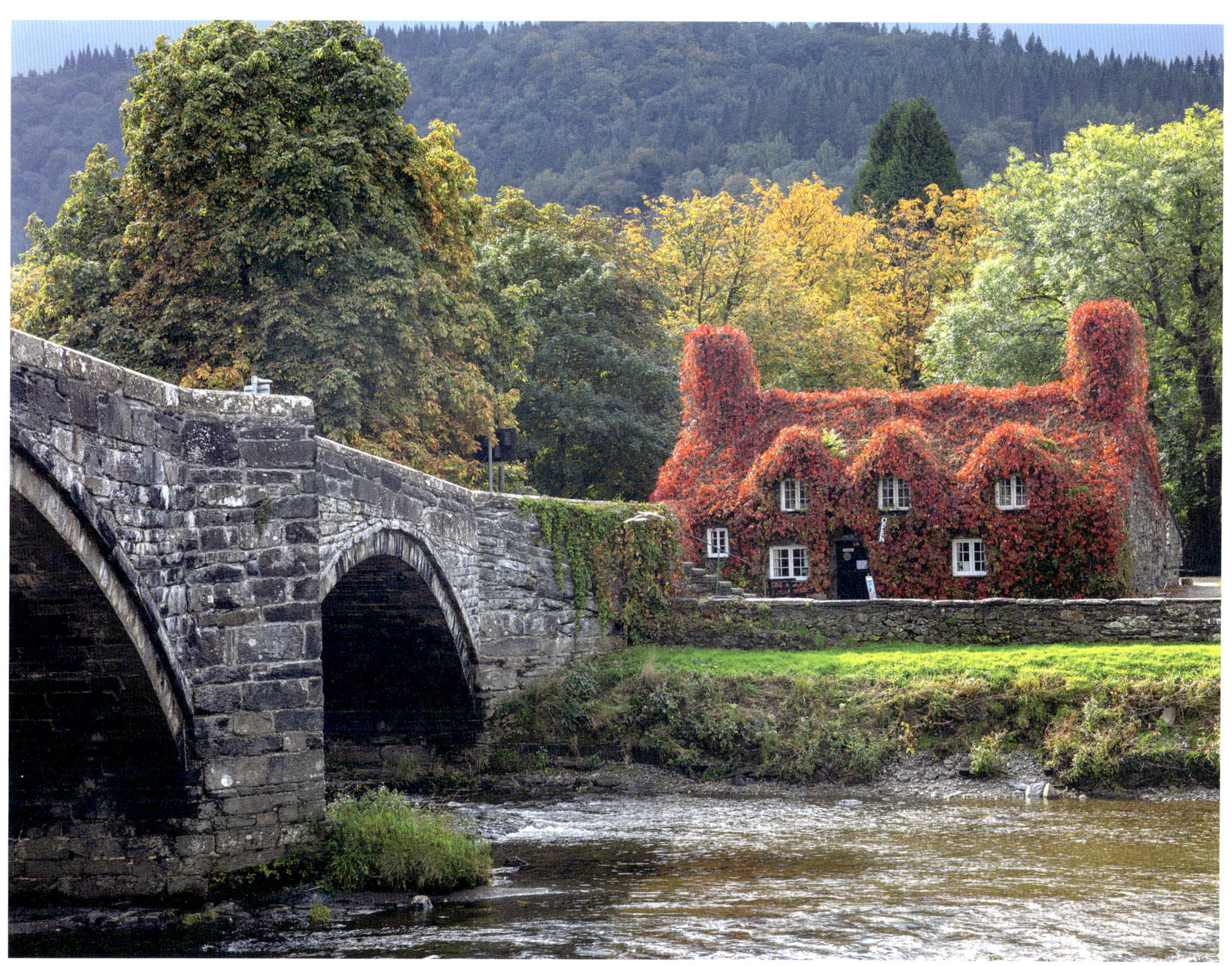

SH 79850 61527

RHOSSILI BAY, GOWER, SWANSEA

2014

Lonely Planet's 100 Best Beaches in the World 2024 says the beach "dazzles with its almost three miles of honey-toned, Atlantic-beaten sands."

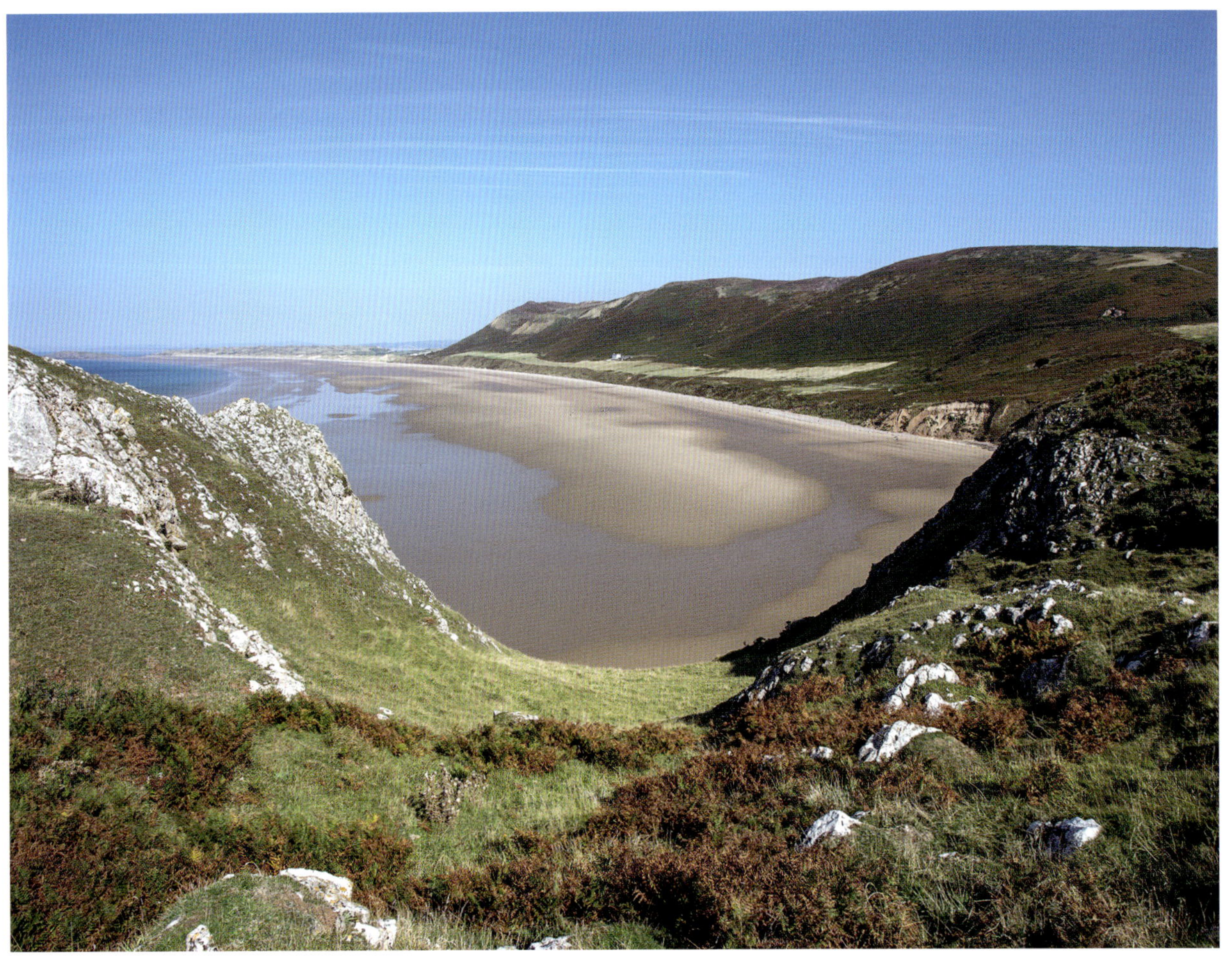

SS 53801 87669

THREE CLIFFS BAY, GOWER, SWANSEA

2014

The bay was a draw for nineteenth century camera enthusiasts and captured in a salted paper print dated 1854 taken by Swansea's Mary Dillwyn, considered to be Wales' earliest female photographer. Among her images is the first ever taken of a smile.

Her family was related by marriage to William Henry Fox Talbot who claimed to have invented photography in 1839.

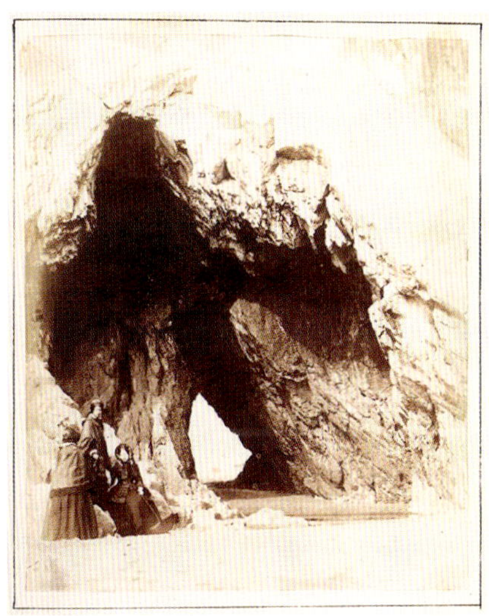

Mary Dillwyn, 1854

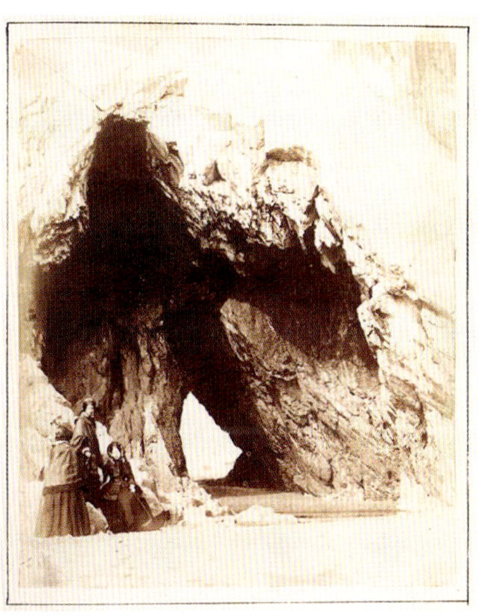

BETWS-Y-COED, CONWY

2016

The Victorian fascination with fairies and folk lore produced some of the earliest photographs of Ffos Noddyn (deep ditch) also known as the Fairy Glen, a secluded gorge on the River Conwy, which has long fired the imaginations of storytellers and poets.

Curiously, the photographs taken on different occasions by Francis Frith and Francis Bedford – both held by the V&A – are shot from the same vantage point. But there is no mystery. On descending into the valley there is one flat stone which made it easier for both to set up their cameras.

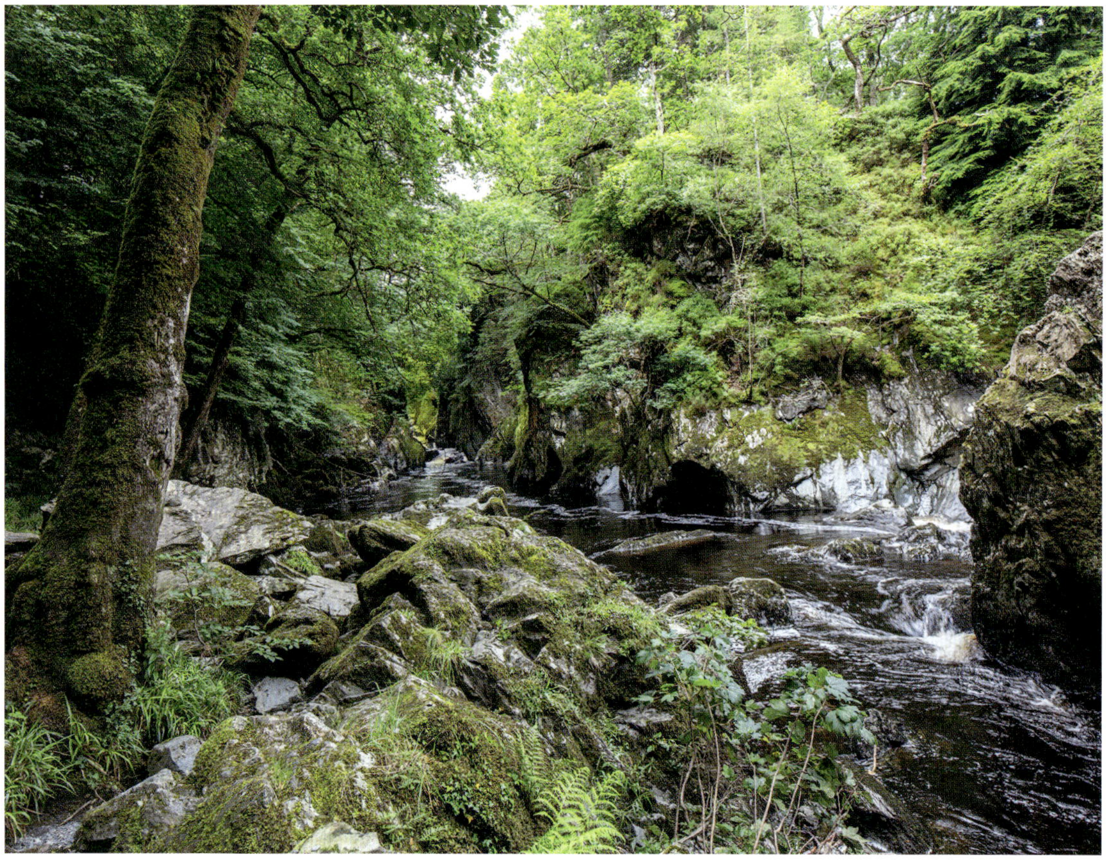

SH 80073 54311

DEVIL'S PULPIT, MONMOUTHSHIRE

2024

The view that inspired William Wordsworth's 1798 *Lines Composed a Few Miles Above Tintern Abbey*.

One of the poem's principal themes is the power of communion with nature and boy, the scene looking down from the rocky outcrop high above the River Wye is quite extraordinary.

Ancient tales told of the platform being used by the devil to tempt the monks below in the abbey.

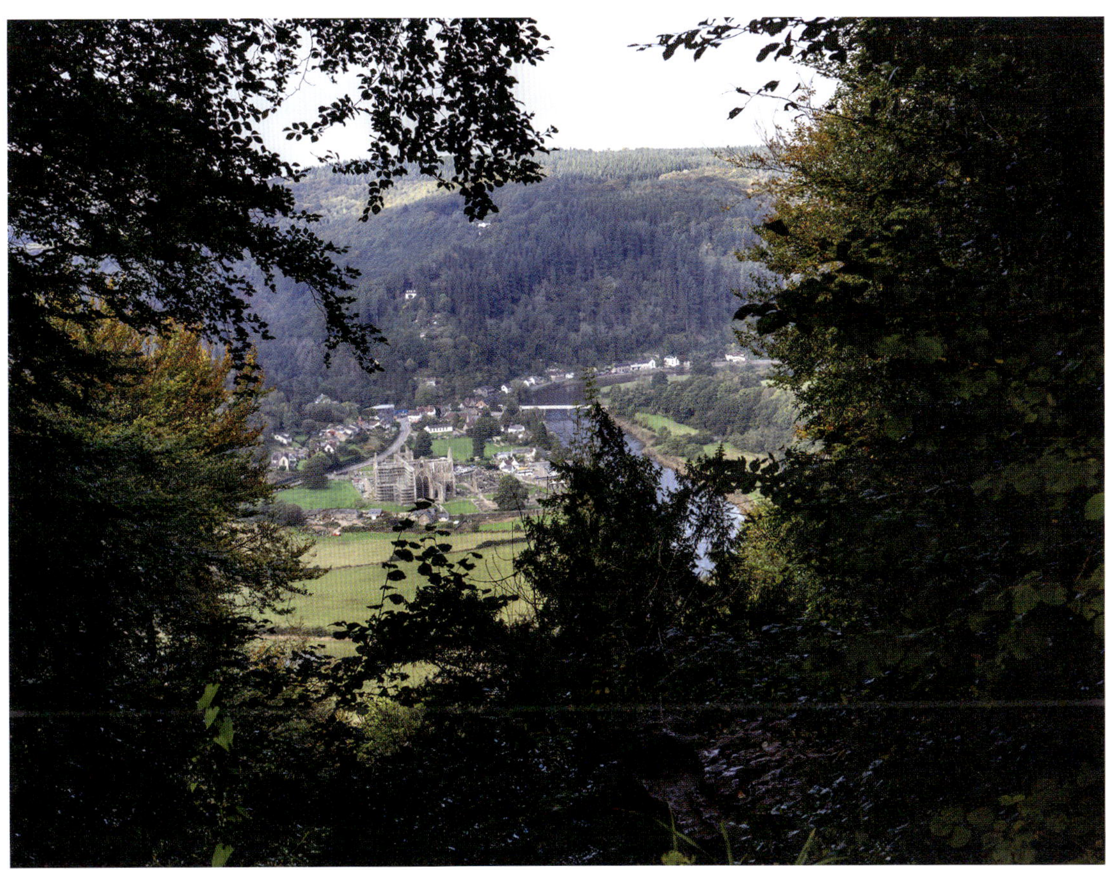

ST 54298 99258

PONT PEN-Y-BENGLOG, GWYNEDD

2017

A favourite view of Victorian photographer Francis Bedford photographed around 1860.

Reassuring maybe to note that the passage of over 150 years had done little to alter the split in the waterfall's flow.

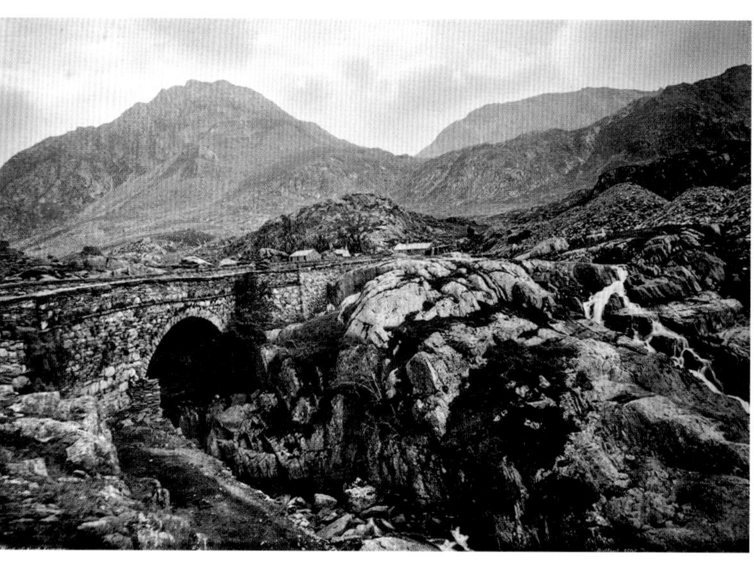

Francis Bedford, circa 1860

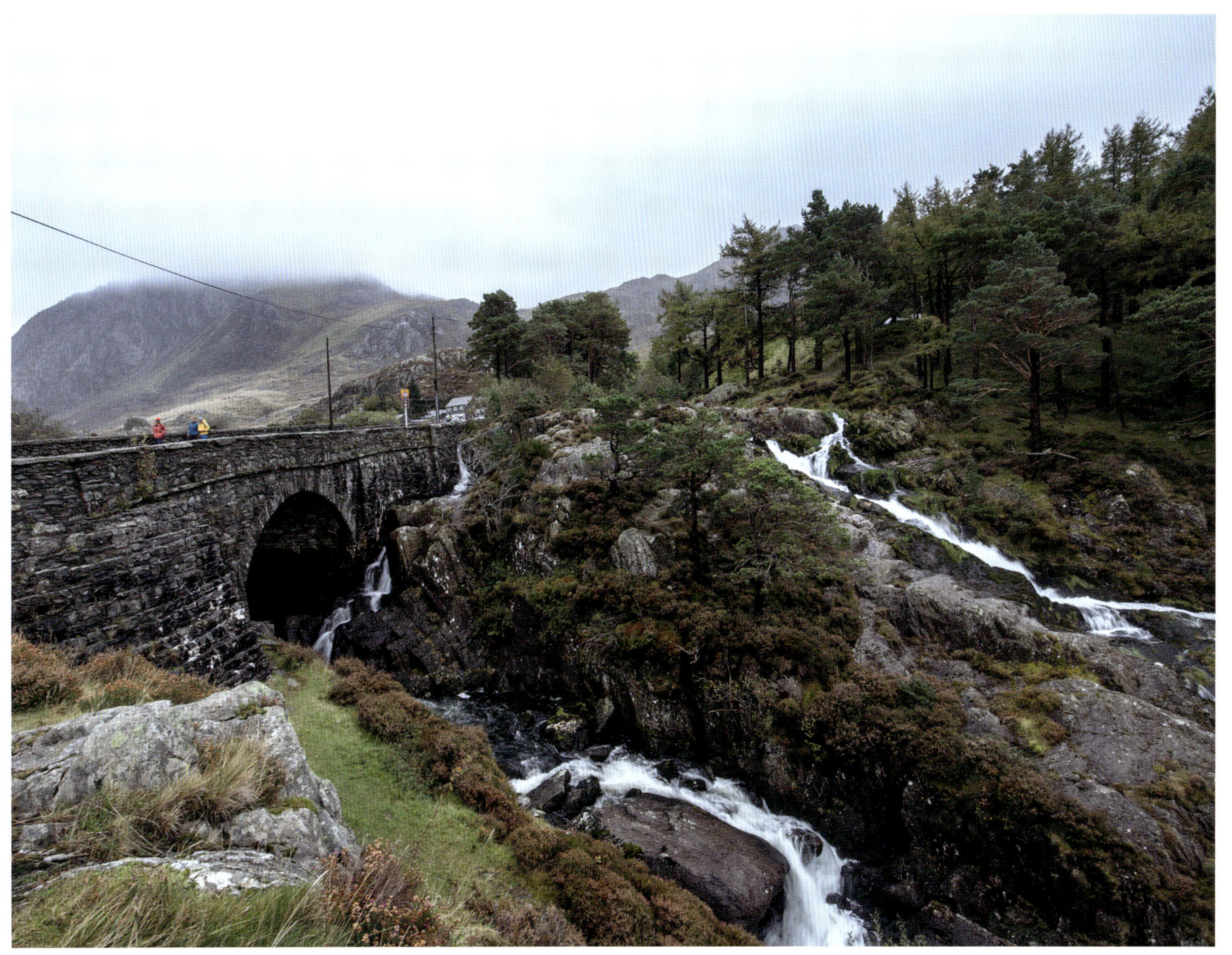

SH 64753 60376

"There is no finer walk than Barmouth to Dolgellau other than from Dolgellau to Barmouth," wrote John Ruskin, one of the greatest writers and social reformers of the Victorian era.

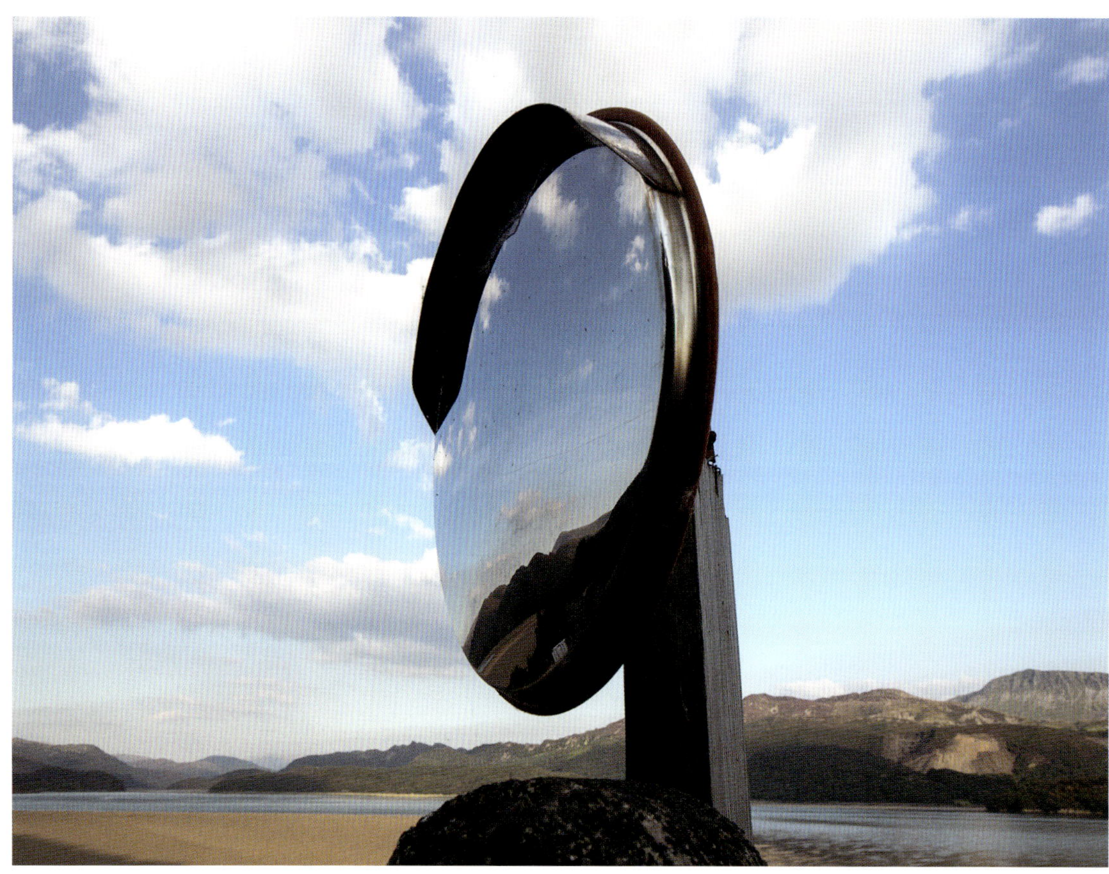

SS 53801 87669

"Time passes. Listen. Time passes."

The view from a converted wooden garage in which Thomas wrote many of his most acclaimed works and where he fished out his unfinished draft of *Under Milk Wood* in 1949.

The "tree room on the cliff" as he described it, is 100 yards from the writer's final home, The Boat House, perched high above the estuary of the River Taf as it flows into Carmarthen Bay.

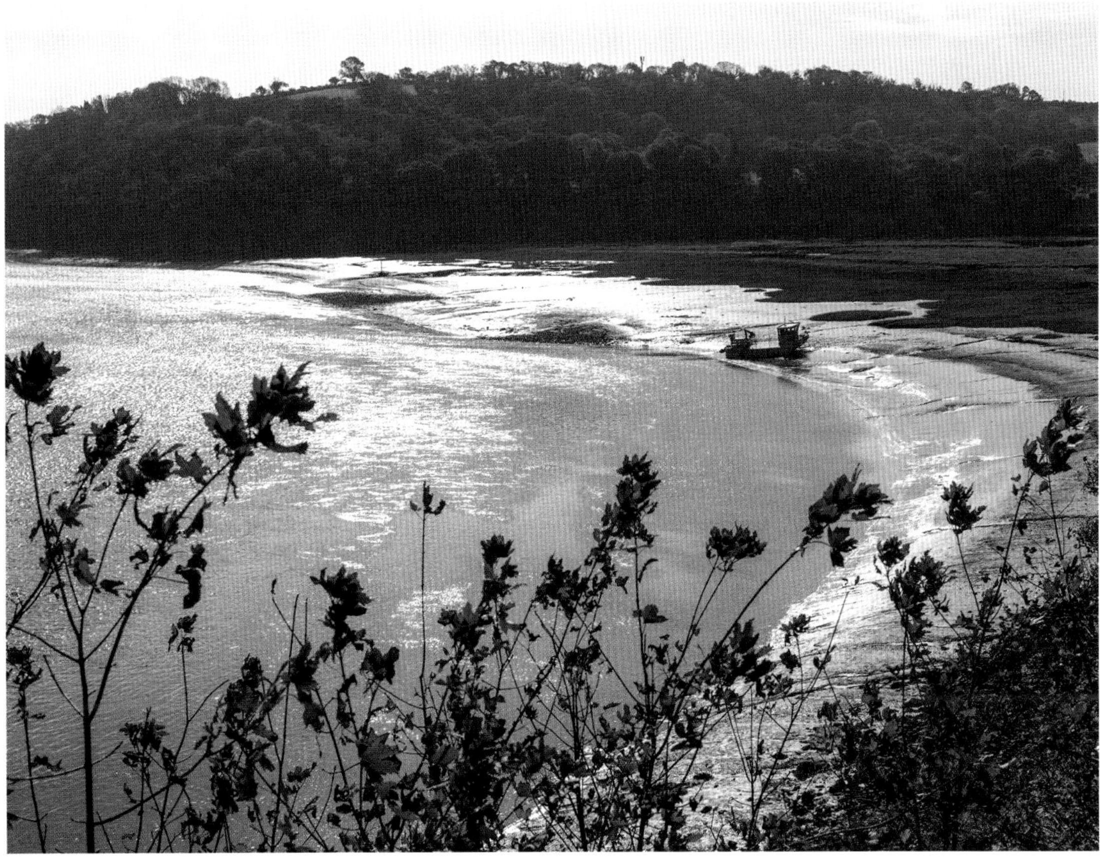

COWS BY THE RIVER WYE, MONMOUTHSHIRE

2013

The view from David Hurn's front door.

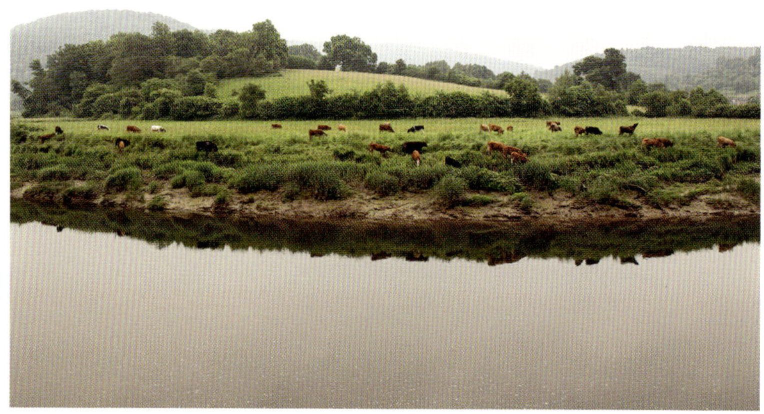

SO 52847 00807

TENBY, PEMBROKESHIRE

2018

The view from photographer Martin Parr's apartment.

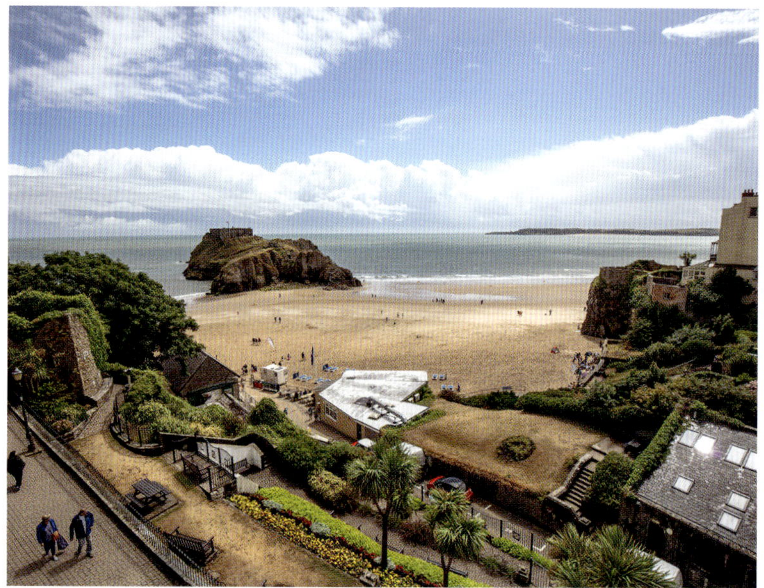

SN 13651 00567

In the opening chapter of *The Matter of Wales* by the late writer Jan Morris:

"The most famous first; the view of Yr Wyddfa, Snowdon, the highest mountain in Wales, from the waters of Porthmadog Bay, looking over the artificial embankment which there crosses the estuary of the Glaslyn River. This grand prospect is like an ideal landscape, its central feature exquisitely framed, its balance exact, its horizontals and perpendiculars in splendid counterpoint."

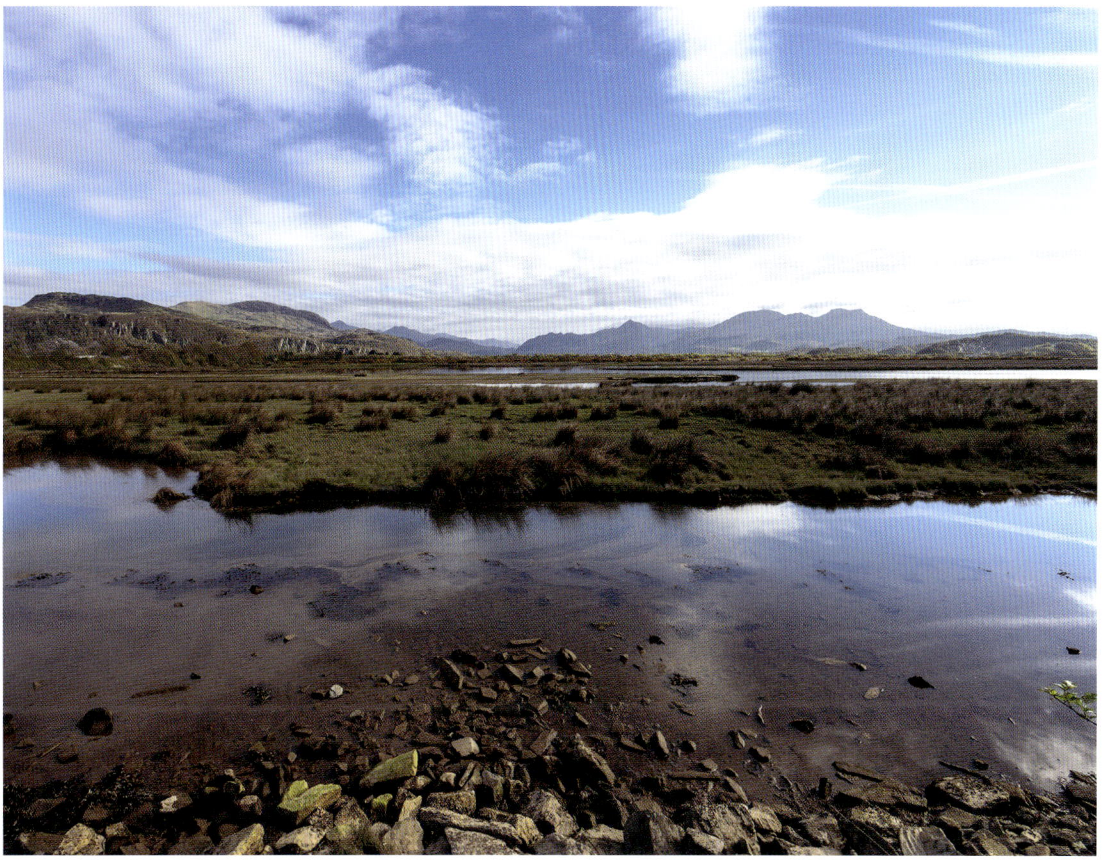

SH 57349 38361

One of the UK's best-preserved Roman roads runs the length of Wales, 160 miles from Neath in the south to Conwy in the north. Its 2,000-year-old cobble stones are exposed as it cuts through the Bannau Brycheiniog (Brecon Beacons National Park). Its name can be translated into English as the Causeway of Elen.

So tangled in lore, it is difficult to define Elen's story with any certainty but she does feature in *The Mabinogion*, a collection of medieval Welsh tales. She ruled alongside her husband, Magnus Maximus, a Roman emperor who ruled Britain, and ordered roads be built across the land for her people, and became known as Elen of the Ways.

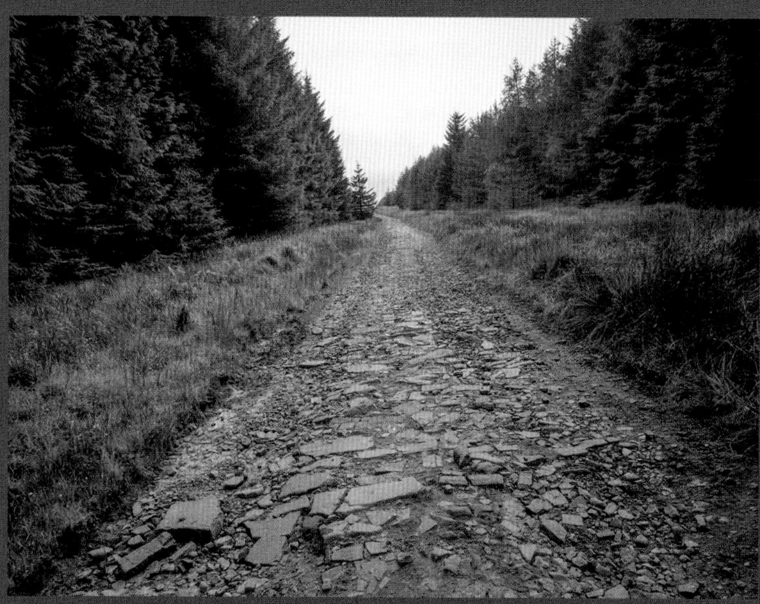

ROADS

SN 92239 16103

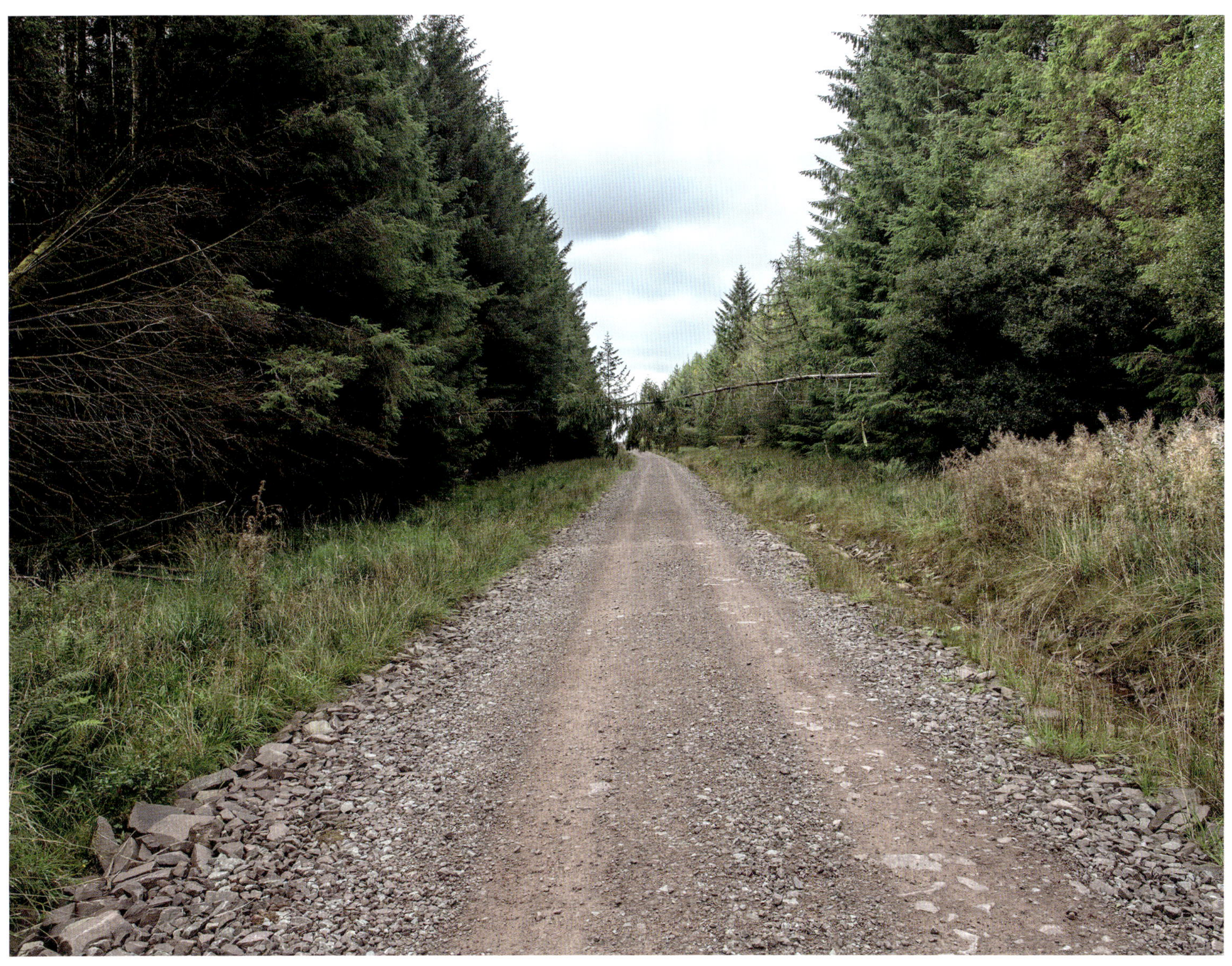

Twelve years later, the cobbles have been overlayed.

Offa, King of the Mercians of the Midlands, had come to power at a time of unrest in the border region of England and Wales.
Around the 780s AD, in a move designed to quell what he saw as the unruly Welsh, he ordered the construction of a great earth wall and ditch, or dyke, running from "sea to sea".

The earth bank border which runs for 82 miles and reaches a height of 12 feet in places, remains a testament to his life which ended in 796. His kingdom was later crushed by the Vikings.

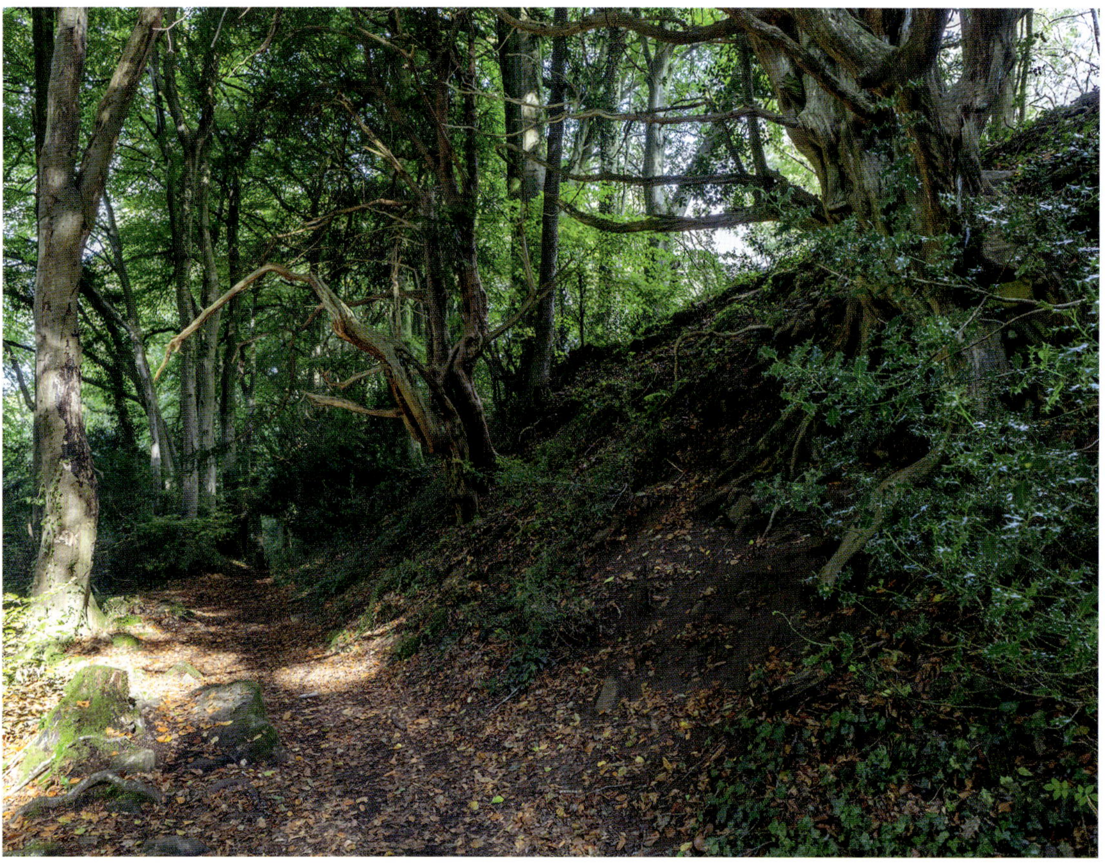

ST 54299 99618

HAFOD-DINBYCH, CONWY

2015

Drovers endured months on the road corralling thousands of livestock each year on the arduous journey from the uplands of Wales to the markets of southern England. Cattle were iron-shod and the feet of game birds protected with tar and sand as the noisy convoys wound their way along a network of rural routes, studded by inns – some to this day bearing Welsh signage in the depth of England – offering board and lodgings.

The once thriving trade promoted the growth of banks, the threat of highwaymen deterring drovers from carrying cash which they would deposit at points along their journey.

The railroad finally put paid to the drovers' skills and livelihoods with many said to have emigrated to America and Australia to take up work as cowboys.

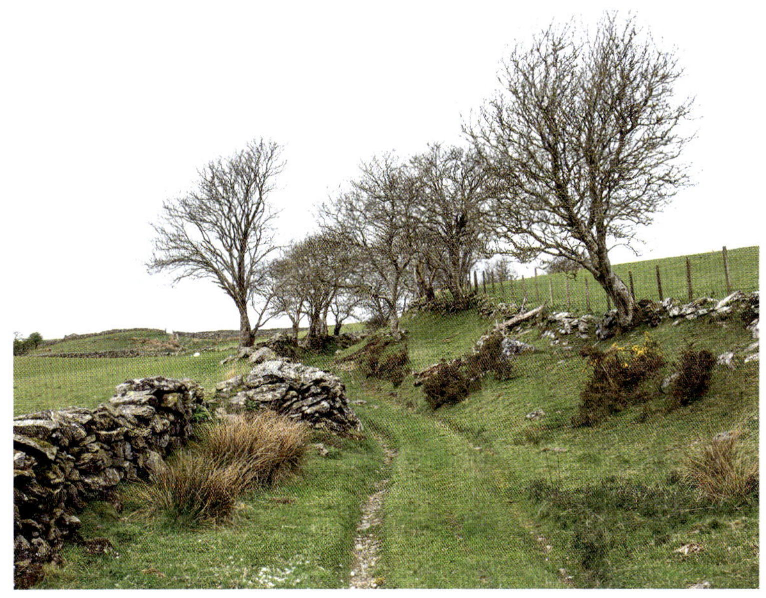

SH 89039 53105

CILYCWM, CARMARTHENSHIRE

2014

A section of one of the main drovers' routes which criss-cross the Cambrian Mountains, showing the original drain designed to provide drinking water for livestock.

Cows, sheep, geese or turkeys in herds of up to 400 would be moved long distances either to market or summer pasture by drovers who revelled in their social standing as important, skilful and hardy.

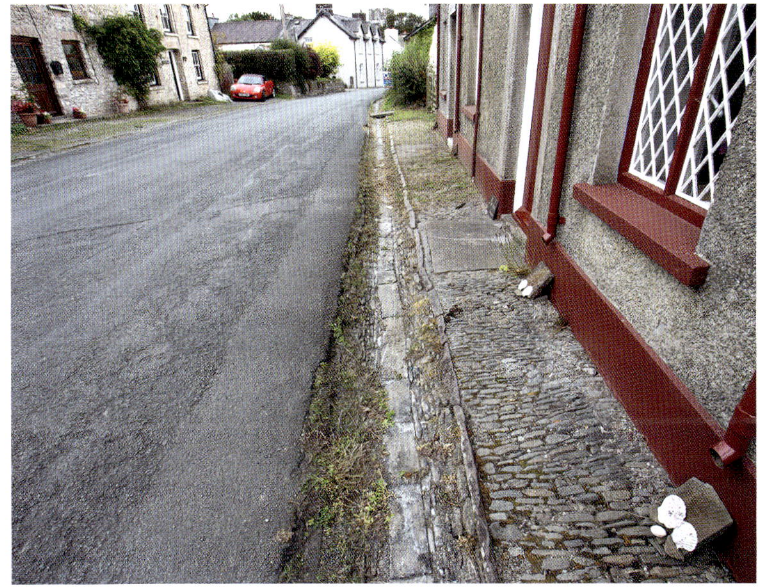

SN 75278 40143

The 'path of the cross', also known as 'Hellfire Pass', is one of the UK's highest public road mountain passes.

Between the wars it was regarded as the best motor vehicle test hill and used by Austin and Triumph to put prototype cars through their paces, later becoming renowned as the most challenging climb for cyclists in the once prestigious round-Britain Milk Race. The ascent is included among the hundred greatest cycling climbs in Britain.

The cross has been positioned at the junction since medieval times, intended to provide a comfort to travellers.

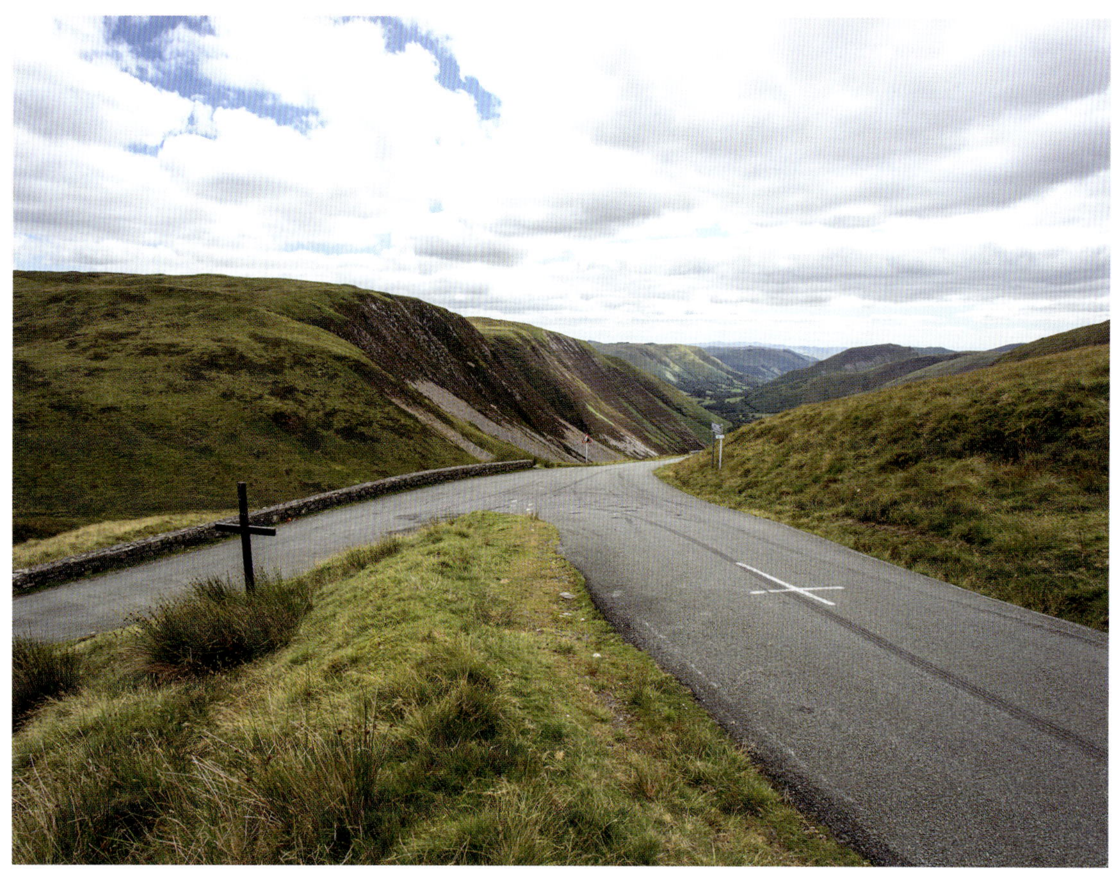

SH 91427 22824

GANLLWYD, GWYNEDD

2018

Rock art along the A470 at Gelligemlyn, where bolts or anchors stabilise the hill and shield traffic from potential rock falls or slides. Installed on a grid, the bolts fasten the unstable surface to more solid rock behind.

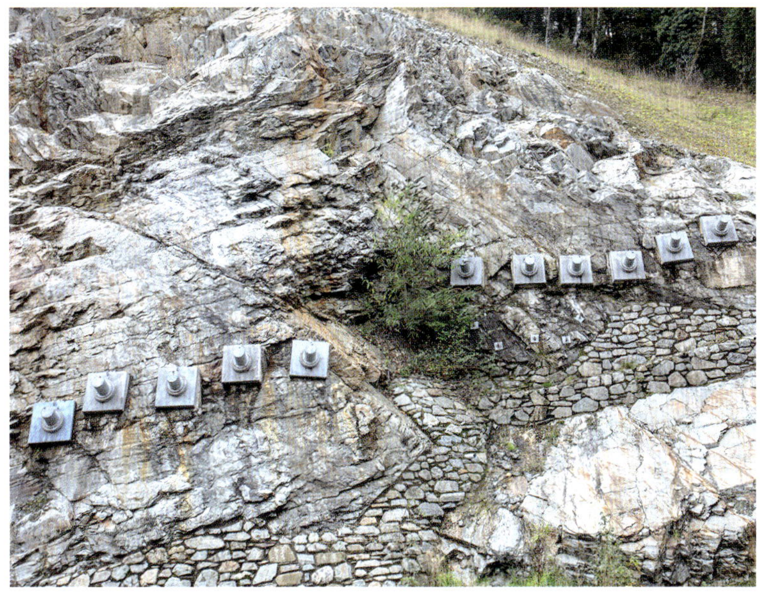

SH 73267 22300

MYNYDD YSTRADFFERNOL, RHONDDA CYNON TAF

2007

Sections of mountainside are commonly draped with wire mesh to prevent rock falls and landslips while still allowing plants and vegetation to thrive.

It could be seen as art. Bulgarian and Moroccan artists, Christo and Jeanne-Claude, were known for their environmental art, wrapping parts of the landscape, including The Gates in New York's Central Park, in various materials.

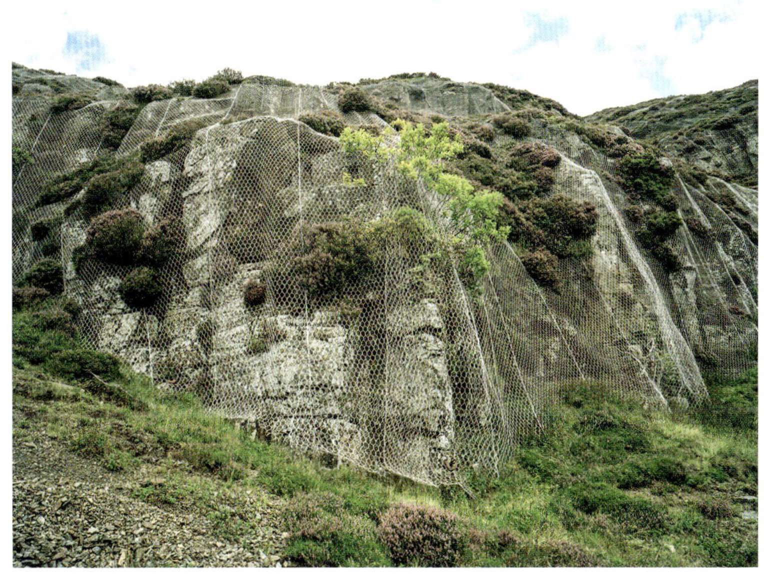

SN 92939 00994

HEADS OF THE VALLEYS, BRYNMAWR TO TREDEGAR, BLANAU GWENT

2014

The biggest-ever road project commissioned by the Welsh Government began in 2000 to turn the 25-miles of the A465 between Abergavenny and Hirwaun into a dual carriageway.

With an estimated cost of £590 million, this was number three of a total of six phases, the final of which is scheduled for completion in mid-2025.

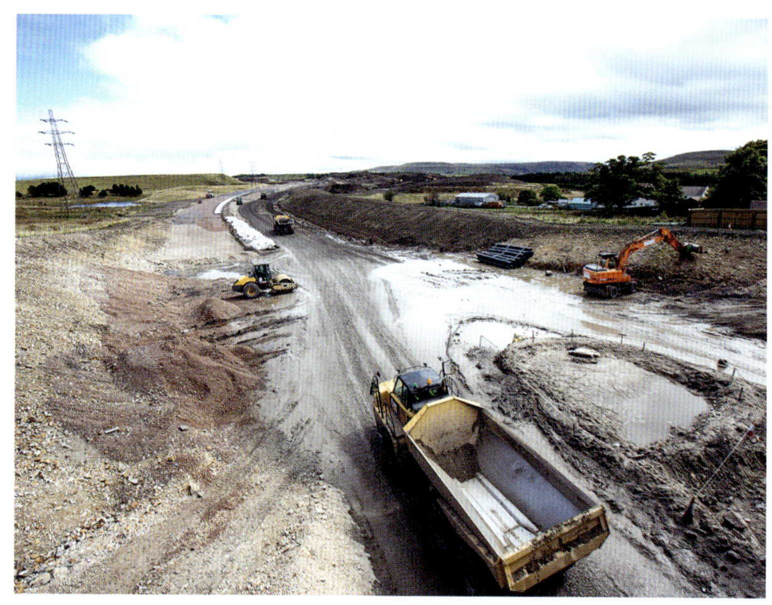

SO 16839 13051

DOLWYDDELAN, CONWY

2006

A wall of slate along a section of the A470 near Betws-y-Coed, that underwent rock blasting as part of road-widening works.

Today, the wall's colour has faded and blends with its backdrop.

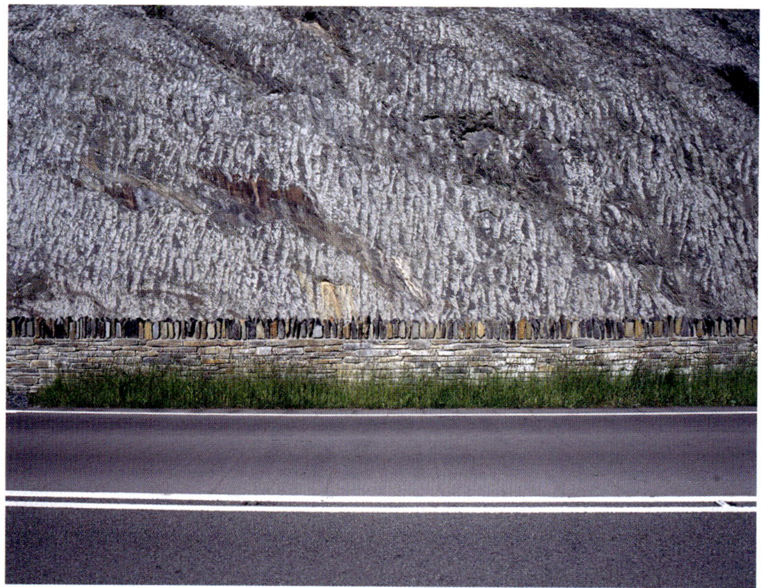

SH79808 54539

The Pembrokeshire Coast Path, a 186-mile mostly cliff-top walking route was first mooted by Welsh naturalist and author Ronald Lockley. After seventeen years of work to cut safe access, building more than 100 bridges and erecting 479 stiles, the path was opened in 1970.

Its success in boosting the tourist economy as well as promoting health and well-being, led to the establishment in 2012 of the Wales Coast Path, the first dedicated coastal path in the world to cover the entire length of a country's coastline.

CONSERVATION

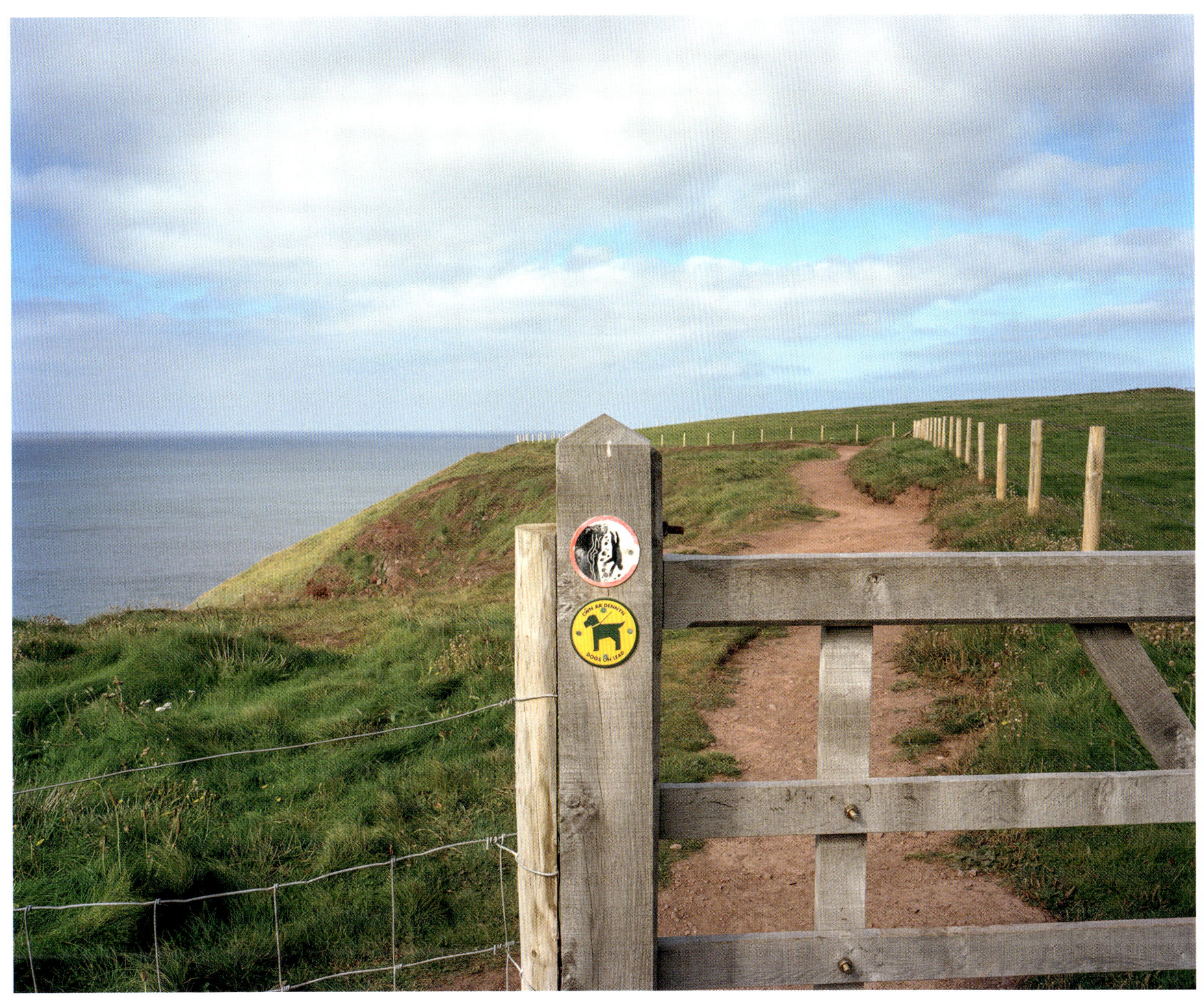

SM 80631 03020

'Citadel of Light' was the first ever donation made to the National Trust, in its foundation year, 1895. The estate's owner was Fanny Talbot, a philanthropist, who lived in a cottage on the gorse-covered hillside overlooking Cardigan Bay.

Writing of her hope that that the 4.5 acres would never be "vulgarised", Talbot said:
"I have no objection to grassy paths or to stone seats in proper places but I wish to avoid the abomination of asphalt paths and the cast-iron seats of serpent design which disfigure so largely our public parks."

In response, the National Trust founders said:
"We have got our first piece of property. I wonder if it will be our last?"

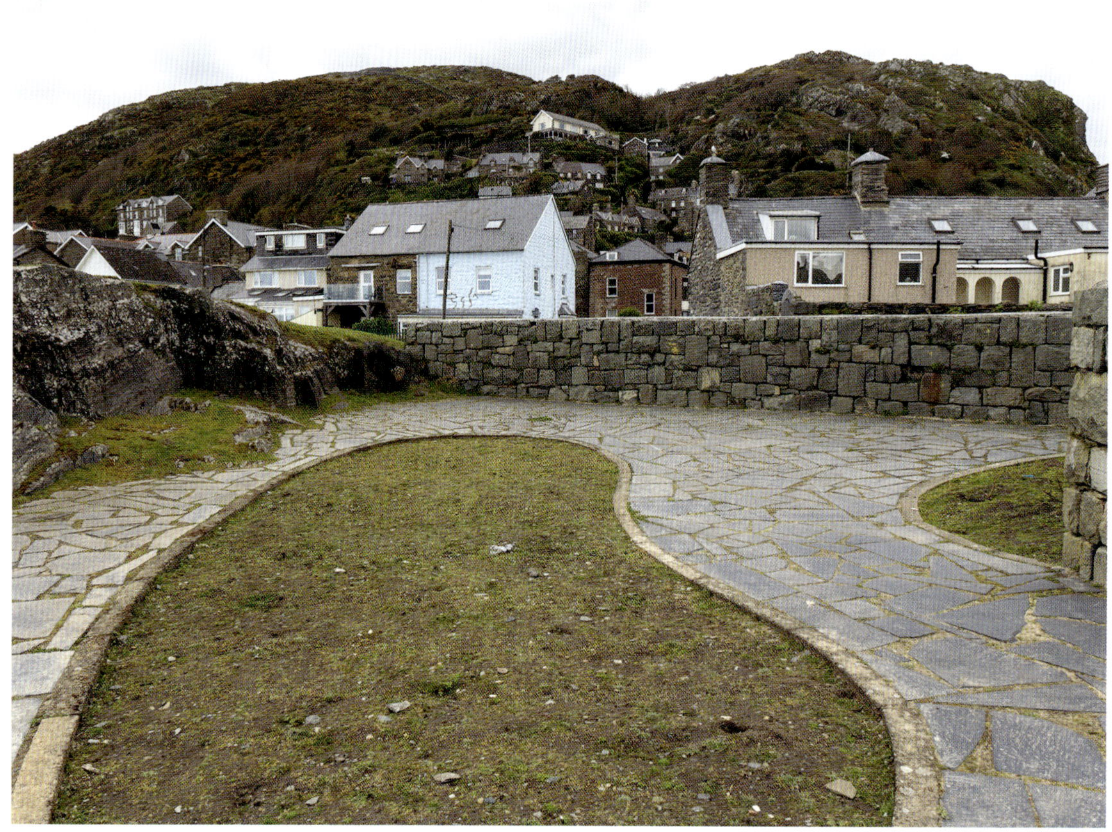

SH 61401 15501

A reserve at the top of the Wye Valley ridge traditionally managed by Gwent Wildlife Trust.

"The diversity and colour of the wildflowers in these traditional hay meadows", the Trust says, "steals the show in spring and summer before giving centre stage to the autumnal hues of fungi."

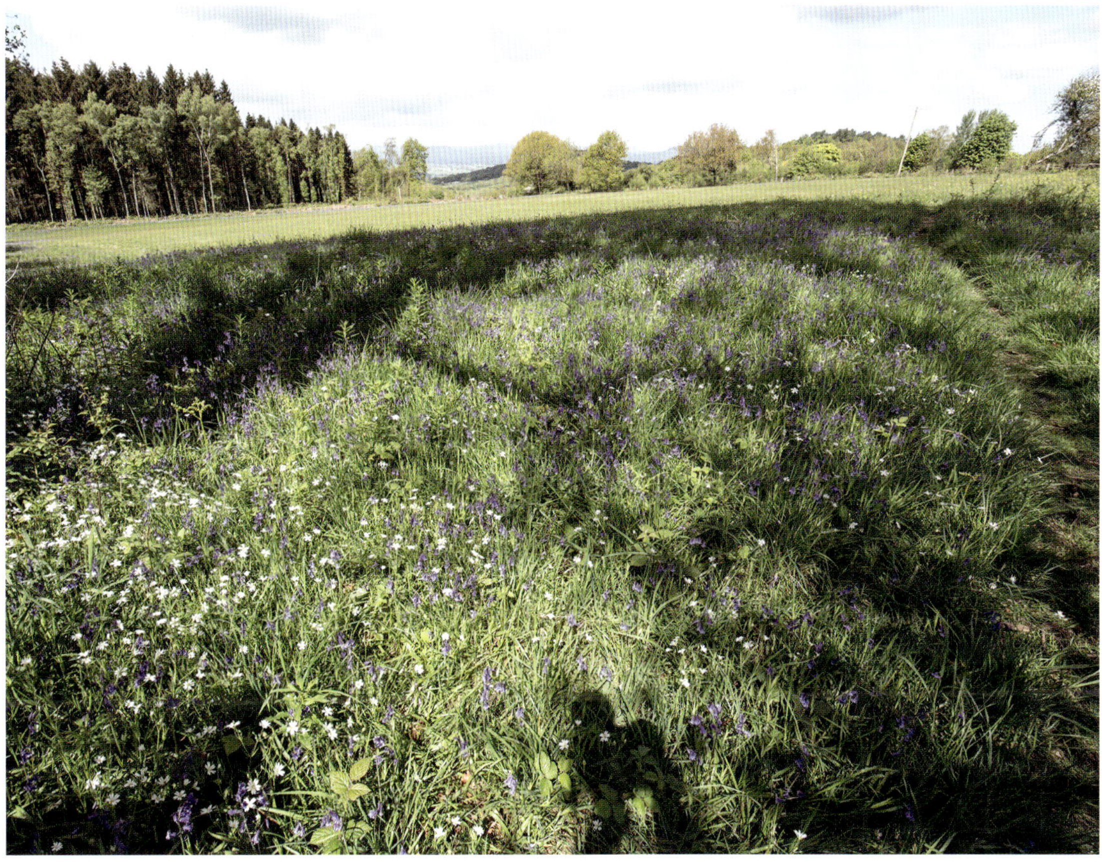

SO 501443 06910

ABERCYWARCH, GWYNEDD

2014

Before the Enclosure Acts of Parliament which began in the 1600s, the countryside was made up of large, unfenced or unhedged open fields worked by tenant farmers who cultivated scattered strips of land.

The legislation redistributed land from common or public ownership to private and led to land being sliced up by boundaries of varying nature.

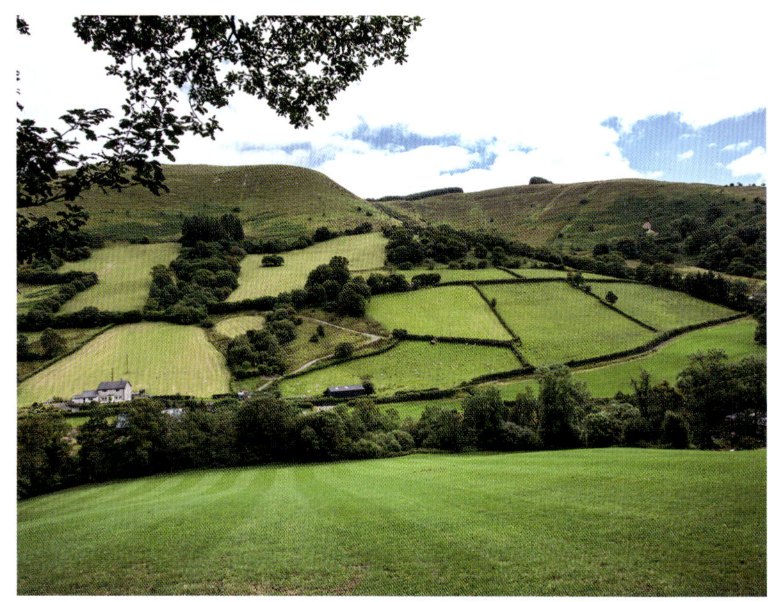

SH 87531 16424

HENRYD, CONWY

2016

Between 1604 and 1914 over 5,200 individual acts were passed covering 6.8 million acres of land.

Boundaries in many parts of Wales typically comprise of rocks cleared from fields at the time of the Enclosure Movement.

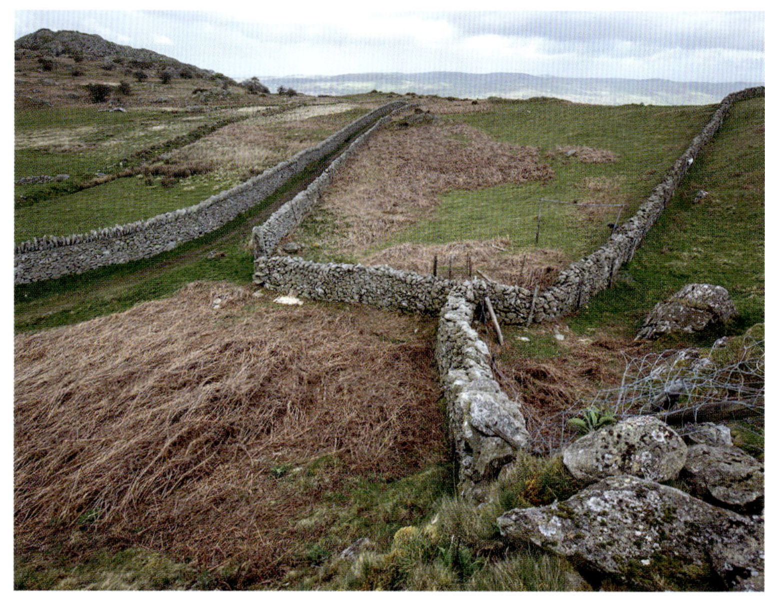

SH 75156 73669

LLANERCH, CARMARTHENSHIRE

2007 (top) & 2013 (below)

When work began on this section of the South Wales Gas
Pipeline – the UK's largest, running 197 miles from Milford
Haven in Pembrokeshire, to Tirley, Gloucester – the farmer in
question was promised his field would be left exactly as it had
been found.

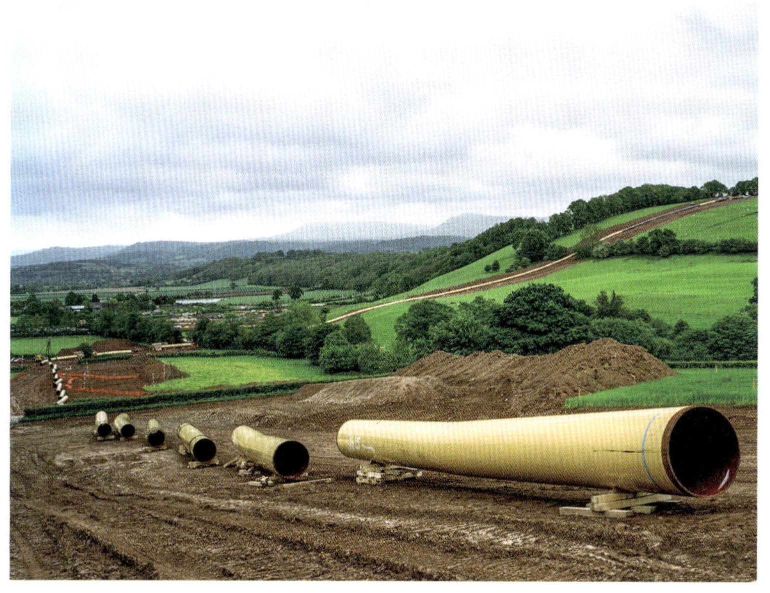

SO 13127 37447

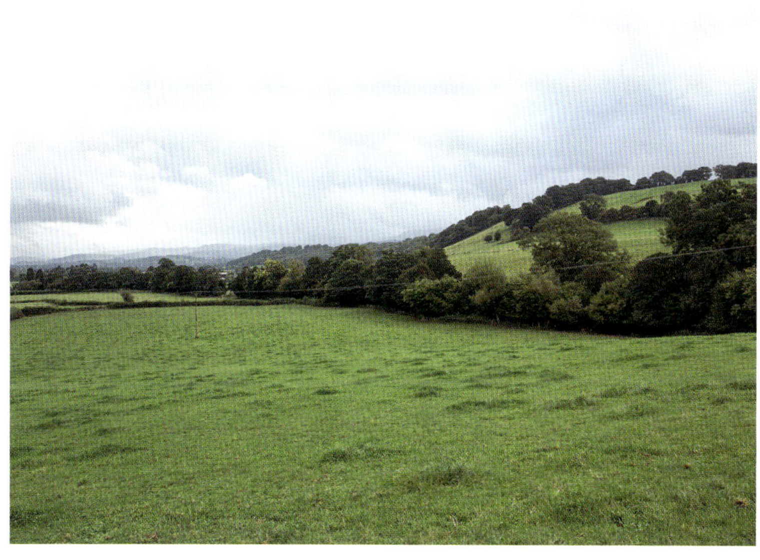

SO 13127 37447

2011

This nature reserve is the largest lowland fen in Wales and one of the most important wetland sites in Europe. Despite being close to dense industry, its extensive reed and sedge beds are home to a wide variety of wetland plants, birds and insects. And ponies.

In September 2024, BBC Wales reported that the bogs are under threat due to damage caused by drainage, pollution and neglect. They are currently part of a £5m restoration project.

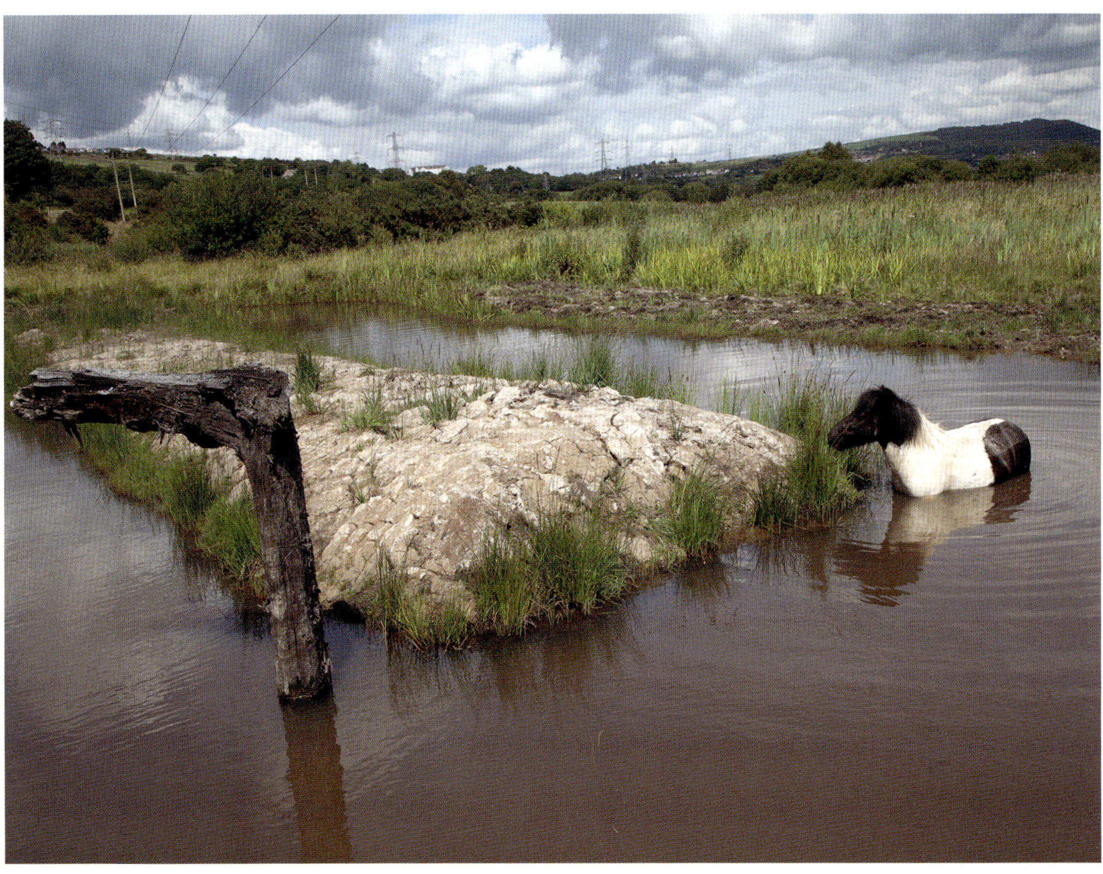

SS 68673 9433

The flow of the River Wye – the second highest tidal river in the world – is almost always uninterrupted as it courses through the village built along its banks. However, if there is one force strong enough to take on water, it is wind.

On this rare occasion, the direction and powers of the gusts caused the tidal flow to back up, causing the Wye to burst its banks.

CLIMATE CHANGE

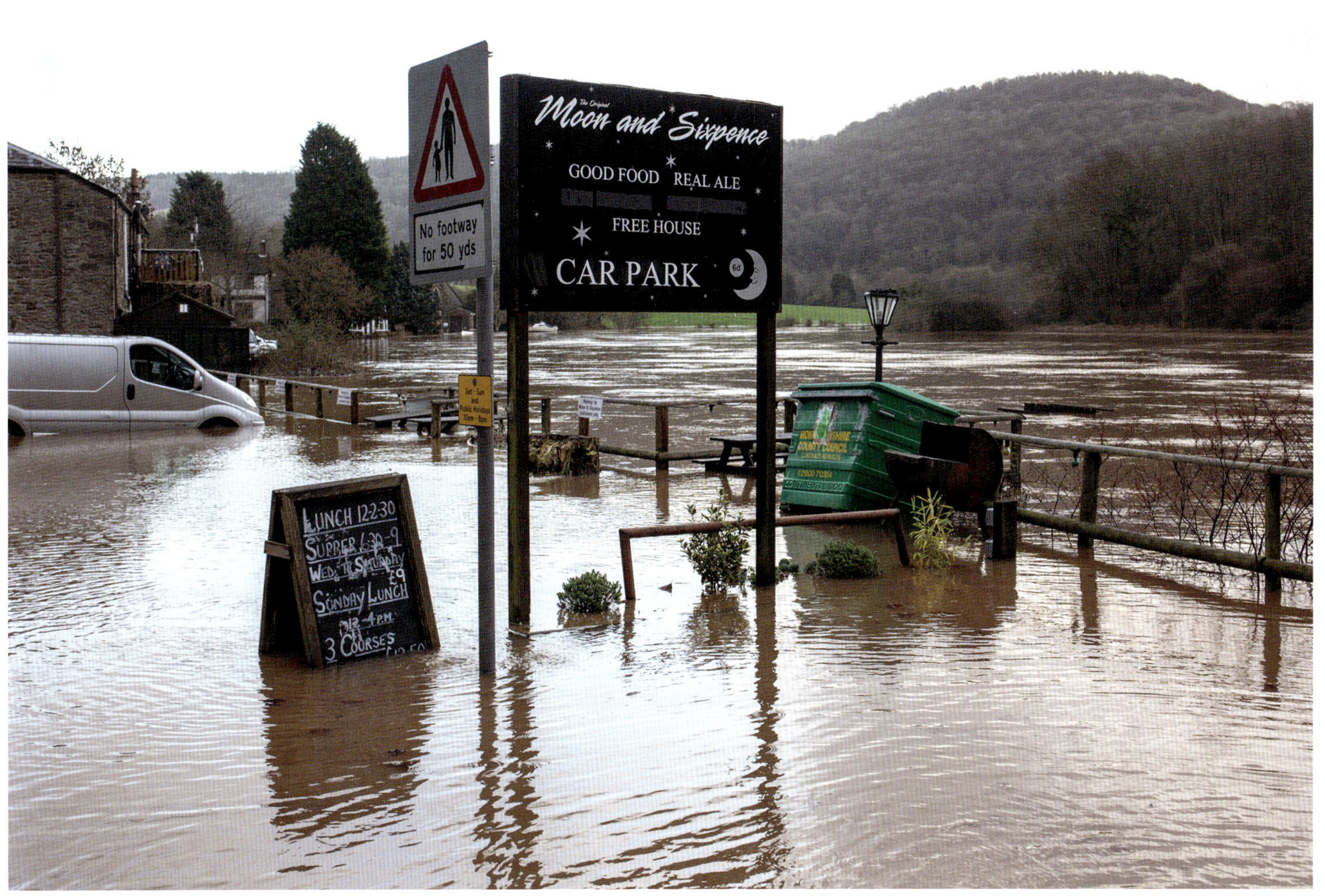
No footway
for 50 yds

The Original
Moon and Sixpence
GOOD FOOD   REAL ALE
FREE HOUSE
CAR PARK

LUNCH 12-2·30
SUPPER 6·30-9
WED. to SATURDAY
£9
SUNDAY LUNCH
12-4 PM
3 COURSES

The seaside resort home of the UK's first climate change refugees.

With millions already spent on flood defences, in 2013 the local authority and Natural Resources Wales declared a 'managed retreat' with no further action against rising sea levels. The 850 occupants of around 400 homes have been told they must move, with little prospect of compensation.

In 2021, officials declared that by 2052 it would no longer be safe to live in the village, a warning that has been disputed by a number of research reports.

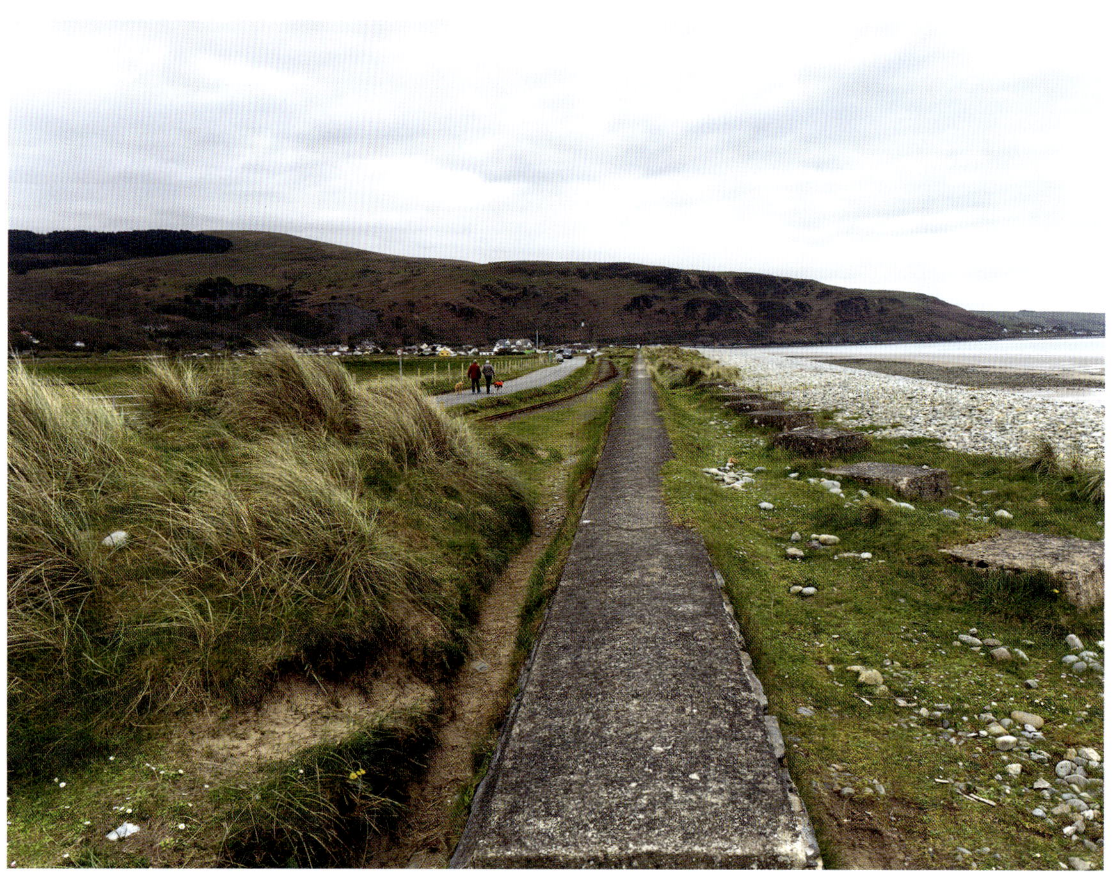

SH 61101 14301

BEACONS RESERVOIR, POWYS

2019 (top) & 2018 (below)

Before and after a heatwave.

As one of the wettest parts of the UK all it takes is a couple of weeks of sun to dramatically change the landscape.

Despite the reservoir's parched appearance, water supplies still operated within normal ranges.

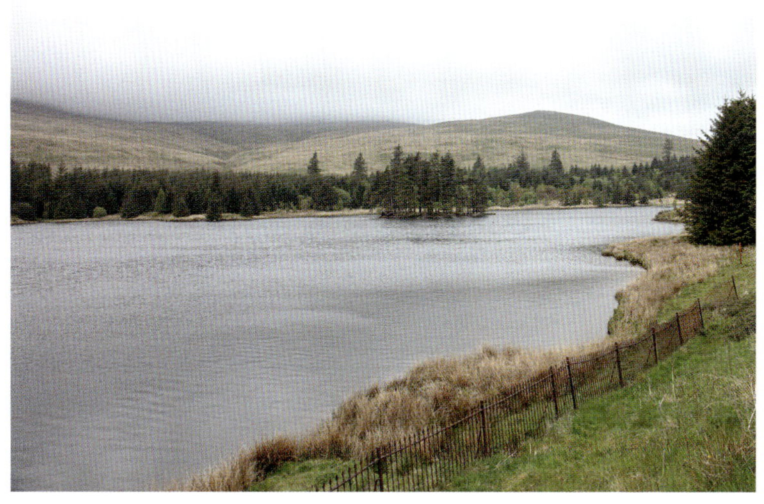

SN 98839 18738

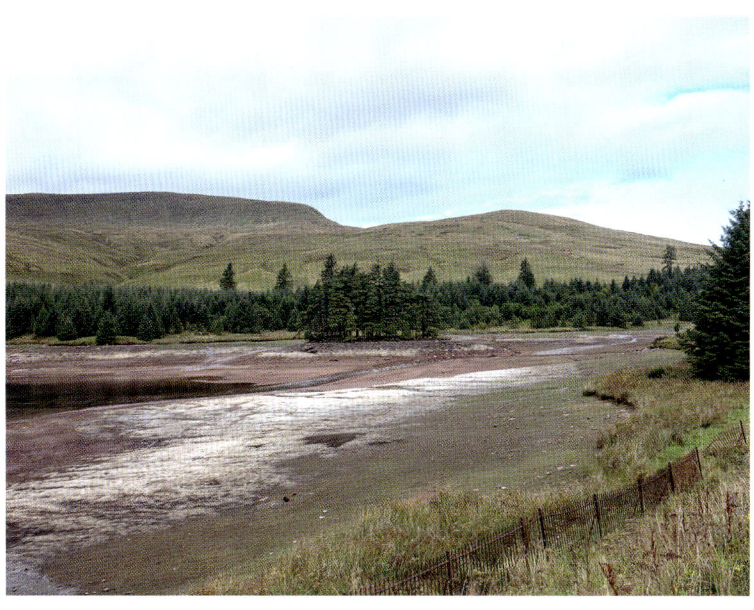

SN 98839 18738

WILD FIRES, BRECON BEACONS, POWYS

2011

In May that year the worst heath land fire in 30 years burned for five days and destroyed nearly five square miles of peat bog including one of the most important SSSI sites within the Bannau Brycheiniog National Park. Firefighters, assisted by the military also attended hundreds of other fires that same year, many of which were started deliberately.

Recovery from such catastrophe can take around ten years.

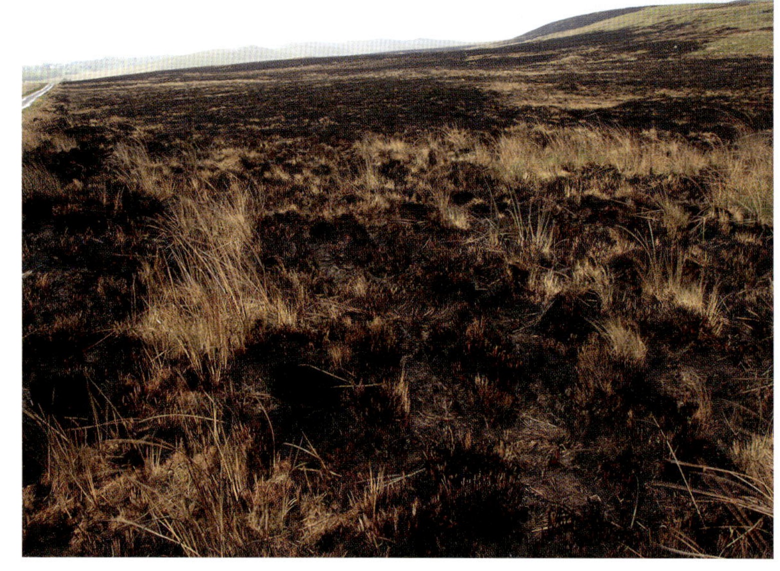

SN 66807 16328

PONTERWYD, CEREDIGION

2007

A tree scorched in half at the end of the firewall.

Between 2000-2008 there were 55,000 recorded grass fires and nearly 500 forest fires in Wales.

Statistics published in 2023 showed almost one in four Fire and Rescue Service call outs were grassland, woodland or crop related.

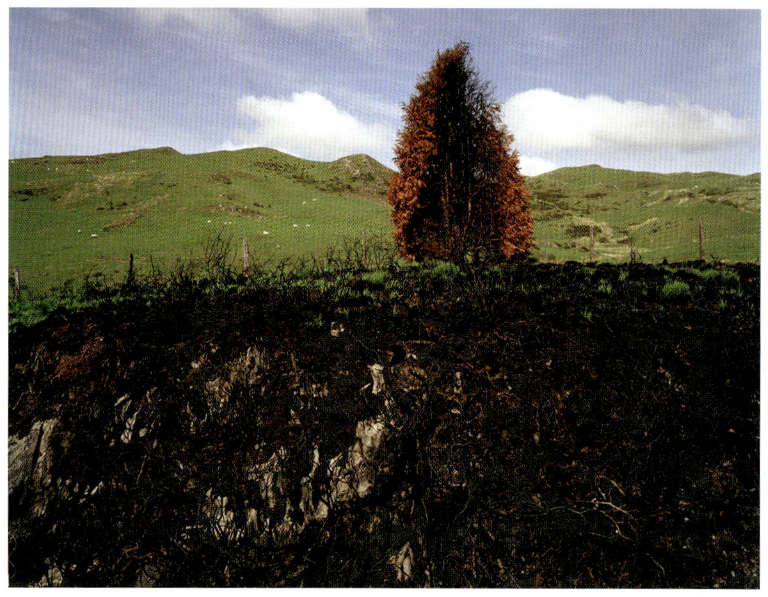

SN 74100 80503

The ancient art of hedgerows, an often overlooked but vital feature of the landscape not only because of their beauty, but for the benefit of its wildlife and ecology.

While there are 69,000 miles of hedgerows in Wales, an estimated 25-30% have been lost since 1945.

They are an important part of Welsh heritage. Established and maintained by farmers using traditional skills over generations, they are protected by law.

BOUNDARIES

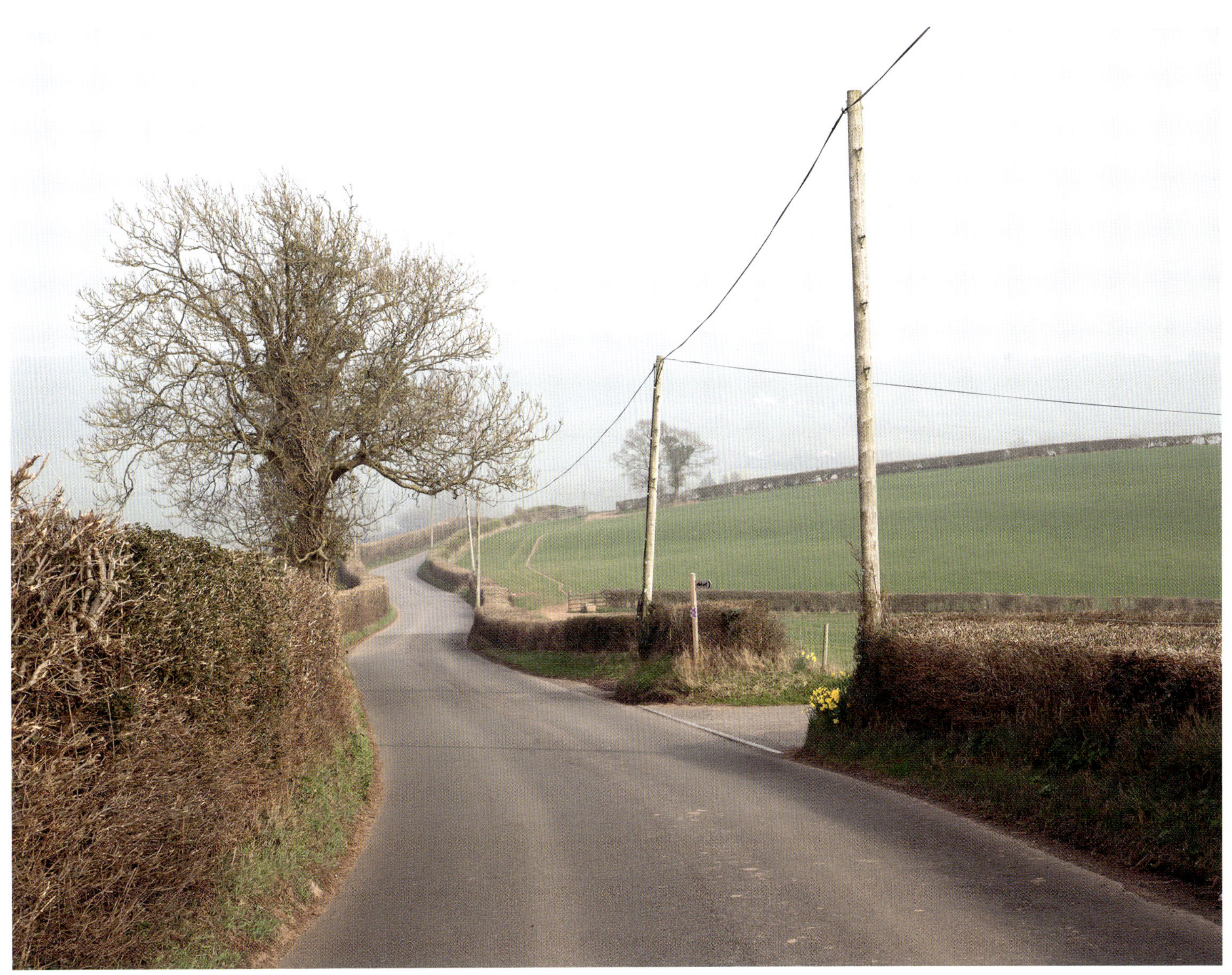

SO 45096 02474

LLANTHONY VALLEY, MONMOUTHSHIRE

2018

Hedge laying at the Valley and District Hedging Match which involves partially cutting and bending the stems of shrubs or young trees to create a living fence and is best done in winter when sap has stopped running.

A properly laid hedge needs no additional fencing and will remain impenetrable year-round.

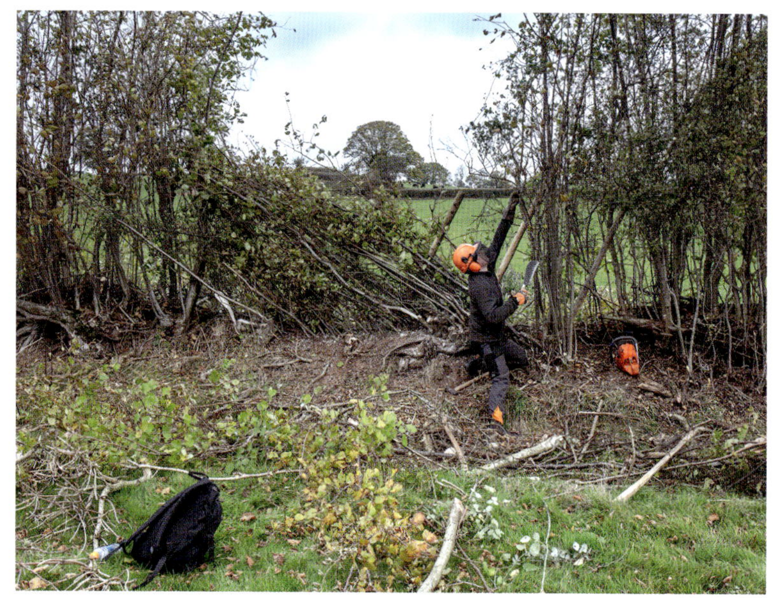

SO 32523 21425

FLAILING IN TINTERN, MONMOUTHSHIRE

2024

Another of various hedge management approaches, flailing involves a tractor mounted mower to uniformly trim the tops and sides.

This example lining the local football pitch shows how this method renders the hedges more open and less dense.

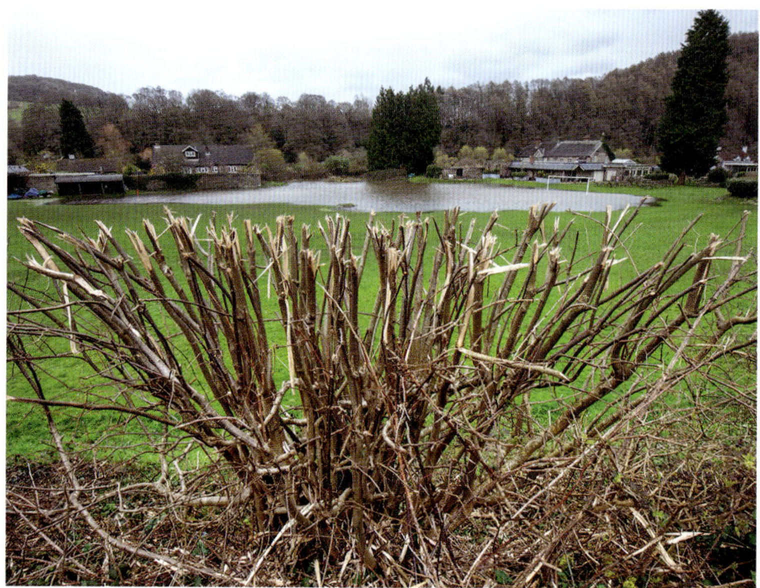

SO 53118 00087

LABURNUM HEDGES, CEREDIGION

2019

The mysterious Laburnum hedges of west Wales. In spring time stretches of hedges lining the roads in south Ceredigion and north Pembrokeshire are ablaze with the 'golden chains' of Laburnum. Why a plant whose every part is poisonous – bark, roots, leaves and especially the seed pods – would be planted along fields near livestock is unknown. Thankfully, there are no reports of any harm.

One theory is that the ballast and pallets of Laburnum wood dropped from old Spanish sailing ships were turned into fencing posts. Another is that it spread from the gardens of residents who had been influenced by its prevalence in grand Victorian country house gardens. And another, that miners at old lead mines were in the habit of chewing the plants' seeds before spitting them out.

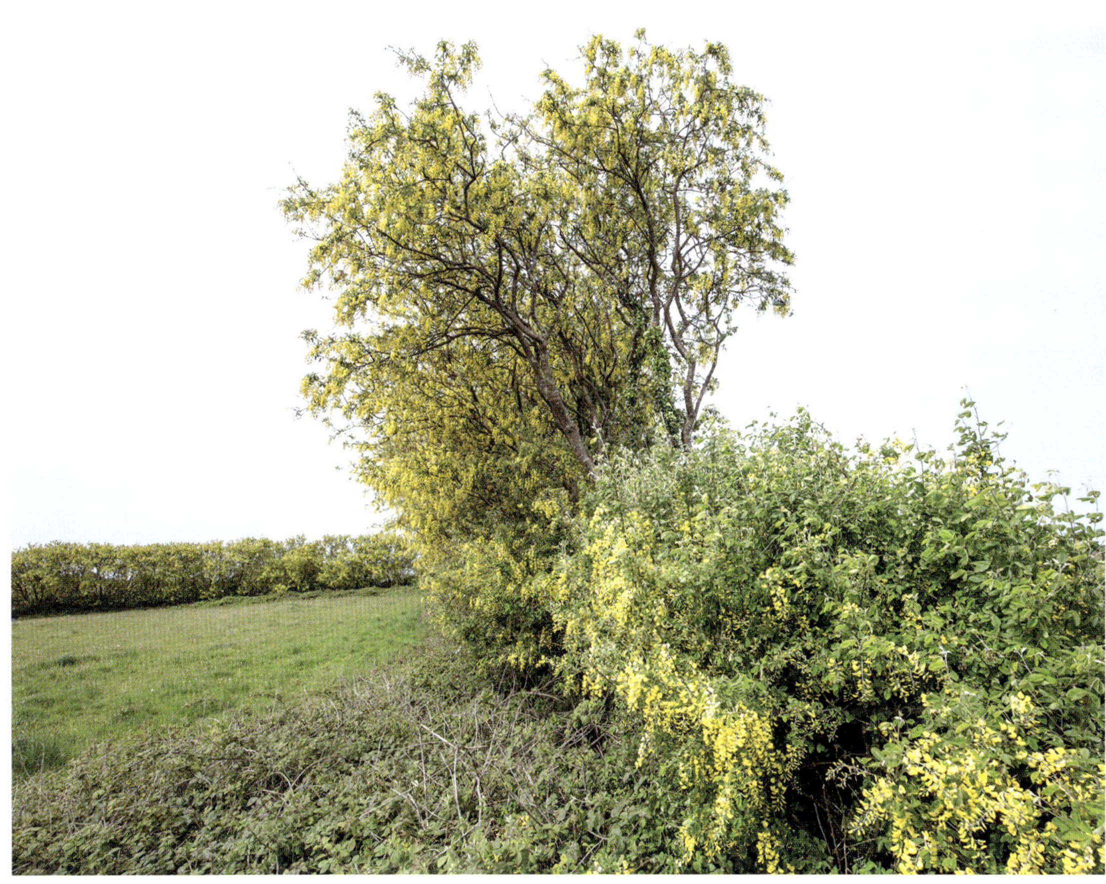

SN 30463 50610

A 2024 report by campaign group Nature 30 called for road verges to be used as wildlife corridors to save Britain's biodiversity. It was supported by global charity Plantlife which is leading the charge on the way the UK's verges are managed. I'm convinced this has had an impact throughout Wales.

The variety and density of roadside blooms seems evidence of the campaign's success. A new phenomenon?

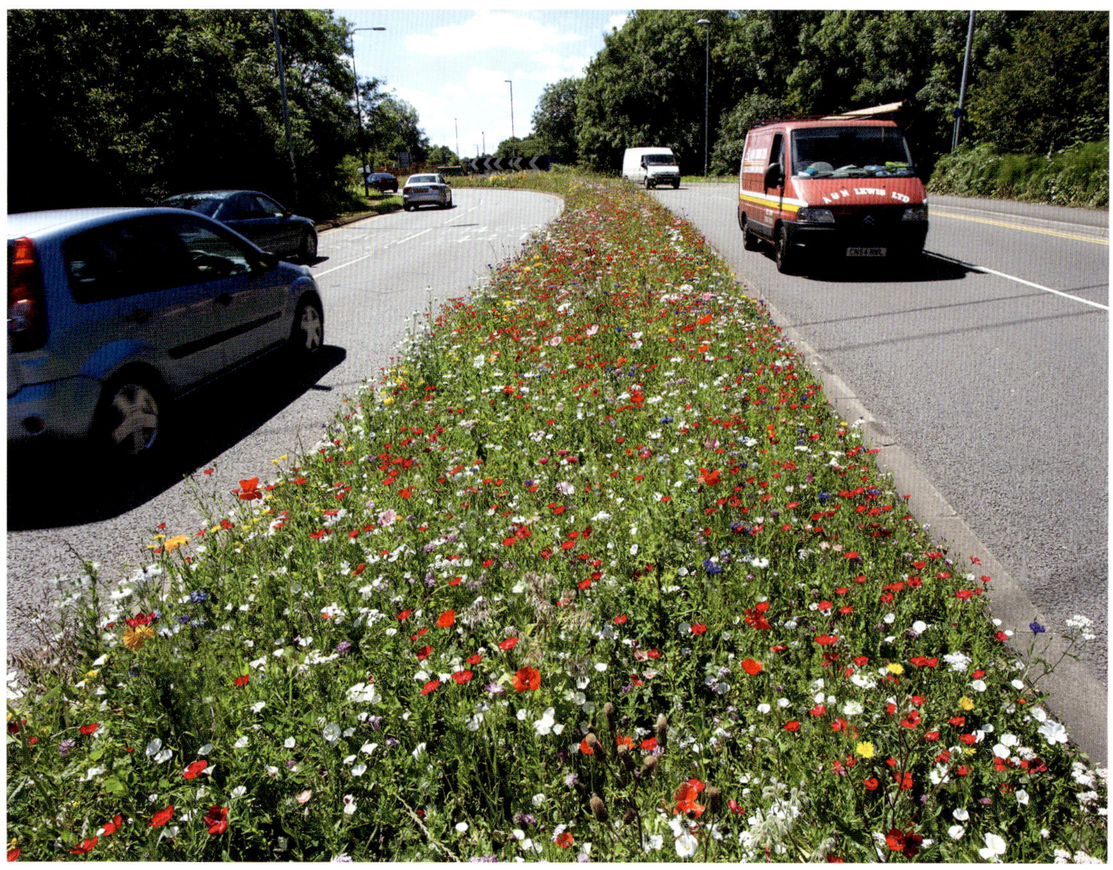

ST 52709 92970

Heralded as a 'garden of firsts' by the National Trust, the grounds boast one of the finest collections of rhododendron species and hybrids in the UK. Such was their demand after explorers brought the shrub back from Asia, America and Australia in the late-1800s, that the ornamental plants spread like wildfire across the grounds of stately homes, public parks and back gardens alike.

But there was a catch.

As a result of cross-breeding different species to help adapt to a colder climate, some plants became invasive and sturdy, their height blocking light from native species, further endangered by the toxicity of their extensive root systems and leaf litter which could also poison grazing animals.

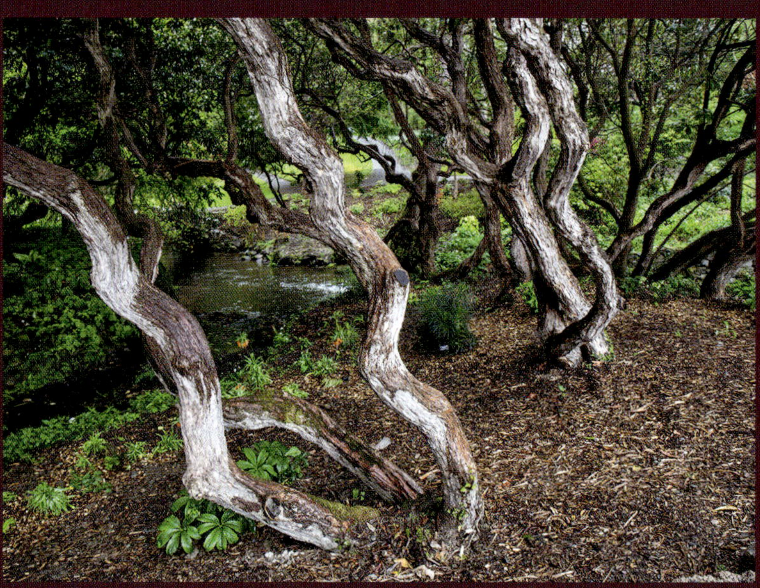

GARDENS

SH 79927 71622

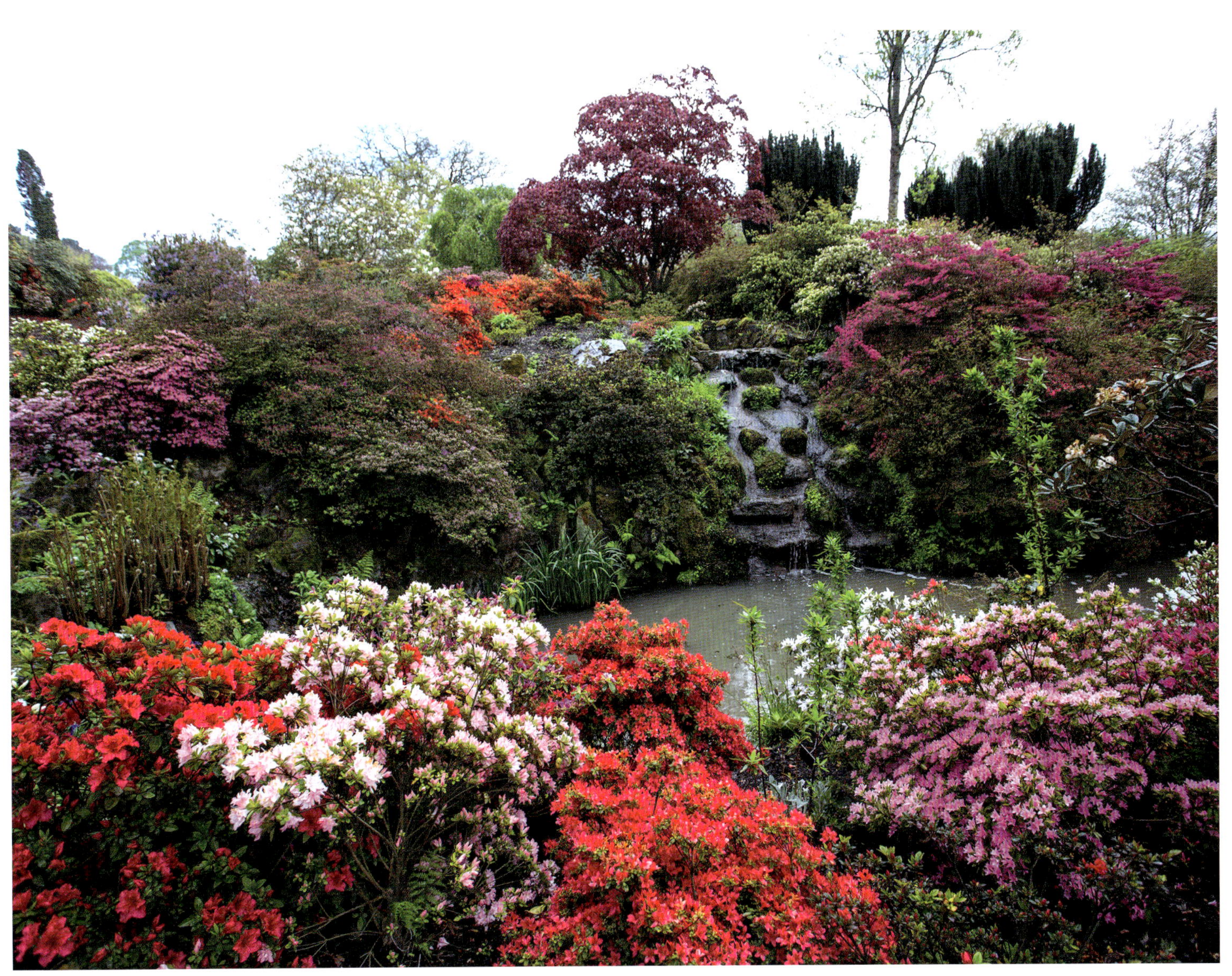

2011

Matt Collins wrote in *The Guardian*, January 2021:

"Aberglasney in south-west Wales is one of Britain's finest heritage gardens. Saved from dereliction in 1995, the elegantly remodelled cloister and three gardens (kitchen, woodland and shrub) surrounding its restored 15th-century mansion are testament to a vibrant, open-minded horticultural approach that has kept me coming back for a decade.

"But more recently, my attention has turned to Aberglasney's hidden gem: an unconventional indoor garden, part of the house itself, called the Ninfarium. It consists of two storeys of ruined walls in the oldest part of the building, topped with a modern glass roof. The exposed walls and window cavities are overgrown with exotic greenery; ginger and voodoo lilies spring through a doorway; Spanish moss drips from the mortar; and hefty bananas stretch to the roof, all concealed Narnia-like behind a heavy oak door."

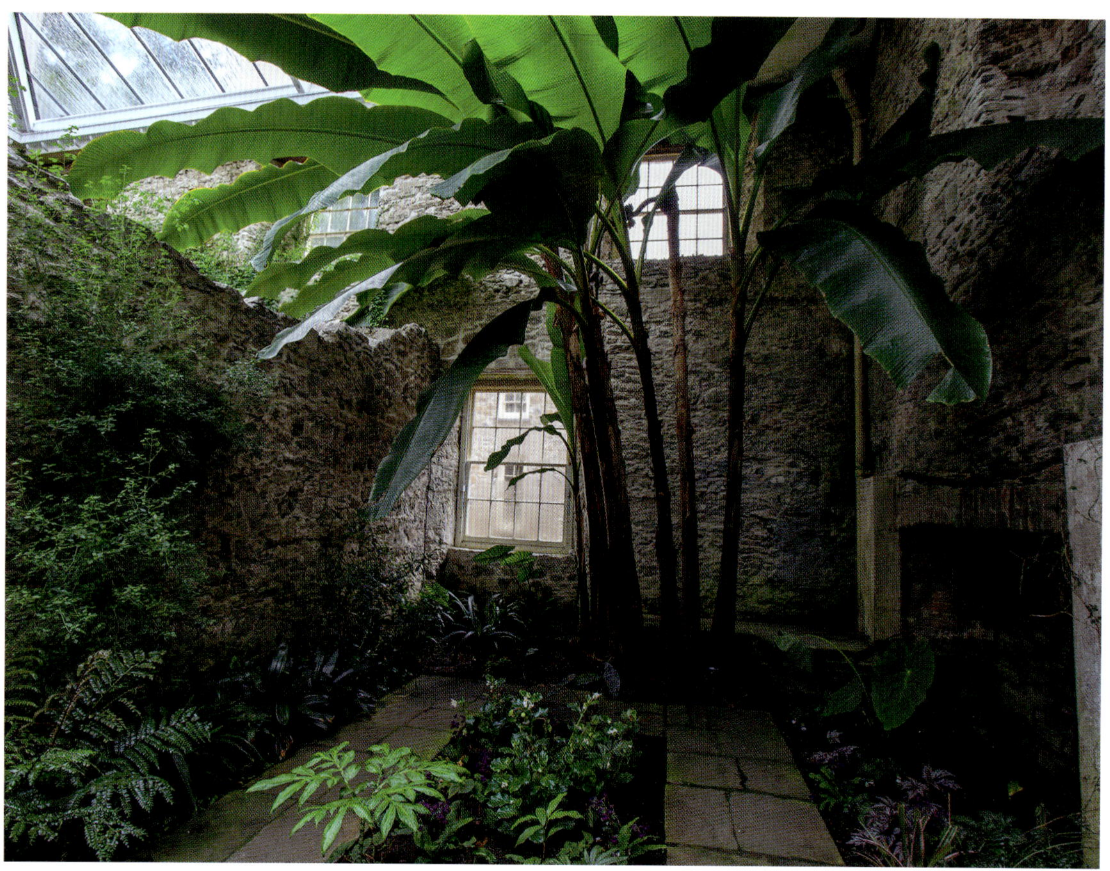

Three continents seen from the Great Glasshouse:
Europe through the window, South America to the left and Australasia
to the right.

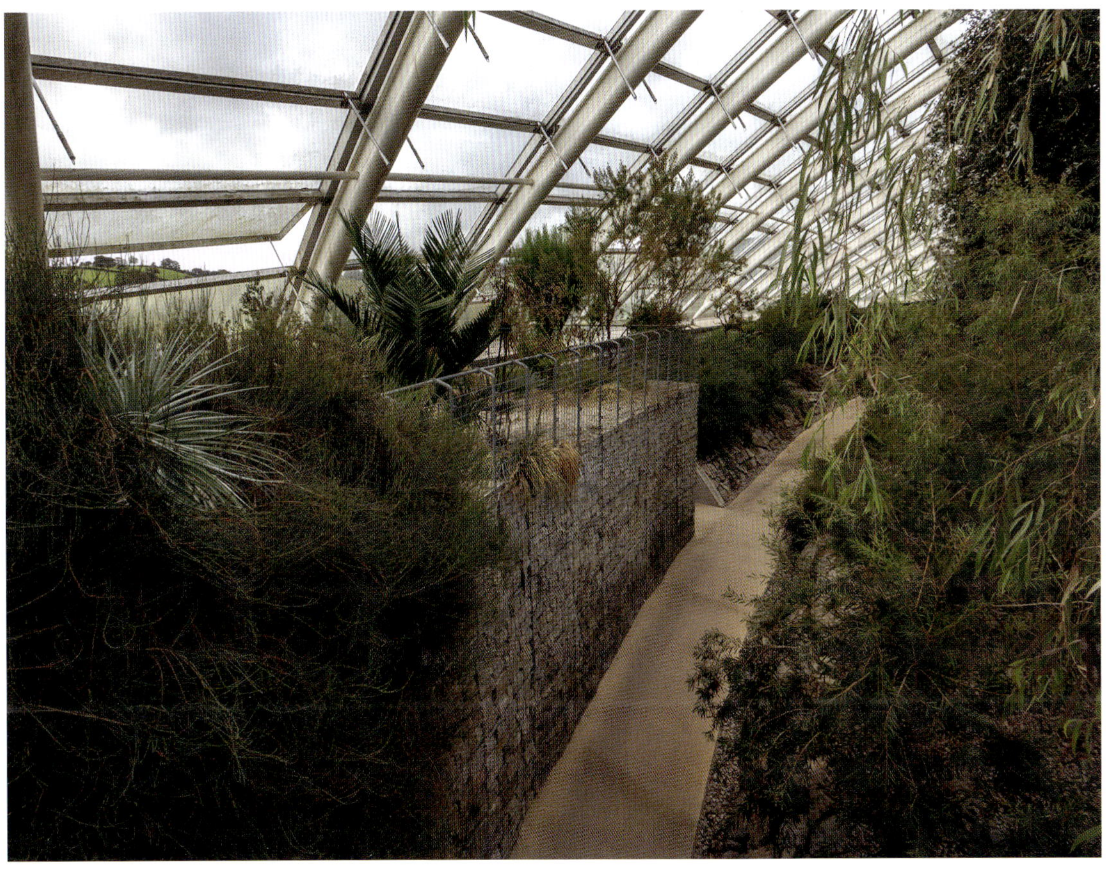

SN 52102 18113

USK, MONMOUTHSHIRE

2016

Every gardening competition Marion Powell enters, she wins.
Having begun by keeping her borders tidy when her children
were small, she expanded her ambitions with a pond then a
greenhouse. Among her accolades is the prestigious Wales in
Bloom's Best Front Garden which she has won three times!

Over the years she has welcomed Alan Titchmarsh, the
Duchess of Cornwall and a host of TV weather presenters.

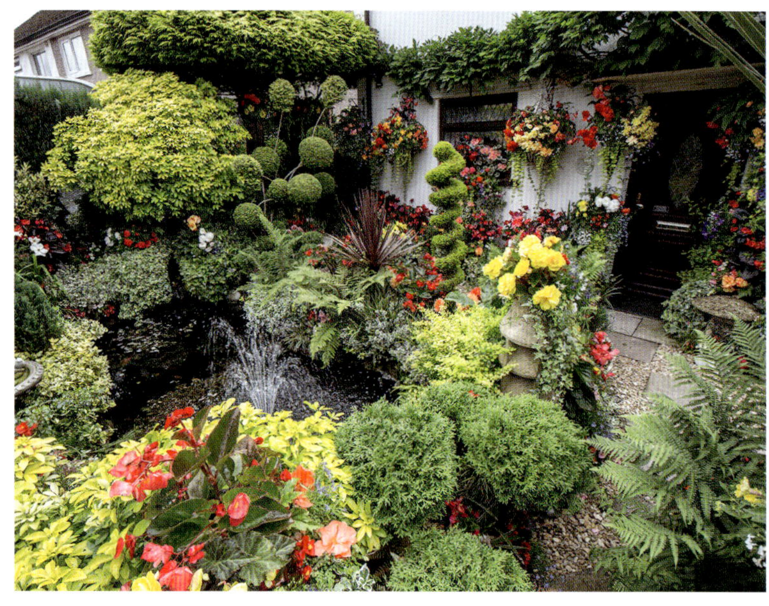

SO 38014 01281

TINTERN, MONMOUTHSHIRE

2018

"I dislike landscapes.
I only like people and plastic flowers".
– Elliott Erwitt, photographer

Inventive, inexpensive, instant, low maintenance and resilient.
Not all are plastic, some are fabric.

What's not to like?

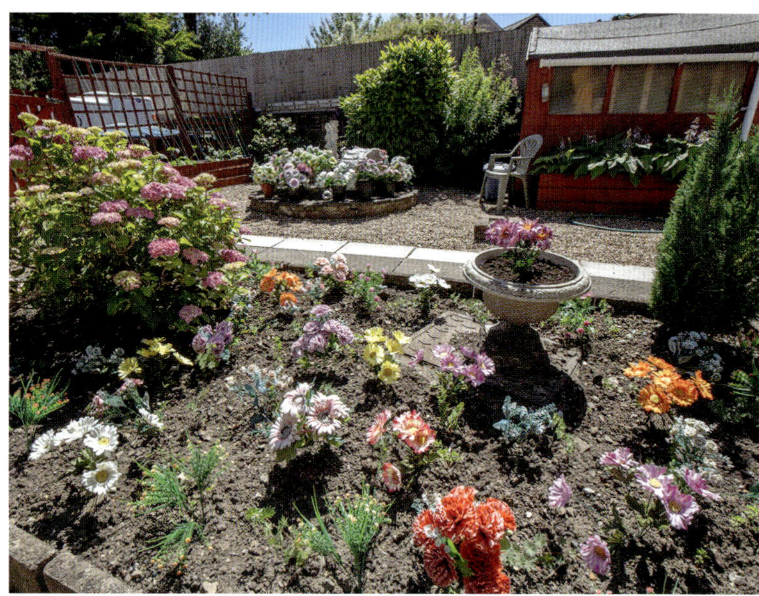

SO 52997 00189

GILWERN, MONMOUTHSHIRE

2016

A creative transformation of tiered walls on a section of the 35-mile Monmouthshire and Brecon Canal, considered to be one of the most scenic waterways in the UK.

The bank provides a modern-day take on the mileposts, weight restrictions and tunnel entrance signs once fitted along the 35-mile waterway, designed by the engineering mastermind Thomas Dadford Jr, who died aged just 40 and is buried a few miles away.

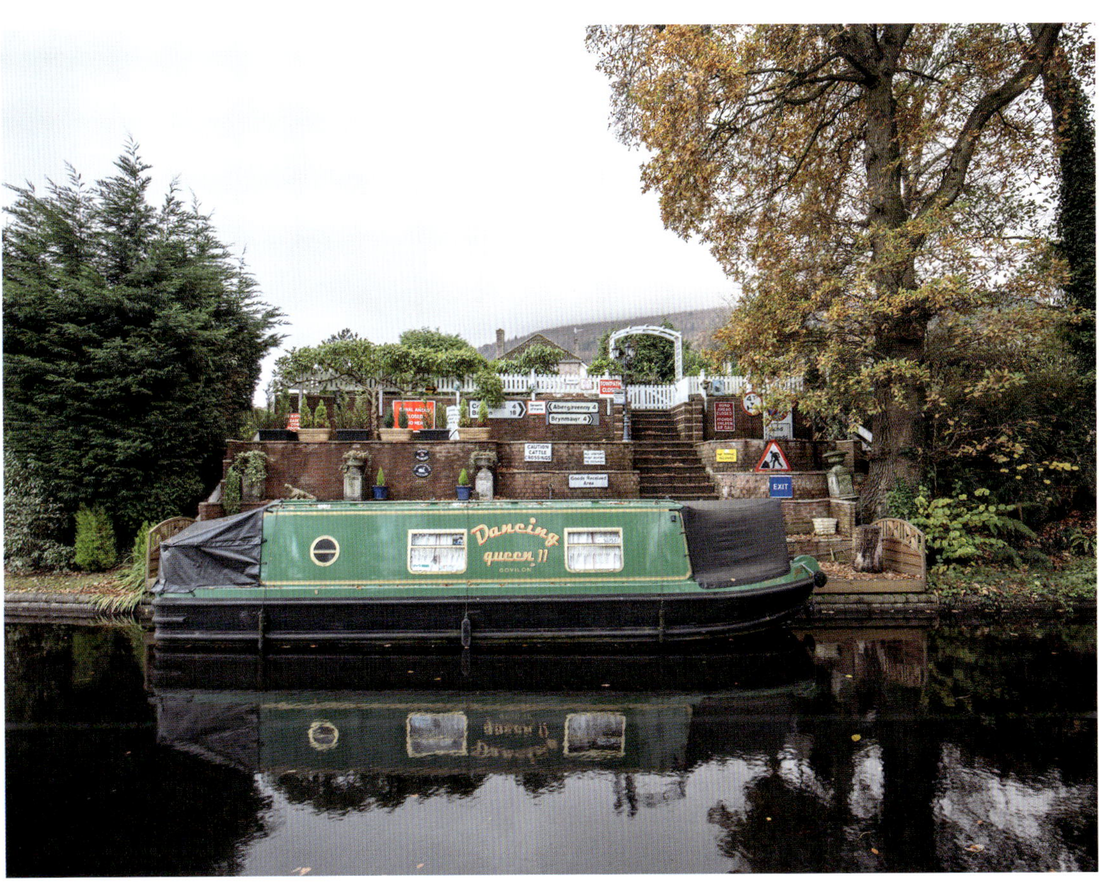

SO 24151 14801

It is said the daffodils can be used to produce a drug called galantamine
to fight Alzheimer's disease.

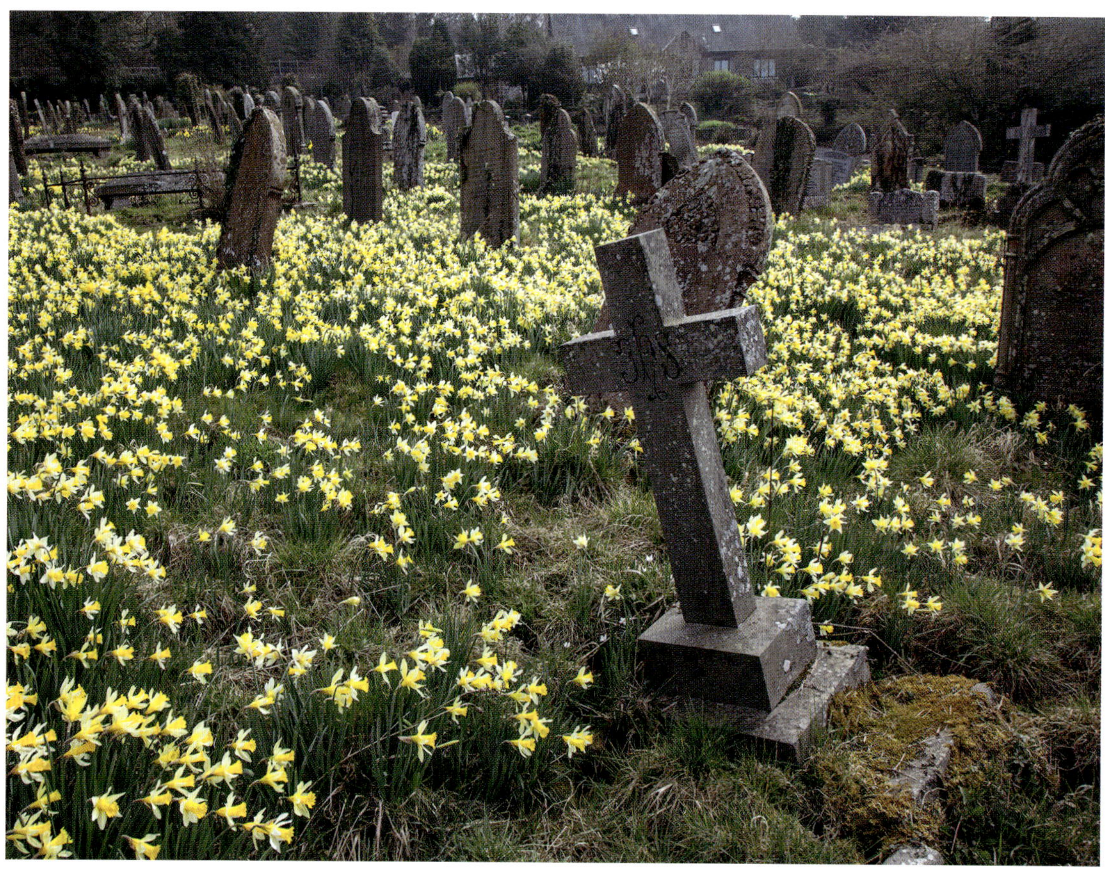

OS 17686 38509

The man-made waterfall on the estate of botanist and pioneering photographer John Dillwyn Llewelyn remains virtually unchanged in over 140 years.

Once one of the great gardens of Britain, Penllergare fell into dereliction and remained unattended for 60 years before a Trust was set up to restore it.

Twenty years later, its miles of woodland and lakes are visited by more than 150,000 people a year.

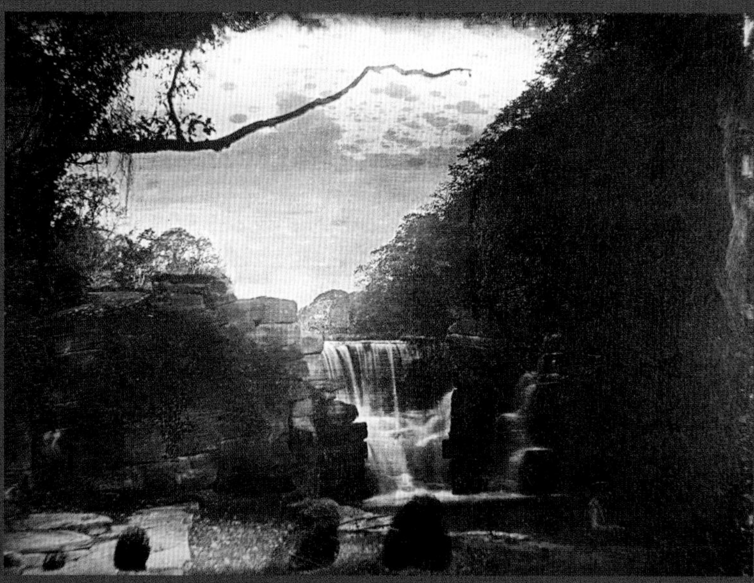

John Dillwyn Llewelyn

WATERFALLS

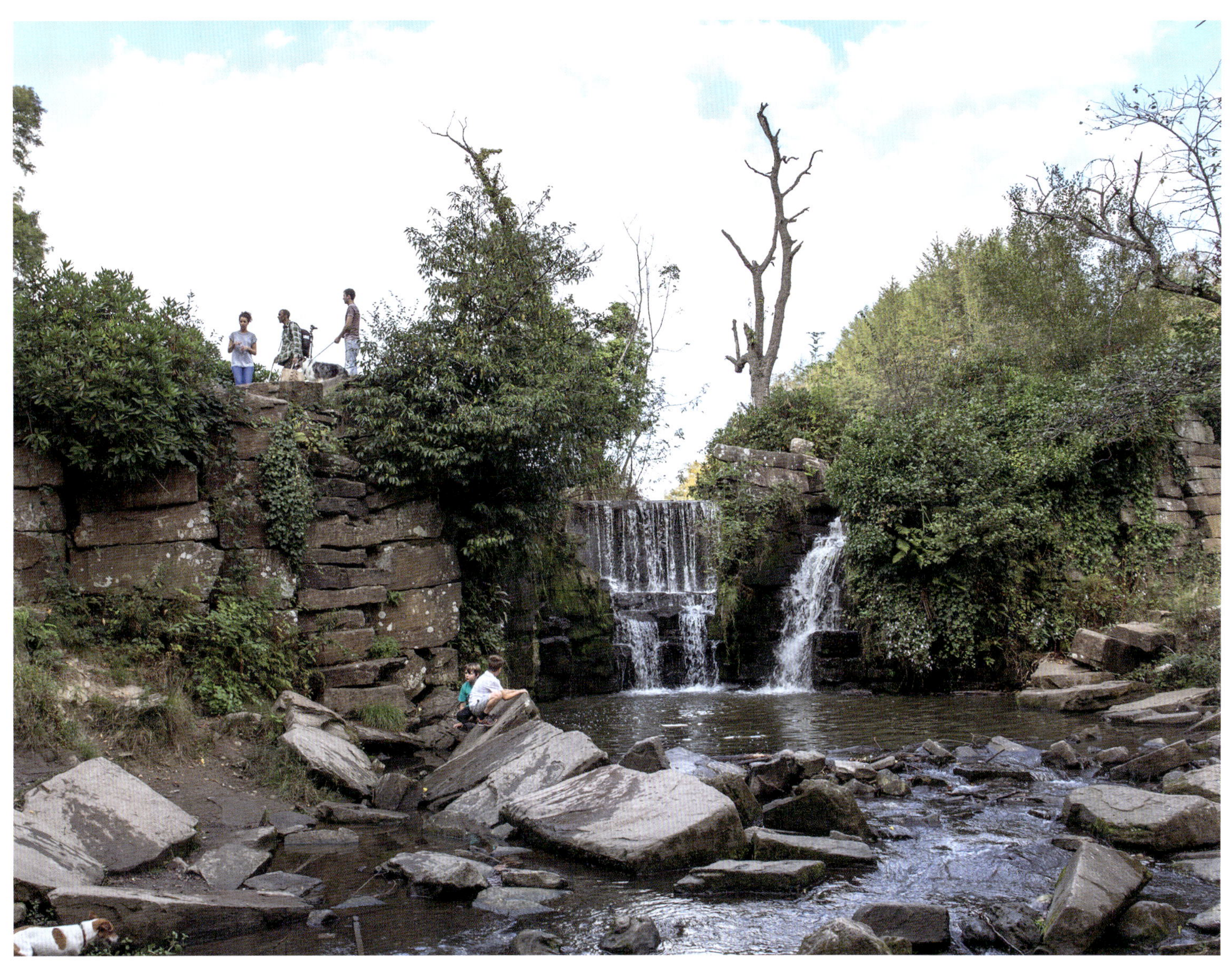

SS 62481 98947

2015

Memorial slabs on trees overlooking the UK's biggest-single drop waterfall where the Afon Rhaeadr plunged 240-feet off a cliff-face.

It is counted as one of the Seven Wonders of Wales and the country's 1,000th SSSI. In his book entitled *Wild Wales*, nineteenth century author George Borrow wrote:

"What shall I liken it to? I scarcely know, unless it is to an immense skein of silk agitated and disturbed by tempestuous blasts, or to the long tail of a grey courser at furious speed. I never saw water falling so gracefully, so much like thin, beautiful threads as here."

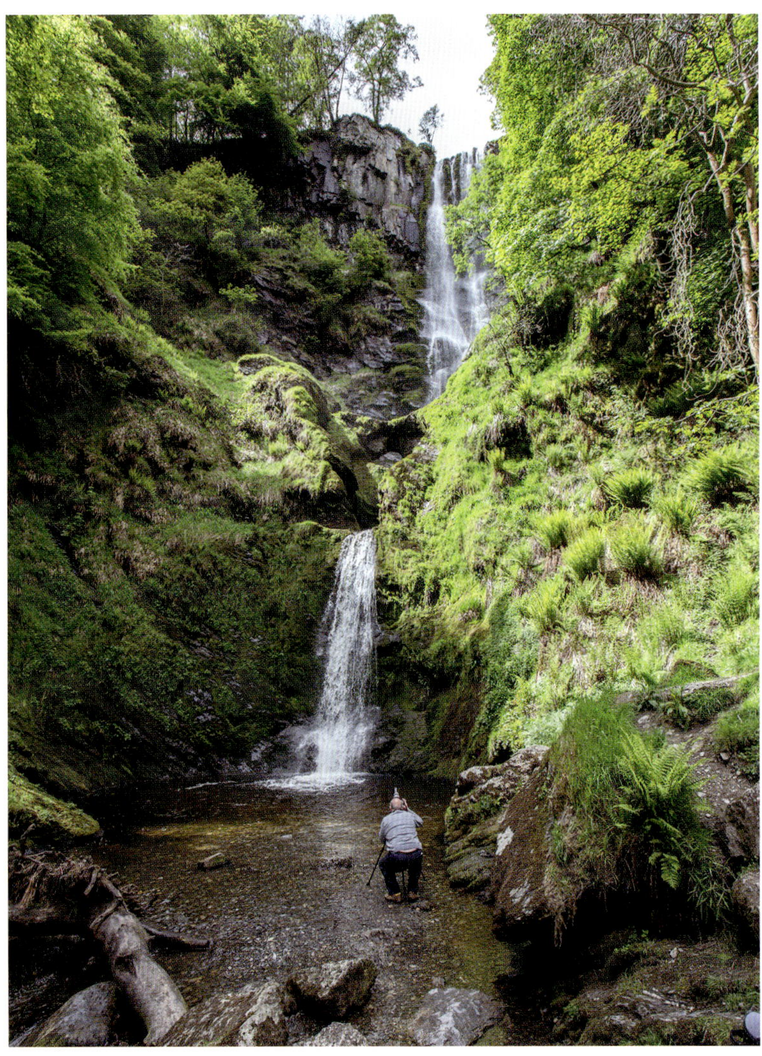

SJ 07344 29486

2015

Wales' highest waterfall cascade 90ft over a sandstone edge known as 'Farewell Rock' within a wooded gorge on the southern end of the Bannau Brycheiniog's Nant Llech valley.

The waterfall in drought reveals the entrance to Batman's cave featured in the final scene of *The Dark Knight Rises*.

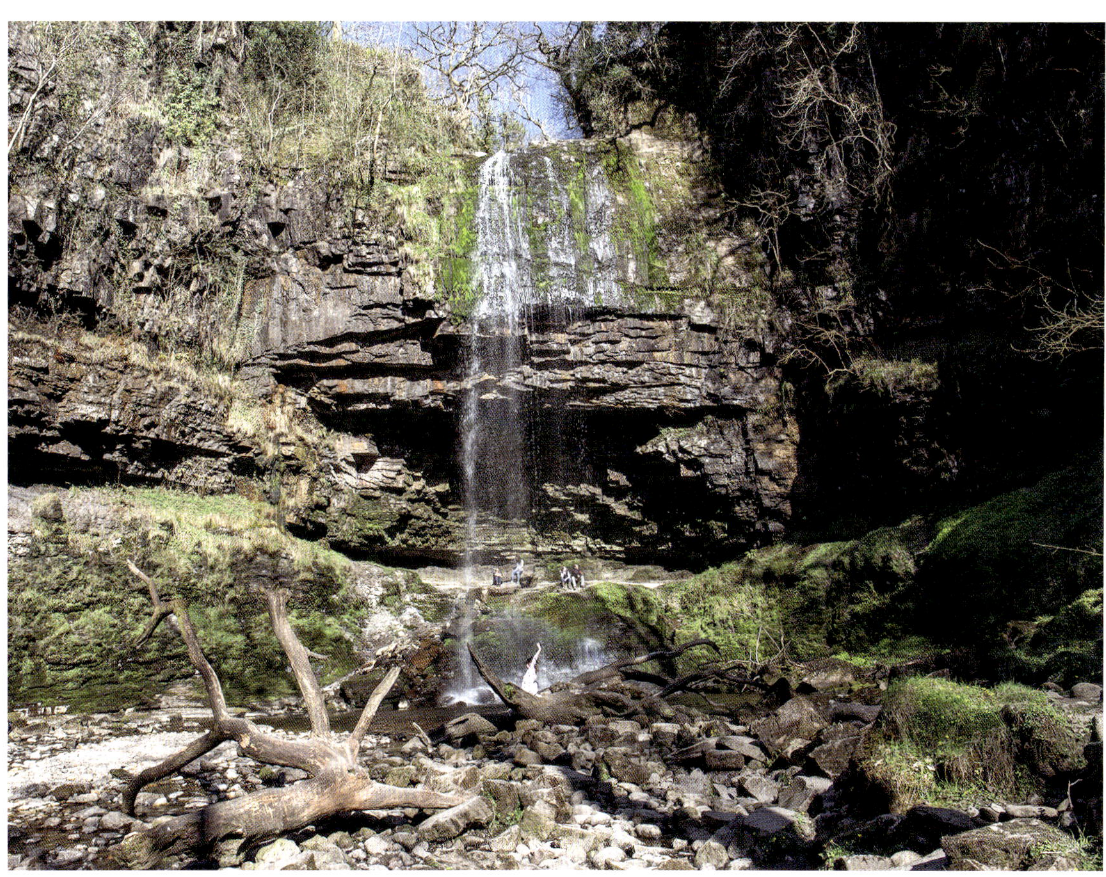

SN 85322 11851

How Swallow Falls came by its name is not clear. The 42-metre torrent – made up of multiple streams from the River Llugwy – is split at one point by a large rock from which the water flows in the shape of a swallow's tail. Another theory is that in Welsh it is known as Rhaeadr Ewynnol which translates to 'foaming waterfall' and, at some point, a confusion arose over the word 'wennol' meaning swallow.

In 1913 a charge was introduced to view it in order to pay for the installation of water and electricity supply to the nearby village. The charge continued long after the costs were covered, resulting in the area boasting the lowest bills in the country.

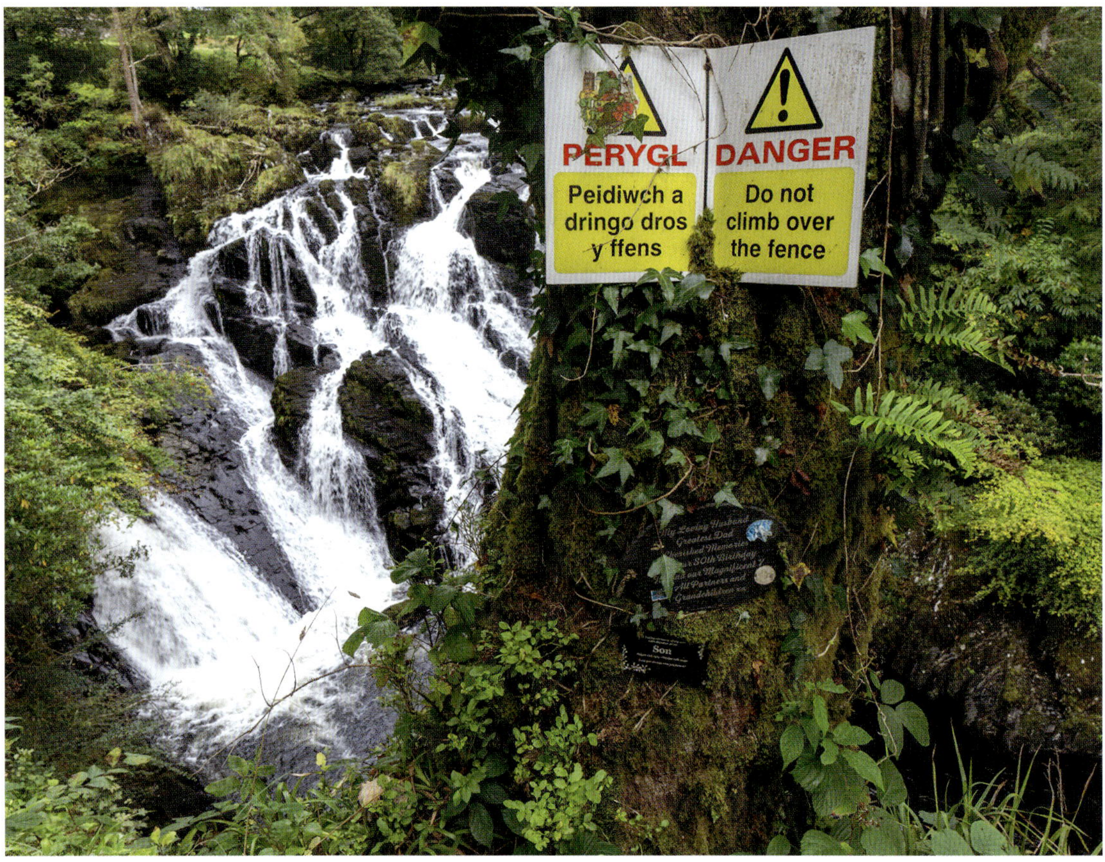

SH 76493 57728

The mountain also known as Snowdon is Wales' highest point.

Standing on its peak on a clear day, visibility stretches down to Pembrokeshire, up to the Peak District in England and across to Ireland.

COMPASS POINTS

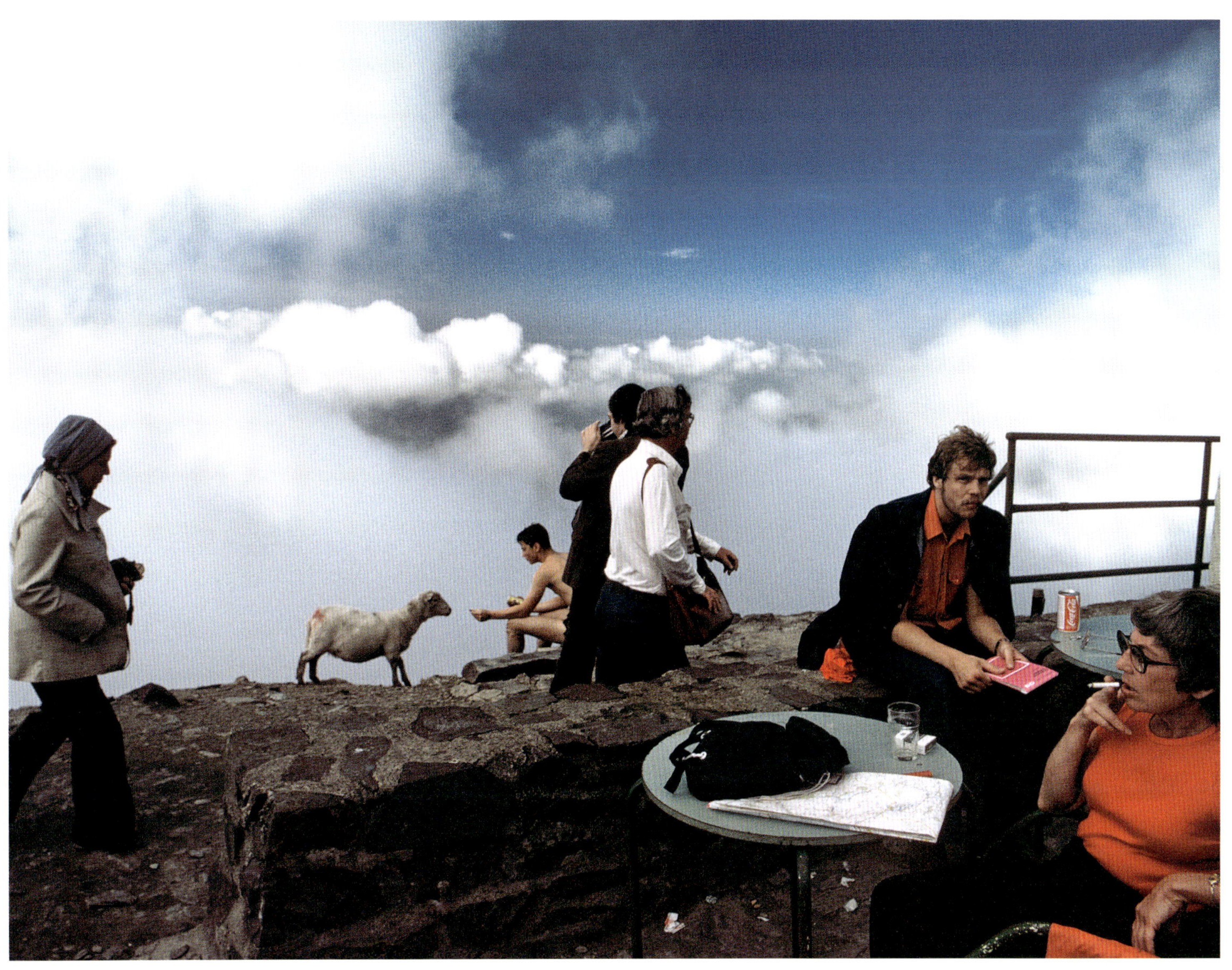

SH 61016 54389

POINT OF AYR LIGHTHOUSE, FLINTSHIRE

2018

Also known as Talacre Lighthouse, the Grade Two listed beacon built in 1776 stands at Wales' most northerly point.

A ghost story featuring its last keeper inspired the installation of a seven-foot stainless steel figure looking out from its balcony to the Irish Sea.

The sculpture was removed in 2012 when planning permission for the figure expired.

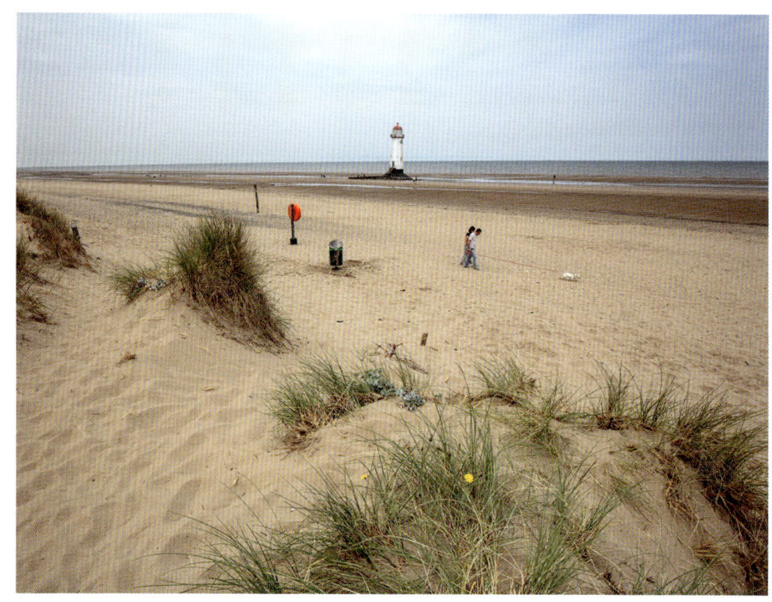

SJ 12198 85124

RHOOSE POINT, VALE OF GLAMORGAN

2013

A stone circle and slate obelisk officially mark the most southerly point in mainland Wales although some argue it should be at nearby Breaksea Point.

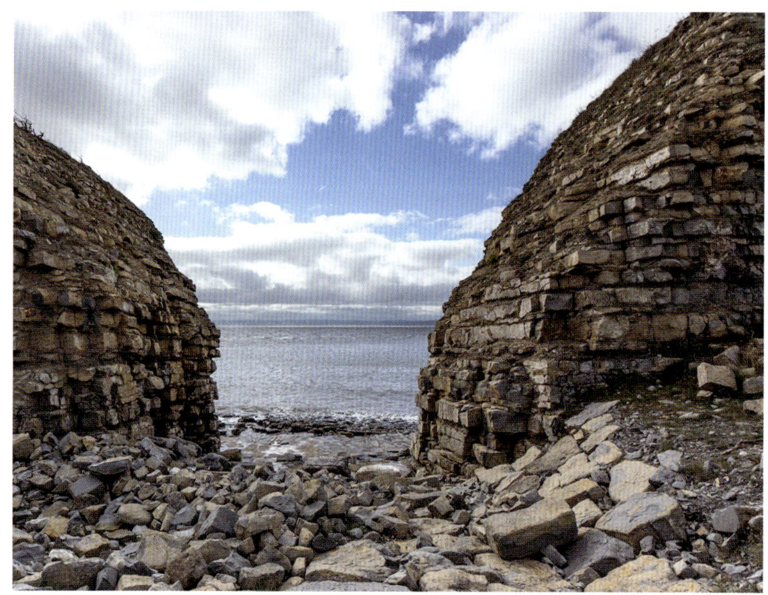

SS 38526 33650

LADY PARK WOOD, MONMOUTHSHIRE

2014

Straddling the border with Gloucestershire in England, this national nature reserve of ancient broadleaved woodland is Wales' most easterly point, named after the estate to which it formerly belonged.

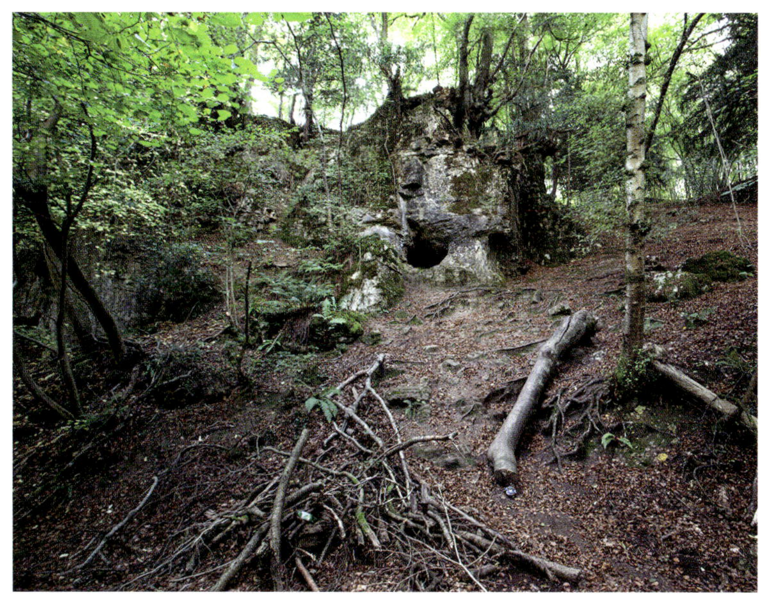

SO 55235 14310

PEN DAL-ADERYN, PEMBROKSHIRE

2018

Protruding from the convolutions of the Pembrokeshire Coast National Park, 'bird-catching head' south of St David's Head, marks the mainland's most westerly point.

Next stop Ireland!

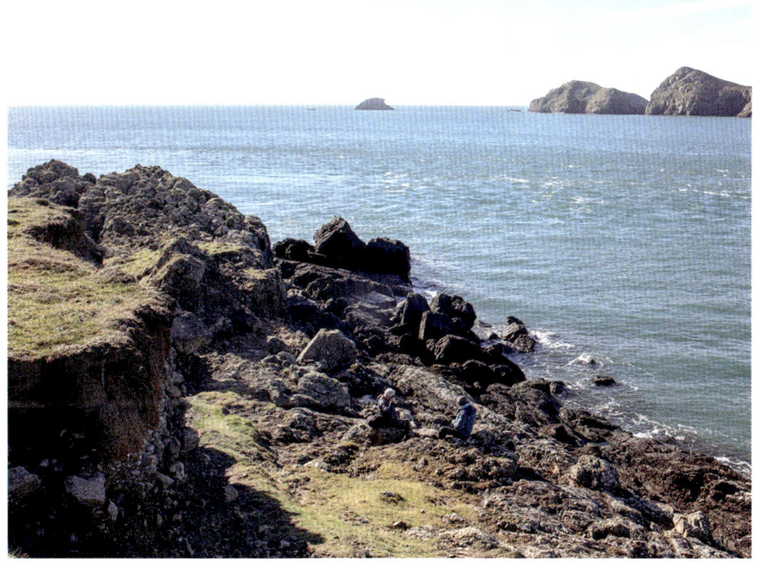

SM 71540 23387

2018

Seemingly marked with a flag, the centre of Wales is about 2.5km (1.5 miles) from the village near Devil's Bridge, according to calculations by the Ordnance Survey.

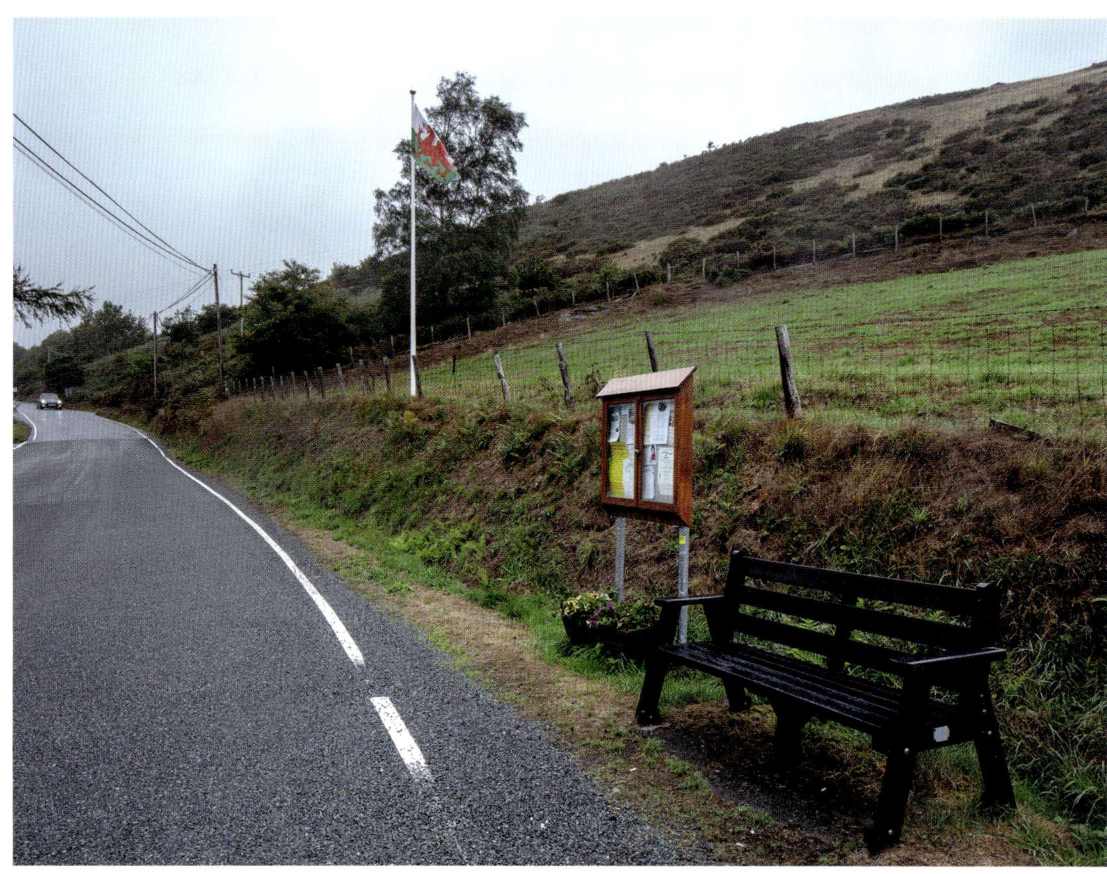

SN 78188 74214

At the highest tides, this village near the city of Newport lies below sea level and is protected by a labyrinth of drains and ditches. In the local church there is a plaque in memory to the 22 who lost their lives in the great Bristol Channel flood of 1607.

The disaster caused the largest loss of life – between 500 and 2,000 – from any sudden natural disaster in the UK within the past 500 years and there are arguments as to its cause, tsunami or storm surge.

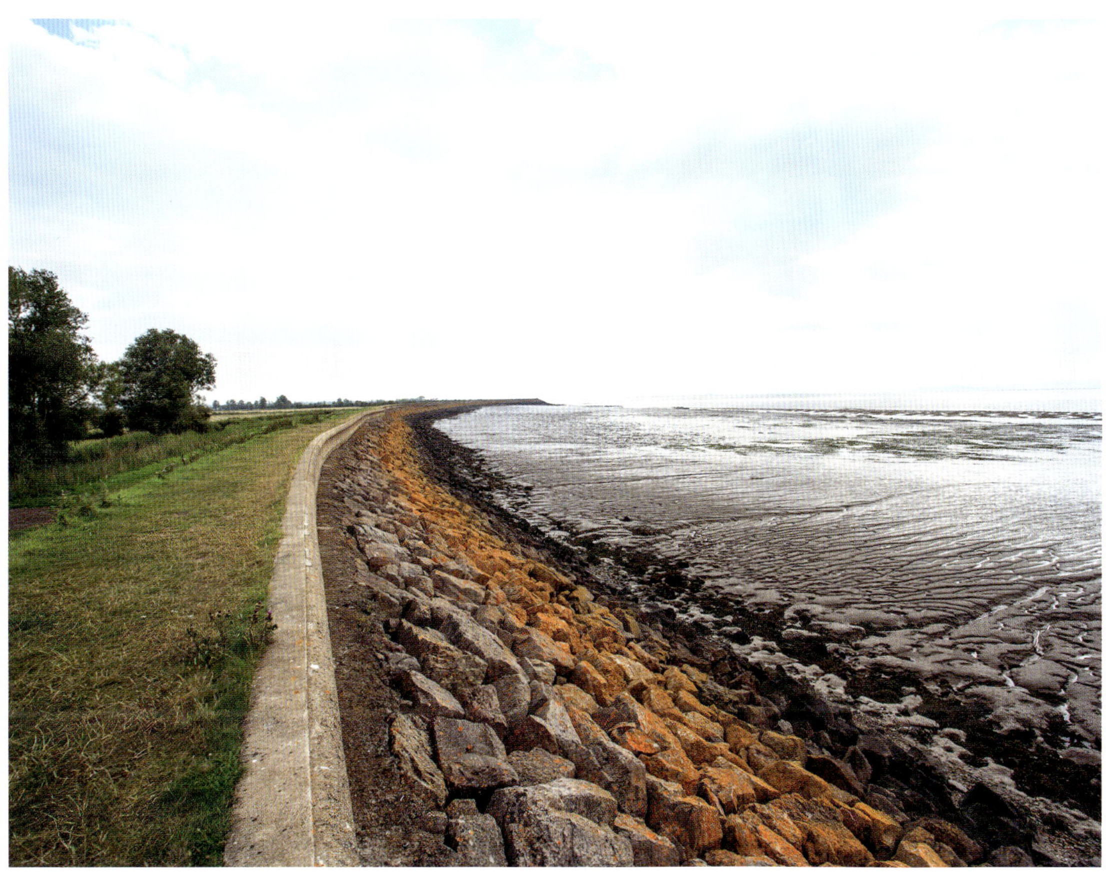

ST 37520 82166

Earth sculpture entitled 'Fold' by Trudi Entwistle.

"Inspired by an exploration of plant material, I wanted to use grass in a unique and geometric way. A ripple through a meadow on the hillside was the result. These sculptural folds in the earth provide a place to nestle and an excuse to spend time in the meadow."

ARTISTS

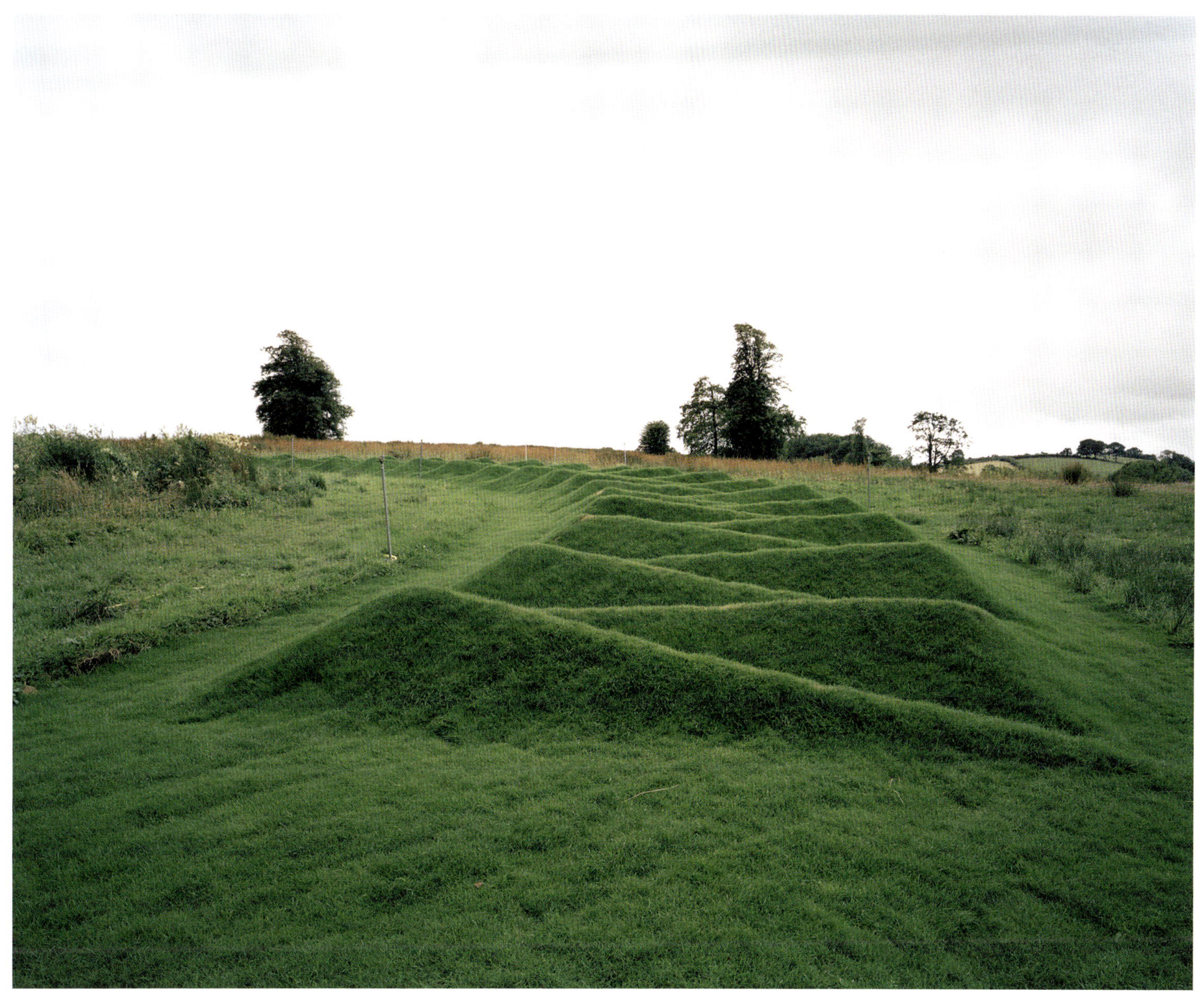

SN 52137 17920

'BOUND', MONMOUTH

2007

Wrapped trees by Philippa Lawrence:

"The work linked to my interest in Japanese packaging and their aesthetic regarding wrapping and packaging. I had previously been interested in placing work outside of the gallery and to quote Christo was also 'revealing through concealing'. Binding the tree in cloth I freed the form and could it offer back to the public to see anew. It followed a concern with unearthing qualities in the commonplace that were worthy of note and were mainly overlooked. Bound referred to the process of binding and swathing the trees in cloth, to the time and intention in making the work – and connecting to place and also to boundaries."

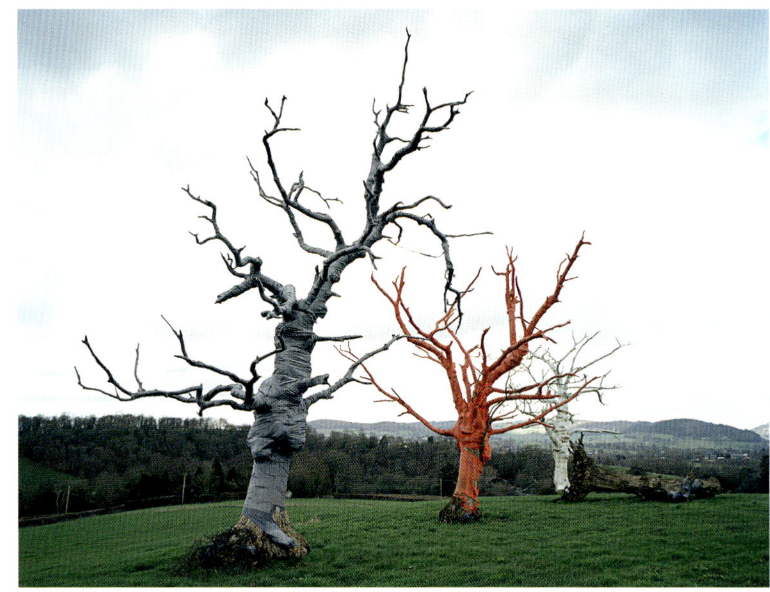

SO 50617 11102

2014

The dead trees unwrapped.

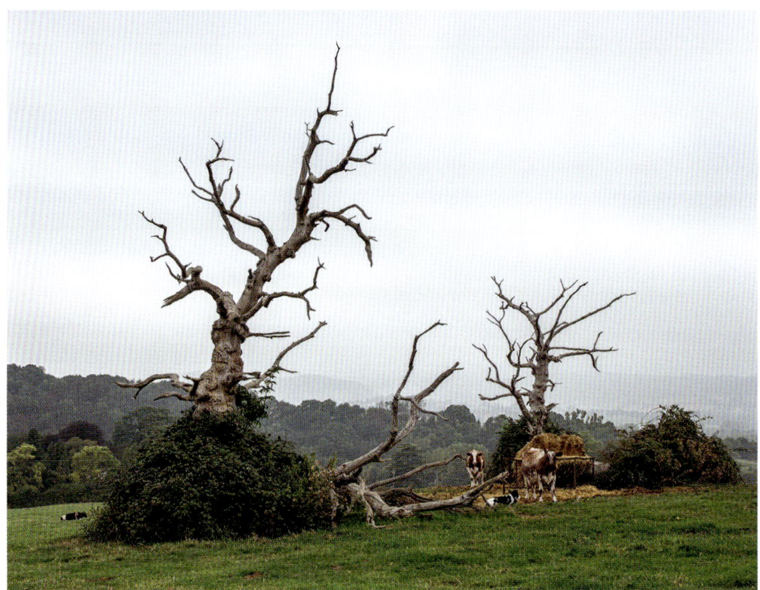

SO 50617 11102

A Facebook post from the owner of a Slovenian garden centre:

"It took seed before the British Empire and is older than the United States, but the 46ft tall yew hedge is still wowing visitors to a
National Trust property – thanks to a dedicated team of gardeners…

"The 14 yew trees, named 'the tumps' were planted in the 1720s by the second Marquess. They were kept intricately clipped for about 100 years,
until in the early 1800s, Powis passed first to the son, then the grandson of Robert Clive, the man who brought India into
the British Empire."

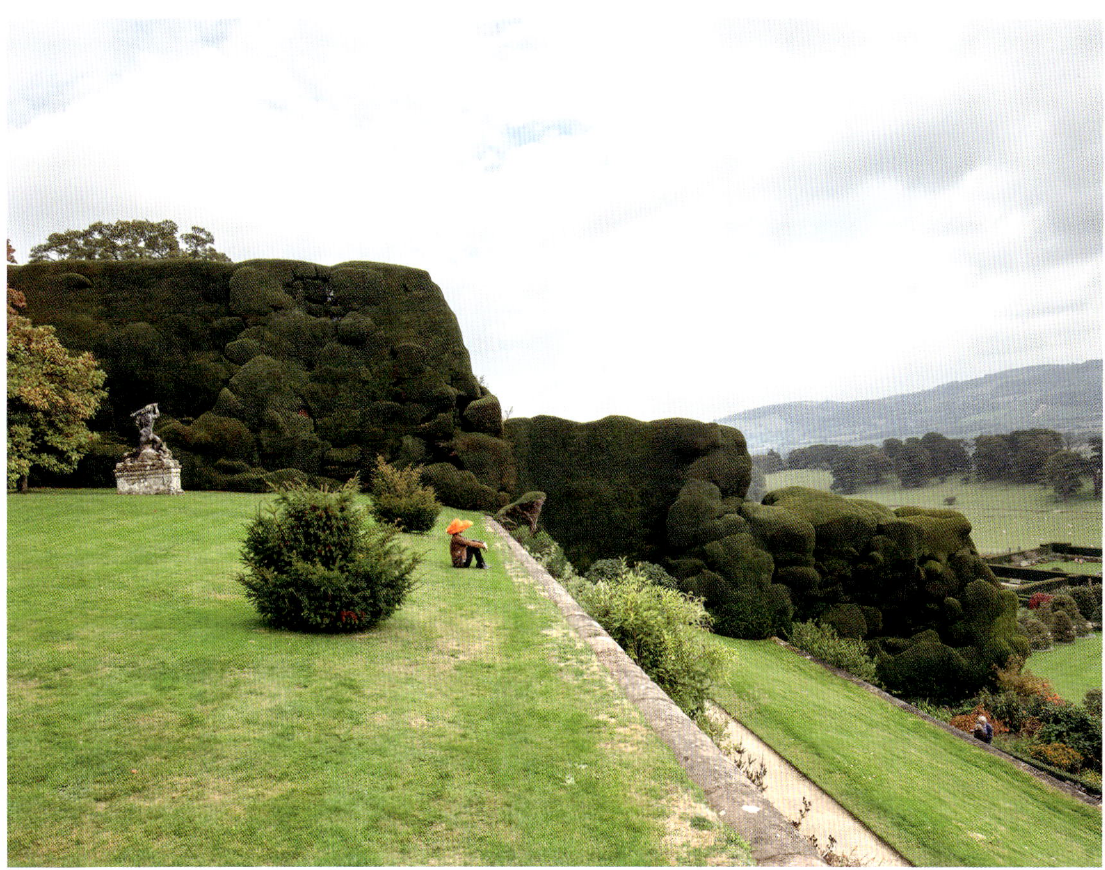

SJ 21640 06470

WILCRICK, NEWPORT

2011

An everyday line of electricity pylons. Here they are reminiscent
of the exquisite geometry and eye-drawing perspective of
Meindert Hobbema's *The Avenue at Middelharnis*, a masterpiece
of the Dutch golden age, painted in 1869 and said to have inspired
Vincent Van Gogh and David Hockney.

The presence of pylons – the original design by the Miliken brothers
in the 1920s having changed little over the years – continues to
divide opinion.

To some they are elegant sculptures, to others a blot on the landscape.

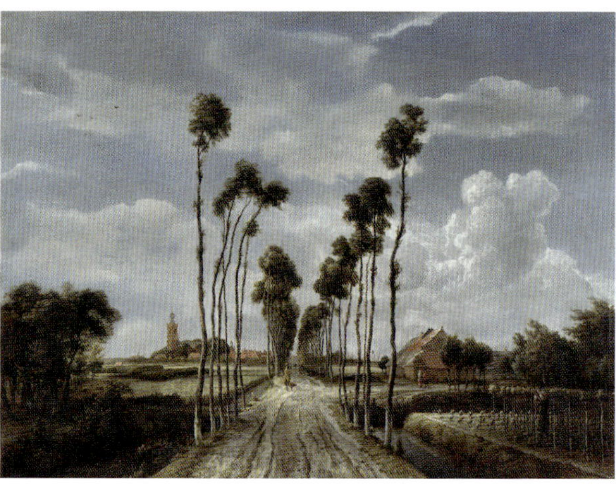

Meindert Hobbema, The Avenue at Middleharnis, 1689
The National Gallery

ST 39783 85655

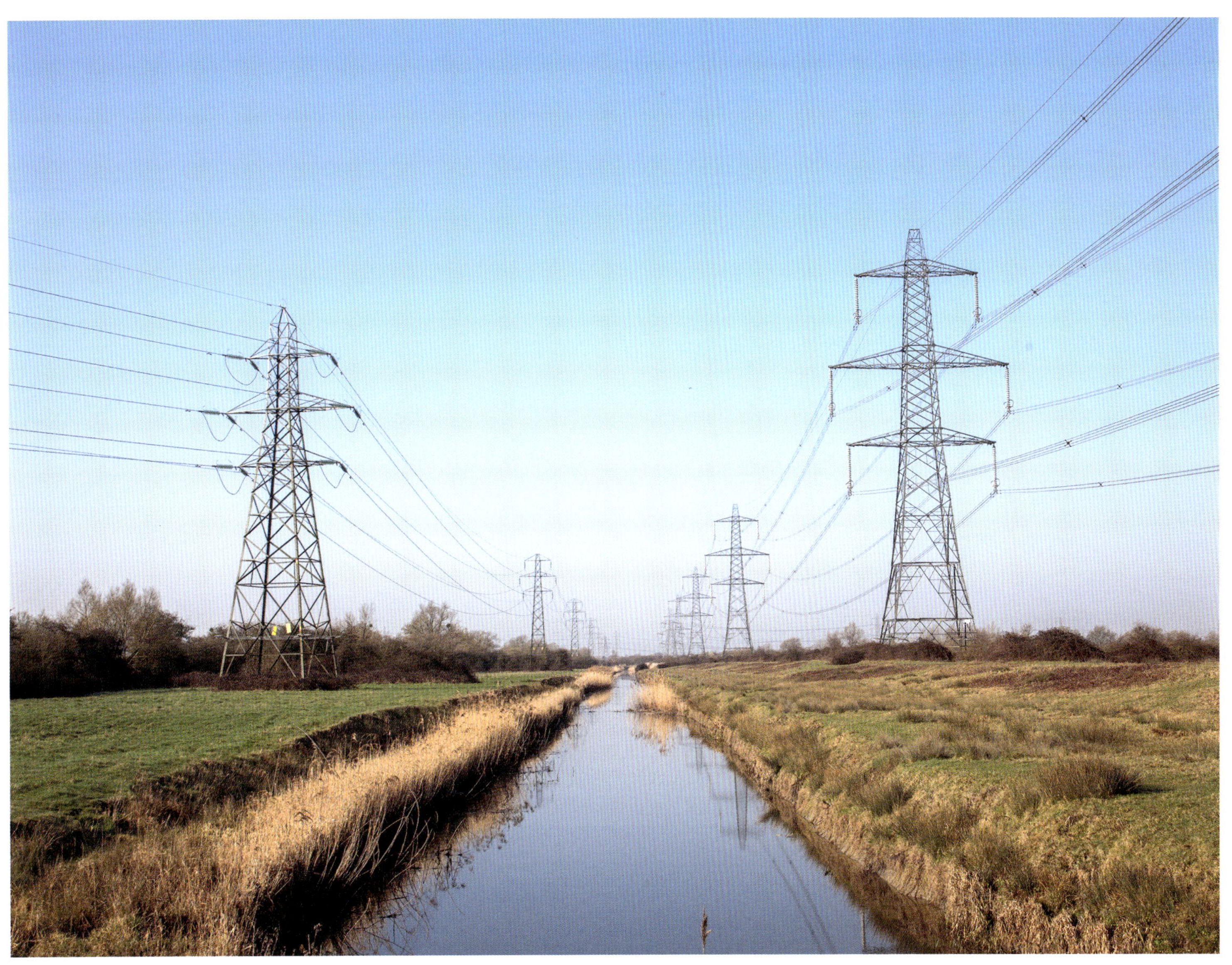

ST 39783 85655

A tale of Christmas past.

The tree, like many treasured memories brought to mind during the holidays, is no longer around, but the traditional dressing of its ailing trunk still glimmers as brightly in the minds of so many who loved it.

In the mind of this photographer in particular.

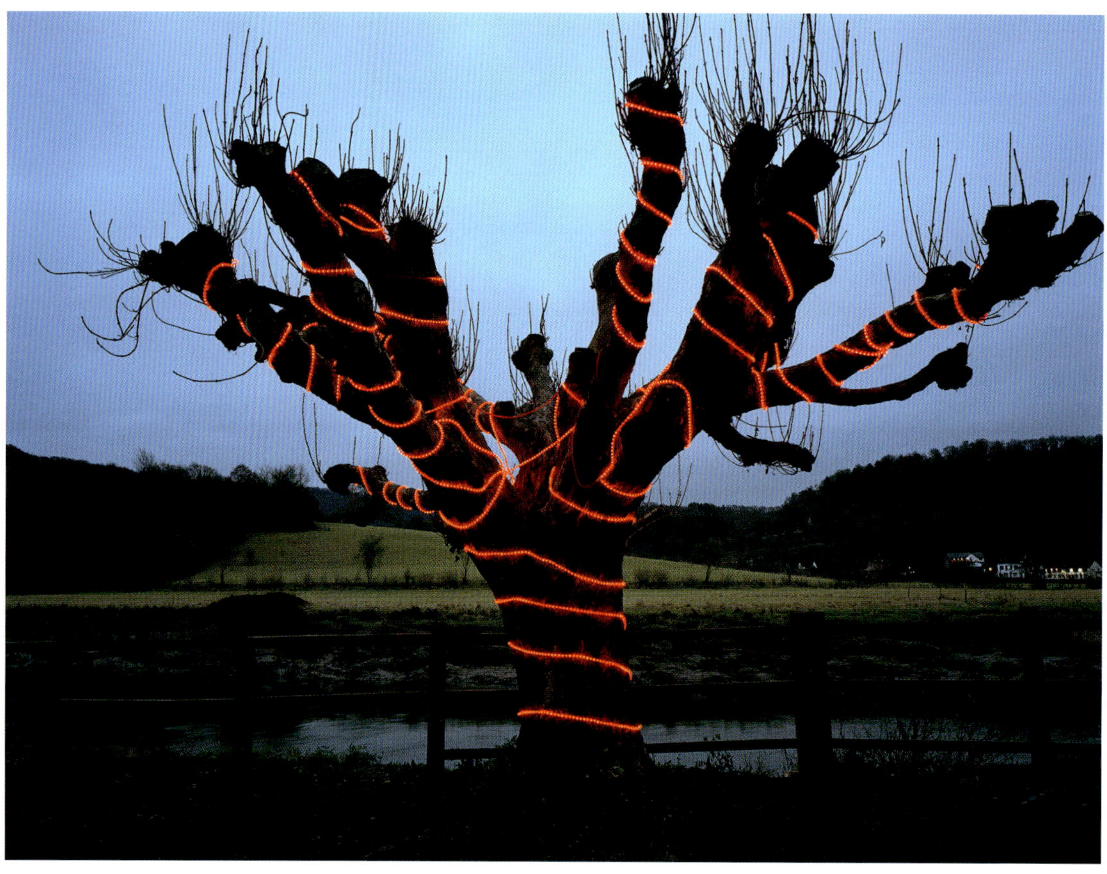

SO 52897 00766

2015

"Pot bunker: small, deep and round; easy to enter, hard to escape." – Royal Porthcawl Golf Course.

This design on one of Wales' oldest golf courses – the club founded in 1891 by the wheelers and dealers of Cardiff's booming coal port – conveys an air of menace akin to a bomb or small meteor impact crater.

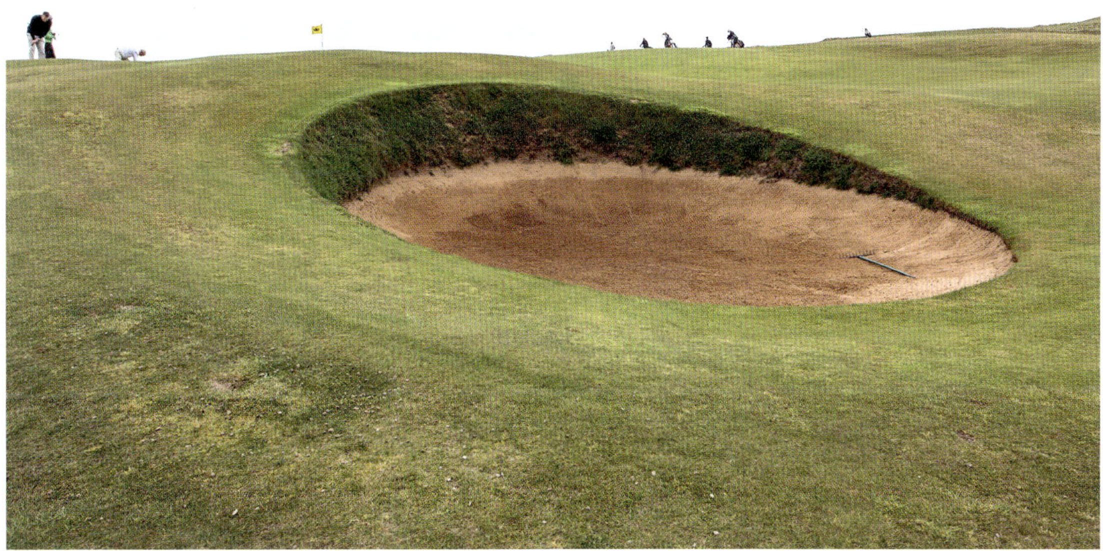

SS 90718 82902

DOLOSSE, COLWYN BAY, CONWY

2017

I am happy to interpret this as one of the best examples of sculpture in Wales.

A total of 22,000 concrete geometric forms, each weighing five tonnes, were laid during the construction of the A55 in the 1980s to protect the road from the breakwater during most severe storms. A type of tetrapod, their interlocking design works in harmony with the sea, dispersing energy from waves with each dolos numbered so movements can be tracked.

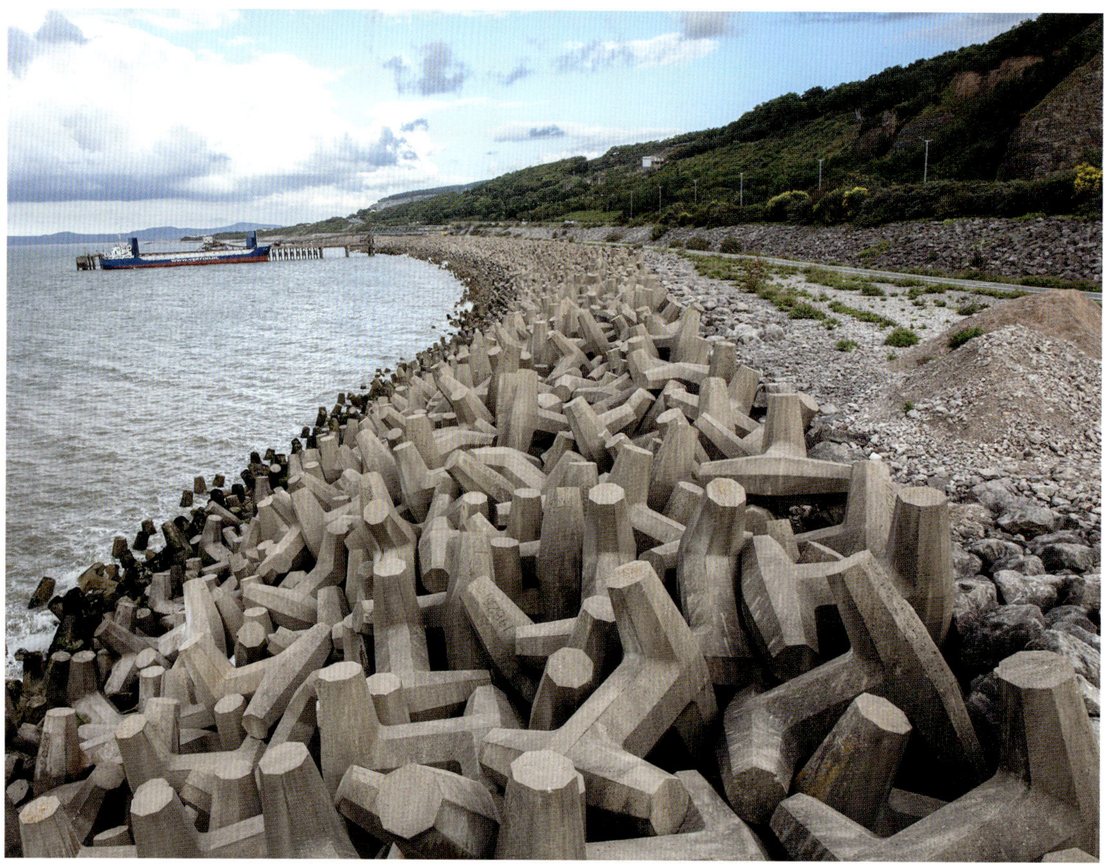

SH 88169 78783

PORTHCAWL, BRIDGEND

2011

In 1984 tarmac was laid on Porthcawl beach to defend the promenade from the sea. It was originally covered with a layer of sand to disguise its appearance but, perhaps unsurprisingly, this was instantly swept away by the first incoming tide.

The infamous 'tarmac beach' remained until 2018 when Bridgend County Council began a new £3 million flood defence project to replace it with more aesthetically pleasing sand-coloured concrete terraces and 'rock armour'.

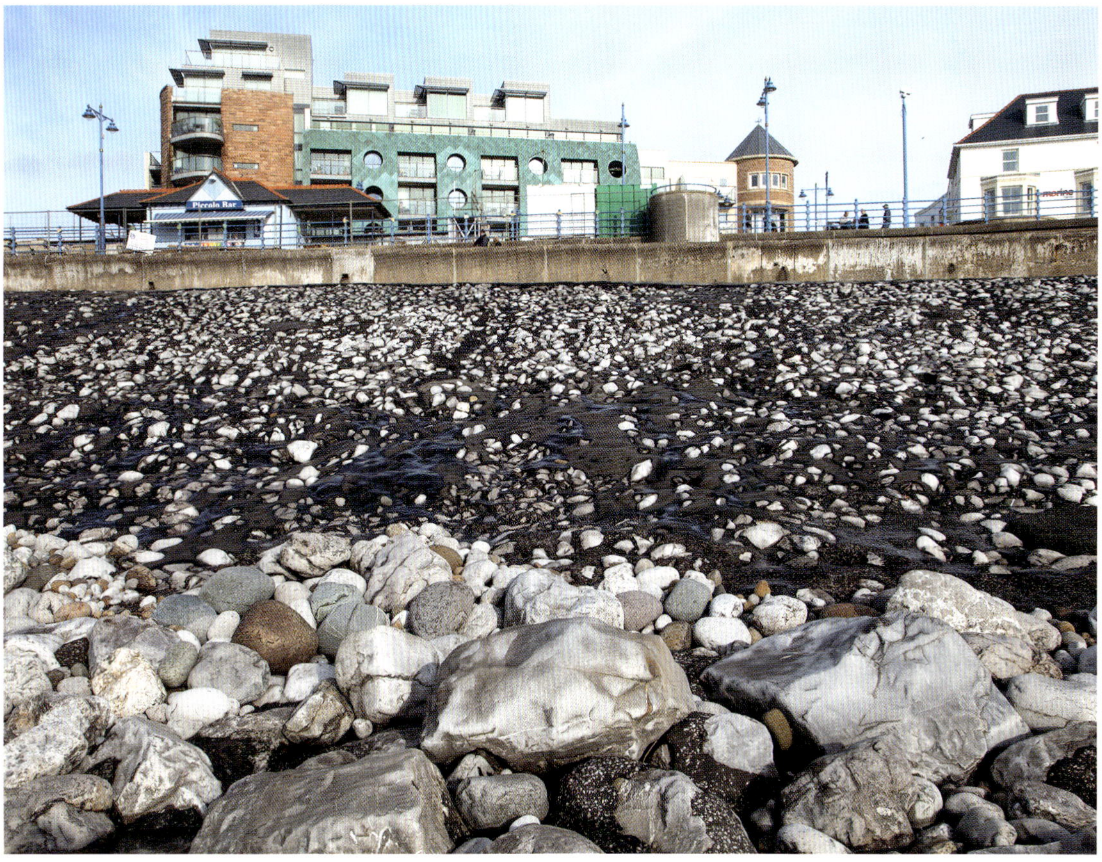

SS 81675 76571

TREHERBERT, RHONDDA CYNON TAF

1993

Naïve sculptures by George Cole, a watchman employed to keep the section of the A4061 which runs over the Rhigos mountain clear of sheep and rocks.

During his sixteen years in post, he became something of a celebrity. So much so, HRH Prince Charles, as he was at the time, stopped by for a photograph. Mr Cole retired in the early 1990s after wire mesh was installed over the mountainside to prevent rock fall.

Perplexingly, his sculptures were not conserved.

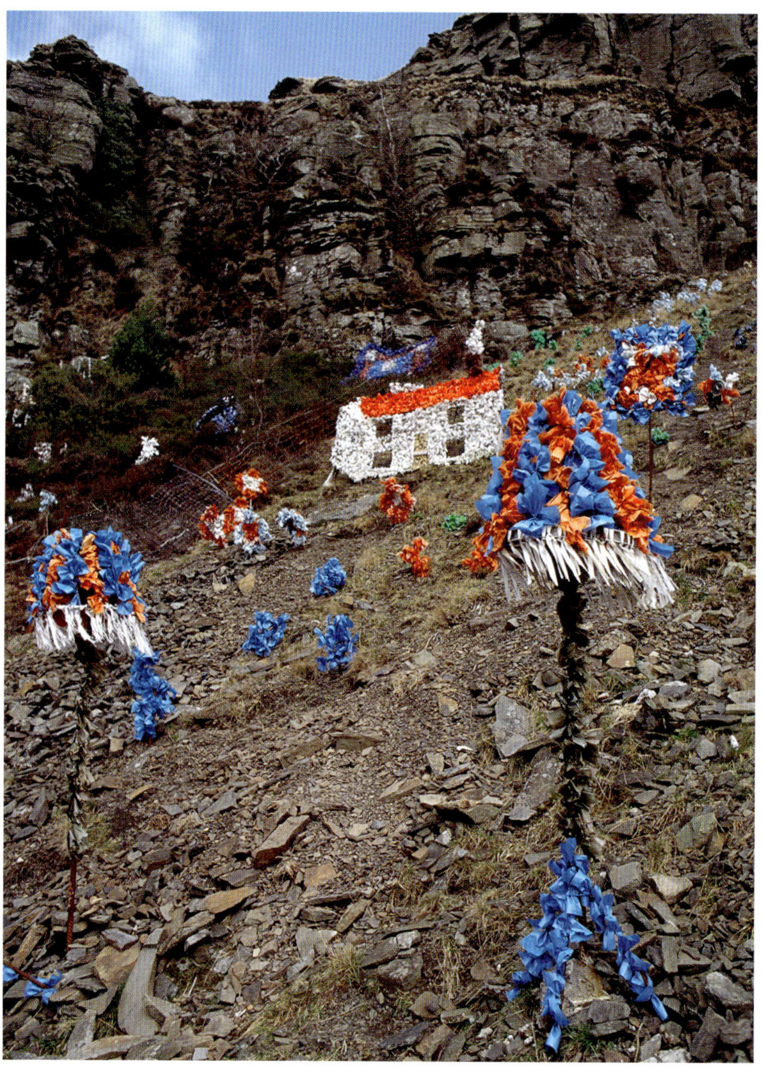

SN 92941 00956

The Huffington Post, February 2013:

Grounded Boat Attracts World's Graffiti Artists To North Wales by Sam Parker

"A grounded boat can be a sad sight, particularly when it's old and rusting to pieces. In North Wales, a former passenger ferry is avoiding that undignified end with the help of several street artists. The Duke of Lancaster has been dug into the Dee estuary in Flintshire since 1979, where it acquired the status of a local landmark. Throughout the early 80s it was used as a bar and market space called 'the Funship' before closing down. Since then, The Duke's hull has attracted graffiti artists from around the world. Eight paintings have been added so far, including works by Hungarian Mr Zero, French artist GOIN and Fin DAC from Ireland.

"Other artworks are the handiwork of street art collective called DuDug – a wordplay on the Welsh for black duke – who now want to turn The Duke into an open-air gallery."

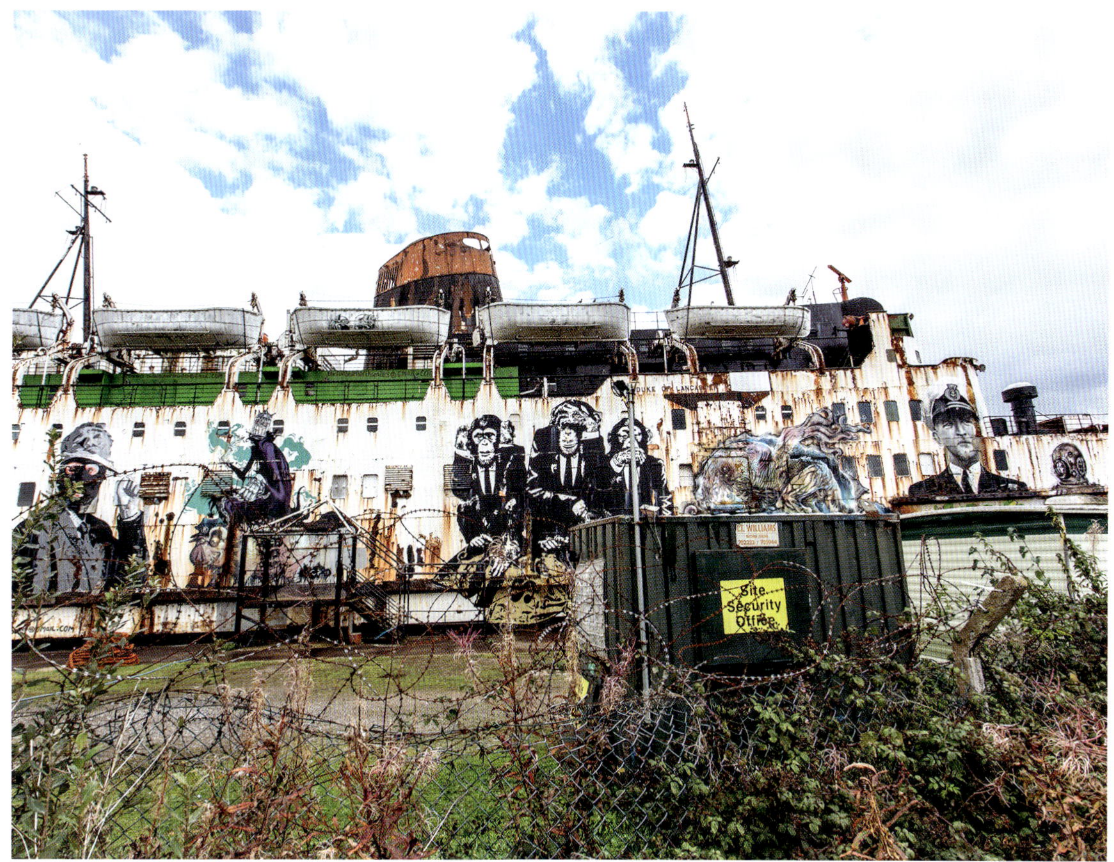

BLACKWOOD MURAL, CAERPHILLY

2015

Seeing something of this quality makes you stop.

A panorama of the Sirhowy and Rhymney Valleys by artist Bryce Davies. To have a mural is fine but to have one this good is extraordinary. Surely it is no more difficult to do it well than to do it badly, nothing to do with technical ability but the endeavour and imagination, of pushing the boundaries of what you are doing to it limits?

Its impact in old and young minds alike, is incalculable.

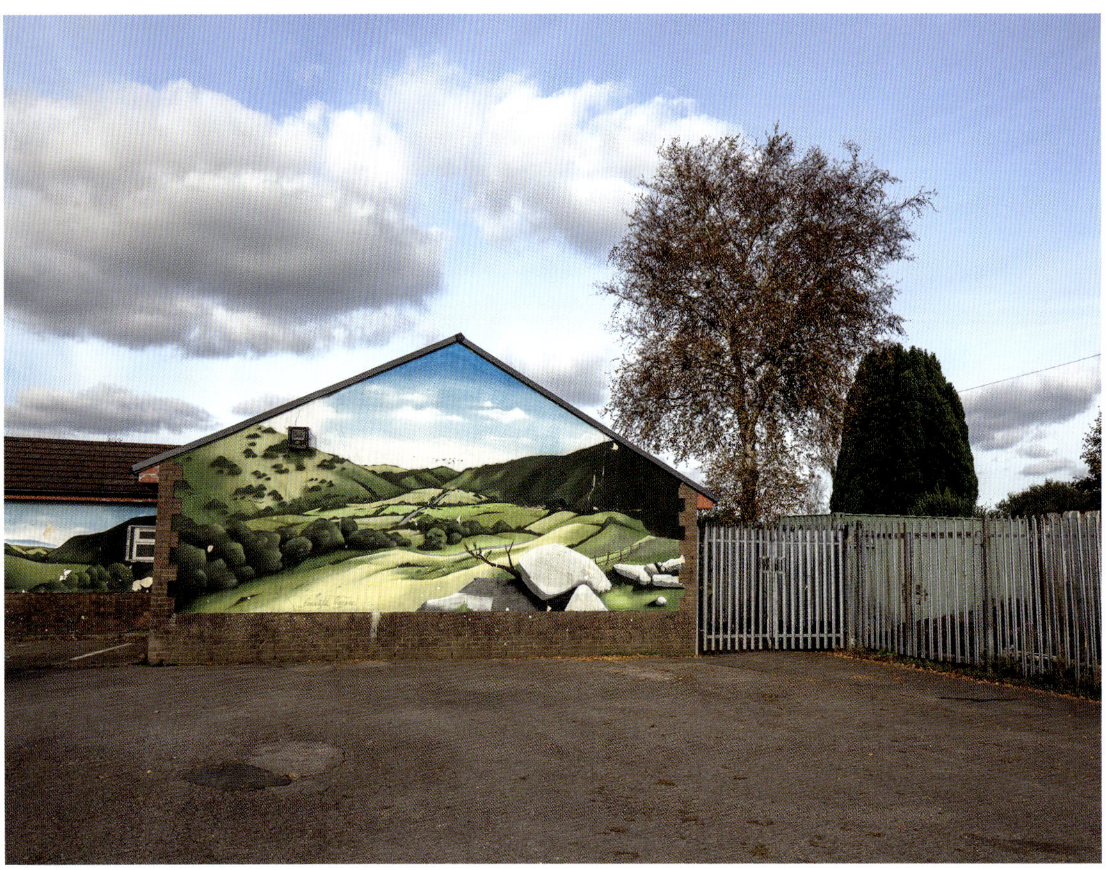

ST 16907 97888

MURAL ON SHOP FRONT, ABERGAVENNY, MONMOUTHSHIRE

2016

Millennium mural in the high street by Frances Baines depicts a background of the town in 2000 while windows into history show key places in the town in 1100 and 1665.

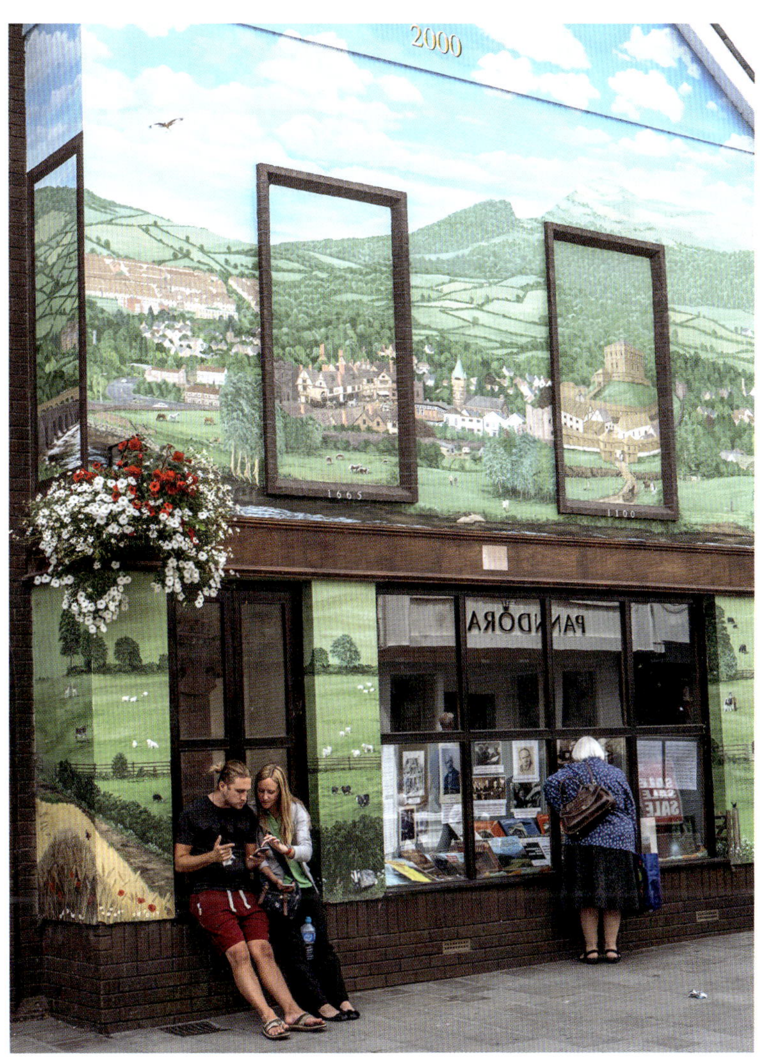

2024

An interesting hotel interior décor choice.

The restaurant had been recommended purely because of its landscape mural of nearby Chepstow Castle.

The food might be good but it never stands a chance of being the most memorable aspect of a visit.

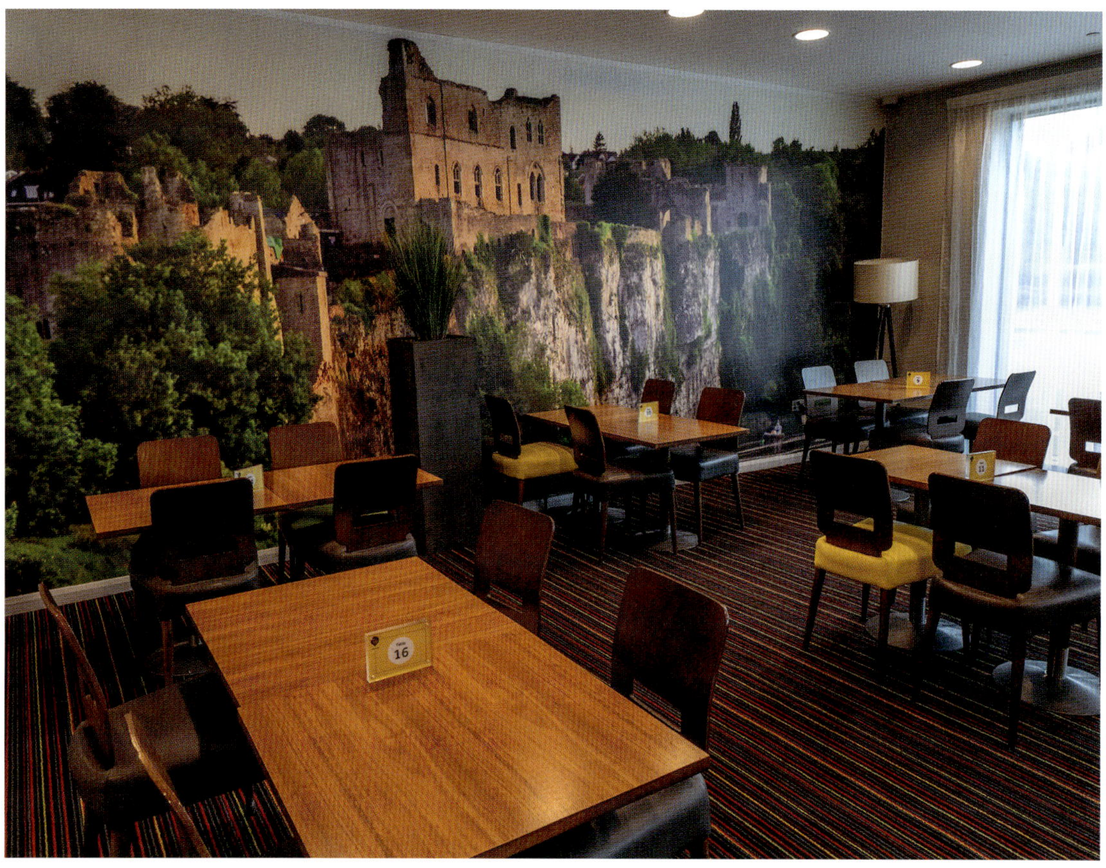

Entrance Ty Hotel   ST 41822 87848

2013

When photographs become a puzzle.

The windows of a Victorian carriage at the Old Station.

What are you looking at? Are you looking at a view through the window?
Or a reflection of a view from behind?

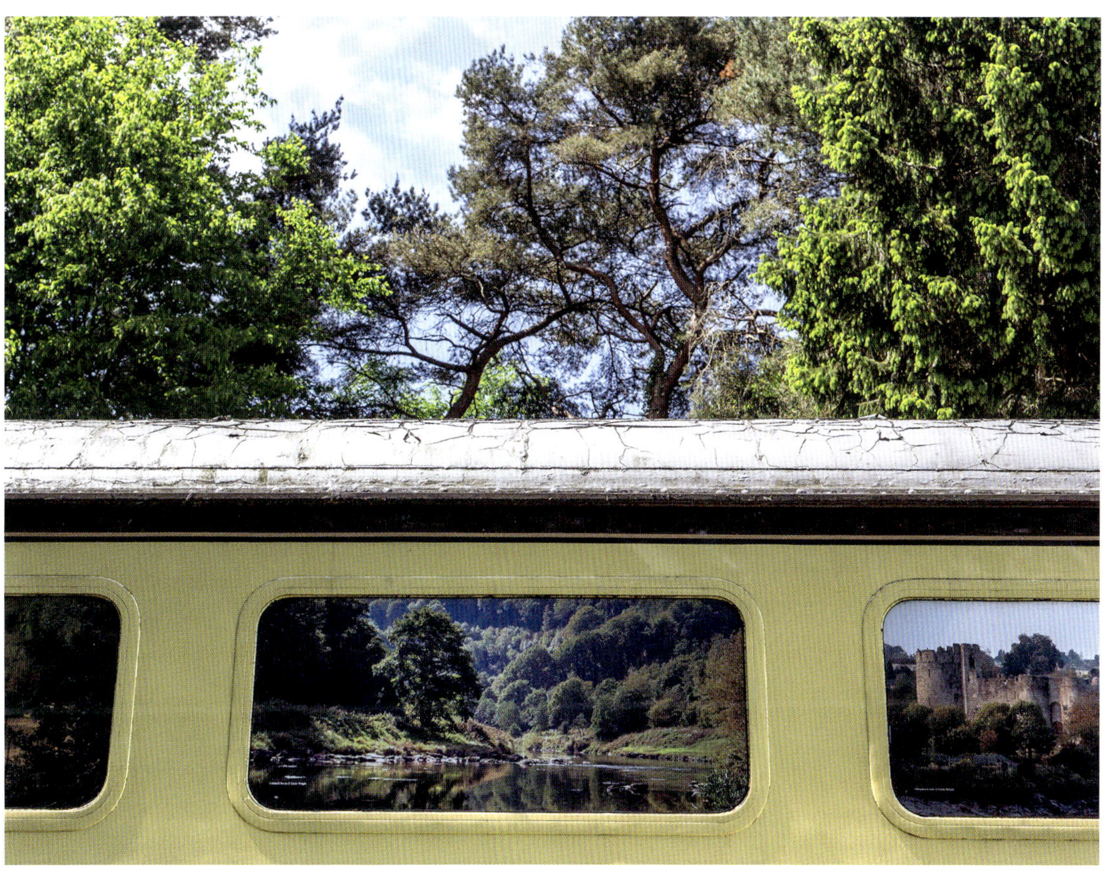

SO 53704 00632

When photographs warp reality.

A visitor to the exhibit would clearly see an artificial background in front of which stuffed birds hang by nylon thread.

The image can easily portray real birds in flight. A reminder to be careful of interpretation.

We can be easily fooled.

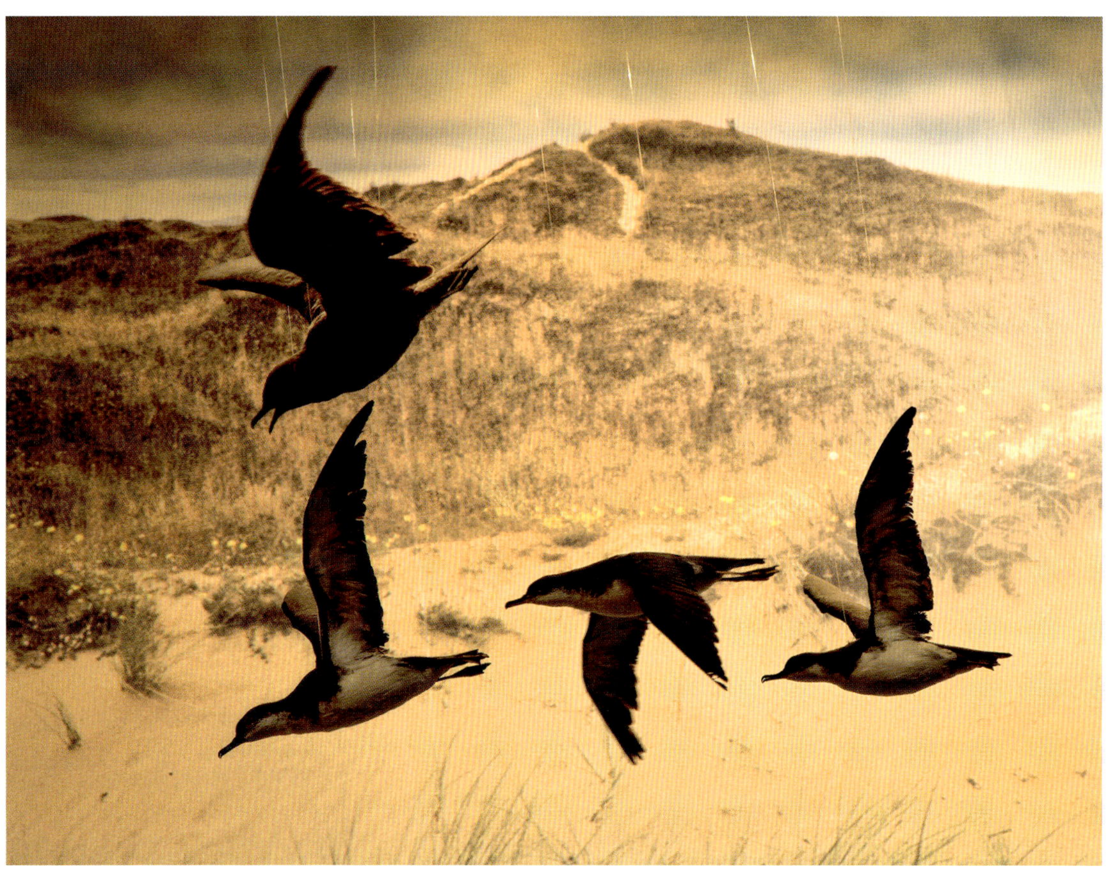

National Museum Wales   ST 18365 76951

The words 'Remember Tryweryn' were first painted on the stone wall of a ruined cottage near the village of Llanrhystud in the early 1960s, and have since been replicated countless times across Wales.

The slogan refers to the flooding of the Tryweryn Valley in Bala in 1965 to form a reservoir to supply Liverpool with water. It was done without the agreement of Welsh authorities and most Welsh MPs.

A ten-year campaign was fought to save the village of Capel Celyn but an Act of Parliament sanctioned the submergence of its homes, post office, school, chapel and cemetery.

SIGNS

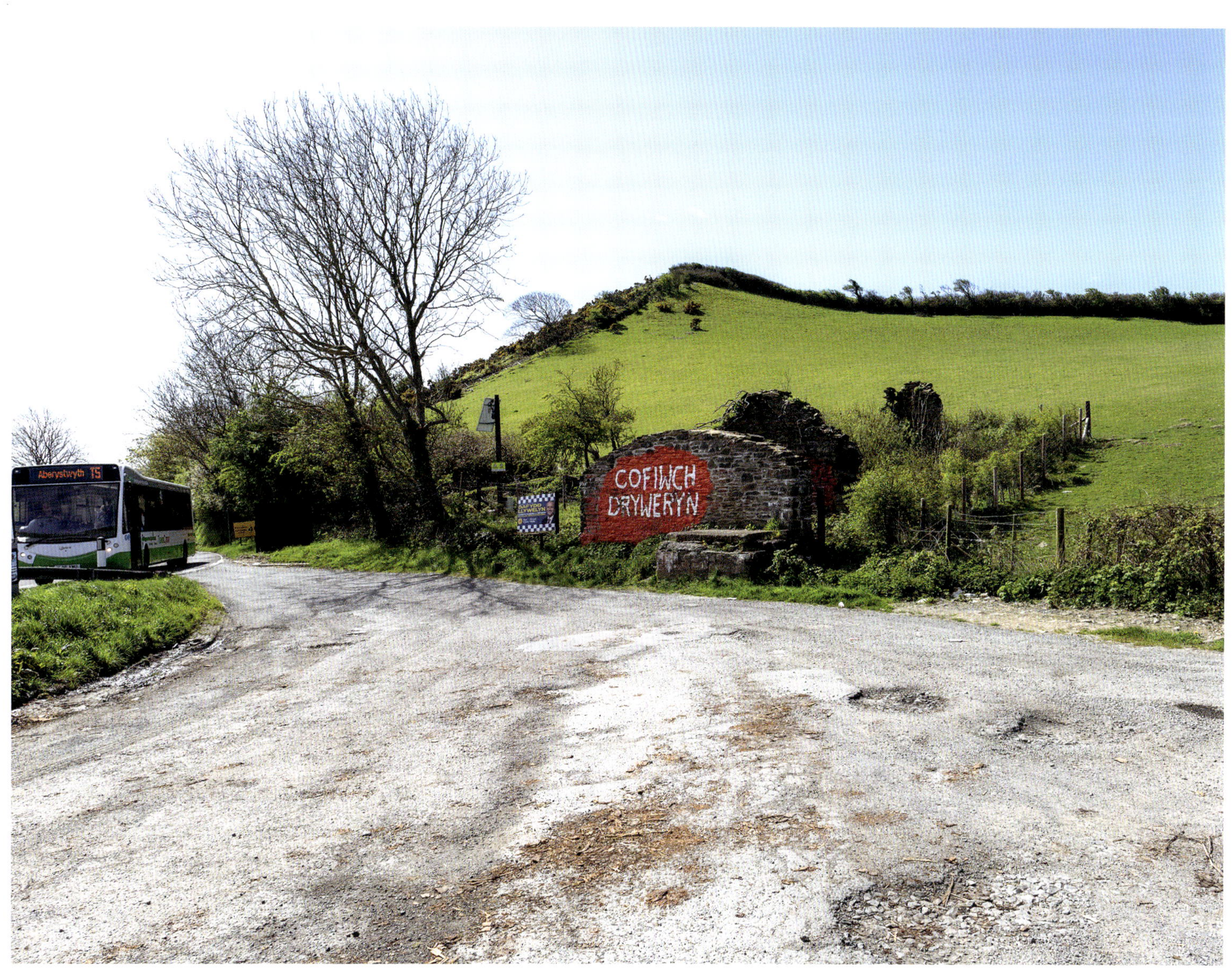

SN54748 70973

The once world-famous community of Tiger Bay, the residential area of Cardiff Docks which was one of the world's busiest sea ports in the early twentieth century.

The district was once said to be the home of individuals from some 57 different countries, living cheek-by-jowl in mutual respect of one another.

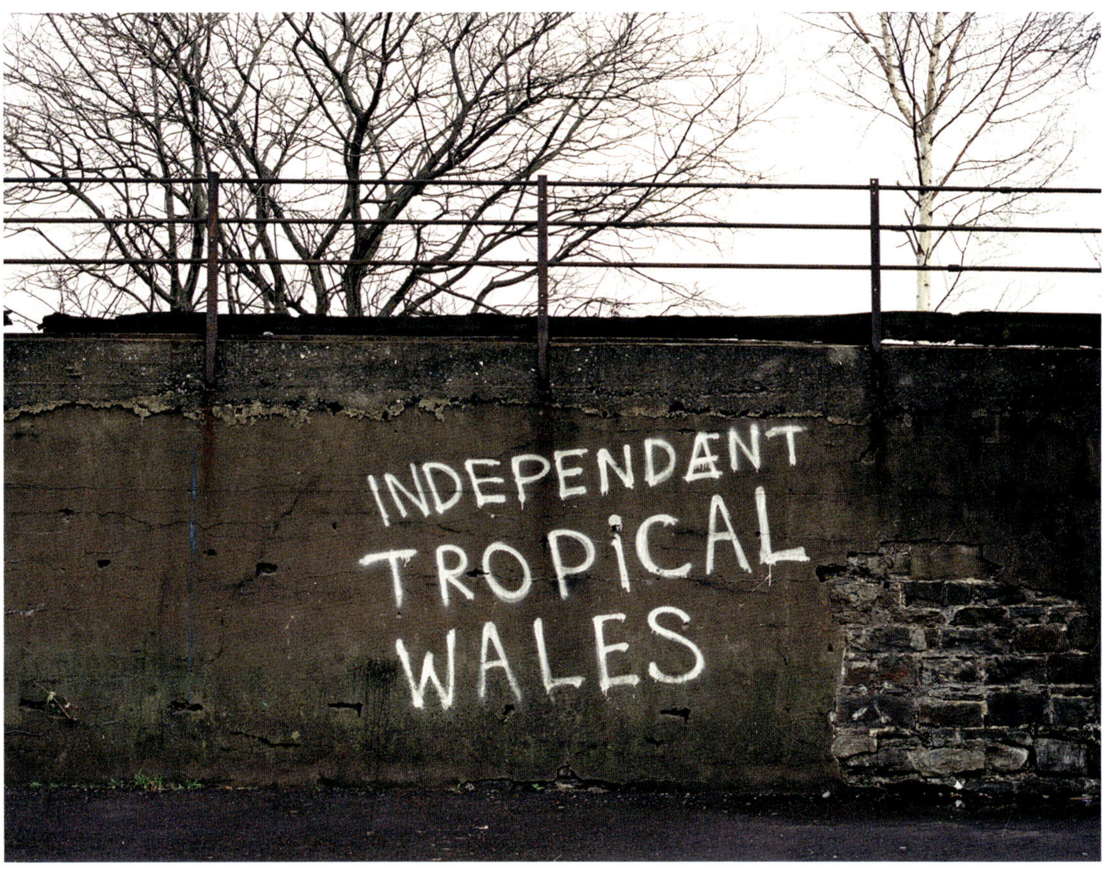

ST 18761 75528

Spotted driving along the A48 east of Carmarthen. Taken with care from the central reservation.

Banksy: "A wall is a very big weapon. It's one of the nastiest things you can hit someone with."

Or, in this case, a pillar.

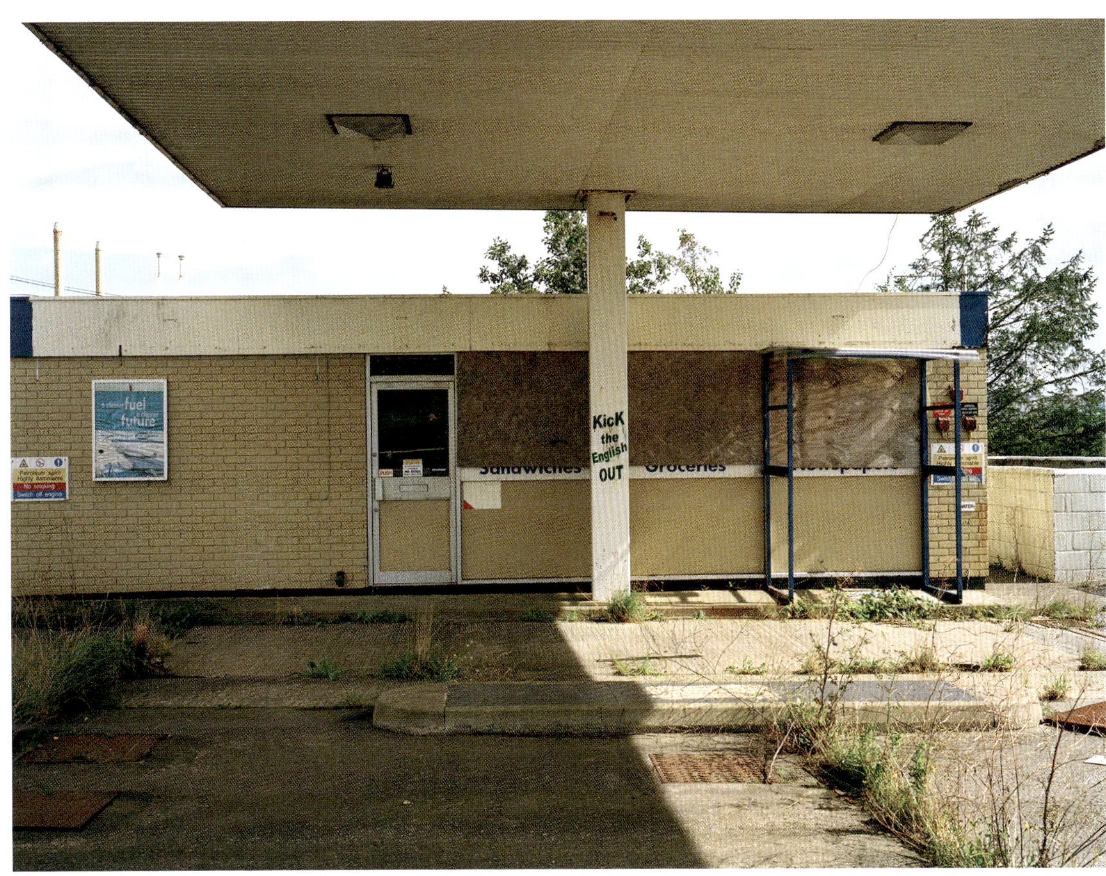

SN 47300 17952

EISTEDDFA GURIG, CEREDIGION

2011

The council kept removing it but it always seemed to reappear.

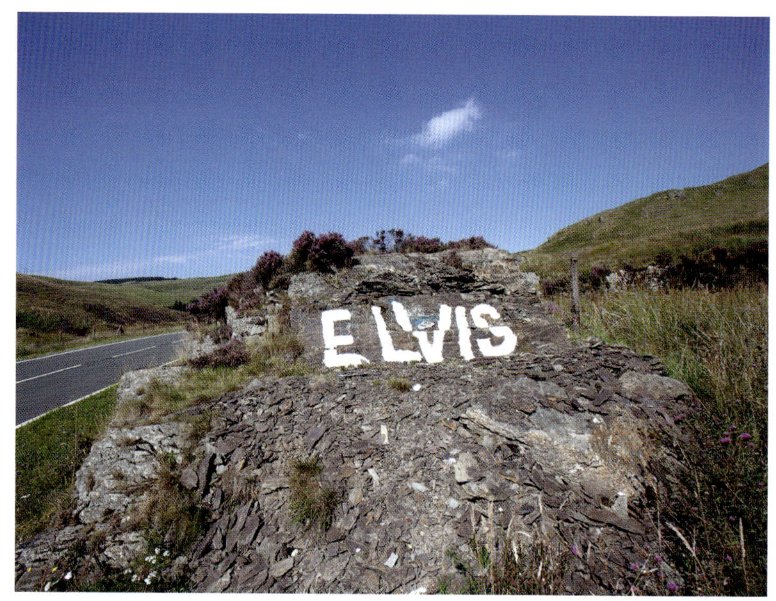

SN 80229 84027

LLANDOVERY, CARMARTHENSHIRE

2014

The beauty of signs.

Naïve art at its most wonderfully unpretentious. Someone that day decided to do their job well

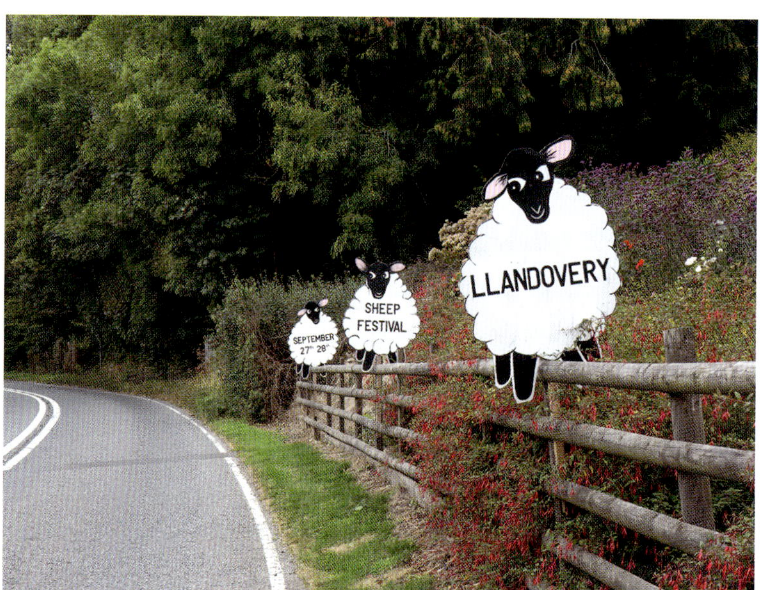

SN 76395 34533

The faces and comment on the plastic of the silage bales,
an unfiltered, un-self-conscious expression. Brings a little joy.

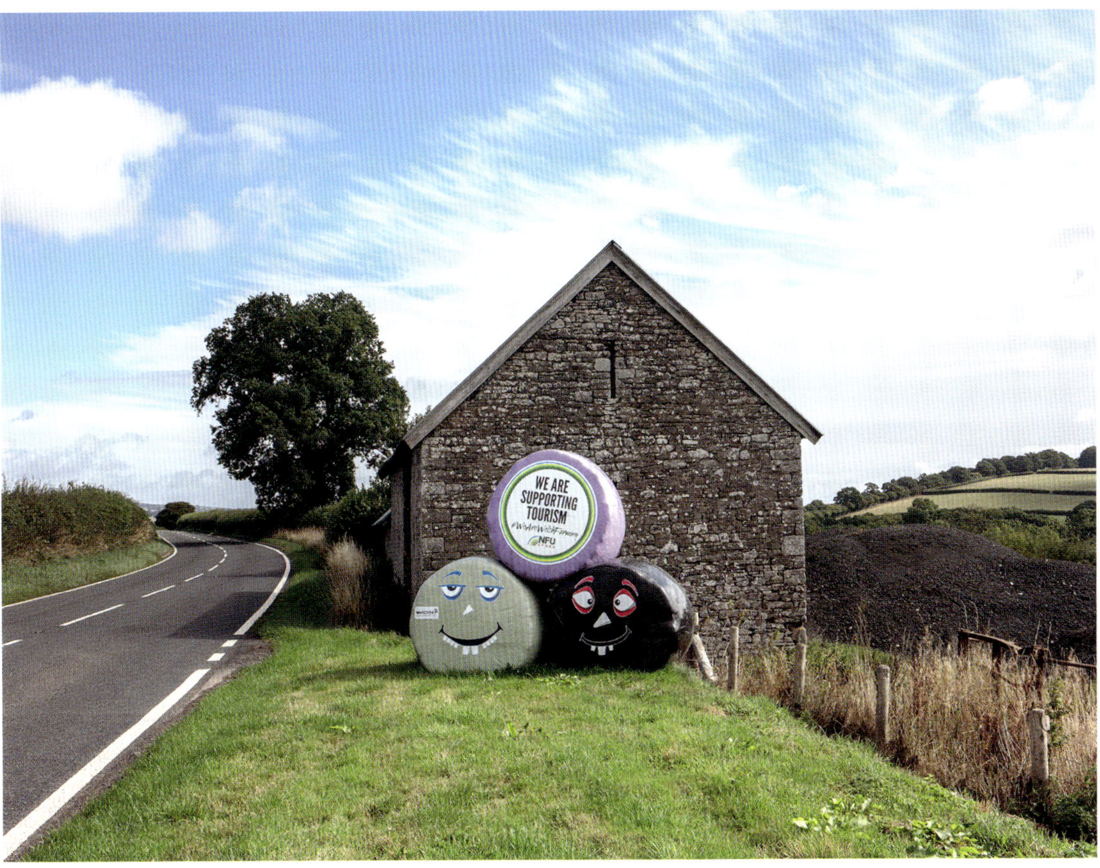

SO 12574 26596

School children carve them on desks, teenagers on toilet walls,
lovers on trees…

It seems we are compelled to write our names on things.

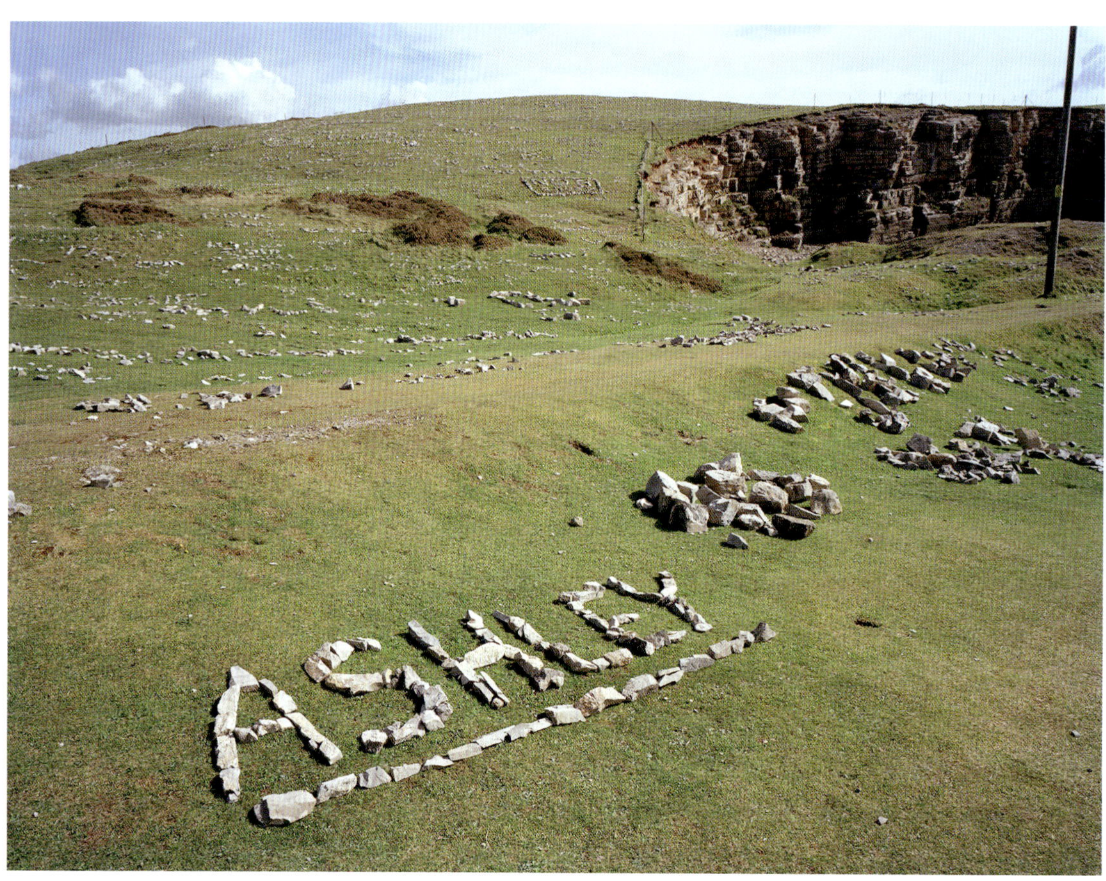

SH 76613 83128

RHOSSILI BAY, GOWER, SWANSEA

2011

We are all 'writing in the sand', an expression of the impermanence and fleeting nature of our lives, our words and achievements erased in time by the shifting tides and wind. Even so, as anyone who has experienced the stress of an exam and the elation of passing knows, these significant milestones in life are worthy of celebrating.

Belated congratulations Julia!

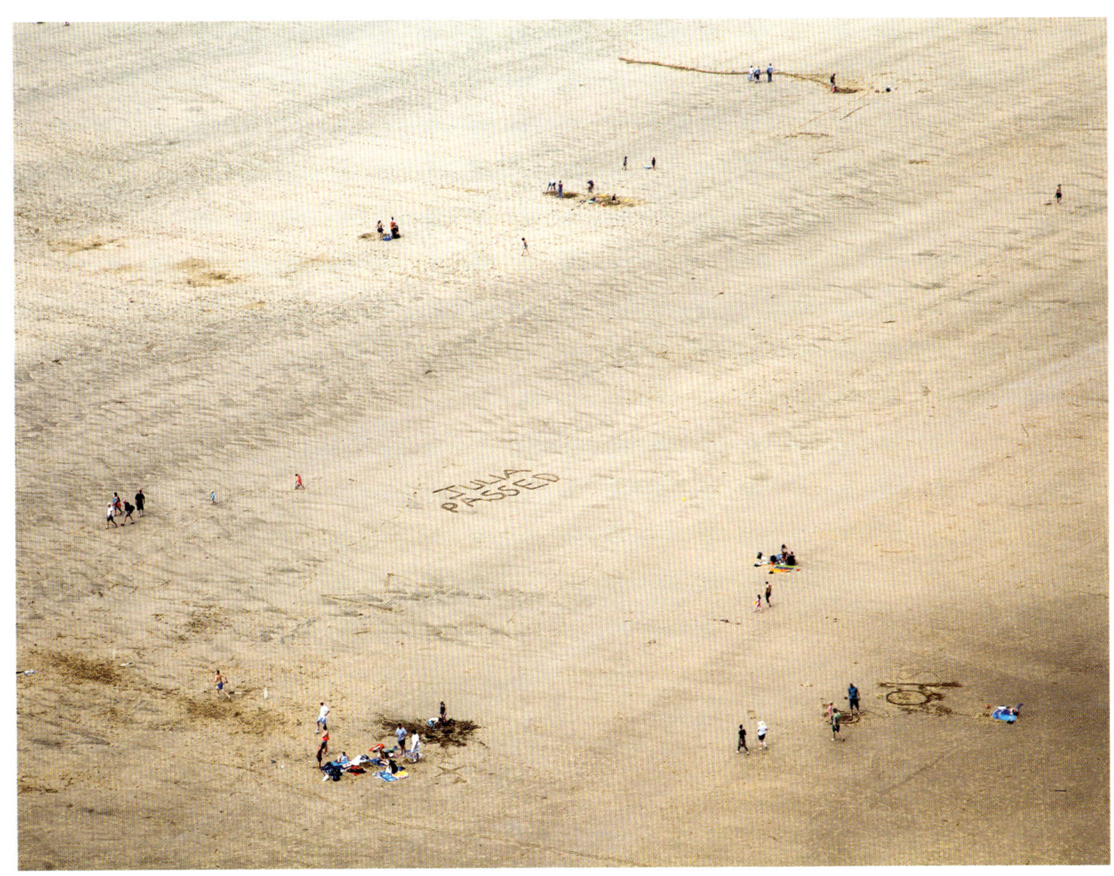

SS 41490 88171

A question along the A484. Heaven or hell?

Stop and think

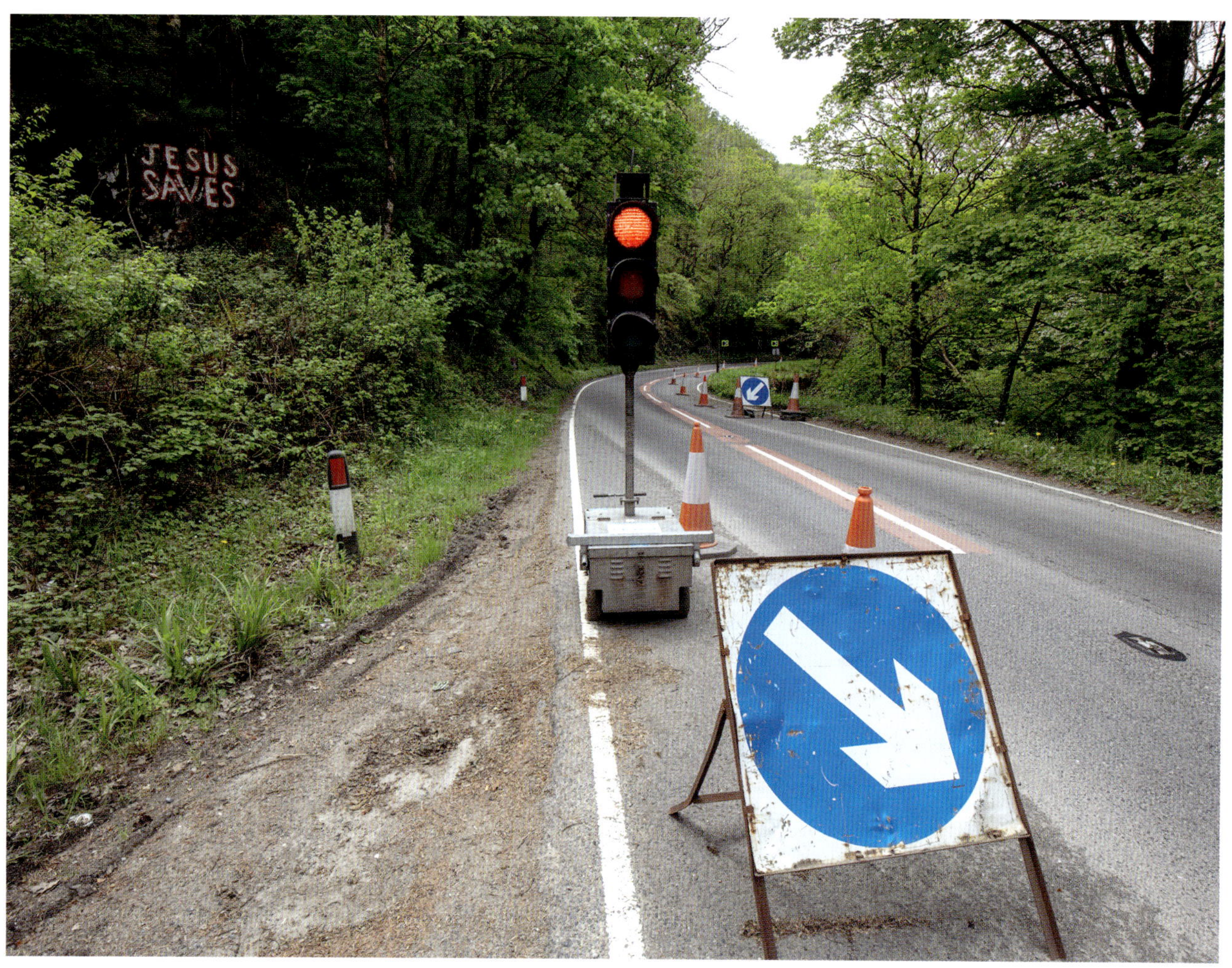

SN 39195 25792

Philosopher Bertrand Russell: "All the labour of all the ages, all the devotion, all the inspiration, all the noonday brightness of human genius are destined to extinction. So now, my friends, if that is true, and it is true, what is the point?".

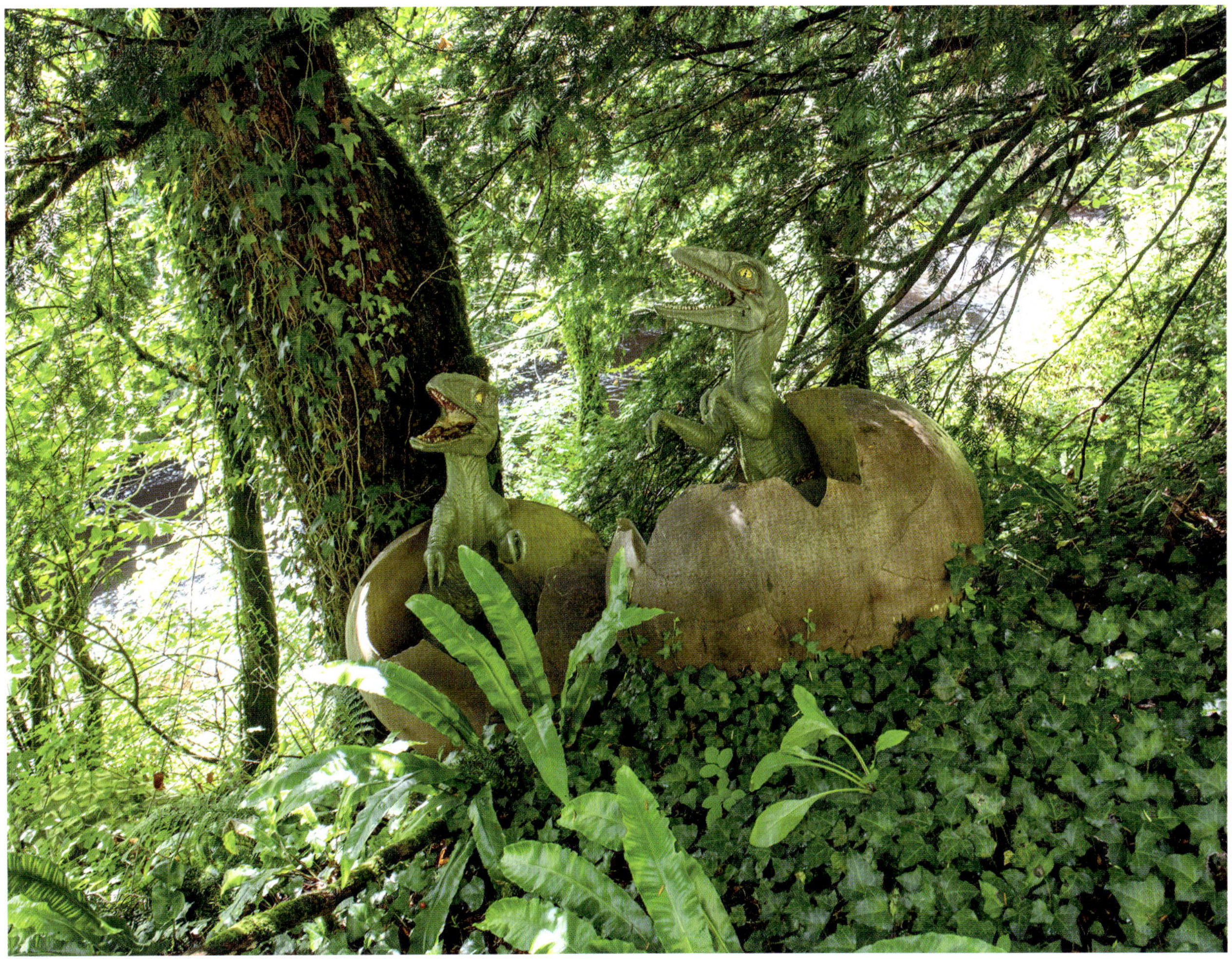

David Hurn

David Hurn was born in 1934 of Welsh decent. He grew up and had early schooling at De La Salle School for Boys in Cardiff (now St John's College). He began his photography career in 1955 and gained an early reputation with his photographic reporting of the 1956 Hungarian uprising. He became part of the social revolution of the 1960's, and photographed many iconic figures from film and music, including The Beatles, Sean Connery (as Bond), and Jane Fonda.

Hurn eventually turned away from coverage of current affairs and celebrities, preferring to take a more personal approach to photography and, in 1973, set up the famous School of Documentary Photography in Newport, Wales. Since leaving in 1989, besides continuing to photograph, he has been in constant demand for lecturing and workshops around the world.

His collaboration in 1997 with Professor Bill Jay produced *On Being a Photographer*, which has had over ten print runs. However, It is *Wales: Land of My Father*, published by Thames and Hudson that truly reflects his style and creative impetus, reviewed by the BBC as "determining the look of Wales for the next decades." Several other books of Hurn's distictive documentary photography have been published in recent years, including *Living in Wales* and *Writing the Picture* – both published by Seren.

David Hurn's longstanding international reputation as one of Britain's most influential documentary photographers continues to see his prints acquired by many private collectors and museums. In 2016, he was awarded an honorary fellowship of the Royal Photographic Society and, in 2021, the Lucie Awards International Honoree: Achievement In Documentary – presented in Carnegie Hall in New York. Back home in Wales, the long-time resident of Tintern in Monmouthshire was celebrated at the 2024 Welsh Media Awards in Cardiff with the award for 'Outstanding Contribution to Journalism' – acknowleding his 69-year photographic journey.

He has been a member of the international Magnum Photos co-operative since 1967.

Richard King

Richard King is a cultural historian, whose work focuses on the themes of identity, subculture and place.

His books include:
How Soon is Now? (2012), which was named Sunday Times music book of the year.
Original Rockers (2015), shortlisted for the Gordon Burn prize.
The Lark Ascending (2019), shortlisted for the Penderyn Prize,
Brittle With Relics (2022), an oral history of Wales 1962–1997,
Travels Over Feeling, Arthur Russell, A Life (2024), shortlisted for the Penderyn Prize.
All published by Faber.

King's recent appointments include:
Visiting Simon and Industrial Fellow, University of Manchester;
Royal Literary Fund Fellow, Cardiff University School of Journalism and Media;
Director – Trustee, Literature Wales.

King was born in Newport, South Wales and has lived in Radnorshire, Mid Wales since 2002.